THE SOULS OF MIXED FOLK

THE SOULS OF MIXED FOLK

RACE, POLITICS, AND AESTHETICS IN THE NEW MILLENNIUM

Michele Elam

Stanford University Press
Stanford, California

Stanford University Press
Stanford, California

Printed in the United States of America on acid-free, archival-quality paper

Library of Congress Cataloging-in-Publication Data

Elam, Michele.
The souls of mixed folk : race, politics, and aesthetics in the new millennium /
Michele Elam.
p. cm.
Includes bibliographical references and index.
ISBN 978-0-8047-5629-7 (cloth : alk. paper) -- ISBN 978-0-8047-5630-3 (pbk.
: alk. paper)
1. American literature--21st century--History and criticism. 2. Racially mixed
people in literature. 3. African Americans in literature. 4. Race in literature.
5. Race relations in literature. 6. Passing (Identity) in literature. I. Title.
PS231.R34E43 2011
810.9'352905--dc22

2010036789

Typeset by Bruce Lundquist in 10/15 Sabon

Dedicated to Harry J. Elam, Jr., "Jay"

Table of Contents

Illustrations

Preface

IN DECEMBER 2003, the *New York Times* celebrated "Generation E.A.: Ethnically Ambiguous"[1] as members of society's hip new A-list, hailing racially mixed people as ambassadors to a new world order, the fashionable imprimaturs of modernity. Galvanized by the Office of Management and Budget's Statistical Directive 15 of the 2000 Census—which allowed for an unprecedented "mark one or more" (MOOM) racial option—advocates for mixed race legal identification have gained tremendous political leverage and national recognition. Focused on spreading the "Good News" of the mixed race experience, dozens of advocacy organizations, websites, magazines, media watches, public awareness campaigns, mixed heritage centers, support groups, summer camps, festivals, podcasts, and blogs have emerged since the 1990s, networking an evolving coalition of interracial couples, families with transracial adoptees, and young people self-identifying as mixed race. U.S. multinational industries regularly exploit mixed race as a hot commodity, showcasing ethnically ambiguous spokespeople as corporate representatives.[2] The dramatic increase in the public visibility and popularity of mixed race has also drawn academic attention, according it the status of a sub-speciality in philosophy, political

FIGURE P.1. *Maintaining*, July 22, 2009. MAINTAINING © 2007 & 2008 Nate Creekmore. Reprinted by permission of UNIVERSAL PRESS SYNDICATE. All rights reserved.

science, sociology, psychology, and education, among other disciplines. As I explore in *The Souls of Mixed Folk*, education, in particular—as both an academic field and a commercial industry—has been especially active in canonizing certain normative models of mixed race as a uniquely post–civil rights identity and experience.

Critical attention to the proselytizing of mixed race acquires some urgency, in part, because its fêting as an up-and-coming legal and experiential category has occurred in inverse relation to the perceived irrelevancy of race, in general, and civil rights campaigns, in particular. Not accidentally, the ascension of mixed race popularity has been enabled in the post-race, "post soul"[3] era, and in concert with the quiet dismantling of affirmative action and the weakening of traditional civil rights lobbies. In 1995, Maria P. P. Root hailed mixed race as the "new frontier";[4] the next year, Stanley Crouch proclaimed that "race is over."[5] Since then, others also have rung race's death knell: Holland Cotter in a 2001 piece in the *New York Times* stated that the time for "ethno-racial identity" is past, that we are now witnessing the coming of "postblack or postethnic art."[6] Debra Dickerson demands the "end of blackness."[7] Anthony Appiah advances a "new cosmopolitanism"[8] that celebrates cultural contamination over what he casts as antiquated tribalism and identity politics. Ethnic hybridity, we are told, heralds a liberating "racelessness" (Naomi Zack),[9] a step "beyond race" (Ellis Cose),[10] the "end of racism" (Dinesh D'Souza),[11] a gesture "against race" (Paul Gilroy),[12] a "new racial order" (G. Reginald Daniel)[13] freed of a supposedly irresistible essentialism (Walter Benn Michaels).[14] Shelby Steele opines in the *Chronicle of Higher Education* that "black-studies programs" are already dinosaur relics of politics past.[15] However, such epitaphs might seem not only premature but suspect: as Toni Morrison in "Unspeakable Things Unspoken" asks, how and why now, after three hundred years of institutionalized racism in the United States, are some people claiming by fiat that "race" is over?[16] And, some skeptics might legitimately also ask, just how and why now does the notion of mixed race acquire such cachet amidst this welter of race transcendence?

This book seeks a middle way between the competing hagiographic and apocalyptic impulses in mixed race scholarship, between those who espouse mixed race as the great hallelujah to the "race problem" and

Mixed race = solution to the problem or a covering of the problem?

those who can only hear the alarmist bells of civil rights destruction. Both approaches can obscure some of the more critically astute engagements with new millennial iterations of mixed race by the multi-generic cohort of contemporary writers, artists, and performers discussed in this book. *The Souls of Mixed Folk* offers case studies of creative works that consider the claims of mixed race to modernity—particularly in relation to antediluvian blackness—as an aesthetic challenge as well as a social concern. I move from a brief discussion of artist Lezley Saar's installation, *Mulatto Nation* (2002), to extended considerations of two nationally syndicated newsprint comic-strips, Aaron McGruder's *The Boondocks* (1996–2006) and Nate Creekmore's *Maintaining* (2006–2009). I then turn to the novels of Philip Roth, *The Human Stain* (2001), Colson Whitehead, *The Intuitionist* (2000), Danzy Senna, *Caucasia* (1998) and *Symptomatic* (2005), and Emily Raboteau, *The Professor's Daughter* (2005), as well as to performances of Carl Hancock Rux's play, *Talk* (2002), and Dave Chappelle's late-night television episode, "The Racial Draft" (2004), from *The Dave Chappelle Show*. All are examples of literary and expressive arts that critique and expand the contemporary idiom about mixed race in the so-called post-race moment. With this focus, *The Souls of Mixed Folk* also seeks to reorient academic and public attention towards the humanities' largely overlooked but crucial participation in the production of mixed race's cultural meanings. As Susan Koshy argues in "Why the Humanities Matter for Race Studies Today," transformations in racial understandings frequently elude social science frameworks, for they "often erupt and are manifested in films, stories, theatrical and quotidian performances, and new media before they assume a social density and critical mass that enable empirical analysis of these phenomena. In other words, they inhabit and operate in a dimension of the human and the social that the humanities are uniquely positioned to investigate and illuminate."[17] At stake is the future direction for mixed race critical inquiry: specifically, how might new millennial expressive forms suggest an aesthetics of mixed race? And how might such an aesthetics productively reimagine the relations between race, art, and social justice in the twenty-first century?

The title, *The Souls of Mixed Folk*, is taken from a frame in Creekmore's *Maintaining* in which two mixed race characters, Lepidus and Marcus, argue about loyalty to what Marcus has cleverly coined the "Halfrican [American] Movement," discussed at length in Chapter Two. I borrow Lepidus' line for the title of this book for several reasons. First, the expression ironically invokes, of course, W. E. B. Du Bois' famous *The Souls of Black Folk* (1903) as part of the comic strip's send-up of the overreaching ambitions and hyperbolic rhetoric of some in the mixed race movement who advertise mixed race people as new millennial beings with special souls that warrant their own manifestos. Second, Lepidus' appropriation of Du Bois reflects the intraracial anxiety of influence common in mixed race advocacy efforts that seek to establish a tradition unique to the "new colored people"[18] by laying claim to early intellectual thought and literature historically associated with African American culture. Many of the authors and artists examined in this book directly address this tension and explore the possibilities for a mixed race expressivity that is continuous with, rather than parallel to, a capacious African American tradition constantly in dialogue and debate with itself. The title's oblique summoning of Du Bois in particular is also significant because so many of the works discussed here often explicitly pay homage to his theory of double consciousness as social insight, his meditations on the political claims of art, and his fascination with the narrative possibilities of mixed race. Third, and perhaps most significantly, I draw the title from *Maintaining* because it samples an alternative vehicle for representing mixed race politics, in this case the middlebrow form of the graphic narrative, and thus is emblematic of one of the many experiments in aesthetics and politics at the heart of *The Souls of Mixed Folk*. I hope, therefore, it is obvious that far from the impudence of implying any comparison between this book and Du Bois', I intend the title to signify on Creekmore's own humorous and gentle dig at all those who might, in fact, wish for a treatise about mixed folks' souls. The title is meant to both evoke and unsettle expectations, to prepare the reader for examples of art, literature, comics, and drama that collectively reframe any such conversations about the "spiritual strivings"[19] of mixed race people.

Several aesthetic, historical, and political rationales tied to post–civil rights politics, history, and identity yoke especially McGruder, Creekmore, Senna, Raboteau, Whitehead, Rux, and Chappelle. I lay them out here also as a road map to the Introduction, which explores more fully the public discourses and debates shaping and being reshaped by these works. Despite their many generic differences, an aesthetic principle uniting all here is the commitment to art as a subtle form of social action—an "aesthetics of resistance,"[20] or as Du Bois puts it, a way of seeking "with Beauty and for Beauty to set the world right."[21] They collectively gesture towards a political aesthetics that imagines art as both an instrument and an end in itself. These works are not propagandistic, but neither do they bear only an attenuated or ornamental relation to social justice concerns. Their engagement emerges both through a thematic interest in mixed race politics as well as through formal aesthetic structures that together interpret the Rorschach blot of the national angst and ambition that is mixed race.

Most often, these works' alternative modes do not involve explicitly imagining or narratively thematizing a vision of a better world or even necessarily a better way. Their aesthetic style more frequently *enacts* the limitations on forms of expression or political sensibilities that might inhibit the imaginative realization of an alternative world, performing a formal meta-commentary on the problem of representing hard-to-solve and sometimes hard-to-see social and racial inequities. This species of text, even when deploying humor, is not especially joyful or uplifting. The works do not offer manuals for enlightenment (which is precisely what so many mixed race memoirs and popular publications do); they do not offer exemplary characters who model "the answer" (which, unfortunately, is repeatedly expected of ethnic literature generally); and neither do they offer one of the most popular forms of compensation for decades of pathologizing mixed race: the creation of professional guidelines for rearing healthy multiracial children. In fact, these texts might rightly be censored reading for those looking for "positive identity formation and empowerment in children of mixed heritage."[22] Instead, they offer experiments across genre (narrative, graphic, performance) that validate mixed race experiences as opportunities for social insight without administering prescriptive morals or promising emancipatory politics.

Furthermore, they are all artistic creations responding directly to the perception that post–civil rights politics are bereft of substance and meaning. Specifically, they represent rejoinders to the absence of a robust new millennial political language for social justice. Part of the challenge they address is a growing appreciation that the packaging of multiracials as the vanguard of the future too often casts traditional civil rights organizations and ethnic studies programs as outdated, associated with 1970s tribal politics by old-fashioned "monoracials." Obama's millennial multiculti cool just seems so much more du jour than Jesse Jackson, Sr.'s last-century ethnic pride. In fact, one of the most acute challenges facing the National Association for the Advancement of Colored People (NAACP), which celebrated its 100th anniversary in 2009, is the creeping sense that black people will become moot in the next century.[23] The texts dramatize a profound political aphasia, a frustration with much of the language of self-possessive individualism and personal choice invoked by mixed race advocates, but an inability to articulate other options or initiatives for discriminated peoples because the discourses of civil rights have been so delegitimated. Paul Gilroy terms this malaise "postcolonial melancholy": the result of "a widespread reluctance to engage racism analytically, historically, or governmentally" because questions about "'race,' identity and differentiation have a distinctive, mid-twentieth century ring to them. They sometimes seem anachronistic because they do try to return contemporary discussion to a moral ground that we feel we should have left behind long ago," and tend to elicit impatience or apathy. As Gilroy argues, "these questions have only a minimal presence in today's incomplete genealogies of the global movement for human rights" and remain "'on hold' and therefore a muted part of the history of our present."[24] McGruder, Senna, Raboteau, Whitehead, and Rux, especially, call on and call up this civil rights history placed on hold. They do so not to revive the "racial, ethnic, and national absolutes" (14) with which this history is often associated and peremptorily dismissed. Rather, these writers and artists invoke it because they still see race as part of the "history of our present," even though there is a recognition that their revivification might be met with eye-rolling impatience. Their work arguably effects some measure of artistic redress for the impotency and speechlessness of post–civil rights discourse.

Gilroy's suggestion that conversations about race are often treated as voices from a past perceived as best over and done with begins to explain what at first may seem this book's retrograde impulse to come *back* from the "beyond black and white" paradigm in order to focus on the particular implications and significance of black-white mixes. The fact that looking at race through the lens of black and white is now considered so very twentieth-century, so been-there-done-that, so *tired*, is precisely part of the challenge of a post-civil rights politics that defines what is or is not passé, that licenses what can or cannot be said and heard. This book's "back from beyond black" orientation, justified in greater length in the Introduction, fully appreciates the importance of comparative racial studies, of the "need to understand race through the lens of intersectionality as well as through an analytic of interracialism."[25] But rather than see these imperatives in tension, *The Souls of Mixed Folk* considers its singular focus on the particular complexities and nuances of black-white mixes as complementary to broader comparative racial projects. In resisting the pressure common in mixed race studies to account for any and all racial combinations and variables, *The Souls of Mixed Folk* seeks to understand better the very specific cultural work of representations of the diversity of black-white mixes as a necessary precursor to analyzing their function and saliency within wider comparative racial dynamics.

Most importantly, this particular group of works are united by their aesthetic repositioning of mixed race priorities from questions of racial privacy to those of civil rights. Noting the increasing emphasis on the "personal, private, individual, and idiosyncratic rather than institutional, ideological, collective, and cumulative,"[26] they critique the narrowing of mixed race discourses from those of "power and economics and history"[27] to those of individual rights, psychological health, and family genealogy. One can see this narrowing in the debates over the U.S. Census. Some mixed race advocates, recognizing the constitutive power of the Office of Management and Budget to legally create racial identities, argue that "multiracial identity was only truly born in the U.S. with the passing of Statistical Directive 15."[28] But the works examined in *The Souls of Mixed Folk* challenge the imaginative and political sufficiency of what I call in the Introduction the "box fetish"—the commitment to box-checking as *the* site for social change. Instead, all explore mixed racial identity not as a special interest but as a performative mode of social engagement.

This consideration of racial identity as socially constituted and historically imbricated rather than as an Adamic self-invention informs the gender- and genre-bending plots and images of mixed race that reimagine both self and history in this book. The first chapter, "The Mis-education of Mixed Race," focuses on how disciplinary practices in the social sciences and in the field of education, especially, powerfully canonize or delegitimate particular images and scripts in the national conversation about mixed race and modernity. In Chapter Two, Aaron McGruder and Nate Creekmore refigure the visual conventions of mixed race to illustrate how politically situated and implicated is the act of "seeing" race. Danzy Senna, Philip Roth, and Colson Whitehead, in Chapter Three, exploit the trope of racial passing in their re-visioning of new world orders that are projected well beyond the "mulatto millennium."[29] Chapter Four examines other post-race fantasies in the works of Senna and Emily Raboteau in what I identify as anti-bildungsromans. These novels explore mixed race coming-of-age as a coming into the social longing for an affiliative community of people "just like us," a separate mixed race same-sex nation within a nation. The performances of Dave Chappelle and Carl Hancock Rux in Chapter Five turn from the yearnings *of* to the yearnings *for* mixed race people—dramatizing the national, commercial, academic, and erotic investments in mixed race that point to the collaborative negotiation that defines all racial identities. Chappelle and Rux especially resist the triumphalist historical teleologies that so often anoint mixed race as cause and proof of social evolution. Notably absent are the quest narratives of climactic self-discovery so predictably commonplace in many mixed race memoirs and fiction. In these works, the meaning of racial experience emerges not through linear advances of time, narrative, and enlightenment but by sifting through dynamic palimpsests of cultural history and possible futurities that, in Senna's, Whitehead's, Raboteau's, Chappelle's, and Rux's works, arouse a continual process of self- and national reassessment. But across all their different strategies, the novels, plays, comics, and performances in *The Souls of Mixed Folk* seek an aesthetic connection to the ethical in expressive gestures that move us towards a poetics of social justice in the twenty-first century.

Acknowledgments

THIS BOOK COULD NOT HAVE BEEN WRITTEN without the personal and intellectual support that I have received from so many of my Stanford colleagues in English, American Studies, African and African American Studies, and others affiliated with the Center for Comparative Studies in Race and Ethnicity (CCSRE). I am deeply grateful for the friendship and goodwill of too many colleagues to name here, but I would like to acknowledge especially Shelley Fisher Fishkin, Arnold Rampersad, and John Rickford, who have been most dear and supportive friends, mentors, and inspirations and who have always wished the best for me, my family, and my work. Sincere thanks also to H. Samy Alim, Richard Banks, John Bender, Carol Boggs, Eavan Boland, Al Camarillo, Clayborne Carson, Prudence Carter, Terry Castle, Gordon Chang, Sandra Drake, Jennifer Eberhardt, Martin Evans, Charlotte Fonrobert, Denise Gigante, Ursula Heise, Allyson Hobbs, Gavin Jones, Teresa LaFromboise, Jacyn Lewis, Andrea Lunsford, Saikat Majumdar, Hazel Markus, Paula Moya, Stephen Orgel, David Palumbo-Liu, Patricia Parker, Robert Polhemus, Nancy Ruttenberg, Ramón Saldívar, Gary Segura, Matthew C. Snipp, Stephen Hong Sohn, Claude and Dorothy Steele, Jennifer Summit, Vered Shemtov, Ewart and Odette Thomas, Hannah Valantine, Blakey Vermeule, Tobias Wolff, and Alex Woloch. Though no longer with us, Jay Fliegelman and George Fredrickson had many a helpful conversation with me on the topic of mixed race and were influential to this project. Caroline Streeter has long been part of our black mixed sisterhood. When visiting scholars at Stanford, Houston Baker, Glenda Carpio, Henry Louis Gates, Jr., Lani Guinier, Charles Ogletree, France Winddance Twine, and Howard Winant were all brilliant interlocutors.

I would also like to thank the Michelle R. Clayman Institute for Gender Research and Op-Ed Project, especially Katie Orenstein and my "mentor-editors," Joe Loya and Katharine Mieszkowski, as well as Corrie Goldman,

Stanford Humanities Outreach Officer. Another important community for me has been members of the Future of Minority Studies Project, including Linda Martín Alcoff, Johnnella Butler, Sandy Darrity, Michael Hames-García, Danielle Heard, Amy MacDonald, Ernesto Martínez, Chandra Talpade Mohanty, Satya Mohanty, John Riofrio, Tobin Siebers, and Rosemarie Garland-Thomson.

I am most deeply indebted to all the fabulous undergraduate and graduate students in my courses on African American literature, mixed race, and "post-race" studies who have shaped, and continue to shape, my thinking on race and identity. I want to thank especially Kiyomi Burchill, Guadalupe Carrillo, Maggie Chen, Elda Maria Gomez, Doug Jones, and Jennifer Harford Vargas, with whom I have had many long, rewarding conversations that have profoundly influenced my work and my life at Stanford.

Thanks must also go to the very helpful comments by my manuscript reviewers, to my Stanford editor, Emily-Jane Cohen, who made several very insightful comments on portions of the manuscript, and to Norris Pope, who first solicited the book. Sincere gratitude goes to Nigel De Juan Hatton for all the early editing and permissions work, to Ron Davies for his good-spirited edits, and to the administrative support by the staff of the Program in African and African American Studies—associate directors Dr. Cheryl Richardson and Dr. Cheryl Brown, and administrative associates Marisa Juarez and LaSundra Flournoy. For technical and moral support, sincerest thanks also to the irreplaceable Alyce Boster, Dagmar Logie, Matthew Jockers, and the entire, amazing, English Department staff "dream team."

I CANNOT BEGIN TO GIVE ENOUGH THANKS to my extraordinary husband, best friend, soul mate, love of my life, Harry (Jay), who has always been there for me and always in the ways that matter most. He is the best person to talk to when words most matter, and the best person to be with when words are not enough. We often say to each other: "You are always in my head when I write"; it is with an especially intimate pleasure that I see the living presence of our many, many conversations in this book. Also at the very center of my heart, Claire Elise—my insightful, thoughtful, witty daughter—kept me both highly entertained and honest during the years of work on this project. I am so grateful every single day for her sweet, wondrous presence in my life. Finally, I am grateful for my family's enduring support and belief in me, which includes my in-laws, with whom I've shared delightful evenings at the kitchen table in Buzzards Bay discussing, race, literature, and politics.

MANY THANKS to the Foundry Theatre for locating and sharing a video copy of a performance of Carl Hancock Rux's *Talk*. Artist Lezley Saar was very generous in not only giving me permission to reproduce her work but sending me my very own Baby Halfie to play with.

Portions of this book have appeared in print and are included, in a different version, here with permission:

"The 'Ethno-Ambiguo Hostility Syndrome': Mixed-Race, Identity, and Popular Culture." In *Doing Race: 21 Essays for the 21st Century*, ed. Hazel Rose Markus and Paula M. L. Moya (New York: W. W. Norton, 2010), 528–544.

"The Mis-Education of Mixed Race." In *Identities in Education*, ed. Annie MacDonald and Susan Sánchez-Casal (New York: Palgrave-MacMillan, 2009), 131–150.

"Mixed Race and Cultural Memory: Carl Hancock Rux's *Talk*." In *Signatures of the Past: Cultural Memory in Contemporary Anglophone North American Drama*, ed. Marc Maufort and Caroline De Wagter (Brussels: Peter Lang, 2008), 83–100.

"Passing in the Post-Race Era: Danzy Senna, Philip Roth, and Colson Whitehead," *African-American Review*, 41, no. 4 (Winter 2007): 749–768.

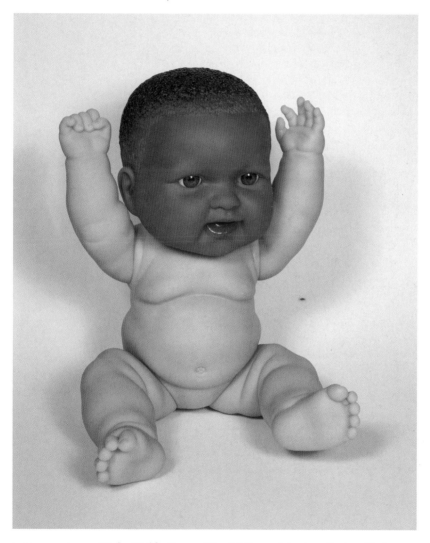

FIGURE C.1. "Baby Halfie Brown Head." Part of the installation *Mulatto Nation* found at mulattonation.com. Courtesy of the artist, Lezley Saar. (This image is discussed in the Introduction.)

FIGURE C.2. "Tillary," listed as African American/Caucasian in the Real Kidz catalog. Molloy Toys, Inc.
(This image is discussed in the Introduction.)

FIGURE C.3. *Boondocks*, June 6, 1999. THE BOONDOCKS © 1999 Aaron McGruder. Reprinted by permission of UNIVERSAL PRESS SYNDICATE. All rights reserved. (This image is discussed in Chapter Two.)

FIGURE C.4. "The Racial Draft," Dave Chappelle and Neal Brennan, writers/producers. Originally aired on Comedy Central network, October 2004. (This image is discussed in Chapter Five.)

Introduction

"BABY HALFIE BROWN HEAD" appears as part of Lezley Saar's art installation titled *Mulatto Nation*, first exhibited at the List Gallery at Swarthmore College in 2003 (See Fig. C.1).[1] The baby doll's bifurcated, manufactured body draws attention to many of the most heated cultural debates over what mixed race reality is (or is not) and represents a new generation of critical aesthetic and political provocation that is the focus of *The Souls of Mixed Folk*. Perhaps most strikingly, Baby Halfie's brown head and white body are unreconciled racial parts. Politically incorrect in an age seeking to answer ever more earnestly the philosophical and democratic problem of "the one and the many," its body will not deliver the desired whole. Baby Halfie is not tastefully merged into sepia consistency nor pleasantly rainbowed into an image of multiethnic unity. Nor does Baby Halfie aspire to representational accuracy; the doll is not an effort to capture how a person of mixed black and white descent might actually appear in the flesh. Rather, the matte skin colors are the generic commercial version of black and white. Retro 1950s, the skin tones evoke a time when peach "flesh-colored" Band-Aids and Crayola crayons caused no stir, when racial types and their placement in the social order were taken for granted. The doll's molded and articulated limbs, despite its folds of newborn fat, call attention to the fact that Baby Halfie is plastic, without personhood or personality. The racial parts are stiff, constructed, interchangeable; in fact, its exhibition mate, "Baby Halfie White Head," models its physical reverse, suggesting that Baby Halfie is host to no unique identity, no character so special that it cannot be replaced with a twist-off part. The doll is an intentionally soulless representative of mixed race in direct contrast with ethnically correct, anatomically correct, or "reborn" baby-doll realism. In fact, because its exposed but erased crotch leaves its gender unassigned, it appears not just asocial but asexual as well.[2]

So just what kind of plaything is Baby Halfie? Who would want to hold and cuddle this doll? Might Baby Halfie's charms be lost on the multiracially identified child and parent interested in the look and ethic of Molloy Toys' Real Kidz series or Dolls Like Me, Inc., which is committed to "building self-esteem in children of color, one toy at a time"?[3] As Ann DuCille asks in her discussion of Mattel's mass-marketing of "real dolls," "What does it mean when similarity and difference . . . are calculated according to a like-me or unlike-me that is not only a code for race but a code for race as skin color? Just what are we saying when we claim that a doll does or does not look like me?" Is the new vogue for mixed race dolls just another attempt "to reproduce a heterogeneous globe, in effect to produce multicultural meaning and market ethnic diversity . . . not by replicating the individual differences of real bodies but by mass-marketing the discursively familiar—by reproducing stereotyped forms and visible signs of racial and ethnic difference"?[4] Baby Halfie is unlike anyone; it resists the visual norming of mixed race implied by, for example, the light-skinned, blond-afroed doll Tillary, which like the rest of her similarly fair-complected middle-class Real Kidz family—Willough, Remsen, Quincy, and Goodwin—participates in the production and mainstreaming of the visual "forms" and "signs" of mixed race identity (See Fig. C.2).

Baby Halfie's arms are raised high as if asking to be lifted up for parental comfort and affirmation, but I suspect no parents will embrace it, let alone purchase it for their tots in hopes of inspiring proud mixed race identification or developmental empowerment—and that is no doubt precisely the point. After all, the section of the Saar installation where Baby Halfie can be found, "Materialism and the Mulatto: Souvenir Gift Shop," is an ironic comment on the business of mixed race self-worth, the partnership of the child health and education industries with corporate marketing. One can buy Baby Halfie along with totes, mugs, tank tops, mouse pads, and bumper stickers inscribed with the Mulatto Nation logo—the American Sign Language hand gesture for the letter M (for "mulatto"). Suggesting mulatto self-respect and revolutionary will, this raised fist burlesques both the Black Power salute of the Black Panther Party in the 1960s and 1970s, and the deaf pride movement in the late 1980s, most often associated with Gallaudet University. In fact, the *Mulatto Nation*

FIGURE I.I. "Mulatto Nation Logo." Part of the installation *Mulatto Nation* found at mulattonation.com. Courtesy of the artist, Lezley Saar.

installation in which Baby Halfie appears is a send-up of many of the most cherished aspirations of mixed race organizations and advocacy groups, especially the desire for their own history of achievement, activism, and heroism. Certainly even the antiquated and, for some, offensive language of "halfie" and "mulatto" is apostasy for new millennials wishing to reinvent the legal nomenclature and political status for people of mixed race.

I open *The Souls of Mixed Folk* with this brief discussion of Baby Halfie because its creative affront provides a vivid example of the alternative progressive directions for mixed race art and activism in the post–civil rights era that are at the center of this book. Uncuddly as it is, Baby Halfie enacts the enduring relevance of Du Boisian double consciousness, in which there are "two souls, two thoughts, two unreconciled strivings; two warring ideals in one dark body" ("Of Our Spiritual Strivings," 694)—or, in Baby Halfie's case, one dark head. Both Du Bois and Saar represent head and body joined and yet uncoupled by race; the fact that they remain distinct and distinctly racialized means that no one looking can claim the opthalmological deficiency that Patricia Williams argues characterizes the mistaken political will towards color blindness.[5] Baby Halfie requires one to see both again and anew the interrelation of black and white, the suture marked like a necklace or a noose at the neck. And because it is so explicitly a racialized doll, Baby Halfie shares in the work of other toys that instruct children in cultural literacies: Kenneth B. Clarke's famous "doll tests" with black children, the results of which were used as part of NAACP legal testimony to dismantle the separate-but-equal legal theory in the 1954 *Brown v. Board of Education* Supreme Court decision; the antebellum Topsy-Turvy dolls, "racially reversible . . . so that children could play with the stuffed 'Dinah' or, if one flipped her skirt over, with her forbidden counterpart, the white 'Miss.'"[6] Saar's doll offers a kind of counter-educational test to both of those earlier dolls' "lessons," for it confounds the practices of identification altogether. In fact, it seems to challenge even more radically the principle that identification—seeing facsimiles "like me" in the world—is necessary or even desirable for progressive social change.

Part of Baby Halfie's charm involves this ability to defamiliarize, and thereby enlarge, conversations about mixed race even when at first glance it may appear to participate in the ethnic strip that we have come to associate with the maintenance of the national status quo. Similar to the now-infamous 1993 *Time* magazine cover of a "woman created by a computer from a mix of several races," for example, Baby Halfie is shorn of most secondary cultural and ethnic markers—clothing, jewelry, hair— and of all context and commitments to place, history, or political persuasion.[7] "Eve," as her editor-creators called her, is represented as both wholly racialized (a palimpsest of all races) and yet as racially transcendent (beyond all racial categories), a peculiarly American contradiction in which ethnic difference is often celebrated so long as it is assimilated into the national melting pot. But if the *Time* mulatta is, to use a folk expression, "light, bright, and damn near white"—that is, ethnically palatable, politically non-threatening, and sexually available to the dominant national culture—Baby Halfie, by contrast, is unassimilable, incompatible, and unobtainable (except through PayPal). Although it is a riveting sight, Baby Halfie refreshingly interrupts all the usual scopic conventions involving the assumption of race's bodily legibility, the compulsive effort to taxonomize phenotype, the fetishizing gaze so often aimed at the racially mixed. For, as visually arresting as Baby Halfie is, its mixed race figure is not pretty, not appealing, and not even very safe. Baby Halfie, in fact, scores high on the creepiness factor: both the strange obscenity of its spread legs and undiapered privates and the threat of lynching or decapitation implied by its removable head suggest racial violence and sexual perversion as part and parcel of its doll guile.

Baby Halfie calls for a double—and triple—take, and then it takes advantage of that staring to prompt attention in new directions. True, some may find Baby Halfie a killjoy to the extent that it rejects the warm and cozy celebration of mixed race people as "in style," as Danzy Senna ironically puts it, popular in an era in which "[p]ure breeds (at least the black ones) are out and hybridity is in. America loves us in all our half-caste glory."[8] Baby Halfie, of course, is intentionally unstylish and unsettling, but in ways that signal the desire for a new political language and aesthetics at this fin de siècle. Saar's *Mulatto Nation* illustrates how artistic engagements with mixed race can prompt deeper, more playful, and potentially more critically enriching considerations of political and cultural representation.

I. THE CULTURAL INVENTION OF MIXED RACE

Despite many differing interests within and across the coalitions that identify as part of the mixed race movement(s), most share a central belief: demographics are destiny. It has become a commonplace refrain within these groups and in the news media that there exists a "mixed race baby boom," that this population will continue to increase as a result of the 1967 *Loving v. Virginia* Supreme Court decision lifting states' bans on interracial marriage and rising immigration rates, especially from Mexico, South America, and Latin America. But rather than assume that the numerical count of mixed race people signals a natural tipping point, a rising tide of color that has only just caught the nation's attention, *The Souls of Mixed Folk* examines the cultural creation and interpretation of this "new" demographic, focusing in particular on popular representations that have helped endow certain idea(l)s of mixed race with political significance in the national imaginary.[9] Certainly the *Loving* decision and immigration trends have contributed to the United States' increasingly multi-hued population, but people of mixed descent are not a recent phenomenon: they have existed in often distinct, self-identified communities since the colonial era in the Americas, from Black Seminoles to Melungeons.[10] Scholars Kim M. Williams and Kimberly McClain DaCosta have challenged both of the frequent explanations (increased immigration, enlightened legislation) for the apparently sudden appearance of mixed race people in the new millennium. They cogently document how the impression of an expanding cross-country mixed race constituency is, in part, political desire and market invention.[11] Further proof that the interest in mixed race people is not simply a consequence of their putative statistical weight and exponential growth, data collected since the 2000 Census suggest that the number of people self-identifying as more than one race is actually declining.[12] This decline has occurred since 2006 despite perceptions to the contrary that mixed race people represent the next boom.

So if mixed race people are neither new nor apparently increasing, why the current vogue for mixed race? Why now? With what effect? How does it matter? To answer these questions means moving beyond what poses as the politically innocent "Why are there more mixed race people now?" to inquire instead "Why do we see more people *as* mixed race now?" and, furthermore, "How do people self-identifying as mixed see themselves?" The concept of mixed race as warranting a separate legal, experiential, or soulful category has only very recently been sanctioned and naturalized, and the quotation marks indicating the in-process, provisional nature of "mixed race" have only recently been removed in public discourse. How have very specific ideas about what it means to be mixed race been so aggressively scripted, marketed, and institutionalized that there exists even a nominal consensus about what a mixed race person supposedly looks like, shops for, stands for, votes for, or who she or he partners with? This book takes as a given the political nature, versus a presumed taxonomic neutrality, of mixed race, beginning with the assumption that mixed race is no fait accompli but still very much a category under construction.

The election of President Barack Obama is a case study in the cultural invention of mixed race, for the self-described "mutt"[13] Obama is often heralded by mixed race advocacy groups as proof that multiracials will eventually inherit the earth. Yet, as I argue elsewhere, despite the pre-inaugural hand-wringing about whether he was "black enough," Obama was brought firmly back into the racial fold—symbolically blessed first with Congressman John Lewis' placement of him within the arc of the civil rights struggle in Lewis' speech at the Democratic National Convention, then anointed by the divine concordance of Martin Luther King, Jr.'s birthday on the eve of his inauguration, and finally given a benediction by civil rights icon Pastor Joseph Lowery that opened with lines from "Lift Every Voice and Sing," the "Negro National Anthem." When Obama became president, Barack became black again. The inauguration was the climax of his transformation from a black suspect, to a suspect black, to a mixed race cosmopolitan, to MLK's heir, to, finally, America's Native Son. The fact that he checked "African American" on the 2010 Census was a personal choice that only threw into greater relief the way his racial identity had already been and would continue to be publicly negotiated. This consensus about just who Obama is serves its purposes—America unites over the idea of "the first black president"—and is an example of how the discursive making and unmaking of biracialism is always in large part a function of shifting political imperatives: Obama is black again. For now.[14]

II. MANIFEST MIXED RACE DESTINY

This then is my claim: I am in all America. All America is in me.

Shirlee Taylor Haizlip, *The Sweeter the Juice*[15]

Historian George Fredrickson's comparative study of mixed race in the United States and South Africa offers a compelling argument that the public recognition of mixed race has little to do with "gene flow" (96) and everything to do with political expediency. Only when there is a national interest in naming, regulating, and legislating a population—that is, when a nation has an economic or political interest in counting mixed race peoples as members of the citizenry—has mixed race been granted independent or even intermediate social status in a fraught and precarious place between minority and majority standing.[16] As mentioned, populations marked publicly and often legally as mixed have long existed in this country. The nineteenth-century nomenclature of octoroons, quadroons, mulattos, for example, represented social and legislative attempts to designate and control such people. Thus the legitimation of a mixed race identity is informed not just by individual intention, or even community activism, but also by advocacy efforts that happen to mesh with national aspirations and are then sanctioned by institutional investment and government recognition. It is important to bear this history in mind when mixed race advocates lay claim to an emerging "Interrace Nation," as Cynthia Chamble puts it, a "race apart" that deserves to create, retrospectively if necessary, a "distinct multiracial history."[17] As Sharron Hall, founder of Intermix, puts it, "It's Time for Foundation."[18] This nation is sometimes asserted as either already present and just waiting to be recognized or else as an aspiration achieved through projection. Many mixed race organizations, like EurasianNation, New Demographics, Mixed Media Watch, mixedfolks.com, and others, advance educational claims on behalf of "the movement."[19] Such organizations claim to be representative of and responsible to a large number of people eager and poised to be identified and rallied. In that sense, the community they are trying to reach, to whom they are beholden, is as much a construction as a discovery. As I noted earlier, Williams and DaCosta challenge these kinds of projections qua assertions as a cross between demographic fudging and political wish fulfillment. That said, even if perhaps Chamble and Spencer do not have the numbers to justify the presence of a "mixed race nation," the social presence and potency of these imagined communities lie less in statistical tallies than in the mobilization of a committed constituency of believers. As Ronald Sundstrom argues, "For a social category, such as race or mixed race, to be a real social kind at some site . . . what has to be present are social forces—labels, institutions, individual intentions, laws, mores, values, traditions—combined in a dynamic with enough strength to give the category presence and impact at that site."[20]

Not surprisingly, then, mixed race as a category gains the most political "presence and impact" when it appears to validate the most cherished and powerful "mores, values and traditions" of the national credo. Frequently portrayed as the realization of Walt Whitman's credo in *Leaves of Grass* (1855)—"I am large. I contain multitudes"—mixed race people appear to reconcile that American contradiction of *e pluribus unum*. If once mulattos stood as testimony of racial inequity, now they are frequently invoked as fleshly confirmation that racial equality has arrived and, thereby, fulfilled part of the nation's providential destiny.[21] The idea that the mere act of miscegenation constitutes racial progress supplies the plot motivation for Warren Beatty's film *Bulworth* (1998): as his main character puts it, political agitation is unnecessary; we just need "pro-creative, racial deconstruction. Everybody's fuckin' everybody else till you can't tell the difference." The implication is that interracial union—or at least the issue from it—sufficiently, and more pleasurably, accomplishes political reform. Indeed, people who identify as mixed race are held up as self-evident physical testimony that the glorious post-race apocalypse is a natural evolution of the democratic experiment. This vision that racial mongrelization is progressively anarchic appears also in Tony Kushner's play *Angels in America: A Gay Fantasia on National Themes* (1994), for instance, in a memorable exchange between the white, right-wing Roy Cohn, dying of an AIDS-related illness, and Belize, the African American gay nurse tending to him. Belize's vision of heaven has "everyone in Balenciaga gowns with red corsages, and big dance palaces full of music and lights and racial impurity and gender confusion . . . all the deities are creole, mulatto, brown as the mouths of rivers."[22] Belize's dream that creolization represents a drag queen's paradise of earthly delights (Roy's hell, of course) leads him to imagine the entropic dissolution of race, sex, and class. His lush dream challenges mainstream heteronormative visions of a mixed race future, but it still embraces the premise that mixed race is the "new frontier,"[23] the hope and expectation that mixed race people can begin the world anew.[24]

III. MIXED RACE PROFILING

Much of the emerging scholarship on this "new frontier" in the fields of education, medicine, philosophy, sociology, and psychology tends to focus on the mental and physical health of the mixed race person as an under-studied population. This psychological and sociological orientation focuses often on the mental health "plight" of multiracial people and on what are determined to be the unique needs of the population.[25] The *Multiracial Child Resource Book: Living Complex Identities* has many articles devoted to the theme of mixed race children's "traumatizing" (Kelly and Root, xv) experiences that result from the "pain and confusion of 'check only one race'" (Douglass, 16) and call for the need to recognize that they are their "own community" (Houston, 227) because "multiracial individuals represent a powerful new form of 'diversity'" (Jones and Smith, 9).[26] But this disciplinary invention of mixed race as a separate kind is problematic because it tends, in effect, to produce the type of population characteristics that it proposes to analyze. What Paul Spickard calls the "boom in biracial biography"[27] has evolved into a normative profile of mixed race people. This profiling extends to the development of mixed race educational curricula and parent education manuals, which in turn provide the legitimating credentials for the marketing of purchases for mixed race children and youth—specialized books, hair, skin, and toy products designed to foster "healthy and happy youth" (Kelley and Root, xv) who will grow up to be a "generation of proud multiracial young people" (xvi)[28] and might one day celebrate "Mixed-Race People History Month (May)."[29] All of these efforts cumulatively reinforce the idea that mixed race people are a distinct population in need of support.

Those who offer special professional attention to the mixed race psyche often explicitly insist that such efforts should not be misinterpreted as pathologizing the individual or playing into the "tragic mulatto" stereotype. In fact, the social sciences are more likely to reinscribe subtly onto the mixed race person another narrative, though one no less problematic— that of the American Adam who embodies values such as individualism, iconoclasm, and free will. In the case of the new professional literature, the challenge for the mixed race person is to resist society's monoracial identifications and racial schema.[30] Once represented as an outcast, now the mixed race person is more often portrayed as a trailblazer. This characterization of the mixed race person understandably overcompensates for the historical demonization of the "mulatto" as marginal and degenerate, and arguably glamorization is more benign than denigration. But both the popular and, with important exceptions, the social scientific characterizations of mixed race tend to reinforce the perception that monoracial identification is, by contrast, collective, prescriptive, trapped in the antiquated race mentality of the 1960s and 1970s, and associated with all things conservative. In this context, black identity is frequently seen as a conscripting, discriminating, and oppressive force that is damaging the hearts and minds of the next generation. For many multiracial activists, then, it is not so much racism but monoracialism that needs to be corrected. As Heather Dalmage puts it, "I propose that if we want to more fully understand multiracial experiences we need to 'flip the script' and analyze why . . . people who identify themselves with a single racial category feel the need and right to intrude upon, pass judgment on, and discriminate against multiracial people and their families."[31]

This rejection of anything that seems to impose historical restriction or infringement upon free self-identification informs Maria P. P. Root's much-circulated "A Bill of Rights for Racially Mixed People." Its first-person declarations—each beginning with "I have the right"—are unequivocal statements of free will issuing from an authoritative "I," and make a defensive appeal for an identity through an assertion of rights (where there are rights, there are a people).[32]

I have the right
To identify myself differently than strangers expect me to identify
To identify myself differently than how my parents identify me
To identify myself differently than my brothers and sisters
To identify myself differently in different situations. . . .

"A Bill of Rights for Racially Mixed People" re-enshrines a model of identity that many in the United States find both irresistible and incontrovertible because it dovetails with many of the nation's self-evident truths, most especially the mandate for self-invention and the agonistic relation of self to society. But because the manifesto is such an ode to free choice, it omits mention of any structural, social, or historical constraints that might inhibit the choices qua rights for some people and not others; nor does it consider the political implications or accountabilities of racial identification. Casting mixed race as a state of mind or a question of privacy reinforces the idea that political agency is a matter of picking up a No. 2

pencil and shading in a bubble or two. The ideal of unfettered choice—
the "mark one or more" designation offering a "bouquet of ethnic possibilities"[33]—appeals as a peculiarly late-capitalist consumerist response
to the political murkiness of racial difference.

Danzy Senna is among those seeking to wrest the language of choice from
the multiracialists, claiming her "right" to her monoracial identification.
Challenging what she calls in "Mulatto Millennium" the Mulatto Nation
policing by the "M.N. posse" (19), and refusing to grant them the market on race as choice, Senna identifies as black, she says, but not because
she has caved in to the idea that one drop of blood made her African
American. Her decision is not following some "pseudoscientific rule but
[making] a conscious choice" (16). Perhaps most pointedly, she argues
that the "choice of multiracial was simply not an adequate response to
racism" (18). Senna's reformulation of rights suggests that the hypocriti-
cal and offending forces are those of the Mulatto Nation's interrogating
"officers" imposing their will upon her, inverting the usual claim that the
category of black steals choice from multiracial people of African descent.

This jockeying over the rhetoric of rights recurs in more conservative
form in Ward Connerly's campaigns to end the collection of racial data
on government, education, and police documents.[34] Explicit about his
political interest in doing away altogether with racial identity by redefining it as a discreet private matter, Connerly has proposed multiple state
bills to this end including Proposition 54: "The Racial Privacy Initiative."
The various agendas of mixed race advocates have at times (sometimes
inadvertently) collaborated with or been co-opted by conservatives such
as Newt Gingrich and others who have publicly aligned themselves with
those efforts that seem to promise disabling race-based policies. But what
most links Connerly's initiatives, in particular, to documents like "A Bill
of Rights for Racially Mixed People" is not their political orientation but
the proprietary language of racial self-determination and disclosure. Root
argues that individuals are bestowed with a defensible right to change
identity as often and in whatever way they wish: expressed through the
genre of declaration and in the discourse of unraced universal rights,
Root's "Bill of Rights"—just as Connerly's Proposition 54 does—embeds
and empowers mixed race identity within and through the rhetoric of pos-

sessive individualism. In 2006, the Harvard Civil Rights Project (now at UCLA) concluded that the U.S. Department of Education's extension of the "mark one or more" multiracial options to K–12 and college forms is a setback to civil rights.[35] Precisely for these reasons, it is important to examine the racial call to arms and the rhetorical construction of identity in this and other similar mixed race manifestos.[36]

IV. THE BOX FETISH

These manifestos, like many mixed race advocacy efforts, have focused on the issue of classification. They tend to reify the census box, or its legal cousins like the school requirements to offer racial box selections for incoming students, as the site for identity assertion and political action, and explicitly argue that not being able to mark the correct box rises to the level of an offense requiring government reform.[37] The circumscription and miniaturization of political discussions to matters of the "box" (be it the census, a job application, a school admission form, or a television poll) center political reform on self-expression rather than on systemic change.[38] In 2010 the federal government undertook what it called the 2010 Census Portrait of America Road Tour, to try to convince "hard-to-count audiences" that they should participate in the dicennial census. The Association of Multiethnic Americans lobbied people with an e-mail message marked "URGENT," saying "Multiracial Communities Must Be Counted Accurately in 2010." The press release enjoined people to take advantage of the "mark one or more races" (MOOM) option first made available during the 2000 Census for "all individuals who would like to be counted among the full diversity of their racial and ethnic backgrounds."[39] What better place to exercise the American mandate of individualism than through multiple box-checking as, ironically, a refusal to be "boxed" in racially. It suggests that people can check "black" today, "more than one" tomorrow, and refuse to check anything the day after.[40] In that sense, for many mixed race advocates, the census box represents the new nonviolent resistance, a finger in the eye of the racial status quo.

Yet even the most well-intentioned individuals are often unaware of the political effects of what they see as a private choice. In 2000 a "community empowerment zone" in a mostly black neighborhood in Tacoma,

Washington—targeted for economic improvement based on racial demo-graphics—was threatened by the sudden increase in those identifying more than one race for the census. Overnight, those who had been black became mixed, and the empowerment zone faced potential dissolution. Few could have anticipated the community impact of their box-checking, including the confused city officials trying to tally the results. Federal guidelines have since sought to correct for these unexpected effects, but the point is that the government accounting of race through the census was origi-nally designed explicitly to inform public policy and the distribution of resources. This is not about ethnic squabbling over spoils.[41] It is a recog-nition that the census is an economic tool that was never meant as—nor should it be—a site for self-expression. As Michael Omi and Howard Winant describe the census, its historically changing racial categorization

establishes often contradictory parameters of racial identity into which both individuals and groups must fit. How one is categorized is far from a merely academic or even personal matter. Such matters as access to employment, hous-ing, or other publically or privately valued goods; social program design and the disbursement of local, state, and federal funds; or the organization of election (among many other issues) are directly affected by racial classification and the recognition of "legitimate" groups.[42]

These competing senses of the function of the census—as an accounting of self or as a political instrument—represent a collision of generational understandings of race that cannot be resolved simply by altogether reject-ing the traditional classification schema of the census, as some mixed race advocates suggest, thinking that they are destroying what Mark Twain in *Pudd'nhead Wilson* (1894) calls "a fiction of law and custom." Ironically, this position tends only to reinforce the logic behind categorization, for it assumes the destruction of a racial homogeneity that never existed. Accord-ing to some studies, well over 80 percent of people of African descent in North America are mixed, and Latinos also, of course, comprise mestizo and diasporic mixes. There is no purity to overturn. Others suggest that more refined racial categorization—new and improved boxes—can bet-ter represent individual hybridity. But Brazil and South Africa have long experimented with legal racial designations of every nuance and shade.

Most scholars agree that the two countries' elaborate taxonomies have not been instrumental in effecting racial equity and progress.[43] Another common explanation for checking more than one box is the argument that if one checks "just" "black" (or "Latino" or "Asian"), the person will betray his or her white parent. But the loyalty test is a red herring: Halle Berry's white mother, for one, is on record as being proud that her daughter claimed the 2002 Academy Award for Best Actress as the first African American woman in history to do so.[44] And as I mentioned, even President Obama checked simply "African American" on the 2010 Census form.[45] So it is worth pausing to ask how and why checking a census box became such an iconic moment to prove filial devotion.

The Souls of Mixed Folk examines works that honor, encourage, and study cross-cultural exchanges and multiracial experiences, but do so by going beyond the box. They do so without making mixed race either a political special interest or the national solution to the "race problem," and they suggest better venues in which to represent multi-splendored selves that might more productively ally with social justice efforts.

V. MIXED RACE BEFORE THE END OF RACE: W. E. B. DU BOIS, LANGSTON HUGHES, FRAN ROSS

White men, and colored womens, and little bastard chilluns—
that's de way of de South . . . mixtries, mixtries.
Cora, in Langston Hughes, *Mulatto* (1935)[46]

Africa and Europe have been united in my family. There is nothing unusual
about this interracial history. It has been duplicated thousands of times.
W. E. B. Du Bois, "The Concept of Race," in *Dusk of Dawn* (1940)[47]

The popular emphasis on the mixed race person as nouveau, as sui generis in history, usually necessitates the strategic erasure of a past that might suggest otherwise. Some mixed race advocacy groups have sought to correct the historical record, although they fiercely contest just what that history is, whose it is, and who should (re)write it. I explore the politics of this mixed race historiography across several chapters in *The Souls of Mixed Folk*. In particular I examine late-twentieth-century and twenty-first-century works that call on much earlier uses of mixed race in the African American literary tradition, not as an identity category with its own lost tradition but as a powerful trope to engage issues of civil rights and social change. To this end, I would like to touch on a few of these earlier texts that are too often lost when recovery efforts are invested in defining a distinct mixed race tradition rather than one imbricated with others.

W. E. B. Du Bois' approach to mixed race as a cultural heuristic, for example, is a prescient counter to many of the ahistorical, apolitical post-racial discourses informing much scholarship and public debate. Du Bois was never particularly interested in "the idea of racial amalgamation" ("The Concept of Race," 628) with intermarriage as an end in itself, but he was fascinated by "the various types of mankind and their intermixture" (629).[48] Du Bois' mixed selves always represent the beginning of political possibilities, the climax of his international fantasies of bio-divinity. In his story "Jesus Christ in Waco, Texas," collected in *Darkwater: Voices from Within the Veil* (1920), Christ is a "mulatto," trope of oppressed, harbinger of the Second Coming. In Du Bois' novel *Dark Princess* (1928), the black-Indian baby is raised to the heavens in a Lion King "Circle of Life" moment:

> "King of the Snows of Gaurisankar!"
> "Protector of Ganga the Holy!"
> "Incarnate Son of the Buddha!"
> "Grand Mughal of Utter India!"
> "Messenger and Messiah to all the Darker Worlds!"[49]

In this spectacular gesture, the child is a multi-faith offering—weightily crowned as King, Protector, Buddha's heir, Mughal, Messenger, and Messiah—that impossibly executes everything from the sacrificial contract of Christ and the fulfillment of spiritual reincarnation to the perpetuation of an elite patronymic. On the one hand, Du Bois' melodramatic ecstasy seems to resemble the millennial hagiography of mixed race. But Du Bois' baby heralds the celestial ascendancy of the "Darker Worlds" in particular. Its birth realizes Langston Hughes' dream, in Du Bois' fiction, no longer deferred,[50] and Martin Luther King, Jr.'s "fierce urgency of now," not the glory days of Generation Ethnically Ambiguous.[51]

16

The study of mixed race, Du Bois insists, is key to understanding how race itself is intimately connected to global and interlocking racialized systems of oppression—to how the "coolie" and the "labor classes" are also kept in their places ("The Concept of Race," 629). He calls for critical attention to the study of mixed race, not as a separate identity warranting independent legal representation but because he sees "intermixture" as the hidden code to the economic basis for race discrimination, and it is for that reason that "[w]e have not only not studied race and race mixture in America, but we have tried almost by legal process to stop such study" (629). A true study of race and race mixture, he argues in "The White World,"[52] does not have patience with the specious argument that "there are no races" because "we are all so horribly mixed" (665). Nor will Du Bois be trapped by his own recognition of the heterogeneity of the race, when his imaginary white friend and interlocutor in the essay concludes, "You are not black; you are no Negro." (This confrontation—so familiar to mixed race people—in which a white person tendentiously pronounces upon their race, anticipates the experience of conceptual artist and philosopher Adrian Piper in graduate school, which later informed "Cornered" and many other performances.)[53] Du Bois' fictional friend, noting the great diversity of black people, takes it as an opportunity to challenge race altogether: "But what is this group; and how do you differentiate it; and how can you call it 'black' when you admit it is not black?" Du Bois tidily dispenses with the sophistry: my "certain group that I know and to which I belong" is defined not by blood or color but by a greater "spiritual hope" (666) and social purpose, a theme he reiterates throughout his life and work no matter his evolving politics and definitions of race.

Langston Hughes also mines the metaphor of mixed race for its insight into economic inequity and social possibility in his Broadway play *Mulatto* (1935), the longest-running drama by an African American on Broadway until Lorraine Hansberry's *A Raisin in the Sun* (1959).[54] In the play's resolution, a black woman, Cora, who has borne three unacknowledged children by a white man, refers to what she calls the "mixtries" of biracial children, the way they appear to have been born without daddies, as simply "de way of de South" (31). As Cora's colloquialism—a cross between "mix" and "mysteries"—makes clear, race mixing is historically indexed to covert operations of sex and power. Because these operations exist as wink-and-nod secrets, her racially mixed children are not allowed to name the white parent as father: Cora's offspring are therefore deemed "mysteries," immaculate conceptions in which, putatively, "black women do not know the fathers of their children" (23).[55] Her notion of mixtries is a vernacular lesson in what is, Eva Saks argues, the "national anxiety about miscegenation," which "is more specifically an anxiety about establishing patriarchal lines of property, about the transmission of material goods within the white community, and the corresponding disinheritance of the black mother and any children born of an interracial union."[56] Saks' point, and Cora's experience, are historical reminders that race mixing continues to regulate the traffic of resources in the contemporary moment, whether through the census or through more indirect vehicles. The political economics of mixed race may not be as apparent now that parentage is generally acknowledged and the one-drop rule can no longer effect legal disenfranchisement by having the child follow "the condition of the mother." But race and class continue to be indexed in close statistical relation; people of color who marry white or light tend to move upward in socioeconomic opportunity; mixed race children with one white parent tend then also to have a higher socioeconomic status, attend better schools, live in better neighborhoods.[57] Moreover, as many chapters in *The Souls of Mixed Folk* address, the national popularity and next-generation marketing of mixed race yields dividends for its corporate sponsors even as racial discrimination in both blunt and subtle varieties persists unaffected.

Looking back to some of the earlier twentieth-century engagements with mixed race also allows us to locate examples of formal experimentation and ironic play with the subject. The nonfiction mixed race memoirs emerging in abundance during the 1990s adhere to a fairly predictable linear plot structured by the search for personal identity, for parental recognition, and for social incorporation. But before them, Fran Ross with *Oreo* (1967) offers a prescient send-up of the genre and bears more kinship with Baby Halfie's outré aesthetic. Her fiction, appearing some forty years before representative memoirs like *The Color of Water* (2006) by James McBride became a mainstream staple of the Oprah Book Club, anticipates and annihilates every convention of the contemporary mixed race coming-of-age narrative. In *Oreo*, the biracial protagonist, Oreo (a name usually leveled at a black person who is considered somehow "white" inside—a "sellout"), in search of her white father, thumbs her nose at almost every earnest piety associated with contemporary mixed race memoirs. One of the most devout yearnings in most such memoirs is the reconciliation of competing ethno-racial-religious inheritances. But in Ross' novel of black-Jewish chiaroscuro, equilibrium is not only beside the point for Oreo; it is represented as perhaps the least interesting dimension to her hyphenated identity. Oreo finds imaginative excess and political insight in the cheeky rub between Jewish racism and black anti-Semitism, in the inharmonious clash of Yiddish and Black English Vernacular.[58] In *Oreo*, all epistemological schema are snubbed—diagrams, equations, recipes, menus, appendices, etc., yield not explanation or truths but furrowed brows and belly laughs. Language is flaunted as an opaque rather than transparent medium (the text's "helpful" translations of Yiddish lead only to colloquialisms or neologisms that require even further translation). High and low literary forms are not only collapsed but also mixed and mismatched. The novel plunders so many different forms—detective, picaresque, allegory, myth, slave narrative, vaudeville, soft porn—that genre becomes mélange, and the indiscretions of form reflect, as well, transgressions of race, gender, and identity.

The multiracial stew resembles the anarchic hopes of Kushner's Belize except that *Oreo* repudiates all heavens (on earth or above). Satirizing the Greek tale of Theseus and his search, *Oreo* makes hay of the search for divine origin, family origin, or identity origin. The novel uncouples identity from spiritual foundations, primal sites, grounded verities, and the patrimonies or matrimonies driving many contemporary mixed race autobiographies. The search for answers, genealogies, for any kind of epistemological or ontological certainty, quickly becomes moot in Ross' novel—indeed, becomes the butt of jokes. Oreo's initially serious and forward-marching quest becomes peripatetic jaunt, then Möbius strip, then M. C. Escher maze, and is an important literary forebear, I would argue, to the mixed race anti-bildungsroman that I discuss later in the book. The pre-twenty-first-century ironic, self-reflexive, and social justice uses of mixed race suggested by Du Bois, Hughes, and Ross—to name but a very few—are rarely acknowledged in the more contemporary representations and historiographies of mixed race. Yet they offer counter-perspectives to the cultural invention of a mixed race community, the commercial and academic mainstreaming of a mixed race identity, and the ascension of mixed race popularity too often unnecessarily pitted against broader civil rights partnerships.

VI. MULATTOESQUE BLAXPLORATIONS

Artistically and politically indebted to these earlier works, the texts of Danzy Senna, Colson Whitehead, Emily Raboteau, Aaron McGruder, Nate Creekmore, Dave Chappelle, Carl Hancock Rux, and Lezley Saar offer a prolegomenon to a progressive mixed race aesthetics and activism. Their work fits somewhat asymmetrically into what has come to be called the post-soul era. On the one hand, as Anthony Appiah puts it, mixed race is "one philosopher's hopes for a new world." The description of his 2008 *New York Times* article, "Towards a New Cosmopolitanism"—"Out/In, Peoples/Individuals, Pure/Mixed, Authenticity/Modernity, Tradition/Rights, Preservation/Contamination"—reinforces a notion of hybridity and mixedness as requisite to a democratic future, replacing backward racial "authenticity," defensive purity, and antiquated tradition.[59] Mark Anthony Neal similarly suggests that a post-soul aesthetic renders moot what he calls "traditional" civil rights–era understandings of blackness in particular and, by implication, race in general. The "post-soul," he argues, "ultimately renders 'traditional' tropes of blackness dated and even meaningless; in its borrowing from black modern traditions, it is so consumed with its contemporary existential concerns that such traditions are not just called into question but obliterated."[60] But as Bertram Ashe, in discussing the post-soul, suggests, mixed race identity need not be positioned as reinforcing Appiah's old/new logic or Neal's black obsolescence. Ashe notes,

These [post-soul] artists and texts trouble blackness, they worry blackness; they stir it up, touch it, feel it out, and hold it up for examination in ways that depart significantly from previous—and necessary—preoccupations with struggling for political freedom, or with an attempt to establish and sustain a coherent black identity. Still, from my vantage point, this "troubling" of blackness by post-soul writers is ultimately done in service to black people. . . . These artists do not have a singular, coherent political stance from which to articulate a specific political argument, but post-soul "blaxploration" acts as much on behalf of black people as traditional explorers acted on behalf of whatever nation or people they represented. As such, these post-soul artists maintain a dogged allegiance to their communities, however nonessentialized and gorged with critiques said allegiance might be.[61]

All the artists and writers whose work I examine in the *Souls of Mixed Folk* do precisely this: offer up capacious racial identities fully consistent with heterogeneity, postmodernity, and self-examination; theirs is a worried, stirred-up, touched-up, felt-up, and held-up blackness.[62] As Ashe puts it in his discussion of Senna's *Caucasia*, post-soul blackness should be able to accommodate the main character's perception on the novel's last page that there exist others who are also "black like me, a mixed girl."[63] Significantly, Trey Ellis identifies this aesthetic as part of the black inheritance of the "cultural mulatto," one of those figures who are "tragic . . . only when they forget they too are wholly black."[64] Biracialism and biculturalism for these artists and intellectuals do not replace blackness; they prompt a deeper investigation and expansion of it—what Ashe calls "blaxploration." As he describes it, blaxploration involves "a hybrid, fluid, elastic cultural mulattoesque sense of black identity [which] marks the work of many post-soul artists" (614).

This critical mulattoesque move can, therefore, engender a generous blackness that reconciles pre–civil rights and post-soul conditions and forms an artistic basis for a "new politics of difference," one that can embrace "multiplicity, and hetereogenity . . . the contingent, provisional, variable, tentative, shifting, and changing"[65] that does not require a total eclipse of blackness as we know it. Rather, blaxploration honors a hybridity that is "in service to" and "on behalf of" black needs and ends. Many of the works addressed in *The Souls of Mixed Folk* suggest ways that mixed race studies, aesthetics, and politics can be understood allied alongside this sense of mulattoesque blackness.

VII. BACK FROM BEYOND BLACK

It is in this context that I want to explain why I purposely chose to focus on representations of black mixes rather than to explore the entire galaxy of mixedness in its endless inter- and intra-racial configurations. Many charge that it is necessary to go beyond the black-white paradigm that has structured so much of the U.S. national debate. It is true that popular public discourse tends to equate race with blackness. But the alacrity with which some dismiss an examination of mixed race within constructions of blackness, and the intellectual irritability with which a claim of "narrowness" is often levied at those who look primarily at blackness, are not unlike the impatience with what is perceived as a dated civil rights–era agenda. Both responses are suspect to the extent that they suggest African American studies is a cultural nationalist project interested only in black people—and only in a certain kind of black people—or that monoracialism is equivalent to homogeneity, or that studying blackness is not wholly compatible with (and in fact arguably necessary for) an intersectional, comparative racial analysis. Black mixes are historically integrated with and fluidly interact with other interracial sociopolitical arrangements, of course, but any comparative understanding of blackness benefits from a deeper appreciation of the complex literary and political history of being black in America. This is especially true when antiblackness, as Jared Sexton has argued, is often such a central part of mixed race discourse.[66] My principle of selection makes a case for the rich intellectual yield that can come from focusing on a peculiar literary and political dynamics of a specific mix: it should go without saying that the history of black-white relations and representation in North America is distinct from that of white-Asian or Latino-black or Caribbean or South African mixes, and those histories and experiences warrant critical attention in their own right as well as the ways in which they are entwined. As I argue in *The Souls of Mixed Folk*, the emergent field of mixed race studies risks intellectual dilettantism if it confuses comparative racial study with the conflation of any and all seemingly applicable literary traditions as if all were simultaneously present and equally salient across any set of texts.

Not only does blackness have a distinct, powerful, and troubled status within the study of mixed race, but it continues to have one, intractably, within broader U.S. racial politics. As Orlando Patterson notes in "Race and Diversity in the Age of Obama," the "present wave of immigrants and their children are rapidly assimilating into an ever-vibrant American mainstream culture . . . [in] an endlessly dynamic two-way cultural process." That said, he points out, the "great exception to this process of social incorporation is black Americans," echoing arguments made by Samira Kawash, Eduardo Bonilla-Silva, Lawrence Bobo, and many others.[67] The continued failure of full enfranchisement for black America results from black poverty and "chronic hypersegregation": "Whatever the reason . . . their isolation means that the problem of ethno-racial relations in America remains, at heart, a black-white issue."[68] The black mixes I explore here have been and continue to be pivotal in racial formations underwriting national identity and dynamics, and as I suggested earlier, the civil rights implications of mixed race identification for African Americans are among the most profound. In *The Souls of Mixed Folk*, critical mediations on black mixes emerge across several genres and media: anthologies, novels, comic strips, late-night television, drama, and art installations. Their appearance across a wide spectrum of pop and literary cultural texts becomes part of their meta-commentary on the divides between high and low culture, trade and popular presses, and they resonate particularly with historical tensions between the "folk" and the "talented tenth" that are so especially indexed to black cultural concerns. Indeed, the black mix focus is also an occasion to consider Tommie Shelby's theorization of a new model for black solidarity that dispenses with racial essentialism but retains "blackness as an emancipatory tool."[69] The creative blaxplorations in *The Souls of Mixed Folk* illustrate this refocusing of solidarity to one based on social justice, but they do not rely solely on Shelby's "oppression-centered" model, or on a separation of "social identity" from "racial injustice." The model of racial identity that emerges shares Shelby's nonessentialized premises but also asserts immediate claims to social realities in which there is no demonization of "identity politics," as he puts it.

VIII. SEEING, STARING, SECOND SIGHT, OUT OF SIGHT

> How do I startle someone into seeing racism, even when it indicts oneself? . . . If and
> when that seeing happens, that seeing of an unconsidered link to racism—it comes one
> way in the first instance, sneaks up, soft as osmosis in the second, crashes through with a
> bright flash in the third. The understanding never seems to happen in the same way twice.
>
> Patricia Williams, *Seeing a Color-Blind Future*[70]

This tension between recognizing race as a productive force while still indicting racism is an acute and recurring concern in African American studies and in race studies generally. Many of these debates play out in the politics of visibility, over the role that textual and political representation should (or not) play in effecting social justice. A good deal of mixed race advocacy remains indebted to precisely the visual fetishes and specular epistemologies of race that proponents explicitly claim to overthrow, in part because they never quite address the cultural construction of "seeing" itself. These "ways of seeing,"[71] to invoke John Berger, fit these mixed race subjects neatly back into the established national order even as advocates suggest that we are seeing something new with racially ambivalent bodies.[72] Thus when mixed race advocacy groups argue for visible representation, they frequently enlist people to represent them who meet the tacit criteria of ambiguity. The result of this silent norming is that people who wish to self-identify as mixed but do not appear ambiguous—or ambiguous enough, according to the historically and contextually shifting criteria—are less suited to serve as political representatives.

This issue of representation for mixed people recurs throughout *The Souls of Mixed Folk*, and emerges as well in the related tension between the desire to invoke minority representation as ethnic affirmation and political litmus test ("we can see how far we've come when we see ourselves on the screen, in theatre, on television, as newscasters, spokespeople, and politicians") and the view that the visual is merely a token, or worse, a seduction that inhibits social critique.[73] These approaches to political visibility generate fierce debates: on the one hand, minority representation can help build an important critical mass of people of color, can bring different voices to the table, ideally at decision-making levels behind the screen or scene, can affect people's perceptions of who belongs where in the public domain. On the other hand, the visible presence of people of color in the media can be cynical tokenism, substituting for actual political influence or reform. Or, as in the case of some media consultants currently lobbying specifically for mixed race representation, it can be unclear whether collaborative cross-racial politics will break down under the competition for the already limited venues for people of color.[74]

Certainly many of the works examined here call for challenges to the unimpeachability of sight and recognize that the obsession with seeing race is also a necessarily flawed search for ontological gratification. But several also retrieve and revise the racial value of what Du Bois calls "the gift of second sight"—seeing how others see oneself—which comes already fitted with a bracing appreciation of the oppressive applications of seeing. These works signify on double consciousness—with its bifocal sight yielding no "true self-consciousness," according to Du Bois—in order to develop a kind of doubled vision that sees through others' misseeing. This doubled consciousness potentially enables epistemic insight into a political and racial order maintained by what or how one is supposed to see or not, and explores other forms of making visible the politically unsaid and socially unseen by employing semaphoric symptoms and signs that redirect and refocus the eye. Linda Martín Alcoff is similarly wary of the political privileging of the visible and so offers the similarly Du Boisian proposal that we must *re-see* race and, by doing so, begin to transform its meanings.[75] Understanding fully as she does the limitations of a "vision-centric approach" (197) and the misuse of sight as direct vehicle of knowledge (198), she argues that although the visible does not reveal biological or metaphysical truths, it most certainly indexes social realities. As Alcoff puts it, "[T]he practices of visibility are indeed revealing of significant facts about our cultural ideology, but what the visible reveals is not the ultimate truth; rather it often reveals self-projection, identity anxieties and the material inscription of social violence" (8). This insight capitalizes on Ralph Ellison's notion of visibility (and invisibility) as a function of "the peculiar disposition of the eyes of those with whom I come in contact. A matter of the construction of their inner eyes, those eyes with which they view through their physical eyes upon reality."[76]

In *Invisible Man*, the protagonist's recognition of the obscuring power of these "inner eyes" comes with the constant potential for violence—not only does he feel injured by whites' inability to see him through the cataracts of racial preconception, but he is tempted to kill them for their blindness, understanding that even then the unseeing person will think he has been attacked by a "phantom" (5). Eventually the protagonist views white sightlessness as something he can turn to his advantage, and to that extent Ellison, Du Bois, and Alcoff similarly call for a refocusing of ways of seeing that can afford not merely a defensive but also a productive opportunity for social insight into the intersubjective processes of racial formation.

In *The Souls of Mixed Folk*, this charge to refocus also involves considering the seeming opposite of invisibility: the experience of being stared at, the result of a hypervisibility that is acute and uncomfortable for many mixed race people.[77] The stare is usually considered to be only an aggressive example of visual hostility, but, as Rosemarie Garland-Thomson cogently argues, it can also provide the unlikely opportunity for interpersonal connection and epistemological reconsideration: "We stare when ordinary seeing fails, when we want to know more. . . . Seeing startlingly stareable people challenges our assumption by interrupting complacent visual business as usual. Staring offers an occasion to rethink the status quo. Who we are can shift into focus by staring at who we think we are not."[78] The Baby Halfie doll that I examine in the opening pages is a useful example of the ways stareable bodies can take us beyond "ordinary seeing," not only as an invitation to reconsider racial and visual clichés of mixed race but as a chance to re-imagine social relations through art. In that spirit, *The Souls of Mixed Folk* analyzes mixed race experiments in sightfulness that join aesthetic invention with new forms of social engagement.

CHAPTER ONE

The Mis-education of Mixed Race

The emergence of university courses and student organizations by, for, and
about biracial and multiracial people strongly indicates that this identity
deserves social and academic legitimacy and institutional sustenance.

Teresa Kay Williams et al., "Being Different Together in the University Classroom"[1]

[W]hat I am always cautious about is persons of mixed race focusing
so narrowly on their own unique experiences that they are detached
from larger struggles, and I think it's important to try to avoid that
sense of exclusivity, and feeling that you're special in some way.

Barack Obama, from the documentary *Chasing Daybreak*[2]

I. THE RISE OF MIXED RACE STUDIES

The U.S. national education industry has emerged as one of the most powerful vehicles through which mixed race is manufactured and marketed.
Anthologies, collections, pedagogical manuals, and educational materials in print, media, and Web form have popularized, propagandized, and
institutionalized particular ideas and ideals of mixed race. This chapter
explores the ways in which K–12 and college curricula have begun canonizing the emergent field of "mixed race studies." Its canonization often
occurs with the explicit rationale of inclusiveness and equity of representation, and sometimes lays claim to a revolution that shares much with
radical challenges to education that the black and brown power movements initiated in the 1960s and 1970s. These earlier reforms critiqued the
standard canons of knowledge and content of education—what got taught
and who decided—as well as the way education naturalized traditional
racial and social hierarchies. The opening lines to Toni Morrison's *The
Bluest Eye* (1970), with its incantation, and then revision, of the familiar

and reassuring children's primer, the Dick and Jane story, is an example of this challenge:

Here is the house. It is green and white. It has a red door. It is very pretty. Here is the family. Mother, Father, Dick, and Jane live in the green-and-white house. They are very happy.

The novel immediately enacts a refutation of this ideal through a grotesque orthographic bleed that anticipates the novel's social critique of the domestic ideal:

Hereisthehouseitisgreenandwhiteithasareddooritisveryprettyhereisthefamilymotherfatherdickandjaneliveinthegreenandwhitehousetheyareveryhappy

As the novel suggests, literacy is not just the acquisition of language but also the internalization of cultural and racial norms. How does literacy instruct children and adults in certain ways of thinking about race? about beauty? about family? about the world? And how does not only how we read but also what we read shape or reshape those very early perceptions? Morrison, then a senior editor at Random House, was and is very concerned also about the literary canon—what counts as "good" or "bad" literature, what texts should be validated and taught or not taught in schools. This, too, is related to the racial politics of literacy and cultural education.

Literacy, Morrison understood, implicitly and explicitly introduces expectations of normalcy, of standard cultural practices, and of aesthetic valuation; in short, literacy establishes tacit instructions for social and political relations, naturalizing racism, too, in all its subtle forms. For *The Bluest Eye*, the racism emerges through norms of beauty that render people of color ugly. However, potentially these forms of pedagogical instruction can set up countervailing literacies, and in that sense, their power brings with it both risks and opportunities, a vehicle for social change and justice.

Mixed race educational reforms often evoke this civil rights tradition, and sometimes their proposed curricula do challenge certain social assumptions, particularly promoting the acceptability of interracial unions and transracial adoption. But like the earlier bids for curricular change, this more recent move to integrate the study of mixed race into schools shares much with traditional educational systems that normalize certain acceptable forms of cultural literacy over others, and to that extent, mixed race education functions as a vehicle of both change and not-change, of challenge and yet of accommodation. In the case of mixed race education, the cultural literacy being taught involves and presumes the acceptance of mixed race as a unique and distinct type of racial experience deserving of its own recognition and thus requiring its own special cultural instructions and social prescriptives. Just as educational systems usually pose as neutral "information delivery" mechanisms, so do these; the fact that analysis of their claims is unwelcome—even, at times, represented as politically backward—makes study of them all the more pressing. As mixed race education has been increasingly mainstreamed, and continues to gain influence in shaping perception, it is essential to examine its particular educational mandates and requisites, to explore advocates' assumptions about race and identity that inform their policy recommendations. The cultural instructions in these textbooks and curricula posit mixed race education as for and about the "next" generation: this is education as script and illustration for a projected future, one that both models and prescribes ideal social relations.

Of course, their project does not differ from most children's books or educational programming, some of which also tends towards this didactic impulse. But much mixed race education is particularly unself-reflective of the ways it sometimes replicates traditional prejudices as part of the very process it uses to overturn others. For in the progressive effort to normalize the "atypical" family of multiply raced individuals, targeted consumers are almost invariably cast as an imagined community of light-skinned children of suburban middle-class, heterosexual parents, as well as educators enlightened enough to recognize their peculiar needs. One of the needs that has been identified, and ostensibly requires catering to, is the right to self-identify racially. The educational industry has valorized the notion of race as non-contingent free choice—with its implicit suggestion that racial self-definition is equally available to all regardless of skin color or context. These assumptions are then emplotted into the educational content, including, as I will examine, narratives of literary and political history. From the 1990s through the first decade of the twenty-first century, almost all mixed race educational mandates have been tacitly couched in these similar conceptual frames, frames that both enable and yet complicate the goal of what has been called "oppositional" and "transgressive" pedagogy. Articles such as "Challenging Race and Racism: A Framework for Educators" by Ronald David Glass and Kendra R. Wallace; "Being Different Together in the University Classroom: Multiracial Identity as Transgressive Education" by Teresa Kay Williams, Cynthia L. Nakashima, George Kitahara Kich, and G. Reginald Daniel; and "Multicultural Education" by Francis Wardle are all important contributions to the study of mixed race. But as the titles of their articles suggest, they tend to take as a given that the educational project of institutionalizing the concept and practice of mixed race is, in and of itself, "progressive"—that is, to assume that it ipso facto challenges the status quo.[3] My argument here involves a provisional critique of some of the notions of mixed race that are currently emerging in curricula, but is not meant as an end in itself. Rather, my challenges here aim to clear space for alternative pedagogies that potentially encourage more politically complex understandings of mixed race identification, as well as to lay the ground for the radically different engagements of mixed race in the literature and drama I examine in the subsequent chapters, works unaccounted for within current educational rubrics. I hope, then, that this analysis will not only facilitate the ability of people who identify as mixed race to examine critically their experiential claims as the basis for epistemic social insight, but also, more broadly, to help explain how mixed race studies and politics are affecting and taking shape within the educational realm, civil rights initiatives, and literary studies of race.

II. THE CURRICULAR INSTITUTIONALIZATION OF MIXED RACE

Since the 1990s, the undergraduate classroom has become a locus of advocacy, in part because demographic study of those who identify as mixed race suggests that the vast majority have been people under twenty-five.[4] It is no accident, therefore, that there has been a nationwide mushroom-

ing of undergraduate courses on mixed race in the humanities and social sciences at institutions such as Yale, NYU, Vassar, Smith, Stanford,
UC Berkeley, and many others. Many have hosted student-sponsored national conferences, educational workshops, and leadership summits on the
subject. The national organization EurasianNation offers a link on its Web
page to "The Top 19 Mixed Race Studies Courses" in the United States
and Canada. On that same site is an article, "The Explosion in Mixed
Race Studies" by Erica Schlaikjer (April 2003), which refers to "the new
generation of academics . . . pushing the boundaries of ethnic studies."[5]
Many of the mixed race organizations, Web pages, affinity and advocacy
groups, magazines, and journals that have emerged in the last few years
of the twenty-first century have begun aggressive campaigns for educational reform, particularly regarding reading lists and curricula for, and
representation of, the so-called mixed race experience at the college level.[6]

The explicit goal of much of this work is to educate a cohort; but, in
fact, mixed race constituencies are as often generated by these efforts. The
classroom is a hub for some of the most active work in creating populations who identify as mixed race. In fact, the new crop of undergraduate
courses on mixed race around the country have, to a great extent, pre-
ceded and anticipated the emerging body of critical literature on mixed
race. These courses, often requested by the students themselves, have
become the developing ground for nascent political identities and social
organizing, both the result of and the inspiration for student clubs, youth
leadership summits, and national student conferences devoted to the issue
of mixed race. That educational environments have become a crucible for
defining and refining what it means to be "mixed race" should remind
us that pedagogy is not the mere by-product of research, that these classroom events and practices are more than just the application of theoretical models and principles and certainly more than an inevitable effect of
changing demographics.[7] The activism of students suggests that a certain
youthful populism is reshaping curricula, a very appealing idea to students'
sense of empowerment. And to some extent that is true. But as Chandra
Talpade Mohanty argues, institutions of higher education have, since the
1970s, developed "what might be called the Race Industry, an industry
that is responsible for the management, commodification, and domesti-

cation of race on American campuses."[8] Mixed race studies is no exception—it is driven by student and social interest, but it is highly managed, marketed, and to some extent tamed within the educational system. And if the classroom has become a particularly dynamic engine of invention and community building, the educational and publishing industries have been just as quick to capitalize on this phenomenon.

III. COVERING: THE EYE'S INSTRUCTION

I begin by reviewing what has become an increasing mainstay in these courses—the mixed race textbook, which is commonly a collection or anthology billed as foundational or field-defining. And I am focusing first on a few representative *covers* from this spate of mixed race anthologies. I chose to examine covers over content, first, precisely because they are often seen as insignificant—after all, we are warned from an early age not to judge books (or people) by their covers, to assume that the substance within rarely corresponds to outward appearance. By presuming the general deceitfulness of such sources, readers can complacently assume that they have performed the only necessary critical act required when it comes to them. But this posture of suspicion does not encourage closer examination of all the sorts of subtle cultural and readerly work that covers perform. After all, covers provide the eye's instruction, the prefatory function of visually glossing the pages within. They implicitly sanction certain ways of reading over others, coax certain interpretative moves even before a page has been read. Their readerly orienting becomes especially powerful when the genre or topic is new on the scene: they are one of the first forms of guidance to readers, implicitly telling us what and how to think about a work, what kind of context and frame of reference by which to understand it.

But literary covers can conceal as well as reveal, and unintentionally narrow as well as open perspective. This is a particularly fascinating issue when it comes to covers of texts representing what mixed race is or is supposed to be. How to represent mixed race when some expressions of ethnic identity are socially encouraged and approved of and others are not? when the social performances of ethnic identity occur in the context of a society that rigorously delimits and monitors expressions of ethnicity? Kenji Yoshino argues, in *Covering: The Hidden Assault on Our Civil*

Rights, that "covering," the coerced pressure to hide crucial aspects of one's identity, provides an adaptive strategy for the ethnic minorities that deploy it, but that the conditions for it are necessarily repressive.[9]

And in fact, covers have quietly played a role in the creation of certain restrictive, normative models of mixed race: *The Sum of Our Parts, Mixed-Race Literature*, and *Mixed: An Anthology of Short Fiction on the Multi-racial Experience*[10] people their covers with stylized facial abstractions (Fig. 1.1); *New Faces in a Changing America: Multiracial Identity in the 21st Century* (Fig. 1.2), *The Multiracial Experience: Racial Borders as the New Frontier* (Fig. 1.3), *Multiracial Child Resource Book: Living Complex Realities* (Fig. 1.4), and *Of Many Colors: Portraits of Multiracial Families* (Fig 1.5), as well as *What Are You?: Voices of Mixed-Race Young People, Mixed Blood: Intermarriage and Ethnic Identity in Twentieth-Century America, Blended Nation: Portraits and Interviews of Mixed-Race America*, and many others[11] feature pictures of "real" people, suggesting, similarly, that the mission of the volume is to represent a snapshot of a population

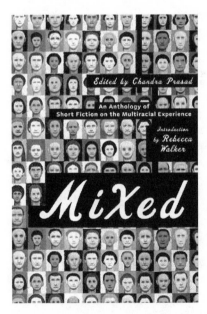

FIGURE 1.1. *Mixed: An Anthology of Short Fiction on the Multiracial Experience*, ed. Chandra Prasad, intro. Rebecca Walker (New York: W. W. Norton, 2006). Printed by permission of Martin Jarrie | marlenaagency.com.

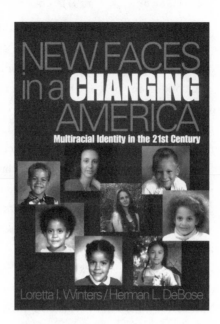

FIGURE 1.2. *New Faces in a Changing America: Multiracial Identity in the 21st Century*, ed. Loretta I. Winters and Herman L. DeBose (Thousand Oaks, CA: Sage, 2002).

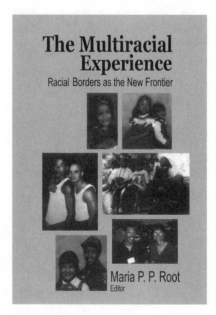

FIGURE 1.3. *The Multiracial Experience: Racial Borders as the New Frontier*, ed. Maria P. P. Root (Thousand Oaks, CA: Sage, 1996).

FIGURE I.4. *Multiracial Child Resource Book: Living Complex Identities*, ed. Maria P. P. Root and Matt Kelley (Seattle: MAVIN Foundation, 2003). Permission granted by Louie Gong, President, MAVIN Board of Directors.

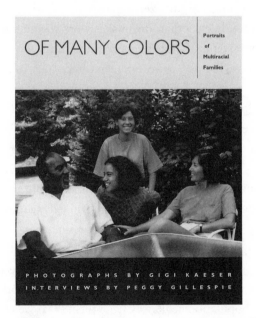

FIGURE I.5. *Of Many Colors: Portraits of Multiracial Families*, photographs by Gigi Kaeser, interviews by Peggy Gillespie (Amherst: University of Massachusetts Press, 1997). Image © Gigi Kaeser, from the exhibit and book *Of Many Colors: Portraits of Multiracial Families*, www.familydiv.org.

previously invisible. In both cases, stylized or realistic, the images function as typological, as marking a diverse but distinct people. Most of these are filled, some to the margins, with middle-class studio portraits of interracial couples and school pictures of their light-skinned, well-groomed children that not only seek to domesticate cross-racial sex, to visually pardon its historical stigma and taboo, but also to trigger the realist commitment to photo-documentary and the putative unimpeachability of the seen. We are encouraged to take for granted the idea that the photoshopped families on the page are but a synecdoche: they imply there must be millions of others similarly miscegenated in Middle America.

The covers equate visibility not only with social recognition but also with political representation. Indeed, mixed race advocacy groups that claim a civil rights–oriented agenda often have as their goal that mixed race people must be seen in the census, onstage, in media, in office.[12] But this act of rendering mixed race intelligible to the eye, understood as a political act, can sometimes actually interrupt more meaningful political engagement. The anthology covers, for instance, in the admirable service of making visible one marginalized population, effectively—and not accidentally—marginalize another: the images work together to codify anew the already iconic status of the heteronormative unit at the expense of other family formations. The photos are not merely reportage of a neutral demographic phenomenon, but the graphic naturalization of a particular political representation of a people. The fact that only heterosexual couples appear (and appear over and over again) on these "family album" covers extends the presumption of heterosexuality to the other images of solitary mixed race children—if they are the biological or adopted offspring of same-sex or intersex couples, we never see it. By implication, these alternative family mixes are not deemed "representative" of the mixed race constituency, and thus are silently omitted from the field of representation. To borrow Toni Morrison's insight in "Unspeakable Things Unspoken," "invisible things are not necessarily 'not there,'" and "certain absences are so stressed, so planned, they call attention to themselves . . . like neighborhoods that are defined by the population held away from them."[13] If we take Morrison's cue, then the covers, in this way, can teach us to see what is left unseen.

But there are historical and social pressures not to see the unseen. These pressures are perhaps made most evident if we remember that the strategy of agitating for racial rights by conforming to a normative sexual model has a disturbing precedent. As Roderick Ferguson argues, "[C]anonical sociology—Gunnar Myrdal, Ernest Burgess, Robert Park, Daniel Patrick Moynihan, and William Julius Wilson—has measured African Americans' unsuitability for a liberal capitalist order in terms of their adherence to the norms of a heterosexual and patriarchal nuclear family model. In short, to the extent that African Americans' culture and behavior deviated from those norms, they would not achieve economic and racial equality."[14] Through the compromises of such imagery, the representations of the mixed race nation make race mixing palatable under cover of conservative "family values." Though it was once beyond the legal and social pale, interracial marriage is rehabilitated as a model for the American Way.

A version of this impulse is also realized on the cover of *Time* magazine that I mention in the Introduction, "The New Face of America: How Immigrants Are Shaping the World's First Multicultural Society," which represents the mixed race woman as proof that America is the melting pot of the world. The twentysomething sepia ingénue on the cover, the cyber-genetic fantasy of the male editors who computer-mated men and women from supposedly all races and regions, emerges as a kind of Jamesian Daisy Miller for the new century. But the heterosexual tradition of miscegenation, William Byrd suggested, offers a most convenient form of internal colonization, for successive generations of people of color will become increasingly, painlessly purged as he understands it in *Histories of the Dividing Line Betwixt Virginia and North Carolina* (1841):

[A] sprightly lover is the most prevailing missionary that can be sent amongst these, or any other infidels. . . . Had such affinities been contracted in the beginning, how much bloodshed had been prevented, and how populous would the country have been, and, consequently, how considerable? Nor would the shade of the skin have been any reproach at this day; for if a Moor may be washed white in three generations, surely an Indian might have been blanched in two.[15]

This new/old vision of the mulatta—as a symbol of "blanching" over bloodshed—functions in perfect concert with the anthologies' similarly appeasing heteronormative photomontages of mixed race. The risk that race mixing will lead to other taboo transgressions and civil rights petitions—same-sex or immigrant rights protests, for instance—lurking in the pages following the cover both occasions "The New Face of America" and explains its function as antidote.

Such images are pivotal in driving our understanding of what mixed race is or should be in the new millennium, and they merge with mixed race identity projects in academic institutions, as both faculty and students will no doubt develop various and perhaps often contestatory educational prescriptives.[16] These contestations are productive, in my opinion; as Kobena Mercer suggests, "Solidarity does not mean that everyone thinks the same way, it begins when people have the confidence to disagree over issues of fundamental importance precisely because they 'care' about constructing common ground."[17] In seeking this rapprochement, those identifying as mixed race might continue to find legitimacy in their experiences, and yet work to develop more theoretically nuanced and politically astute understandings of the identities they claim.

As I mentioned at the outset of this chapter, classroom materials—survey courses, teaching manuals, major press anthologies—all have played a quietly powerful role in the mainstreaming of these prescriptives and understandings. The anthologies perhaps deserve special note here. In her essay on the processes of ethnic canonization, Barbara Christian astutely notes "what anthologies can do" for both good and ill:

Anthologies do chart a field, as the cultural nationalist anthologies of the sixties and the women's anthologies of the seventies demonstrate. They can be a significant cultural force in creating interest in a field. . . . They are not fixed in stone, as revisionist women of color anthologies exemplify. Anthologies as an intersection of many identities do develop, change, revise themselves. Obviously, the process of anthologizing is worth it for those of us in "new fields." And yet I am struck by the limitations of anthologies. . . . Is there a false unity camouflaging dominance and subordination? Do anthologies reproduce exclusion or dominance? Anthologies can appear to be comprehensive when they are not, since specific historical moments affect their shaping.[18]

Christian's points about the ability of anthologies to define and empower particularly a new field of study are especially resonant in the field of mixed race studies. But she is also, rightly, wary of the way they imply unity, inclusion, and equity of representation where there may be little, and of the way they may only rarely flag the limits of their comprehensiveness because of a studied inattention to their own historicity. This inattention probably results from the impulse of these fields to situate themselves as "new," which tacitly imagines a progressive teleology in which they are the latest, the next, the cutting edge. In short, their very project encourages the tendency to see themselves as representing the breaking wave—that is, *ahead* of the times—rather than *in* the times. This is certainly true, as well, of mixed race studies, which often positions itself as the future for the study of race, specifically, and as a requisite for understanding the new millennial world, more ambitiously. Certainly it is challenging for anthologies, which are in the very act of defining new fields, to historicize themselves; but self-reflection requires not only the distance of hindsight. As Christian insists, critical attention to "structures of dominance and exclusion" must be brought to bear in the earliest conception of anthologies, at the moment of their making.

IV. MARKETING FOR THE NEXT GENERATION: EDUCATIONAL PRODUCTS FOR THE SPECIAL CHILD

This curricular packaging of mixed race is echoed and enhanced in its commercialization. Kimberly McClain DaCosta's excellent analysis of the market targeting to and profiling of multiracials in the 1990s notes that the advertisements featuring images of mixed race people and interracial couples "requires no knowledge about multiracials and their putatively unique habits and needs. Rather, their impact, and the advertisers' motivation for using such images, lies in their symbolism—the ability to evoke for a viewer positive qualities, feelings, or desires. Multiracialism's capacity to evoke such desirable qualities, and even what is considered 'desirable,' are historically and context specific."[19] These desirables include the branding of multiracials as a distinct population associated with a hip, young, new people, "drawing on existing culturally resonant narratives of the meaning of racial mixedness for the purposes of selling stuff. In doing so, they shape social perceptions that multiracials exist as such. Through the marketplace, multiracials are being constituted as subjects."[20] Those narratives of mixed race are culturally resonant, I argue further, because they dovetail with American tenets of individualism, iconoclasm, and forward-looking modernity. It should be no surprise, then, that this creation of a mixed race subjecthood has been increasingly targeted at and for both the very young and the parents of youth, the anticipated heirs to and stewards of America's future.

Consuming mixed race has been represented as expressing oneself, a form of national obligation to self-realization—no better fulfilled than through the active support of one's children's efforts to "find wholeness."[21] Certainly many of the children's books illustrate the same heteronormativity as the anthology covers, combined additionally with a salubrious dimension that suggests multiracial health is just a page (or product) away in, for example, fiction like *Black, White, Just Right!* and *I'm Chocolate, You're Vanilla: Raising Healthy Black and Biracial Children in a Race-Conscious World* as well as parental guidance texts like *Does Anyone Else Look Like Me? A Parent's Guide to Raising Multiracial Children* and *Tomorrow's Children: Meeting the Needs of Multiracial and Multiethnic Children at Home, in Early Childhood Programs, and at School.*[22] They have become part of a related and growing niche market associated with educational mixed race products, products pitched as necessities for a "healthy" multiracial identity: parent resource handbooks for mixed race childrearing, specialized toys, dolls, and books for biracial children, signature clothing for youth identifying as mixed race, "unique" hair care products for "blended" tresses, and new lines of healthy "multiracial" skin lotions and creams. These products advertise good self-esteem through proper care of one's specialized epidermis, package a step-by-step program to happier family life in detailed "mixed" hair instruction fliers, and promise a better world through a multiracial literacy achieved through subscription to a children's library of mixed race-friendly picture books.[23] The Web-based company Like Minded People ("clothing for the conscious, inspired by life") offers items that create a sense that the socially enlightened can and should wear garb that reflects their evolved perception, including T-shirts with scripts across the front like "[Not] Other," "Everyone Loves a Mixed Girl," and "What Are You?" These messages signal in-group code references that take a stand on or "talk back" to putatively mixed race issues and interests—in this case, the statements take up positions, announcing the refusal of a U.S. Census category of "other," which was an option considered briefly by the Office of Management and Budget during the 2000 U.S. Census deliberations; offering social affirmation to a girl who might feel denied it; and turning on its head the most commonly asked question of people perceived to be racially ambiguous, asking the would-be offender instead, "What are *you?*" These T-shirts are represented as forms of social bonding through social intervention—those who wear them form the "like-minded," a community of belief more than of blood.

Of course, in the effort to represent the like-minded, some sheep might be lost. What if one identifies as mixed race but would have found perfectly acceptable the "other" census option? What if the claim that everyone loves a mixed race girl, in its effort to counteract the implied view that someone somewhere does not love her, slides into the historic tendency towards colorism and the privileging of light-skinned females as special beauties? What if the challenge "What are *you?*" does *not* lead to the kind of "conscious" self-reflection on the part of the viewer who might be tempted to ask that question that the company suggests it hopes for, but instead leads only to a straightforward non-ironic interpretation of the question: that is, "What am I? Oh, well . . . ," and then goes on to list dutifully his or her own genealogy. In other words, what if someone reading this T-shirt is not prompted to think, "Hmmm, why do I not ask that question of myself? Why would I ask what are you versus who are you? Why would I ask that question of this racially ambiguous person and not someone else? What are my own presuppositions about who is what or who belongs where? What is it about my own uneasiness about being unable to racially classify this person?" What if, instead, he or she misses the intellectual challenge and the question only reinforces the practice of asking others "What are you?" My point is not to suggest that the messages ought to be honed to defend against such misinterpretation, but rather to note the ways in which these are all posited as sites of education for the "like-minded" that tend to advocate positions more than raise questions, to exclude those who are unlike-minded, and, even more dangerously, it seems to me, to create a consumerist climate in which, as

DaCosta cogently puts it, "'recognition' (be it in the form of representation in advertisements or in the census) is substituted for a politics of civic and economic equality."[24]

V. LITERARY HISTORY IN THE MAKING: CANONIZING MIXED RACE

One of the most significant moves in mixed race education has been the revisioning of literary history, and, in turn, the surveys and period courses usually based on it. This revisioning is in many ways billed as a great awakening to a lost past, a truth to put the lie to monoracial identity. But the new ideal of mixed race is also about forgetting as much as it is about any recovery, for the recent project of finding a "mixed race literary tradition" involves what Mireille Rosello calls "amnesiac creolity." Identity, Rosello suggests, is always

the product of forgetting or repressing the inherent hybridity or creolity that constitutes it. The politics of hybridity then calls for the remembering of the truth that was always already there, for the recovering from the amnesiac sleep of identity. It is almost as if the error or illusion of our misplaced faith in identity can now be replaced with a new creed of hybridity: I once was lost but now am found, was blind but now I see. But is not this teleological narrative of redemption similar to modernity's promise of history as the gradual emergence of humanity into the dazzling light of the truth? The narrative of the beyond—beyond identity, beyond race, beyond racism—is in many ways a revision of the Enlightenment narrative of the universal subject which gradually shed all particularity and contingency to emerge into the light of its true being, with the signal difference that this has now been recast as essentially hybrid rather than essentially singular.[25]

Rosello's insight holds, similarly, for the proposals for some of the new literary histories canonizing mixed race literature. Their advocates celebrate the "truth" of lost-but-now-found hybrid literatures putatively eclipsed by monoracialist biases, but end up, just as Rosello suggests, merely making the hybrid subject a new kind of Enlightenment universal ideal. This is particularly ironic because mixed race advocates often claim to challenge the political processes of literary canonization, yet remain wedded to the same processes by which certain writers get placed in certain categories—they may change the racial calibrations, but the system itself, in which writers of one color are categorized by race and not by genre or style, arguably changes little.

The United States' literary canon has long and problematically coupled race and genre, perhaps beginning with William Dean Howells, the "Father" of American realism, who in the late nineteenth century, praises Paul Laurence Dunbar as most true to his race when writing poems in dialect.[26] In their challenge, however, multiracial advocates have begun a problematic reinterpretation of African American literary history by redefining authors previously identified (or self-identified) and anthologized as "black" according to the racial discourses of the day, ascribing to them a new multiracial identity. Through this presentist gesture—imposing contemporary values and designations onto past events and people—many of these writers and their texts are being "saved," redeemed and relieved of their blackness, celebrated and canonized through a process in which bi- and multiraciality become an index of heroic self-definition in the move to define some lost mixed race literary tradition.

The sometimes proselytizing politics of this new literary-history-in-the-making often involves what used to be called the "mulatto/a"—now reconceived not as a "neither/nor" or even a "yet both" figure but as a New Age pioneer who seeks to transcend racial categorization through the synergism beyond "the sum of our parts," to borrow from the title of one recent anthology.[27] Charles Chesnutt, Jean Toomer, W. E. B. Du Bois, Nella Larsen, and many others are all re-presented in this latest canon as misunderstood trailblazers.[28] Jonathan Brennan in the introduction to his edited *Mixed Race Literature*, applauds Jean Toomer's comment that people like him are "in the process of forming a new race" and praises him for breaking free of the "corral"[29] of monoracialism imposed on him by his black contemporaries and current black critics—namely Henry Louis Gates, Jr., according to Brennan. Some critics suggest that the putative misrepresentation of those of mixed race is the legacy of tyrannizing forces of literary history circa 1960s and 1970s, a literary history that was crudely forged, according to literary critics like George Hutchinson and Gene A. Jarrett, in the fires of anti-white resentment and race pride.[30]

In his biography of Nella Larsen, for instance, Hutchinson notes that the book is not only about her but also about the "suppressions demanded by the constant work of maintaining the color line";[31] his criticisms are mostly leveled at black scholars who, he argues, pathologized Larsen's biracial identity and grossly distorted earlier accounts of her life because they were wedded to a racial binary. Jarrett similarly insists that black nationalist literary histories so privileged a certain kind of protest literature that contemporary critics have ignored or devalued the "raceless" and "anomalous," as he calls it, fiction by writers like Frank Webb and Frank Yerby, among others. All of these are valid points: certainly the political and aesthetic prescriptions of the Black Arts/Black Power movements often narrowed critical interpretation of texts by authors of African descent and crafted a literary history that favors certain kinds of form and content over others. But to argue that narratives of the mixed race experience do not fit comfortably within any known literary tradition, as Brennan suggests, or that they are an unequivocal finger in the eye of monoracial hegemony, as Hutchinson at times implies, or can pose a lost alternative tradition, as Jarrett argues, perhaps risks at times overstating these works' distinctiveness and the post-race promises they might hold. After all, many of the nineteenth- and twentieth-century narratives that they reference clearly extend rhetorical and racial acts of self-definition that appear across texts as varied as antebellum slave narratives or late-twentieth-century black bourgeois memoirs. This is not to say that self-identified mixed memoirs since the 1990s have not begun to assume their own literary shape, sharing and trading in increasingly common generic features and even clichés: for instance, most of these texts assume some form of the quest narrative, in which the protagonist seeks identity, parentage, cultural connection, culminating in acceptance/celebration of one's multiraced self as an explicit counter to the tragic mulatto story. But even as these contemporary narratives tell stories of proud iconoclasm, and the trials and blessings of racial ambiguity, they usually operate very securely within literary convention and traffic in similar tropes, devices, narration, and traditional constructions of self and other. As I mentioned in the Introduction, Fran Ross's *Oreo* (1974), in its exuberant contrast in both form and content to these contemporary explorations of mixed race, is cautionary of all the earnest racial pieties of nationalism—black, mixed, or otherwise. Ross throws into great relief the ways much literature promoted as mixed race is not necessarily "new" or immune to the same tendentious inclinations of the literary traditions it may criticize.

My concern is that an insistence on mixed race uniqueness, particularly as something that has been intentionally excluded from a black literary tradition, can eclipse the ways many of these texts directly participate in genres and literary practices historically associated with not only black but also ethnic literary traditions in general. More importantly, not to see these connections, not to see how a mixed race "tradition" is situated within and against other ethnic traditions, can lead to critical blind spots, as David Palumbo-Liu wisely notes. This is not to make narratives about mixed race less "special," but to suggest that their specialness might not require separation or independent status. At the very least, the critical attention to narratives warrants scrutiny of the canonization of mixed race literatures. As Palumbo-Liu argues,

In addressing the issue of critical multiculturalism with regard to the canonization of ethnic literatures, three topics are of utmost importance. First, it is crucial to obtain a sense of the *history* of forming a "canon" of minority literatures and how the convergence of certain political claims (i.e. race and gender) had to be negotiated. It is also necessary to consider how the texts of a particular "group" may occupy *specific* institutional positions. Second, turning to specific texts, one needs to critique how ethnic "voices" are constituted within the interstices of dominant aesthetics and ideologies and minority discourses. How are minority discourses generated differently within the dialectic of dominant and ethnic discourses? And how are tribal and ethnic communities "represented" in these discourses? Finally, moving beyond U.S. national borders, how do ethnic texts become canonized and reconfigured as they move across national cultural spaces? And how do race, class, ethnicity, and gender intersect in the aggregation of an ethnic canon?[32]

Palumbo-Liu's call to examine who, when, why, and to what end canons emerge as intraracial projects and not simply as challenges to a white Western canon is extremely helpful precisely because in this case so few of the questions he asks are ever asked about the rise in press interest and critical popularity of mixed race literatures. Yet it is essential to place the canonization of mixed race in the history and context of the current power of post-race discourses in dominant cultural discourses; to explore how mixed race literature is increasingly being held up as a progressive good that is too often defined against so-called monoracial literatures; and to examine how the mixed race "voice" is being culled, refined, and cultivated as the voice of the future.

It is important to distinguish the critical gestures I mention above from some other contemporaneous engagements with racial hybridity. Werner Sollors' study of ethnic modernisms and important anthologizing of primary texts that suggest a literary history of interracialism, and Henry Wonham's critical anthology revealing hybrid texts as cohabiting within and across Anglo and African American traditions, are quite different from the new and separate literary history that seems to be proposed in different ways by others. Sollors does argue in *Neither Black nor White yet Both* that "'race mixing' has its [own] tradition, an interracial tradition that needs to be explored."[33] And he takes to task scholar Richard Bone for his 1975 interpretation of Charles Chesnutt's story "The Wife of His Youth" (1898), in which Bone treats the light-skinned protagonist, who belongs to the exclusive Blue Vein Society, as black rather than mulatto.[34] Indeed, Sollors lays special responsibility for what he sees as a critical miscalculation in scholarship that emerges during the Black Arts era, stating that it was upon the reissue of the Chesnutt collection of stories in the "1960s . . . [where it] received . . . readings as a 'black text.'"[35] But if he does resist the reduction of racially diverse experience to a monochromatic and one-note blackness, he does not deny that fiction concerning the "mulatto" is an integral part of a black literary tradition. Similarly, Wonham's anthology, bringing together work by scholars like Shelley Fisher Fishkin and many others also interested in the cross-fertilization of ethnic literary traditions, is, as Toni Morrison puts it in the opening essay, not a move beyond race or to a new racial order. As she notes, readers should be mightily wary of willing away "race" or "Afro-American culture"[36] in the process of—and certainly not in the name of—exploring how multifaceted, heterogeneous, and interethnic its influences are. If Sollors' project is descriptive and Wonham's interpretive, Brennan's, Hutchinson's, and Jarrett's are a bit more acquisitive, seeking, it seems, at times to claim not only past narratives that might be redefined as mixed but also the recent plethora of mixed race memoirs, quasi-fictionalized autobiographies, essays, and fiction.

The literature usually marketed as part of a mixed race and race-mixing canon—despite their many differences—to which I have been referring includes, to name only a very few published since 1994:

Shirlee Taylor Haizlip, *The Sweeter the Juice: A Family Memoir in Black and White* (1995); Lisa Jones, *Bulletproof Diva: Tales of Race, Sex, and Hair* (1994); Barack Obama, *Dreams from My Father: A Story of Race and Inheritance* (1995); Judy Scales-Trent, *Notes of a White Black Woman: Race, Color, Community* (1995); Gregory Howard Williams, *Life on the Color Line: The True Story of a White Boy Who Discovered He Was Black* (1996); Marsha Hunt, *Repossessing Ernestine: A Granddaughter Uncovers the Secret History of Her American Family* (1996); Scott Minerbrook, *Divided to the Vein: A Journey Into Race and Family* (1996); James McBride, *The Color of Water: A Black Man's Tribute to His White Mother* (1997); Toi Derricotte, *The Black Notebooks: An Interior Journey* (1999); Danzy Senna, *Caucasia* (1999) and *Symptomatic* (2004); Lalita Tademy, *Cane River* (2001) and *Red River* (2007); Rebecca Walker, *Black, White, and Jewish: Autobiography of a Shifting Self* (2002); Neil Henry, *Pearl's Secret: A Black Man's Search for His White Family* (2002); Ronne Hartfield, *Another Way Home: The Tangled Roots of Race in One Chicago Family* (2005); Emily Raboteau, *The Professor's Daughter* (2005); Essie Mae Washington-Williams, *Dear Senator: A Memoir by the Daughter of Strom Thurmond* (2006); Kym Ragusa, *The Skin Between Us: A Memoir of Race, Beauty, and Belonging* (2006); June Cross, *Secret Daughter: A Mixed-Race Daughter and the Mother Who Gave Her Away* (2007); Bliss Broyard, *One Drop: My Father's Hidden Life—A Story of Race and Family Secrets* (2007); Elliott Lewis, *Fade: My Journeys in Multiracial America* (2006); David Matthews, *Ace of Spades: A Memoir* (2007); Judith Stone, *When She Was White: The True Story of a Family Divided by Race* (2007); Victoria Rowell, *The Women Who Raised Me: A Memoir* (2007); Lise Funderburg, *Pig Candy:*

Taking My Father South, Taking My Father Home: A Memoir (2009); and Heidi Durrow, *The Girl Who Fell from the Sky* (2010). We can also include collections of autobiographical narratives that contain pieces by those who variously identify as mixed: Carol Camper, ed., *Miscegenation Blues: Voices of Mixed Race Women* (1994); Lise Funderburg, ed., *Black, White, Other: Biracial Americans Talk About Race and Identity* (1995); Claudine Chiawei O'Hearn, ed., *Half and Half: Writers on Growing Up Biracial and Bicultural* (1998); Pearl Fuyo Gaskins, ed., *What Are You? Voices of Mixed-Race Young People* (1999). Recent biographies that also emphasize and explore mixed race identity include Kathryn Talalay's *Composition in Black and White: The Life of Philippa Schuyler: The Tragic Saga of Harlem's Biracial Prodigy* (1995), and George Hutchinson's *In Search of Nella Larsen: A Biography of the Color Line* (2006). Perhaps the ultimate stamp of institutional approval is the publication of *Mixed: An Anthology of Short Fiction on the Multiracial Experience*, edited by Chandra Prasad and published by W. W. Norton (2006).[37]

Other major academic as well as popular presses have begun producing and marketing collections and literary surveys of mixed race writing; these volumes and anthologies quite literally institutionalize and commercialize an alternative literary history.

Part of my critique is of the tautology at work in many well-meaning arguments for a distinct literature by mixed race peoples. Brennan, for instance, calls for—but then in the same breath somehow also presupposes—a "mixed race tradition"[38] in which to place literature. He insists we must consider the mixed race writer's work within every single ethnic literature tradition corresponding to the writer's "mix": Langston Hughes, he says, is "African-French-Cherokee-European American" (29), and thus one should see his work as a "hybrid text" that is the sum of all those traditions, as if each were itself singular and internally homogenous. Susan Graham of Project RACE has been criticized by Jon Michael Spencer for claiming that, were he alive today, Langston Hughes, often called the black poet laureate, would have self-identified as "mixed." But Brennan even bypasses Graham's hypothetical scenario and asserts as self-evident fact that Hughes *is* a "mixed writer."[39] Thus appears, only twenty pages into the book, the kind of conflation of blood ancestry and literary category that Brennan earlier says he wants so much to avoid.

Paul Spickard's interpretation of "mixed race" in *Mixed Blood: Inter-marriage and Ethnic Identity in Twentieth-Century America* is similarly engaging and yet also similarly problematic, arguing, for instance, that mixed race peoples "draw their life-force from fashioning and refashioning the story of the ethnic self,"[40] but he then turns what could have been a move towards literary analysis into a taxonomy of multiracial traits and tropes. Citing Reginald Daniel, Spickard claims, "For multiracial people, you live your racial narrative by creating it. The created element is particularly strong in the case of multiracial people. There is an element of fictionalizing to it, but it's not falseness. It is choosing the proportions and the proper fit of the various ethnic elements one possesses."[41] His argument that fictionalizing is not falsity importantly addresses the common charge that people of mixed race are "inauthentic" or racial posers. That said, Spickard's sartorial metaphor for self-fashioning suggests that identity can be selectively styled like pieces of clothing chosen for the correct "proportion" and "proper fit," implying that people identifying as mixed race can and should creatively suit themselves up in whatever racial garb they choose.

If, for the select few perceived as racially ambiguous by a dominant culture, race does involve a heightened ability to make situational choices about one's racial identity, then by "choice" we must not merely mean a willingness to buy into, literally, the commercialization of race affects; that is, "choosing" race, one hopes, ought not to translate into, for example, simply purchasing hip-hop wear. Such an exercise of choice reduces "crossover dreams,"[42] as Noel Ignatiev puts it, into a point-of-purchase sales gimmick that markets race as apolitical and endlessly portable. Yet this free-market view of race reinforces the idea that one can just slip in and out of identities without political commitment or ethical consequence.[43]

In these ways both the thematic and the multi-tradition approaches strike me as useful but limited in analyzing the phenomena and representation of mixed race because they risk resuscitating the very racial categories they say are on their last gasp, risk dehistoricizing the literature, hazard inattention to the literary and cultural specificity of this peculiar form of literary production, and risk participating in the global commodification of race. These approaches also make evident, and no less problematic, how literary histories are made and unmade according to varying cultural priorities. For instance, many literary critics rehearse a common mantra of mixed race advocates in their discussions of the census: we merely wish to value equally our parents, both white and black antecedents. When transposed to the literary realm, however, this bid for filial interraciality threatens constructing literary history on the basis of a sense of genealogical debt.

Perhaps more productive would be analysis of this literature not in terms of genealogy but in terms of its genre of choice, for instance, which has been to date mostly autobiography and memoir. These have often been received as a transparent reflection or sociological description of the mixed race parentage or experience, but as with all autobiography, they are a function of ethnic narrative and practices of literary self-representation. Thus the critical and literary scholarship of David Palumbo-Liu, Ramón Saldívar, Amritjit Singh, Robert Young, and others might better place texts called mixed race narratives within, rather than as a reinvention of, literary history. The latter approach would allow us to see how such literature can be situated, and how it participates, in respective ethnic literary traditions; it also, importantly, invites closer attention to the ways hybridity is narrated already within these traditions and where it can be more fully articulated and elaborated. Also, rather than mixed race individuals' being viewed as sui generis and "outside history," they might better be considered as racialized subjects *in* history. Thus even if novelist Jean Toomer loved the writer Georgia Douglas Johnson's literary salons as a sanctuary "out of time" where his "new friends . . . were not concerned with being either coloured or white," such a claim says less about a unique identity movement that emerges out of history than one deeply embedded in its historical time and place.[44] Toomer identified over time across a racial spectrum, but his preference for Johnson's salon must be understood, Elizabeth McHenry argues, in terms of the concerns of the Washington, D.C., upper-class, light-skinned elite, the center of black aristocracy from the end of Reconstruction to World

War I,[45] an elite that distinguished itself sharply from the black masses until the Red Summer of 1919 and the race riots throughout the country that sharpened the race line. In other words, the desire to be outside history has its own history.

VI. CULTURAL INSTRUCTION AND PEDAGOGIES OF MIXED RACE

Much recent fiction and drama try to account for multiple racial affiliations within any one group and to work against the notion of homogeneous and totalizing racial categories implicit in, for instance, both black cultural nationalism and what Harold Cruse calls white "racial particularism."[46] These texts beg the question: Does the mixed race category productively complicate all racial boundaries or does it risk instituting and reifying yet another kind of racial categorization—in effect, does the designation of "mixed race" dissemble or merely replicate reductive models of race? Prompted by the recent work on a "post-positivist realist" politics of identity,[47] I would like to ask: What *would* a politically progressive and theoretically sophisticated mixed race politics and aesthetics look like? To that end, we might join caution about the popular and scholarly appeal of mixed race with curiosity about what multiple racial identification *does* allow for intellectually, experientially, and artistically. Something understood as mixed race literature will be taught as these debates rage on about its literary status and its social implications, so the answer is not to resist teaching it but to teach it critically in the very midst of these debates and as central to the emerging scholarship.

For some invested in mixed race as a populist, grassroots movement, however, all academic engagement with the issue is poisonous. Francis Wardle, in her article "Academics Are Enemies of the Multiracial Movement," argues that there exists a conspiracy of professors, presses, and conference-goers who, through a campaign of indifference and hostility, wage war against the movement:

As the American population is becoming more and more accepting of interracial relationships and multiracial identities, the academic community is leading the opposition to the progress of the multiracial movement. This opposition is manifest in a number of ways, 1) multicultural education textbooks, articles and conferences simply ignore this population, 2) there is a group of university professors who stridently and unrelentingly publish articles and books opposing all aspects of the movement, and 3) university publishing presses publish these aggressive anti-multiracial tomes.

She concludes by saying that "the concentrated attack on the multiracial movement through the publication of books and journal articles, and presentations at diversity conferences, are a very clear example of institutional racism," and she finds it a "travesty" that these "institutions (which pay the salaries of these professors and subsidize university presses) are funded by the average American citizen."[48] Wardle targets those who teach in African American studies and ethnic studies programs as the worst offenders, with the assumption that they are wedded to the antiquated "single-race view of diversity"—a version of the monoracialism-is-the-culprit syndrome—leveled here not at the NAACP or Urban League but at centers of higher education. It is a poignant irony that these programs—most of whom produce interethnic, comparative, interdisciplinary analyses of race, class, gender, etc. already and are the most likely, after all, to host and sustain the study of mixed race—are demonized. Notwithstanding Wardle's threat of trying to cut funding for universities that house people and presses who say things she does not like, I want to argue against such anti-intellectualism: as I suggest in the Introduction also, W. E. B. Du Bois early intuited that scholars must study, analyze, and critique the cultural and political field of mixed race. Never a shy one for vigorously interrogating his own ever-evolving conceptions of race, he understood that considerations of mixed race were always grounded in an analysis of psychology, power, history, and economics.

To this end, inclusion of so-called mixed race literature alone is not a satisfactory pedagogical response to what Wardle sees as the invisibility of mixed race peoples. Appropriate here is Michael Hames-García's critique of the usual modes of canon-inclusion in which he notes that, ironically, incidental representation of marginalized literature in an anthology can function to highlight and heighten the status of the traditional literatures, which dominate it in terms of page numbers and length of selections. Furthermore, inclusion that occurs in the absence of considerations of "oppression and resistance"[49] (versus the safer and more commonly preferred theme of innovative "discovery" and sanitized "contact") leads merely to "risk-free diversity."[50] This "additive"[51] approach to multicultural education also fails to be much use if it advances only an understanding of different cultures' putatively discrete experiences instead of encouraging appreciation and analysis of "how cultures are interrelated and connected by historical practices and systems of domination."[52] Considering cultures and socially located identity in these more charged terms in the literature will surely raze the ideal notion of polite and "uninvested democratic discussion" (31) in which the protocols of civility can unwittingly coerce silence. Scholars could anticipate—and set the context for—more vigorous and productive conversations.[53]

One of the important and yet rarely discussed issues related to the study of mixed race in the context of cultural interaction, including oppression, is whether mixed race individuals and communities can be considered oppressed, marginalized—and often even whether they can be considered minorities. On the one hand, mixed race peoples can to some degree lay claim to being among the most *representative* of oppressed populations. They are representative not because those of "crossed blood" bear a uniquely "heavy cross" (vii), as Berry Brewton puts it. For Brewton, these are the über-outcast, "pathetic folks of mixed race ancestry . . . raceless people, neither fish not fowl, neither white, nor black, nor red, nor brown" (vii). Yet to argue that they are victimized primarily by racial categorization itself because it cannot reflect their experience lays blame rather conveniently at the foot of theoretical abstraction—blames "race" rather than racism. As Kimberlé Crenshaw cogently argues,

The embrace of identity politics . . . has been in tension with dominant conceptions of social justice. Race, gender, and other identity categories are most often treated in mainstream liberal discourse as vestiges of bias or domination—that is, as intrinsically negative frameworks in which social power works to exclude or marginalize those who are different. According to this understanding, our liberatory objective should be to empty such categories of any social significance. Yet implicit in certain strands of feminist and racial liberation movements, for example, is the view that the social power in delineating difference need not be the power of domination; it can instead be the source of social empowerment and reconstruction. The problem with identity politics is not that it fails to transcend difference, as some critics charge, but rather the opposite— that it frequently conflates or ignores intragroup difference.[54]

Crenshaw's theory of the need for identity politics to account for intra-group difference is especially useful in recasting the oppression of mixed race people: rather than seeing mixed race people as oppressed by racial categorization itself (the liberal argument, according to Crenshaw), I argue that mixed race people bear oppression because, historically, their bodies have borne physical testimony to sexual violation as an exercise of racial privilege, what Hortense Spillers has called "the will to sin,"[55] by a dominant culture. They represent the reference point, the very nexus of cultural collisions, conflicts, and conjoinings; those of mixed race heri-tage can be the issue of loving relations, surely, but also, overwhelmingly from a historical perspective, they are the result of hypergamic relations, in which one party, usually the woman, occupies a significantly lower social and racial status. That history is carried forward in various ways, and certainly the long-documented comparative, unequal status of people of color to whites, even in "loving" interracial relations, is an ongoing negotiation for couples, as Calvin Hernton and so many others after him have documented.[56]

Deciding whether or not mixed race people qualify and identify as oppressed minorities is not a matter of assessing historical injury based on some impossible measurement of blood quantum, which leads only to unproductive debates about whether some fictive percentage of black or Latino heritage outweighs the white blood, with its historic dominance. As social scientists have long argued, racial advantage or disadvantage in terms of income, health care, social leverage, likelihood to be incar-cerated, and a host of other indicators is not, and ought not to be, de-termined anew with each individual case but by the "class" of people to whom individuals most likely belong.[57] That is, race, *and this holds for mixed race identification as well*, is socially and politically salient even if the particular experiences of individuals vary. Historically, so-called mulattos, mestizos, and hapa individuals have been singled out as part of the threat of the "growing tide of color" in the United States even if any particular person identifying as mixed race does not consider herself oppressed (or does not, as might very well also be the case, recognize the particular ways in which he or she is oppressed). In that sense, mixed race people can most certainly be considered among those minorities who have been historically oppressed.

Yet some argue, with much justification, that in the last decade a temporal shift has lent great cultural prestige to the "mulatto."[58] Those who are light-skinned, who do not identify with any particular racial community, or who are aligned with a civil rights agenda, are held up high as exemplary symbols of the melting pot, representatives of racial harmony, ambassadors of cultural and racial appeasement. Many mixed race individuals who claim to be oppressed by—through their sense of exclusion from—monoracial communities and relate more to white people, indeed have the racial profile of white people to the extent that they do not fully recognize themselves as racialized and thus are oblivious to color hierarchies from which they benefit socially. This nevertheless does not change the view of mixed race individuals as having a valid association with marginalized people. Rather, many of them participate in what Moya calls "neoconservative minority identity politics."[59] They bear all the typological features: "ambivalent relations with the minority communities with which they are identified by others" (132) although allowing themselves to be exploited as "exemplary" representatives of that community, even serving occasionally as "native informants" (133) for those "outside" the group. Those who engage in neoconservative identity politics also tend to "overlook the structural and inegalitarian nature of society," ignoring the "structural inequities that contribute to the correlation between the likelihood of incarceration and nonwhite racial status, and between poverty and the female gender." Instead, inequalities are attributed to the "cultural character of the subordinated individual or group," and thus, consistent with the focus on culture in this sense, "neoconservative minorities have a liberal understanding of individual agency" (133). Still, Moya sees these neoconservatives as "fellow travelers" even as she sees their ways of negotiating racial discrimination and inequality as problematic, and I would argue that to the degree mixed race advocacy is all about identity—and racial identity, in particular—they share a certain political fellowship.

Nonetheless, that does not mean that people who identify as mixed race have, necessarily, special critical insight or epistemological acumen regarding either their experience or race in general.[60] Thus it is important in teaching mixed race literature to discuss the conditions and circumstances behind most historical race mixing, which in Brazil, Cuba, Jamaica, South Africa, Suriname, and the U.S. American South, to name a few, leads us directly to a history involving cross-racial exploitation.[61] Too often students' historical memory is extended only to *Loving v. Virginia* (1967), the Supreme Court decision that rendered interracial marriages legal: with that as the originary marker, students tend to associate race mixing only with marital free will, with the brave, free choice of partners, with what looks like the transgressive personal politics of interracial love. But to shrink the meaning of mixed race to the present historical moment creates the impression that race mixing has always been or is now always inherently "progressive." Even in liaisons from the post–civil rights era, power relations are never absent, although the repeated invocation of the *Loving* decision as page one of a heroic American narrative about overcoming state discrimination often suggests just this. The retroactive scripting of that decision as the foundational moment in a narrative of love transcending race and nation can distract us from analysis of how interracial unions and the children born of them do, in fact, necessarily participate in the racial, economic, and social policies of a nation. The rest of *The Souls of Mixed Folk* considers creative works that take for granted that participation and seek new ways of imagining and representing mixed race art and activism.

CHAPTER TWO

The "Ethno-Ambiguo Hostility Syndrome" of the "Halfrican American"

MIXED RACE IN
AARON MCGRUDER'S *THE BOONDOCKS*
AND NATE CREEKMORE'S *MAINTAINING*

Laughter and its forms represent . . . the least scrutinized sphere of the people's creation.

Mikhail Bakhtin, *Rabelais and His World*[1]

[L]et The Boondocks go on its merry, subversive way ("Hey, it's just a
cartoon") and hope that, somewhere down the road when we all live in
a more just America, we will look back and say that in the beginning,
the revolution wasn't televised, it was on the comics page.

Michael Moore, foreword to *A Right to Be Hostile*[2]

IN CHAPTER ONE, I consider the emerging field of mixed race studies, including the way that the marketing of curricula, textbooks, and
anthologies is perhaps the most visible institutional vehicle for canonization of an ethnic literature. But there are other less unconventional, but
potentially even more influential sites simultaneously engaged in defining the meanings of mixed race identity: and one that is perhaps especially under-explored includes the syndicated comic strip. In its various
forms—in print, online, occasionally translated to television—comics can
reach millions of people across regions, generations, and demographics.
Although not as overtly didactic as anthologies (they rarely come with a
mission statement), comics also often intervene in the most pressing public
debates and controversies. Because they generally appear daily or weekly,
they also can take—and possibly quicken—the pulse of a hot subject in
an even more immediate way, and as Bakhtin and Moore suggest in the
quotes above, their humor is the more politically potent for being unscru-
tinized. Most importantly, the two comics I discuss productively refigure

the visual politics of race through their graphic medium. In the work of both Aaron McGruder and Nate Creekmore, racial identity cannot be located through visual convention: rather, it is reframed as a matter of public negotiation, social location, cultural affirmation, political commitment, and historical homage. Race is not arbitrary imposition for Huey, the black main character in McGruder's *Boondocks*, or for Marcus, the mixed race protagonist in *Maintaining*; for both, race is a renewable and usable occasion for social insight and historical sensibility.

In that respect, Aaron McGruder's *The Boondocks* and Nate Creekmore's *Maintaining* represent particularly distinctive forays into mixed race, new millennial representation. Both cartoonists are of African American descent and represent a generation of younger artist-commentators interested in the subject of mixed race. McGruder, born in 1974, created *The Boondocks* in 1996 (it was nationally syndicated in 1999) and then paused the newspaper version of it when he moved to produce an animated version of it for television beginning in 2004. By most measures one of the most popular and controversial comic strips in U.S. history, *The Boondocks* has garnered McGruder many accolades, including an NAACP Image Award, and a Chairman's Award, both in 2002, as well as indictments from, among those most vocal, Bob Johnson of the Black Entertainment Network (BET), who has been frequently and ferociously lampooned by McGruder. Several major newspapers boycotted the strip in 2004, refusing to run episodes that featured an imaginary reality TV show hosted by rap impresario Russell Simmons titled *Can a N***a Get a Job?* McGruder has also created other works, including a graphic novel, *Birth of a Nation* (2004),[3] a collaboration with writer Reginald Hudlin and cartoonist Kyle Baker. Creekmore, born in 1982, has twice won the Scripps College Cartoonist of the Year Award and an Associated Press award for achievement in college cartooning. *Maintaining* appeared nationally with the Universal Press Syndicate in 2007, although UPS ended his contract in August 2009.[4]

A decade apart in age, these cartoonists have different political orientations, perhaps reflecting a highly controversial cultural trend that is represented by the racial identifications of their primary characters. McGruder's interest is in exploring interracial (especially black-white) and intraracial (especially black-black) relations from the perspective of a black-identified character; Creekmore's interest is in exploring interracial (especially black-white) and intraracial (especially black-white but also including transracially adopted) relations from the perspective of a character who identifies as biracial. McGruder's critiques of the multiracial movement most often occur through the mixed race figure of Jazmine. The main characters in *The Boondocks* are two ten-year-old boys, Huey and Riley, described in the strip as "angry black men stuck in the suburbs," who occasionally interact with Jazmine, who lives next door and who "must deal with being the child of an interracial relationship, and withstand the teasing of Huey and Riley."[5] Creekmore's strip makes more central the issue of mixed race with its focus on "life's peculiarities and absurdities through the eyes of a biracial adolescent named Marcus," whose best friend, Anton, is identified as black.[6]

McGruder has come under severe critique for what many have perceived as an attack on the character of Jazmine, and by extension, on the mixed race movement. This "bashing," as one critic calls it, has been almost obsessively cataloged by date and insult, and vilified as committing sins of the highest order, as represented by the following rant offered by *The Multiracial Activist* (*TMA*). TMA, which describes itself as "An activist journal dedicated to the struggle for and preservation of civil rights for biracial and multiracial individuals, interracial couples/families and transracial adoptees," is a popular link hosted by dozens of mixed race advocacy sites and claims that *The Boondocks*

presents a militant, afrocentric view of America through the eyes of "Huey," its chief character and protagonist. It also promotes an intolerant view of mixed-race ancestry and interracial marriage. Many installments of the strip, specifically those run on April 28, 29 and May 5, 6, 8, 11, 12, 24, 25, 26, 27, 28, 29 are dedicated to "Huey" bashing another character "Jazmine" for choosing to identify as biracial as well as belittlement of interracial marriages. This type of message only breeds further intolerance and hatred. This is not comedic expression. It is bigotry disguised as a comic strip and leveled at an already oppressed segment of the population, biracial/multiracial children and adults as well as those monoracial individuals who choose to marry across color-lines.

Quoted within the article is an even more passionate diatribe by a self-titled "white multiracial," suggesting that McGruder is guilty of not only bigotry but war crimes:

Ms. A.D. Powell, a political activist and self-identifying white multiracial author and contributor to the INTERRACIAL VOICE website had these words to describe "The Boondocks":

"Aaron McGruder's hate propaganda is especially harmful to children who see the bullying and harassment of the multiracial character, 'Jazmine,' into a false 'black' identity presented as a positive thing. Indeed, the message that 'Jazmine' is too inferior to also claim her European ancestry but is a 'confused cutie-pie' for white-hating black males appears to be the main theme of 'The Boondocks.' McGruder has spent more time on this theme than any other. Adults should know that they have the legal, social and moral right to call themselves multiracial or even that 'godlike appellation "white."' Children, however, are vulnerable. They are the targets for McGruder's 'We'll take you against your will' advocacy of 'ethnic rape.'"[7]

This response forms part of a documentary archive and brief against *The Boondocks* that comprise a searchable library on the TMA site. If McGruder has been vilified as an ethnic rapist, Creekmore is embraced as a lover, feted and congratulated by those associated with multiracial movements.[8] In fact, McGruder and Creekmore are often explicitly contrasted. As one reviewer puts it, "Unlike *The Boondocks*, this strip doesn't appear to carry a black agenda nor the anger that was Aaron McGruder's hallmark. This feature seems more engaged in discovery of truthful observations about teen life and being biracial."[9] Despite their differing receptions, Creekmore's "discovery" about biraciality is not antithetical to a "black agenda." Both McGruder and Creekmore understand multiraciality projects within black advocacy and offer aesthetic commentaries on the racialization processes of both multiracial and black identifications.

As Michael Moore's foreword suggests, McGruder is the twenty-first century's Gil Scott-Heron, the renowned poet sometimes called the father of spoken word poetry. McGruder's nationally syndicated comic strip, *The Boondocks*, like Scott-Heron's 1970 poem "The Revolution

Will Not Be Televised," is a similar nose-thumbing of the status quo and a clarion call to a new generation. Needless to say, when Moore wrote his foreword, he did not know that McGruder *would* take the revolution to television—the show premiered on November 6, 2005, in the "Adult Swim" block of the Cartoon Network—but Moore's point still holds: comics are dismissed as low entertainment only by the culturally elite or the politically naïve.[10] *The Boondocks* is renowned for its acute, often controversial, cultural commentary on racial politics in America, and correspondingly the millennial phenomenon of "mixed race" identification has not escaped McGruder's eye (nor his ire). I analyze *The Boondocks* as a form of pop-cultural intervention in contemporary debates over multiracial identity, generative debates that offer what McGruder calls a "space for a kind of playful black intelligentsia."[11]

Although often relegated to low-culture art form, comics—also called sequential art, graphic storytelling, or visual narrative—ought to have the same aesthetic status as literature and art, Scott McCloud argues.[12] I would add further that they, like other arts, have powerful claims on social reality: those peculiar claims of fiction on the world are not mimetic but mutually constitutive. So what world is Aaron McGruder both commenting on and creating? His internationally acclaimed and assailed comics are a thorn in the side of both the political right and the left, offering searing send-ups of nearly everyone in the Bush administration, calling President Bush a "moron" and offering Condoleezza Rice a personal ad, opening with "Female Darth Vader type seeks loving mate to torture":

High-ranking government employee with sturdy build seeks single black man for intimate relationship. Must enjoy football, Chopin, and carpet bombing.[13]

One of his favorite targets is the aforementioned Black Entertainment Television (BET)—or as the main character in the strip, Huey, calls the BET network, "Black Exploitation Television" or "Butts Every Time."

My focus here is several episodes of *The Boondocks* in which McGruder features a twenty-first-century "mixed race" character, one prepubescent, ten-year-oldish Jazmine Dubois, whose black father, Tom, and his white wife, Sarah, are both lawyers. (The Dubois surname's resemblance to "Du Bois" only highlights just how imperfectly aligned are their visions of what an integrated world might look and act like.) The Dubois family has just arrived in the largely white "upscale neighborhood of Woodcrest" (*The Boondocks: Because I Know You Don't Read the Newspapers* 10), where the black protagonist, Huey, and his younger brother, Riley, have also recently located. Woodcrest, significantly, is based loosely on the middle-class suburb of Columbia, Maryland, where McGruder was raised, an intentional community, an interracial social experiment which, according to *New Yorker* journalist Ben McGrath, was "envisioned as a sort of integrationist, post-civil rights utopia developed by the Rouse Company in the mid-nineteen sixties . . . featuring an official 'Tree of Life,' and streets and neighborhoods with names like Hobbitt's Glen and Morning Walk and Elfstone Way. (Huey and Riley live on Timid Deer Lane, one block over from Bashful Beaver)."[14] Jazmine is light-skinned, with what she calls "frizzy hair," which she defensively and repeatedly insists is not an afro. This new millennial mulatta is, according to Huey, a "textbook case" of "Afro-Denial" and "Ethno-Ambiguo Hostility Syndrome" (*Because I Know* 23), a case study of a black person in pathological denial and self-delusion. And, as Huey tells her parents, he believes he has the cure: "an immediate intervention of positive Nubian reinforcement" to lead her down the "long hard road to afrocentric wellness" (23). Jazmine is weak from a kind of racial anemia that only the drip of righteous Africanity can correct.

FIGURE 2.1. *Boondocks*, May 26, 1999. THE BOONDOCKS © 1999 Aaron McGruder. Reprinted by permission of UNIVERSAL PRESS SYNDICATE. All rights reserved.

FIGURE 2.2. *Boondocks*, May 27, 1999. THE BOONDOCKS © 1999
Aaron McGruder. Reprinted by permission of UNIVERSAL PRESS SYNDI-
CATE. All rights reserved.

The parents are not so subtly to blame for her malaise, suggests *The
Boondocks*. Several panels make clear that, despite their self-congratula-
tory claims to the contrary, those in interracial unions do not necessarily
embrace a progressive politics. Jazmine's white mother, for instance, may
show Huey pictures of her parents at the "'63 March on Washington"
and of herself at both "an anti-apartheid rally in '88" and the Million
Man March (35) to prove her liberal bona fides. But when Huey asks to
speak to Jazmine's black father, she insists, both defensively and condescendingly, that "[t]here's a 'black thing' at the door" (35), referring both
to Huey's subject topic of conversation *and* to the person of Huey. That
said, Mrs. Dubois' comments suggest the possibility that she recognizes
that there might be some experiences that many black people have, about
which she cannot always presume to speak authoritatively. On the other
hand, Huey's own condescension does not allow her the possibility of that
recognition. He implies that the best he can ask of her is only "cooperation," not insight. In that sense, the frame suggests a criticism of both.

These exchanges are amusing, of course, but they also cogently explore
the political options for all people in the post–civil rights era. The art
provides an imaginative space for the gestation of ideas that both respond
to and shape public perceptions and political consensus. Specifically, *The
Boondocks* offers a call for a new type of racial literacy, one attentive to
a wider spectrum of racial experiences, and more keenly informed about
the social and political possibilities for cross-racial cooperation. Part of
McGruder's twenty-first-century education—very different from the kinds

of mixed race pedagogical mandates discussed in Chapter One—also involves an appreciation of popular culture's potent role in generating and shaping those identities, experiences, and histories.

1. "COMPULSORY BLACKNESS"

Because the issue of race is so often cast among mixed race advocates as an issue of free will, arguments for and against mixed race identification are often pitched as battles between liberatory self-definition and vulgar group attribution. McGruder's comic series directly challenges the frequent assertion among mixed race advocates that they are not free to identify as they please because black people, in particular, coerce them into a stifling monoraciality. As Coleman Silk cynically describes it in Philip Roth's *The Human Stain* (2001), discussed in Chapter Three, race is "the tyranny of the we that is dying to suck you in."[15] In Jazmine's words, this is translated into her complaint, emphasized in the strip with childish foot stamping: "I resent racial categories!" (*Because I Know* 13).

But despite these high-minded assertions of independence, Jazmine's white mother is, ultimately, the architect of her daughter's position. Mrs. Dubois grants herself proxy legal authority to represent her child's interests, but in doing so she inadvertently flags the limits of the autonomy she touts. Autonomy is always circumscribed, McGruder reminds us, whether by legal guardianship and age restriction, in this case, or more generally, by historical constraints of free will and choice.

In one series of *The Boondocks* panels, for instance, Mrs. Dubois adamantly explains to Jazmine's school principal on the phone that Jazmine should be the author of her identity (*Because I Know* 71). According to Mrs. Dubois, the choices she makes on her daughter's behalf should be immune to unseemly school, state, government, and political interests—that is, should be legally protected by the likes of Ward Connerly's "Racial Privacy Initiative," discussed in the Introduction (Connerly, who insists he is not black but "Creole," is explicitly named as a "great villain" in McGruder's dedication in *Because I Know You Don't Read the Newspapers*). But the principal's quick cut to the chase makes it clear that what he hears through the multiculti talk is the buried claim and ultimate point: "never black." The principal *is* annoyingly dismissive

FIGURE 2.3. *Boondocks*, September 17, 1999. THE BOONDOCKS
© 1999 Aaron McGruder. Reprinted by permission of UNIVERSAL PRESS
SYNDICATE. All rights reserved.

of the parent's direction and *does* officiously challenge her authority to
dictate her daughter's race; but the exchange also dramatizes the cultural
fact that Jazmine alone does not get to declare her race (or racelessness)
by fiat, and neither does Mrs. Dubois get to be the sole and self-ordained
arbiter of race. The mother thinks family determines racial identification;
the principal thinks race affiliation is a filial kinship with black people
that trumps her authority as mother. McGruder precisely captures the
tension between what Kimberly McClain DaCosta calls the "'racialization
of the family' (how racial premises came to be buried in our understanding of family, in which genetic/phenotypic sharing is coded to signify
cultural sharing, intimacy, and caring) and the 'familization of race'
(how it came to be that members of the same racial group feel a kin-like
connection and how that familial understanding is used politically)."[16]

The white mother is McGruder's special target, and culturally significant in this scenario because, as I suggested in the Introduction, white
middle-class mothers were among the first to exert pressure on the legisla-
ture to change racial categorization.[17] Erica Chito Childs, in her analysis
of multiracial websites, finds this irony common: mixed race advocates
tend to proscribe and prescribe multiracial identification as dogmatically
as the monoracialism they "vilify" for *its* dogmatism.[18]

So it is particularly salient that in *The Boondocks'* battle—framed
as maternal rights vs. state's rights—Jazmine's mother thinks calling her
daughter black is an institutional act of racial conscription. The claim that

black people are twisting the arms of their lighter-skinned brethren, basically bullying them into enlistment, is the refrain one hears frequently in the reader criticisms of the comic series."[19] In fact, Maria P. P. Root provocatively argues, mixed people are "oppressed" by black-identified people for this reason, saying that "multiracial people experience a 'squeeze' of oppression *as* people of color and *by* people of color,"[20] mostly through racial coercion (insisting they are inescapably black) but also as often, though contradictorily, by racial gatekeeping (saying they're not "black enough"). Jayne Ifekwunigwe—adapting, she says, Adrienne Rich's notion of "compulsory heterosexuality"—calls this "compulsory Blackness." But this disturbing collapse of "oppressions" equates blackness with the hegemonic norm of heterosexuality, a move that locates "mixed race" as victimized not by the dominant white racial culture in the United States but by a black monoracialism. Certainly painful acts of gatekeeping and colorism in both personal and public forums are historically well-documented, and the injurious practice reflects an anxiety about boundaries, privileges, and entitlements and causes pain and confusion. But this reimagining of blackness as a tyrannical rather than liberatory force in the mobilization of civil rights has become a mainstay in "mixed race" discourses—monoracialism is increasingly cast as an antiquated and reactionary holdover from black nationalism, ill-fitted for today's demographic and political realities. To call black identification oppressive is a reimagining made possible, ironically, by turning Rich's expression against many of those who had fought before and alongside her feminist struggles. And, sadly enough, the notion of "compulsory Blackness" demonizes black identification at the expense of analytical opportunity to the extent that the expression evokes heterosexism yet offers no analysis of, for instance, the way certain constructions of mixed race or blackness may function in concert with heterosexism. It is to blame the victim, or at the very least to distribute unfairly culpability in the oppression of peoples wishing to identify as "mixed race."

At any rate, this sort of recasting of the players in the political scene (such that the oppressed are billed as oppressors) is precisely what gets challenged in *The Boondocks*. Huey, for instance, thinks calling Jazmine black simply amounts to the historical recognition of heterogeneity within blackness itself (since so many African Americans have mixed heritage, calling oneself black *and* mixed is a kind of redundancy from this perspective). Thus, both the principal's and Huey's eye rolling at the Dubois family's (multi) racial equivocation makes clear that they understand race as something neither she nor her mother can simply waive or command away. Furthermore, both Huey and the principal suspect that the Dubois family's refusal of racial categories is less about "accurately" accounting for genealogical diversity than it is about opting out of blackness in particular. Accordingly, when Huey tells Jazmine, for instance, that it's "good to have more black people around," she replies with racial goose-stepping: "um . . . gee, um why . . . why would you think I was . . . um . . . black . . . . I just want to be human" (10, 11). Rather than admit a racial connection, she waxes at length about her "special" and "lonely" status, offering up a maudlin soliloquy to the heavens about being "different from everyone else" (27). (See Fig. C.3.)

Huey already takes as a given Jazmine's inclusion in the "black race," so her pleas of alienation ring hollow. Through such scenes, Jazmine's histrionic hand-wringing are portrayed as not merely self-indulgent but moot.[21] His "You're black. Get over it" (27) sounds the same as the principal's assertion of her blackness, but it is very different: the principal simply reduces race to expedient administrative categories. But Huey's reality check of Jazmine rejects the narrower notion of racial identity as individual private property and returns racial experience to a larger, and enlarging, historical conversation.

II. FRIZZY HAIR AND FAMILY TREES

[B]lack women artists have stolen a march on both visual theory and criticism.
Having emerged in record numbers and gained unprecedented visibility in the past
two decades, they have frequently engaged aspects of current body/gaze discourses.
But in doing so, they often push these preoccupations into unfamiliar territory—
invoking the intricate, aesthetic and social histories of black "hair" politics.
Judith Wilson, "One Way or Another"[22]

One of the most incisive challenges to mixed race identification is most illuminating in Huey's frequent insistence that Jazmine's hair is an afro.

Although it may seem that Huey is simply racially tagging Jazmine, in fact he does not equate race with Jazmine's locks, or any other physical or physiognomic marker, for that matter. Indeed, Huey's harassment actually challenges visual ascription as a legitimate process by which to assign race. Huey, after all, comes from Chicago, wherein reside a great variety of black people. He is not trying to reconcile Jazmine to blackness or to racially shoehorn Jazmine; she already appears to him as one familiar type on the historical and visual spectrum of black people. In fact, he suggests she is *representative* of black people. In his review of a 1999 speech by McGruder to a university audience, Daniel Witter quotes him as saying that *The Boondocks* is "my attempt to tell a story about black America" and that "the black struggle for identity . . . is personified [by] Jazmine Dubois . . . She is part of who we (the black community) are." Further, McGruder insists, his portrayal of Jazmine is, as Witter characterizes his words, "not a slam on mixed-race people, as some have taken it to be; instead she exemplifies the exploration of what it means to be black." In the speech McGruder suggests that "the lack of understanding about problems biracial people face every day reveals a lack of discourse between racial and ethnic groups."[23]

It is no accident, then, that his insistence that Jazmine's hair is not just "frizzy," as she keeps insisting, but akin to Angela Davis' famous 'fro, visually locates Jazmine in a political history in which black women appear in all shapes and colors—including those with straight hair, blond hair, light skin, light eyes, and so on—from Frances E. W. Harper to Nella Larsen, and from Diane Nash to Adrian Piper and Angela Davis, to name but a few. To him, she is never beyond the pale of blackness: she is black, front and center. Jazmine, however, admits she has no idea who Angela Davis is. The fact that she knows nothing of the radical black feminism that Davis stands for, nor how Davis' afro signified black resistance for an entire generation of women—*this* is what Huey criticizes. (Even Jazmine's black father is culturally illiterate, thinking Huey's name—Huey P. Newton, cofounder of the Black Panthers—is the name of a contemporary rock singer). And when Huey calls Jazmine "Mariah" (10)—as in Carey—he feels that her ambivalence about being black smacks of celebrity angst, a petty complaint that could be made by only a privileged few—rich and famous or just very light-skinned. Huey, then, is not simply a slave to the biological sophistry and legal fiction of the one-drop rule, for his commitment to monoracialism suggests an awareness of race and its cogency as fully historical and political. In that sense, the new "race problem" is that as a latter-day Du Bois (as in W. E. B.), Jazmine represents a disturbing twist on double consciousness, one that amounts to an *un*consciousness of the processes and politics of race altogether.

For similar reasons, *The Boondocks* also critiques one of the mainstays of mixed race representation: the obligatory rehearsal of one's multiracial family tree. Replacing calls for social justice or racial equity, the most often repeated goal of "mixed race rights" is merely to "name all the parts of myself." The rhetorical or graphic display of the family tree (almost de rigueur in the growing genre of mixed race narratives) participates in a racial gaze that can interrupt political reflection. For Jazmine and her family, description has come to stand in for politics, genealogy substituting for political discussions of the body politic. The family tree is paraded as revelatory and socially transforming fact. It has come to serve as proxy for social change, in which representing one's family tree has become a political end in itself. The exercise of those rights often amounts to making identity a category of genealogical documentation, documentation which, to the extent that it is complacently represented as an end in itself whose social good is somehow self-evident, obscures identity as social index and mode of analysis. When Huey asks Jazmine, "OK . . . if you're not black, then what are you, hmmm?" she responds dutifully with a list documenting down to the fraction her ethnic racial portfolio: "My mother is one-quarter Irish, one-quarter Swedish, and one-half German, and on my father's side is part Cherokee, and my grandfather is mostly French, I think, because he's originally from Louisiana, and his father was from Haiti I believe, which makes me . . ." Huey intervenes: "Which makes you as black as Richard Roundtree in 'Shaft in Africa'" (*A Right to Be Hostile* 15). Huey disparages not so much her mixed genealogy as the idea that a recapitulation of ethnic and national descent really says anything meaningful about racial identity. At the very least, he suggests, her genealogy is neither progressive nor has sufficient explanatory force. Rather, her accounting retroactively ratifies the idea of racially homogeneous categories and national identities by suggesting that each parent's race or ethnicity is unitary.

Her laundry list also collapses blood and nation and then fractionalizes both—how else can the notion of "one-quarter Swedish" make sense— and looks less like the new millennial model of post-race and more like an uncritical revival of classic nineteenth-century positivist racialism. Huey interrupts her—and the discourse itself—by insisting instead on the political nature of racial identity: he teases her by saying, "I understand, Jazmine. I'm mixed too." We see an up-close shot of her face, which lights up as she says hopefully, "You are?" only to have him sarcastically claim, much to her disappointment, to be "part Black, part African, part Negro, and part colored." Significantly, his designations do not pretend to be descriptive; they all carry heavy historical and political implication. He then walks off wailing, "Poor me. I just don't know where I fit in," as she cries after him (again): "You're making fun of me!" (16). Of course, Huey *is* making fun of Jazmine in this exchange. However, his send-up is social critique to the degree that it does not concede the reduction of racial identity to the sum of one's parts; he thinks of race not in terms of blood but in relation to representation. *Shaft in Africa*, after all, is late in the series of 1970s campy sex-and-adventure Blaxploitation films. Huey's invocation of the hyper-blackness represented in the Blaxploitation genre of film is a spoof *of* them—he is concerned not with black authenticity but with cultural figurations of blackness. Race, for McGruder, is always cast as a matter of historical consciousness, social play, and political engagement. This perspective is reinforced in his comments on the racial status of Barack Obama, when he notes, "We all share the common experiences of being Black in America today—we do not all share a common history."[24] In such scenes, *The Boondocks* replaces mere optic confirmation of race with black cultural performance and historical citation as more useful markers of racial identity. His coherent sense of "Black" is historically informed, historically evolving, and historically heterogeneous in both community composition and cultural practice.

III. PLAYDATES:

NAT TURNER AND SCARLETT O'HARA

Seated with Stuart and Brent Tarleton in the cool shade of the porch of Tara,

her father's plantation, that bright April afternoon of 1861, [Scarlett] made a

pretty picture. Her new green flowered-muslin dress spread its twelve yards of

billowing material over her hoops and exactly matched the flat-heeled green

morocco slippers her father had recently brought her from Atlanta. The dress

set off to perfection the seventeen-inch waist, the smallest in three counties, and

the tightly fitting basque showed breasts well matured for her sixteen years.

Margaret Mitchell, *Gone with the Wind*[25]

Instead of seeing racial identification as the place to map genealogy (as
laudable and politically innocent documentation) or to honor one's parents
(which translates familial fealty into political requirement), Huey shifts
the question of mixed race from one of being a good child to a reminder
of the sexual politics of race always inhering in genealogy and parentage.
His undermining of Jazmine's "plight" is not merely a retreat to some kind
of Old World monoracialism; it is a refusal of historical amnesia. Thus it
is no accident that McGruder's challenge occurs through the figure of the
mulatta, who is not just a little girl with one white parent and one black
parent but is, as Hortense Spillers puts it, "a locus of confounded identities, a meeting ground of investments, and privations in the national treasury of rhetorical wealth . . . an example of signifying property *plus*."[26]
Jazmine's family sees her as the literal, physical embodiment of America's
shining idealism, proof that the American Way is right and true, corporeal
testimony that it has overcome its "race problem"—overcome race itself.
And Jazmine's parents understand NAACP membership—and, of course,
their intimate coupling—as the only political acts required. But, their liberal credentials notwithstanding, as McGruder reminds us, Jazmine as
mulatta still exists as the nexus of history, fantasy, and desire.

We learn, for instance, that Jazmine's parents have a serious black
man/white girl fetish (*Because I Know* 77) and despite their unimpeachable liberal credentials, still get hot over the taboo of interracial sex:
every Halloween they play Desdemona and Othello, or if bored, we are
told, Nicole and OJ (89). Again, as with his reference to *Shaft in Africa*,

FIGURE 2.4. *Boondocks,* June 30, 1999. THE BOONDOCKS © 1999 Aaron McGruder. Reprinted by permission of UNIVERSAL PRESS SYNDICATE.

McGruder evokes the cultural trafficking in blackness and the power of representation in the sexual politics of race.

Huey gets his periodic payback for this liberal objectification, however: when Jazmine wants to play scenes from Margaret Mitchell's *Gone with the Wind*, he drily suggests playing Nat Turner to her Scarlett O'Hara (37). As Jazmine says, it's not simply that Huey doesn't "play nice"; he does not "play right" (37), indicating that there is a right and a wrong history to which he is clearly not subscribing. How better to impeach the so-called right history—the mainstream and largely Southern apologist history of Mitchell's plantation nostalgia—than to juxtapose it with a bloody slave rebellion, to put Scarlett arm in arm with Nat? Huey and Jazmine have inherited history's scripts as well as its parts, but that does not mean they have to play them, McGruder suggests. He cleverly "rights" history by rewriting some roles. To his credit, he never writes his characters out of history even when they imagine themselves to be.

IV. PREPUBESCENCE FOREVER: COMIC TIME, COMIC FORM, AND SOCIAL COMMENTARY

It is striking how *The Boondocks* both invokes and refuses the graphic narrative's conventions of time and form in the service of social commentary. As Will Eisner reminds us,

[t]he format of the comic book presents a montage of both word and image, and the reader is thus required to exercise both visual and verbal interpretive

skills. The regimens of art (e.g. Perspective, symmetry, brush stroke) and the regimens of literature (e.g. Grammar, plot, syntax) become superimposed upon each other. The reading of the comic book is an act of both aesthetic perception and intellectual pursuit.[27]

On the one hand, time and "timing" are "critical to the success of the visual narrative." Timing is, as Eisner puts it, "the manipulation of the elements of time to achieve a specific message or emotion, panels become a critical element. . . . In music or the other forms of auditory communication where rhythm or 'beat' is achieved, this is done with actual lengths of time. In graphics the experience is conveyed by the use of illusions and symbols and their arrangement" (26). Therefore speech balloons, the size and spacing of comic panels, the conventional pace of visual scanning, and so on can all impact timing in graphic narratives. But representing Time with a capital T, more generally, is a bit more complicated. In what Eisner calls the "sea-scape" of our sensory world, sound is measured audibly, relative to its distance from us. Space is mostly measured and perceived visually. Time is more illusory: we measure and perceive it through the memory of experience (25). Thus to evoke the dimension of Time itself, comics must rely on some "memory of experience"—which, as he explains it, is the remembered repertoire of personal experiences from which readers draw to make sense of the world and thus also of the page. From infancy onward, we learn the idea that Time "passes," according to Eisner, through our experience in the world and from repeated social convention. (So, for instance, remembering that a body thrown out of a window will hit the ground allows a panel to jump from an image of a body thrown out of a window to a panel where a body is on the ground, and readers will understand, through the memory of experience, that the body fell not just through space but in time.)

McGruder, I believe, expands for his own political ends Eisner's theory of representing time. The graphic comic medium allows for, and McGruder's social critique exploits, a sense of both horizontal, progressive time (the implied momentum of time suggested by the visual movement from panel to panel) and vertical, synchronic time (the characters never age, are frozen in this place beyond time, even as they are, paradoxically, always *in* time and history). Jazmine is prepubescent, for instance, which puts her, like Mark Twain's children, in the supposedly prelapsarian pre-social realm, the site of superior social critique. She is sexually and racially coming of age, but she is no ingénue; in McGruder's work, she is neither sexless nor history-less, pointedly *not* prior to the social realm but, as I hope I have suggested, poised as an index to it.

Importantly, McGruder retools comic conventions not only of time but also of bodies. According to Eisner, "the artist must work from a 'dictionary' of human gestures" that are drawn from both "personal observations and an inventory of gestures, common and comprehensible to the reader" (101). McGruder's distinctive use of Japanese anime-based manga, a Japanese pop-comic style that had its origins as a low-class protest form, has a characteristic typology—high brow, large eyes—that is often described as flat, two-dimensional, static. Anime tends toward the hyperbolic, suggests a "type," a timeless or fixed quality to ethnic character: this is, of course, especially risky when one considers the nineteenth-century history of racial caricature in which black people's permanent immaturity, their putative atavism, is encoded through exaggerated features. As Henry Wonham notes in *Playing the Races: Ethnic Caricature and American Literary Realism*, one formal and political response, then, to caricature is realism: "Realism, as the representational antithesis to mere caricature . . . performs the work of liberation, disentangling the human individual from the distorting grip of ethnic typology."[28] And indeed, as he points out, the link between a "realist aesthetics and the politics of emancipation" has become something "approaching a literary-critical doctrine" (5). This commitment to the high moral earnestness of the Real (as a genre within supposedly a liberal politics) is especially true when dealing with certain kinds of subjects: so, for instance, when Art Spiegelman's *Maus I: My Father Bleeds History: A Survivor's Tale* first came out in 1986, there was much disquiet among many who felt that representation of the Holocaust demands the strictest forms of realism, requiring first-person testimony, authenticated facts, and photo-documentary as well as a posture of reverence, needless to say, and, therefore, the comic genre was a wholly inappropriate, even sacrilegious, form for these purposes. Similarly, the race problem is seen as no laughing matter, as sacrosanct; and social protest, some argue, is better waged on the streets, through the ballot box, in sober editorials. Furthermore, because the comic medium has been used *against* racial advances, for some it is a particularly unfit mechanism to be reappropriated for racial justice—a kind of taking up with the devil. It seemed to point to McGruder's hubris in trying to use the "master's tools" to dismantle the house, to borrow from Audre Lorde, or as McGruder puts it, to put a "foot in the ass of The Man."[29]

Aesthetic form and political effect cannot be conflated, however, and ethnic caricature and realism are not opposite poles on a spectrum. Wonham observes, "[T]hese two aesthetic programs, one committed to the representation of the fully humanized individual, the other invested in broad ethnic abstractions, operate less as antithetical choices than as complementary impulses" (8). Both, he argues, try to "'lay bare' the essence of the human subject, whether through type or character" (10); and in fact, in myriad ways "ethnic caricature performs an integral function *within* the political and aesthetic program of American realism" (8). In fact, McGruder actively manipulates the conventions of racial caricature in order to reveal social reality (and potentially effect social change). McGruder plays with physiognomic taxonomies through anime's distinctive focus on the face. Eisner notes that the face, in particular, "has an essential role in communicating emotion through codified gestures that are culturally recognizable" and as such the face is "expected to act as an adverb to the posture or gesture of the body . . . [and] the head (or face) is often used by artists to convey the entire message of bodily movement" (Eisner 111). McGruder's characters are nearly all head and face, and through them he invokes and revokes traditional stereotyping: he features, for instance, disproportionately large eyes but *no* lips, the corresponding requisite in black minstrelsy. His main black characters are children, calling up the equation of black people as infantile, but McGruder's young people have anime's extremely high brows, which in this context clearly suggest intellect and intense social conscience rather than childish ignorance and civic incapacity. Furthermore, there is almost no attention to the body *below* the head, decoupling the association of black people with the flesh and body rather than the spirit and mind. In this way we have black people on view but not on display. His images do not trigger the visual conventions historically associated with black people, and thus do not further whet the appetite for black spectacularity.

Finally, McGruder does an end run around the supposed racial limitations of black-white technology in graphics, the idea that visual contrast through pixel density limits the ability of print media to represent color variation and distinction. But McGruder's characters are all shades of black; moreover, they register as blacker—or not—only in relation to other characters, emphasizing the provisional, situational perception of race through color. In short, even McGruder's pixels are political.

V. THE MIS-EDUCATION OF JAZMINE

It is true that a sense of mixed-race identity could be a powerful factor
in raising the awareness of all mixed-race people; but it is also true
that . . . that which is well intentioned could become a tragedy.
Richard E. Van Der Ross, foreword to *The New Colored People*[30]

Although *The Boondocks* in one sense freezes time through typology, McGruder's comic strip keeps race and history in motion. His characters never grow up, but they do learn; their bodies are static, but they mature politically.[31] This is one of the many paradoxes of time in the comic strip. For instance, most people self-identifying as "more than one race" on the 2000 Census were under twenty-five, so in that sense—even though Huey and Jazmine are the same age—Jazmine represents a generational break with Huey's mode of seeing blackness. It is true that Huey indicts the basis for Jazmine's racial ambivalence, but the strip suggests that Huey must accommodate or at least better account for Jazmine's unique racial experiences as well. The rapprochement between them occurs through some mutual educating.

Jazmine's education is akin to Carter G. Woodson's famous treatise, *The Mis-Education of the Negro* (1933), in the sense that she learns to leverage her own particularly racialized experience to counter the white social "mis-education" she has received. But even more, and despite Huey's taunts, her mixed-racial anxieties are not entirely dismissed within McGruder's graphic narrative. Her complaints, for instance, of Huey "making fun" of her several times, are a repetition that sounds like both a whine *and* a legitimate refusal to give up entirely the possibility that she might have a different racialized experience than he.

Some of the most powerful moments in the strip occur when Jazmine begins to develop a more theoretically sophisticated identity, one in which she moves from understanding herself in terms of solitary existential angst (a misunderstood girl with bad hair) to seeing herself in relation to history and political imperatives. She comes to understand black critiques of American history not through Huey's lectures, interestingly, but through dealing with a little white neighbor, Cindy. Cindy thinks black people are only hip-hoppers and gangstas (*Because I Know* 16), understands "color-blindness" as a "disease" (16), and does not know that "there were slaves in America during independence day" (38). After these exchanges with Cindy, Jazmine concludes that "maybe Huey was right" when he refuses to celebrate the July 4th holiday, or at least spends it "writing some letters to some of the countless black men in America's prisons" and meditating "on the meaning of liberty" (38). She wants simply to be a "peaceful citizen of earth" (25) and desperately to be "friends again" (23), but he suggests that cannot happen until she accepts her afro and what it represents.

Huey critiques her naïveté and Eurocentrism (95), but it is actually through Jazmine's exchanges with Cindy that she begins to assess her own experience, drop her claims to "racelessness," and move towards not so much a recognition of her "mixed" experience as sui generis but a sense of it as distinctive on a continuum with black experience as represented by Huey and his brother. Her education points to one of the more promising directions emerging in progressive mixed race politics, in which, as Ronald Sundstrom suggests, there must be a "conscious effort to uphold moral obligations to parent communities . . . a commitment to fight racial hierarchy and racism . . . a rejection of white privilege" and a sense of "irony."[32]

But if Jazmine is educated into a capacious blackness, Huey's education requires a complementary hybridization of thought and form. As he puts it in one of the editorial inserts, in which Huey is writing a book titled *Ward Connerly Should Be Beaten by Raekwon the Chef with a Spiked Bat: A Critical Look at Black Conservatives*, he represents himself as poised between academe, which to him seems removed from the world, and a globalized hip-hop culture, which risks giving it up to bling-bling (*Because I Know* 69). A possible cross-over model for his political aspirations, Huey suggests, is represented by Raekwon the Chef (the Wu-Tang Clan's primary lyricist).

Like McGruder's blend of hip-hop savvy and Japanese pop cultural forms in anime, the Wu-Tang Clan fuses black vernacular culture with Japanese camp. The group enacts what Anthony Appiah calls "cultural contamination,"[33] but with an additional political edginess. The Clan (with its anti-Klan outlook) joins its cross-raciality with self-reflective politics, its social critiques of corporate consumerism, and its resistance to gratuitous booty.

Raekwon illustrates Huey's own dilemma as someone trying to bridge a cultural divide: the performer is someone who is, paradoxically, both famous and obscure—an icon in the hip-hop community but, he notes, an unknown to many academics. Huey contemplates a political mid-way, as the speech balloons in his editorial inform us:

Will Huey alienate the masses with obscure references? Can he broaden the scope of his work without corrupting its cultural integrity and unyielding radical tone? Can he discover the elusive middle ground between Frances Cress Welsing and Henry Louis Gates Jr.? Oh, we do not envy the difficult task facing poor Huey . . . (69)

His compromise between the populist Frances Cress Welsing, the black psychiatrist whose *The Isis Papers* offered a radical indictment of white supremacy in the 1970s, and the erudite Gates Jr., world-renowned Harvard scholar of African American studies, is revealed in his revision of the proposed book title: *Ward Connerly Is a Boot-Licking Uncle Tom: A Critical Look at Black Conservatives*. The new title will "transcend cultural barriers" (69) because everyone, Huey philosophizes, knows what an "Uncle Tom" is. In that way, Huey's striving towards a merging of differing worldviews makes him more, not less, like Jazmine with her racial bi-focalism. His synthesis of academic and pop-cultural modes only sharpens rather than suspends his critique of black conservatives, and suggests that Jazmine's accommodation of black and white perspectives might also only intensify her critical mien.

VI. THE HAPPY LAND OF HALFRICA

In an interview with Intermix, a mixed race organization based in England, Nate Creekmore says he was "amazed at the positive reception [*Maintaining*] received," and was praised for creating work that "comes from a mixed-race perspective."[34] There are but few precedents for this: George Herriman (1880–1944), renowned creator of the comic *Krazy Kat*, was of African American descent (both his parents are listed as "mulatto" in the 1880 Census), though he passed as Greek and his death certificate listed him as Caucasian. Many have suggested that his underground racial background made its way obliquely into his comics.[35] But Creekmore is really the first nationally syndicated comic strip artist and illustrator who openly self-identifies as "mixed."

One reason for his popularity might be the fact that Creekmore's comments in the Intermix interview, in a Mixed Chicks Chat interview,[36] and on his own website seem in lockstep with the mixed race movement's emphasis on challenging social categorization by asserting racial self-identification and rejecting the presumption of identity confusion:

I'll avoid the awkwardly forward "What are you?" question and let you know my mother is white and my father is black. There are a myriad of terms (some horribly offensive and others less so) to describe the ethnicity of people like me. . . . Essentially, *Maintaining* is about what it means to be biracial in a society that prefers its people be uniracial. To be biracial is to be a person, so *Maintaining* is about how biracial people (and their families) are people like everyone else. Even today it is rare to see depictions of biracial people (specifically black/whites) that go beyond the stock "tragic mulatto" character. I want *Maintaining* to offer a different perspective that will be recognised by mixed-race people and that will be palatable for everyone else. . . . The strip is loosely based on my own experience. . . . I know who I am regardless of what the perception of me might be, ethnically. So while it might be easier for me to just go around and say I'm black, I think that would be wrong on my part, because I grew up with my mother as well as my father. . . . It's sad that you have to choose between the two groups. I don't even think that should be an issue. I have to rise above that stuff. I'm a part of both cultures. I can't be eternally conflicted with myself.

And yet, if Creekmore is characterized as distinct from McGruder's "angry black man," his strip takes a peek at "Halfrican American fury" (7/10/09);[37] and if he says he writes primarily for "mixed-race people," in the strip Marcus actually directs most of his comments to his best friend, the unambiguously black Anton, who, along with his love interest, Frieda, a Korean transracial adoptee, often disputes Marcus' sometimes grandiose mixed-racial speculations and propositions. And all three of them challenge the assumptions of their white, black-cool-loving classmate Steve. That is, in practice, *Maintaining* is cross-racial discussion that not only addresses mixed race people—with its explicit focus on the experiences of those mixed black and white—but also involves black people and white people. Further, even though Creekmore rehearses the belief that calling himself black involves rejecting a white parent, as I will explore, several of his episodes gently critique the limitation of this routine claim and many others.

In the episode "The Happy Land of Halfrica," Marcus and his little brother, Tavian, gaze upon a vision of a paradise island with dancing, laughing, bikini-clad inhabitants: "There is no race in Halfrica, her people are a blend . . . of black and white ethnicities, and everyone's a friend!" To which Anton whispers to Tavian, "There's no such place as 'Halfrica.' Your brother's lost his mind" (11/2/08). This island fantasy is part of what one could call the rise and stall of the Halfrican American dream that Marcus plays with throughout the strip. The name "Halfrican American" is his effort to distinguish "my people"—that is, those of a black-white mix as distinguished from the more general "biracial" moniker—and to give them a more noble title than "mongrel," "mutt"

FIGURE 2.5. *Maintaining,* November 2, 2008. MAINTAINING © 2007 & 2008 Nate Creekmore. Reprinted by permission of UNIVERSAL PRESS SYNDICATE. All rights reserved.

(6/8/08), "half-breed," "high yellow," "redbone," "lite-bright," "zebra," or "oreo" (2/27/09). In his effort to assert a more positive identity, Marcus often mouths the popular commonplaces of mixed pride: "I traverse the black world of hip hop and the white world of indie as easily as a train" (3/20/09); "Mixed race people are the future, we bridge ethnic and racial gaps! We disprove the ideals of racial purity!" (9/12/08); he calls himself a "mulatto ambassador" (8/11/08) easing interracial fears. And when Marcus needs to declare his mixed race cultural nationalism, he will bring out the "yin yang" or "zebra" shirts, and posters of a scantily clad Halle Berry that whet his teenage dreams. His efforts to imagine a community of mixed race people extend to the hailing of the Oreo as the cookie of choice among mixed race peoples (but only when eaten—otherwise it is the most segregated of snacks): "By eating the Oreo Cookie, we celebrate our Halfrican American heritage" (3/28/08). He even swoons at the idea of a utopic new world:

As blacks become more white and whites become more black, racial divisions will become passé. A new society will emerge . . . a society where everyone is mixed like me. A utopia, if you will. Can't you see, Anton, blacks and whites have been seasoning each other's tastes for years, Music, speech patterns . . . senses of cool. (2/1/09)

Marcus' argument for how this homogenized world will be achieved sounds much like that of the conservative black writer George Schuyler, who argues in "The Negro Art Hokum" (1926) that there were no such things as African American identity (black people are just "lamp-blacked Anglo Saxons") and African American art because social, economic, religious, and cultural integration was rendering such distinctions false. Schuyler, who married a white woman and raised their daughter, Philippa, as a genetic experiment in genius (and in fact Philippa was a child prodigy as a world-renowned pianist), was vigorously criticized by other Harlem Renaissance intellectuals, who pointed out that social, religious, residential, and economic segregation—both de facto and de jure—was in no retreat, and that discrimination coupled with proud self-determination within what W. E. B. Du Bois called a "nation within a nation" had, indeed, created valuable, culturally distinct art and lifestyles.[38] Arguably the same issue holds today, and few would argue that integration has been fully realized; certainly statistics bear out the fact that disparities continue in wealth and health services, real estate redlining, unequal treatment under the justice system, and nearly all sectors of public life. Creekmore's parody, like Schuyler's *Black No More* (1931), is alert to humor both as a means to confront "the maddening illusions of race and the insidiousness of racism" and as a vehicle that is "leery of identities built on victimhood."[39]

In *Maintaining*, all these clichés of "heterogeneous superiority" are skewered, the mainstays of the mixed race movement given some pokes in the side that if not meant to bruise will not tickle either. Anton teases him in one episode: "Some people," he says, addressing the audience, "think mixed race people are the key to racial harmony. Some believe they have the answers and that mixed people are the future." The next image shows Marcus hung up on a fence by his pants bottom with Anton commenting: "The future looks grim." "Some people." Marcus, properly chastened, gets the joke and the point: "Ha Ha. Now let me down before the cops show up" (12/5/07). Even the invention of a new racial categorization— the "Halfrican American"—with the pretentiousness of Marcus, godlike, naming "his people" as though a separate nation, is satirized. Frieda says it is "gimmicky": "[T]hat's the name you give people who are half-black and half-white?" "What?" he says in response: "My people needed a name so I gave them one." She says she prefers simply "Marcus" to "Halfrican American" or his other options, "Caucasianegro" and "Afro-Saxon" (3/29/08). In his efforts to push the idea of a mixed race community to Frieda (usually as part of his efforts to court her), Marcus imagines her his "soul mate" (6/27/09) because she has (adopted) white and black parents though she looks to be of Korean background. Jumping on the coincidence of their parents' interracial union, he announces, "You're Halfricasian!" to which she drily replies, "Or I'm adopted. Whichever" (6/23/09). Even Marcus' frequent calls for "role models" and media representatives are spoofed: "We want Barack back," he chants, because "black people stole Obama!" whom he claims as "one of Halfrican America's finest sons" (2/25/09). He similarly lobbies for theatrical casting that is mixed race sensitive (in a series of episodes, Marcus expresses outrage that his little brother is not selected for the role of the mixed race Obama in his school play (5/2/09, 5/4/09, 5/5/09, 5/7/09) and calls for more Halfrican American role models, such as himself (7/7/09, 7/8/09), though it is unclear if he can even serve as an exemplar for his little brother, let alone his "people." Since most mixed race advocacy websites have lists of and links to people hailed as mixed race celebrities (some who identify as mixed, some who do not), his spoof directly comments on the trend to locate and agitate for mixed race representation in the public and popular culture spheres.[40] Anton's response: "Don't be like that. We left you Joakim Noah" (2/22/09). Noah, of French, Swedish, and Cameroonian descent, is a professional basketball player and often a poster child for multiracial cosmopolitanism.

Marcus' scrambling to find a shared connection between his "people" is recognizable and sympathetically represented, but Creekmore is also precise about the dangerous political risks associated with it and the historical amnesia often informing the effort itself. Nowhere is this critique more pointed than in Marcus' musings at one point that mixed race people should have certain privileges, including a "half white middle section" on the bus, imagining himself as a Halfrican Rosa Parks (8/24/08). In another episode, it is even clear that the creation of a mixed race community comes with some dangers of what Creekmore describes as an "exclusive membership" that is "a sort of apartheid."[41]

ANTON: How do you determine who is a part of this newly labeled ethnic group?
MARCUS: Obviously, a set of standards will be put into place . . . hair texture . . . skin tone . . .
ANTON: I don't like where this is going. . . .
MARCUS: I just don't know if this Halfrican American movement is going to work out, Anton. Some biracial people can't join because they're not mixed enough, and others clearly are mixed but call themselves black regardless. My people have no unity!
ANTON: The downfall of too many minority groups. (6/14/07, 6/15/07, 6/17/07)

The problem, though, is not that there is not unity; the problem lies in the desire for unity itself, the segregations and distinctions made in the name of unity and solidarity if held as the basis for a "people." But Marcus

persists in developing a "list of guidelines for determining whether someone can be Halfrican American," which reads like a cross between South
African apartheid legal determinations of "coloured" people and the black
elite's infamous "paper bag" test of the twentieth century (which allowed
entrance to clubs and parties based on whether one's skin was as light
as or lighter than a brown paper bag). In the episode, Marcus scribbles
down: "One's father must be black and one's mother must be white, or
vice versa. One's skin ought to be noticeably lighter than a brown paper
bag. One should have 'that good hair,' and when a pencil is placed in said
hair, it would slide out easily." Anton says, "The fact that you're actually
writing this down is what I find most disturbing" as Marcus goes on, ". . .
one should have a somewhat 'Puerto Rican look'" (6/18/07). The message
is clear, and though Marcus continues to claim the expression "Halfrican American," the process of articulating his particular experience of
mixed race does not result in the creation of a separate community. His
efforts at mixed race organizing are thwarted not by the illogics of race,
the strip implies, but by an ill-advised refusal of historical memory. This
failure to place mixed race within a past (and its lessons) is coupled with a
fierce competition over which movement is the most "next-gen." Marcus,
for instance, soon finds himself in competition with his friend Lepidus,
who is jockeying for a "TRUE movement for mixed race people. Halfrican Americanism is done! REAL black/whites will rally under the name
Caucafrican American!" Ledipus takes Marcus' bullhorn and shouts,
"Half-black, half-white! Must be all right!" (7/18/09). It seems Marcus'
nascent Halfrican American movement is already obsolete in the mad dash
to the future. This battle over who "we" are and who represents "us"
is particularly important because the very idea of mixed race belonging is
problematic. As author Malcolm Gladwell, of British-Jamaican descent,
puts it in "Lost in the Middle,"[42]

When do I use "we"? In a room full of people I do not know, I always search out
the ones who fall into the middle, like me, out of some irrational idea that we belong together. I worry that this is the wrong thing for the child of a mixed marriage to feel. My parents conquered difference, and we would all like to think
that sort of accomplishment is something that could be passed down from gen-

eration to generation. That's why we're all, in theory, so excited by the idea of miscegenation—because if we mix the races, presumably, we create a new generation of people for whom existing racial categories do not exist. I don't think it's that easy, though. If you mix black and white, you don't obliterate those categories; you merely create a third category, a category that demands, for its very existence, an even greater commitment to nuances of racial taxonomy. (124)

Marcus' naïveté about his own "greater commitment to the nuances of racial taxonomy" is often echoed in the community-building efforts of many mixed race organizations, which frequently sift the believers from those they designate the "haters," from those who demonstrate the proper attitude and those who do not.[43] Marcus' and Ledipus' campaigns suggest that creating certain kinds of communities, whether of like-minded or like-looking members, risks generating the most exacting terms of inclusion. As I suggested in Chapter One, often tacitly committed not only to a certain "ambiguous" look but also to a distinctive ideological position, the racial sorting and political gatekeeping that operates in mixed race organizations is usually invoked around increasingly consolidated principles, attitudes, and understandings about race (as a false god), about identity (as self-selected), about the terms of oppression (not white hegemony or structural racism but often black politicians, black organizations, black studies), about interracial relations (a revolutionary love),[44] about the putative need for mixed race role models, politicians, playwrights, movie stars, novelists, newscasters, and, Marcus says, special school clubs, class presidents, and history lessons in the achievements of mixed race peoples (2/24/09).

VII. PUBERTY, COMIC FORM, AND CROSS-RACIAL DESIRE

In this sense, Creekmore's critiques of mixed race special-interest lobbying resemble McGruder's. But *Maintaining* also has its distinctions, many of which explore a broader spectrum of mixed race experiences, including those that take into account such critiques. One of those distinctions is that Creekmore's characters, unlike McGruder's prepubescent set, are teenagers experiencing the drip of hormones and the initial throbs of desire.

Creekmore's adolescents are not in Huey's and Jazmine's pre-juvenile condition, always prior to an adulthood they analyze. Marcus, Anton, and Frieda are eagerly rushing headlong towards maturity; they cannot wait to grow up and are already dating (or in hot pursuit of a date), driving (when they can get the keys), and (trying to) vote though still underage. Marcus' adolescent insecurities replace Huey's prepubescent certainties. More importantly, it is during adolescence that racial awareness is heightened by the sexual exchange. W. E. B. Du Bois, for instance, writes poignantly of realizing that blackness had a negative association when his "calling card" was refused by a white girl in class that he initially was interested in. In *Maintaining*, the youth identifying as mixed race and obsessively discussing who constitutes a racially appropriate partner becomes a commentary on the way racial and sexual comings-of-age are entwined. In a series of episodes, Marcus asks if he "should *only* date Halfrican American girls" (6/20/09) since his biracial friend, Titus, tells him that, because they themselves are "half-black, half-white," they, in turn, should date only half-black, half-white girls. His motto: "If she ain't half black then send her back" (6/18/09). They are, after all, "the most beautiful women on the planet!" (6/19/09). But then Marcus realizes that they seem to be snubbing interracial dating, which, given the circumstances of their birth, is ironic, but when he tells Titus that he has "always felt mildly offended by non-interracial dating," Titus tells him *he* is being "close-minded" and "offensive" (6/19/09). Both highlight the potential prescriptiveness of both racial exogamy and racial endogamy: is one being close-minded when favoring racially similar partners, and if so, is it not also close-minded to favor non-racially-similar partners? The dig is not leveled at black people for advocating marrying "within the race" (a common charge by mixed race advocacy groups); by contrast, in this episode two youths who identify as mixed race are associated with the kind of race pride so often criticized— whether privileging mixed race partnering or interracial partnering, they flirt with the same kind of cultural nationalism railed against by Jayne Ifekwunigwe and others that I discuss in Chapter One.

Like *The Boondocks*, *Maintaining* also critiques the racial dynamics of the white mothers and black fathers. Creekmore does not suggest that Marcus' parents, like McGruder's Jazmine, have an OJ-Nicole/Othello-

Desdemona complex, but Marcus' parents do share a fantasy that they are progressive trailblazers. Without denying the fact that those who married across racial lines, until very recently, endured legal hostility and social disapproval, Creekmore nonetheless gently warns against too much self-congratulation: in an episode in which Marcus' parents reflect on the mainstreaming of interracial couples, his mother asks with ill-concealed disappointment, "Are we now, as a couple . . . inoffensive?" Her husband cuddles her and insists she will "always be offensive to me, baby." Marcus, observing this display, tells them to "get a room" (3/22/09), responding with a typical adolescent's disgust at parents' affection but also at the recognition that his parents' shared sense of racial transgression juiced their mutual sexual attraction. Virtuous color blindness did not enable this love across the color line—quite the contrary; a stimulating aware-ness of their lover's otherness played a hand. To that degree, Creekmore suggests that interracial couples are invested at the most intimate level in sexualized racial difference.[45] If *Maintaining*'s critique of white moth-ers is not quite as searing as that of *The Boondocks*, in a Mother's Day episode Creekmore's strip does similarly examine the futility of maternal efforts to insist on race as choice (5/11/08).

Rehearsing and revising some of the same assumptions that Jazmine's mother voiced in her discussions with the school principal about her child's

FIGURE 2.6. *Maintaining*, May 11, 2008. MAINTAINING © 2007 & 2008 Nate Creekmore. Reprinted by permission of UNIVERSAL PRESS SYNDICATE. All rights reserved.

racial identification in *The Boondocks*, this time it is the father rather than a school official who suggests that Marcus and biraciality is not "something new," not something that can be left to a child's own discretion, and not something that transcends "standard labels." The episode suggests not only how dissension can occur even within families but also how racial identification is not simply about finding the correct name. His "Hey, negro!" is less a statement fixing his son's identity than it is a play on the rich African American tradition of naming. His signifying employs a name that evokes what Aldon Lynn Nielsen calls "black chant" which, quoting Stephen Henderson, is a form of a "communication of 'Blackness' and fidelity to the observed or intuited truth of the Black Experience in the United States."[46] That is, Marcus' father's name-calling references black experience, not ethnography. Ironically, given that his mother says calling him black would be to crudely simplify things, "Hey, negro!" is, in fact, far more complex: it is a calling up and calling upon all the nuances of affectionate in-group teasing, gaining its humor both because it ironically places his son's minor irresponsibility (he has yet to take out the trash) within the history of white men's charges of black idleness, as much as it places it, equally ironically, within a history of black nationalism in which the antiquated "negro" became synonymous with political sellout. As Amiri Baraka translated it, "negro" was an insult that meant you were not a Black person—the capital B signaling political awareness. This episode, then, is not about his father's insistence that Marcus is black when his mother calls him biracial; it is about the collision of nomenclatures in which "biracial" denotes identity narrowly as a function of parentage and "Hey, negro!" connotes identity as a function of cultural experience and community history. They are referencing very different critical frameworks for understanding identity. Thus, even though Creekmore talks about feeling responsible to his white and black parents, the strip explores how much more complex this issue of racial self-identification is, and how even family members are talking past each other when they talk about race.

Earlier I discussed McGruder's creative use of anime and manga to represent black people and refigure black infantilization. Creekmore has a slightly different but similarly productive aesthetic. In part it is unique in what it does not do: it does not simply counter a visual racial stereotype (in this case, of the tragic mulatto or of debauched mulatto sexuality appearing as early as in D. W. Griffith's 1915 film *Birth of a Nation*). Rather, he has the challenge of representing mixed race as the visual and political conventions are just emerging: how to represent "ambiguity"? Does mixed race always mean light-skinned? If so, how does one represent that in black and white or in color comics? In a podcast interview, Creekmore was asked by a listener how did he "convey 'biracial' in drawings," and he said that he did use skin color to signal biraciality, making Marcus "a little yellow," invoking the whole "high yellow thing,"[47] as he put it. He also mentioned that the parents, one white, one black, appear in the strip for those who miss the cue or when the comic is printed in black and white. But there are in fact many other ways that the biraciality is signaled in *Maintaining*. As does McGruder, Creekmore makes race intelligible only in context and comparatively, and, further, both demonstrate competency in conventions of mixed race representation and make some adjustments to them in concert with the strips' reimagining of the cultural conception of mixed race. Anton is signaled as "Black" because his hair is styled in cornrows and he wears hip-hop garb, while Marcus' hair is close-cropped and he dons Gap jeans; and Anton's nose, while the same shape as Marcus', stretches the width of his face. Arguably these trade in stereotypes of black versus mixed, as if Marcus' whiteness translates into a divestment from what Tricia Rose identifies as the cultural potency and poignancy of "black noise"[48] as well as from the brotherhood of the black barbershop. The marked features seem to return black physiognomy to a focus on the face. Anton's stable visual coding as black parallels his consistent part as black monosyllabic straight man to Marcus' mixed ramblings.

Yet Creekmore also interrupts the racial syntax that he establishes, and not only because the other black and mixed characters all have different hair, dress, affectations. The nose, of course, has special historic status in racial semiotics as a diagnostic tool to "out" the racial depravity within.[49] But the characters' noses across races are often shapeless and randomly assigned. Marcus' friend Lepidus, who identifies as mixed race, has wavy hair and a bulb of a nose, and other black characters' attire and hair similarly vary. Like McGruder's emphasis on the large head, Creekmore renders his characters' eyes as enormous saucers. They evoke not the bugging of minstrelsy but the oversized sensitivity of both his teen-aged characters and the parents trying to make sense of the world. The mouth and nose are diminished beneath those eyes, so that the cluster of racial signifiers associated with people of color also becomes not just rearranged but rearticulated. The forms cue race, but they do not always neatly correlate with predictable racial content. This dissonance is part of the challenge to make both blackness and mixed race supple and capacious enough to engage more fully and accommodate racial experience more generally. In exploring the theatricality of blackness, Fred Moten examines how black artist/philosopher Adrian Piper deploys racial performance "in order to critique racial categories and to investigate what happens when the visual singularity of a performed, curated, or conceptualized image is deployed in order to move beyond what she calls the 'visual pathology' of racist categorization" (234). In *Maintaining*, this performance of blackness versus mixedness also disrupts the presumed class difference between the two. Few references are made to Anton's economic background, but Marcus is working class and his folks are barely keeping a toehold there. The frequent assumptions that the mixed race movement is middle class and liberal do not apply here; Marcus' mother dropped out of high school to marry his father, and she recently had to go to work because of the recession; his father cannot seem to hold on to any employment, having had short stints as a security guard, a telemarketer, and an underground boxer.

VIII. HALFRICA IN WHITE AMERICA:
BLACK WANNABES AND WHITE WANNABES

The conversation between black and mixed race identification is an occasion to discuss, and is understood in the context of, much broader issues of racial aspiration. One of Marcus' white classmates thinks he must be part black because, he argues, he is "so in tune with black culture," adores hip-hop, has two black friends, and "loves white women" (5/17/08). Anton says he is just "half white, half whack" (5/15/08). Steve imagines that if indeed this warrants his inclusion in the race, he could win some "sweet minority scholarships" (5/16/08). Believing he "has so much rhythm and soul" (5/17/09), Steve—so taken with the idea that "black people are just so cool" (1/15/08)—decides to pass as black. With a copy of John Howard Griffin's *Black Like Me* (1961), and, Anton suspects, under the influence of *The Jazz Singer*, Steve goes into blackface by applying shoe polish, thinking it is a gesture of sympathetic understanding (5/24/08).

Although in this episode Steve's desire to participate in black culture is rendered obscene, there is a hint of how whites might more productively participate in and identify with black culture in ways that are less naïve or appropriative. Steve does not understand, but viewers will, that Steve has been subject both to racial profiling by whites who cannot distinguish blackface from black faces and to the indignation of black people offended by his blackface. In the comic, Steve's innocence increasingly becomes less endearing and less an excuse for his racial borrowings. When Steve tells Marcus that he has been reading black literature, Marcus is impressed. After he finds out it is not Richard Wright or Ralph Ellison but *Vibe* magazine that Steve is referring to, his enthusiasm evaporates, suggesting that literature may provide a more meaningful way for whites to access and be involved with black experience beyond hip-hop, and blackface, and reading "Ebony Flavored Hustler Pimps" (5/20/08). That said, *Maintaining* is as cynical as *The Boondocks* about white interest in black people: several episodes feature white liberal girls wanting to touch black hair (4/19/08), white kids inviting black peers over because black people "start the party" (1/22/08), and white classmates talking only to kids of color about sports or hip-hop (6/9/08).

If *Maintaining* explores white obsession with black folk, it similarly speculates on the desire for whiteness among people of color. A topic of conversation in black communities for nearly two centuries, it has been a near-taboo in mixed race groups: the desire and capacity for light-skinned people to pass for white. College graduate Titus, Marcus' erstwhile mixed race hero, has dyed his hair blond and lets people think he is white so he can "survive," as he puts it. He has two degrees, he points out, and yet can get only menial work. Of course, passing as white only means, he admits, that he is upgraded to employment at Starbucks instead of Taco Bell. Marcus cannot convince him that this is the "best possible time to be mixed" (9/13/08), and one is reminded of the protagonist's concession at the conclusion of James Weldon Johnson's *Autobiography of an*

Ex-Colored Man that by passing as white he has passed up a chance at greatness as a black man:

I am an ordinarily successful white man who has made a little money. They are men who are making history and a race. I, too, might have taken part in a work so glorious . . . I cannot repress the thought that, after all, I have chosen the lesser part, that I have sold my birthright for a mess of pottage."[50]

Marcus tries to convince Titus not to give up his birthright just because it is hard being mixed, as Titus insists. Esau's mean "mess of pottage" is not worth the loss of mixed race glory. But Marcus, too, finds it hard to be in the middle: "When I am with blacks I'm white, and with whites, I'm black. That's what it means to be mixed" (5/27/08). Moreover, he, too, is subject to discrimination and daily white suspicion—at one point, in fact, his solution is to anticipate and defuse white anxiety about men of color by wearing a sandwich board that reads, "It's okay. My mother is white" (7/1/08). So even though Marcus believes in the power and rightness of mixed race identification, and sees his friend's passing as betrayal, he cannot deny the reasons for it. They are not in the post-race era just yet.

IX. HALFRICA IN BLACK AMERICA: THE BLACK CHART

Steve not only wants to be black; he feels authorized to question black people's blackness. He tells Anton that Titus is cool but "not very black" based on his barely noticeable "blaccent" (2/23/09). But in *Maintaining*, blackness is also even more highly legislated and regulated by black people. Anton even goes so far as to invent a "Blackness" Chart, complete with equations designed to rank degrees of blackness according to skin tone, speech, parentage (8/28/08). Marcus's ranking is low, so he tries to negotiate his way up, pointing out that Bob Marley and Barack Obama are both mixed, and that Malcolm X was barely darker than him.

Even though Anton tells Marcus that it "is more than skin tone. Black is a state of mind" and that "it's about understanding and embracing African American culture, not just pigmentation" (8/27/08), he nonetheless places the dark-skinned Wesley Snipes as number two in the ranking. Who is black enough, who decides, and what is the basis for the decision are assessments that are as unstable among black people as among white people, the strip suggests—not that that makes it less fiercely policed.

Maintaining is full of meditations on blackness; some of the fiercest critiques are of the narrow confines of blackness, whether they are of the "buffoon of a man" Al Sharpton as the anointed representative of the race (2/3/08) or of Marcus' paternal grandmother, who calls her grandchild a "Nubian prince" and his mother a "white devil" (12/27/07). But the strip also offers up some sermons on the importance of African American culture as central to American culture—"We test her ideals and force her to prove herself! Black Americans *are* America, boy! A living breathing metaphor. We built this country brick by brick" (4/6/08)—and on the fact that, even in this progressive era, even with the cachet of black cool, there is no black privilege (10/12/08). Blackness is critiqued but not demonized in *Maintaining*; it is not the enemy of mixed-racehood.

X. THE RE-EDUCATION OF ANTON

In fact, the most intriguing dimension to *Maintaining* is the re-education of Anton, who, mistrustful of whites, must go through corrective training; Marcus decides to "confront his fear of white people" and takes Anton to a coffee shop, whites' "natural habitat. It's their footlocker and barbershop rolled into one." When Anton says he's "not ready," Marcus gives him a scarf to wear because "they all wear scarves" (8/12/08). Anton is afraid of all white people, but less of working-class whites than of those "white white people" (8/8/08), the ones that voted for Barack Obama. Marcus insists that liberal whites are "harmless" (8/9/08) and eventually takes him to an all-white party as part of his immersion technique (1/25/08). And yet, even as the strip critiques black stereotypes of white people, white people do often prove to be inept and racially obtuse, confirming if not Anton's fear then most certainly his judgment that whites simply do not understand minority experience and need a good poke in the eyes—figuratively or literally (2/17/08).

But *Maintaining*'s re-education, finally, is not of Anton but of all the readerly constituencies, for it is not only Anton who has to reconsider his assumptions. The misunderstandings between whites, blacks, and mixed race peoples are the result of a consumerist, mass-media production of

blackness that markets racial stereotypes that both white and black people then consume. Mixed race people, Creekmore suggests, are not the only ones struggling against such narrow definitions of blackness, and the anxiety over whether they are black enough comes from an artificially created sense of what blackness is. The strip saves its most scathing indictment for the pop-cultural production of blackness that brands black adolescents not in the ghetto as "inauthentic," and equates black culture with "depravity and crime," concluding that "popular culture is kind of racist" because it suggests that "if you're not poor, you're not black" (4/27/08). Anton begins to realize that hip-hop is not synonymous with black culture (9/26/07), that Steve's embrace of "black cool" is really a shared mirage, and that Marcus' exhaustion with R&B may actually allow him license to enjoy a wider range of music without (too much) guilt.

With their focus on the most historically controversial and most politically implicated mix of black-white, *The Boondocks* and *Maintaining* encourage us also to analyze the way that, despite the conscription of several "mixed race" political initiatives to a liberal humanist "color-blind" or conservative "post-race" agenda, comic strips can help us understand that mixed race is not a modern palliative to the "race question" but, instead, a palimpsest of national anxieties and ambitions involving race. Cornel West, in what amounts to both a prophecy and a jeremiad, insists that "[t]he time has come for critics and artists of the new cultural politics of difference to cast their nets widely, flex their muscles broadly, and thereby refuse to limit their visions, analyses, and praxis to their particular terrains."[51] *The Boondocks* and *Maintaining* invite such cultural inquiry in part because their terrain covers no one political platform or clear party agenda. McGruder's diagnosis of the ethno-ambiguo hostility complex and Creekmore's account of the Halfrican American are not apolitical nor post-partisan; rather, they suggest the ways that the humanities work against contracting political discourses and can, more generally, enlarge both intellectual exchange and templates for racial representation in the twenty-first century.

CHAPTER THREE

Passing in the Post-Race Era

DANZY SENNA'S *CAUCASIA*,
PHILIP ROTH'S *THE HUMAN STAIN*,
AND COLSON WHITEHEAD'S *THE INTUITIONIST*

I. PASSING IN THE MULATTO MILLENNIUM

At its best, the comic strip medium that McGruder and Creekmore use allows for a snapshot of a cultural moment. The genre's agility also means that it can nimbly intervene in racial discourses, fret the edges of polemics, tweak stereotypes, or tamper with emerging new profiles—all with a certain temporal immediacy. Its timeliness makes for an ephemerality, at least to the extent that its cultural relevancy is often assessed.[1] The next two chapters shift genre to explore mixed race representation in the more expansive form of the novel, although like the comics, these works also both comment on and reshape African American literary and cultural expression.

In the previous chapter, I noted Creekmore's extensive attention to the issue of passing in the character of Steve, the mixed race youth who tries to make himself over as white. This attention to passing by the teenage set is the more remarkable because the practice is associated with a bygone era. As I suggested in the Introduction, because mixed race has been often represented since the 1990s as hip testimony to American democracy, the corporeal resolution of racial diversity and national unity, it is also represented as a painless antidote to the centuries-old practice of racial passing. Passing, then, seems a particularly antique phenomenon in this "mulatto millennium,"[2] usually invoked merely as a historical footnote supporting a complacent national narrative suggesting that the de facto and de jure discrimination which first led African Americans to pass before the civil rights era has itself passed from this world, given an easeful death by *Loving v. Virginia* (1967). Part of that same teleological narrative of nationalist progress, the 2000 Census "mark one or more" option is also celebrated as the nail in the coffin of the monoracialism that putatively would have forced one to pass in the first place.

Such accounts prepare us for the belief that racial passing has quaintly, almost nostalgically, gone the way of gramophones, congolene, and flappers. Thus, this post-census pop-cultural world at the turn of the twenty-first century makes the question of historical passing seem moot and the very notion of contemporary "passing novels" oxymoronic. Indeed, in 1998, historian Nell Irvin Painter stated that Walter White's 1926 novel, *Flight*, "belongs to an extinct but historically crucial genre of African-American fiction: the passing novel."[3] The rich but deceased tradition to which Painter refers includes racial passing novels of the mid-nineteenth and early-twentieth centuries that variously feature passing as a strategy of survival, as a means to economic gain, or, as James Weldon Johnson's narrator sees it at the outset of *Autobiography of an Ex-Colored Man* (1912, 1927), the wicked realization of a "savage and diabolical desire" to play a "practical joke on white society."[4] This literary tradition has its equally vibrant corollary in the passing movies of the thirties and forties, including *Imitation of Life* (1934, 1959), *Lost Boundaries* (1949), and *Pinky* (1949).[5] M. Giulia Fabi argues that passing (both the historical practice and the literary trope) distinctively emerges from within the African American tradition, although white authors too, from Lydia Maria Child to Harriet Beecher Stowe, and from W. D. Howells to William Faulkner, have long been fascinated with its political and literary possibilities.[6] This fascination has extended even to the curious crossover subgenre of reverse/accidental passing novels in which a white man discovers he is black, among them Charles Chesnutt's posthumously published *Paul Marchand, F.M.C.* (written in 1921), Sinclair Lewis' *Kingsblood Royal* (1947), and more recently Gregory Howard Williams' *Life on the Color Line: The True Story of a White Boy Who Discovered He Was Black* (1995). But whether the works are white- or black-authored, and whether they condemn passing as racial apostasy or as racial affirmation, the passing genre has long been considered passé, as Painter suggests, and its concerns from another time.

And yet the theme of passing lives on—is, in fact, resurrected to assume a rather spectacular new life—in millennial novels such as Danzy Senna's *Caucasia* (1998), Colson Whitehead's *The Intuitionist* (2000), and Philip Roth's *The Human Stain* (2001).[7] These narratives of racial passing by one white and two African American authors have risen seemingly from the dead not to bear witness to past issues but to testify in some of the fiercest debates about the viability of race in this "beyond race"[8] era. In this very context—remarkably, counterintuitively—racial passing is born again, reanimated as an interpretive mode of both social inquiry and literary analysis, representing for some merely a theoretical "mistake" and for others an epistemological lodestar.

In millennial passing novels, racial identity and its transgressions are not outdated abstractions; rather, these works foreground the fact that racial passing offers a challenge to the enduring canards of identity formation itself. As John L. Jackson and Martha S. Jones argue,

passing denotes not social artifice but social absoluteness: the degree to which all identities are constituted through routinized and repeated actions. One passes for what one purportedly is . . . everyday, in thousands of minuscule and major ways. Passing is less about faking prefabbed social identities than it is about demanding appreciation of the idea that all identities are processual, intersubjective, and contested/contestable. It is not about the relative significance of individual voluntarism versus socio-economic predeterminations as much as it highlights the performative scaffolding fundamental to any understanding of self and other.[9]

Jackson and Jones usefully dismiss two of the most common charges against or for passing: either that it makes fake *or* that it makes brave—that is, that it cynically violates one's "true" essential identity or heroically refutes social ascriptions of identity. I would like to capitalize further on their efforts to think past the usual assumptions about passing, and to consider the performative, iterative nature of racial identity as a rich social heuristic, albeit for sometimes competing political and literary ends. In Senna's novel, for example, passing enables incomparable epistemic insight into class and racial inequities; in Roth's work, passing becomes an ultimately reactionary vehicle to critique racial political correctness; in Whitehead's *The Intuitionist*, passing is nothing less than an apocalyptic signal from the future heralding the Fall of the known world. Ironically, the supposed anachronism of passing enables these distinctively modern social critiques—including interrogations of the "multiracial experience" as the "new frontier."[10]

II. WHY PASSING MATTERS

Although "passers" are usually characterized as exceptional, a demographic anomaly (it is a relatively small population who can pass, and even fewer do), passing is at the dead center of, rather than peripheral to, questions of racial identity, including "mixed race" identity. This, in part, is because who can pass and where one can pass is more a complex combination of situational discretion and acculturated perception than of numbers. As Robyn Wiegman asks, "Does the 'fact of blackness,' as Frantz Fanon terms Western racial obsessions, lie in the body and its epidermis or in the cultural training that quite literally teaches the eye not only how but what to see?"[11] What constitutes a supposedly ambiguous body in one time and place may not do so in another; in other words, ambiguity cannot be treated as a transhistorical or positivist given; it is an attribution resulting from an acquired and variable interpretive competency. Furthermore, such competencies are always entangled with, and often motivated by, historically specific political interests. In fact, taking for granted a presumptive consensus about the so-called ambiguous body is to erase the historical and political why's and how's some bodies at some times come to be coded in a particular way. It also extends the visual fetishizing of race, the assumption that race, even mixed race, is always optically available and decipherable.

To move away from the racial optics of passing, given the obsession with sight, requires recognizing that passing's significance lies not in a certain type of calculable body or documented frequency. In fact, its relative statistical irrelevance bears little on its cultural and literary relevance to the national drama over it. What is more significant is that passers, in their supposed orbit of a racial norm, in fact generate that very norm, define it as the circumference does the circle. In this sense, "the possibility of passing is *constitutive* of racial identity."[12] And as several scholars have already noted, the high national stakes in legislating race (of what counts as black or white identity) through the management of passing are evident as early as the anxious segregations enacted by the *Plessy v. Ferguson*, 163 U.S. 537 (1896) Supreme Court decision.[13] As Samira Kawash astutely points out, passing fiction in the late twentieth century endured even though the practice of passing arguably declined: "[T]he ending of

legal segregation and the transformations in racial politics of the 1960s
made the theme of passing politically irrelevant. Passing disappeared
from popular racial discourse and representations. By the 1970s, discussions of passing were by and large confined to literary studies of passing
fiction."[14] Narratives of passing are significant not because they give us
clues to actual extant practices but because they give us clues to extant
cultural fretfulness about perceived practices whether real or imagined.
It is perhaps most useful to ask, then, not what does passing *look* like but
what does passing *do?* What do discourses about passing culturally enable, disable, facilitate, accommodate? Senna's, Roth's, and Whitehead's
novels are very much indexed to racial fears and fantasies affiliated with
the post-race national *Geist*, attentive to the "ambiguous" body up for
grabs in the furious debates over public policy regarding race, from the
Census to Ward Connerly's "racial privacy" initiatives.[15]

III. UNBELIEVERS: RACE AS MISTAKE IN *CAUCASIA*

One of the most controversial aspects distinctive to this post-race condition that *Caucasia*, *The Human Stain*, and *The Intuitionist* take up is
the notion that race is a mistake. According to Walter Benn Michaels in
"Autobiography of an Ex-White Man," passing is moot because even
social constructionist models of racial identity are a "mistake" and race
itself is an "impossibility" (143). Extending arguments developed earlier
in *Critical Inquiry*, Michaels' project involves the exposure of what he
sees as the stubborn "identity politics" represented by the white editors of
Race Traitor.[16] He cites their arguments as particularly egregious examples
of the flawed thinking informing social constructionist commitments. Social constructionism, in Michaels' view, includes those approaches that
do not locate race in biology, soul, or any internal "essence," but instead
define race as "performative." Therein rests the contradiction at the heart
of social constructionism, Michaels argues, for he believes that lurking
within its theories of performance lies an unacknowledged investment in
essentialism (125).

I am using his argument here as representative of others that are, if
not entirely symmetrical, very similar in their insistence that race is a
colossal faux pas. In effect, Michaels argues, race is a misplaced act of

faith, a quasi-religious commitment to a logical contradiction. However, his approach that race is error renders race's fix merely a matter of correction, which tends to circumscribe the entire discussion within the narrow protocols of truth and fallacy. This contraction of race to a yes or no proposition limits because it consigns one to a political therapeutics of assent or dissent. It also, as Toni Morrison has suggested, constricts literary and social accountings of race. As she puts it, literary study should be attentive to the "narrative gearshifts—metaphors; summonings; rhetorical gestures of triumph, despair, and closure dependent on the acceptance of the associative language of dread and love that accompanies blackness."[17] And in her view, the notion that race is irrelevant makes for not only an impoverished aesthetics but also a suspect politics.[18]

Senna's, Roth's, and Whitehead's novels explicitly dramatize this conflict, suggesting that the so-called illusoriness of race is a red herring, and that to treat race as a philosophical dead end is itself a game of sophistry. Senna's first novel takes particular aim at this denomination of racial disbelief. *Caucasia* is the racial coming-of-age of Birdie Lee, the daughter of an African American professor, Deck Lee, "obsessed with theories about race" (22), and Sandra Lodge, a leftist Boston WASP. When the parents separate in the radicalized 1970s with a vague agreement to reunite after the political coast is clear, Deck takes Birdie's darker-skinned sister, Cole, to Brazil with him while Birdie goes underground with her mother, passing as "Jesse Goldman," white and Jewish, in New Hampshire. The search for the "remedy" to race, what Deck calls "somebody else's four-hundred-year-old mistake," amounts to the "myth of fucking Sisyphus" (392), a lifelong labor that has given him nothing but "existential angst." (393). Trying to correct the mistake, he concludes, is like forever trying to push the backsliding rock uphill. His conclusion echoes and would seem to confirm Michaels' position on race.

Yet in the novel, this supposedly irresistible intellectual conclusion is shown up as both specious and opportunist. After all, when we first meet Deck, he is writing the definitive book on race, theorizing that "the mulatto in America functions as a canary in a coal mine," the "gauge of how poisonous American race relations were" (393). By the novel's end he is pontificating to Birdie about his new theory—that race is but a myth—

which he asserts just as dogmatically. This latest theory, the novel suggests, is an equally insufficient "truth," for when Birdie confesses to her father that she has been "living as a white girl" (391), his claims about the total unreality of race merely justify his condescending indifference. Birdie expects him to launch into

a tirade about the evils of passing. But he only shrugged. . . . "But baby, there's no such thing as passing. We're all just pretending. Race is a complete illusion, make-believe. It is a costume. We all wear one. You just switched yours at some point. That's the absurdity of the whole race game." He was turning professorial on me again. (391)

Faced earlier with her father's theory that "mulattos" are a cultural bellwether, and confronted now with his latest theory that "mulattos" are a cultural con, Birdie names the paternal betrayal enabled by such pedantry, bluntly telling him to

[f]uck the canaries in the fucking coal mines. You left me. You left me with Mum, knowing she was going to disappear. Why did you only take Cole [Birdie's sister]? Why didn't you take me? If race is so make-believe, why did I go with Mum? You gave me to Mum 'cause I looked white. You don't think that's real? Those are the facts. (393)

Clearly, Birdie cannot hold him accountable for his perfidy in the face of the social force of color if she concedes that race is make-believe. Furthermore, his denial of the reality of her passing forecloses interpretability of her experience—experience which, throughout the text, she marshals as leverage for both self-assessment and social analysis.

Her passing is key to the way race unevenly arranges her domestic relations as well as to the way race operates within larger social inequalities made vivid to her as she "passes" into them. Her years spent navigating the crepuscular light between the races as "a gray blur, a body in motion, forever galloping towards completion—half a girl, half-caste, half-mast, and half-baked, not quite ready for consumption" (137) bring her in contact with the social detritus and the economically downtrodden who have also slipped unseen between the cracks. She does not have, nor does she need to have, a static, seamless identity, some full-caste, full-mast, fully baked perspective from which to survey the world around her. The novel suggests that it is precisely the moving target of her social location that uniquely positions her to question both colorism and classism. She bears witness to the hypocrisy of her elementary school's ideals—its Nkrumah-inspired nationalism leads students to honor "mulatto heroes" (42–45) and yet to shun her as not black enough—and to the class and race elitism of their New England blue-blood grandmother, who rejects her sister because she is darker-skinned (104–106). Birdie also closely observes her mother's slumming in New Hampshire when trying to pass as working class, and notes the thoughtless cruelty of Sandra's dilettante experiments as a lesbian (144, 172). Her passing is distinguished from her daughter's as a form of indulgent experimentation that leads only to her restless picaresque. In contrast, Birdie's passing is the crucible in which her racial and class identities grow critically self-reflexive. Her identities are "subject to multiple determinations and to a continual process of verification . . . through her interaction with the society she lives in,"[19] and through this critical loop she becomes more aware of the complexity of identity and society. In that sense, her passing proves an epistemic source of insight into not only her own identity but also social arrangements.

Her father's theory that race is a mistaken illusion preemptively undermines, as Birdie complains, "even the ability to speak" (94) about her experience; it also denies him the ability to articulate his *own* experience. On one occasion, for instance, police officers accost him in the park with Birdie because they do not believe he is her father. The police harass him, imply he is a black molester of white girls (60). Shamed, Deck pulls away from Birdie—"as if the touch had burned him" (61)—and turns without a word from the child who witnesses, and is the unwitting occasion for, a public humiliation he desperately wants to forget. His claim, then, that "we were all just pretending" is more defensive repression than enlightened theoretical position, an effort to deny—and thereby somehow provide psychological protection from—the shaming effects of such racialized conflicts. So it is a pivotal reclamation of the significance of her racial experience when Birdie says to herself: "I got what he was saying, but I also knew what I had seen and heard. . . . Who I had become. That was as real as anything else" (396). This calls to mind Tshembe's prescient claim in Lorraine Hansberry's *Les Blancs* (1965):

Race—racism—is a device. No more. No less. It explains nothing at all. . . . It is simply a means. An invention to justify the rule of some men over others . . . I am simply saying that a device *is* a device, but that it also has consequences; once invented it takes on a life, a reality of its own. . . . And it is pointless to pretend that it doesn't *exist*—merely because it is a *lie!*[20]

A driving force in *Caucasia* is the attempt to acknowledge, to name, to theorize the many purposes to which race as device is put, to analyze the compelling realities of the lie. So, for instance, it matters not if race is a moving target or if Birdie's racial appearance is in flux. She says she "looked white" (393); Birdie's mother says she looks like a "little Sicilian"; her father insists, "I know what my daughter looks like, thank you. Maybe you need to cut this naïve, color-blind posturing. In a country as racist as this, you're either black or white" (27). What matters is that race—not despite but because of all its accommodating inventions and competing interpretations—is the deciding factor in both the family diaspora and the parental betrayal.

Part of the political and personal failure of making believe that race is make-believe emerges from Deck's simplistic equation of performance with "costume" (391) and theatrical pretend, with his suggestion that there exists some stripped ur-reality beyond racial parochialism. This notion of a race-free "offstage" revives the tired dichotomies: the "real" versus the "performed," the referent versus the reference, essence versus action—dichotomies that lurk in Michaels' critique of passing as well. As he puts it, "a truly performative conception of race would make passing impossible. . . . Passing becomes impossible because, in the logic of social constructionism, it is impossible not to *be* what you are passing for" (133).

This question of to be or not to be in Deck's—by way of Michaels'—theory loses much in translation when applied to Birdie's experiences. This is because, for Michaels and Deck, racial performance means simply an ensemble of actions abstracted from social relations and context, without the gravitas of identity, without political consequence, and without epistemological authority. Michaels' model and Deck's explanation, by conflating identity with essence and performance with "nonidentity" (133), trap race within a hermetic equation in which one cannot be an ex-colored man or an ex-white man because being an ex-anything presumes that one *is* what one wishes to pass from and thus presumes the "ontological priority of racial identity" (134). But, as Paul Taylor argues, "one most certainly *can* pass without subscribing to racial essence: it is a fact about each of us that we occupy the location that we do, and there are facts about each of us that qualify us for our social locations and that signify to others what our locations are. We can conceal these facts (in other words, pass) and in so doing invite society to misapply its criteria for racial identification, without changing locations."[21] To put it another way, Stuart Hall insists that cultural identity is "not an essence but a *positioning* . . . there is always a politics of identity, a politics of position, which has no absolute guarantee in an unproblematic, transcendental 'law of origin.'"[22] The passer is not necessarily re-inscribing a belief in an a priori racial essence but, rather, manipulating identity as it is imbricated in a constitutive network of social conventions and institutional facts.

IV. PASSING WHILE BOXING:
RACIAL PERFORMANCE IN *THE HUMAN STAIN*

One way to understand the relation between passing and racial performance is to see better how both are not a stepping out of the social field but an immersion in it. Elin Diamond theorizes performance as a dynamic interaction between audience, performer, context, etc.: "Every performance . . . embeds features of previous performances: gender conventions, racial histories, aesthetic traditions—political and cultural pressures that are consciously and unconsciously acknowledged."[23]

Performance, then, is not just an "act," at least not in the sense of act as "false" deed or as a behavior that is an isolated individual choice in a discrete temporal now. The meaning of racial performance, like the staging of identity, can really be understood only through its emergence within interpretive rubrics and socially situated contexts, both the past and the present. In this way, passing is "performative" as a form of historical engagement, as cultural palimpsest, as continuous negotiation with social practices and norms, reminding us that passing is not merely, to borrow from Lisa Lowe, "the simple 'free' oscillation between or among chosen identities."[24] Michaels' model of being and not-being cannot easily account for the historical dimensions to race, the "uneven process" in which "the histories of forced labor migrations, racial segregation, and economic displacement" are always implied in the mulatto figure. This does not mean that the experience of hybridity is historically over-determined, but rather that the experience of hybridity emerges through its uses and practices: as Lowe puts it, "hybridities are always in the process of, on the one hand, being appropriated and commodified by commercial culture and, on the other, of being rearticulated for the creation of oppositional 'resistance cultures'" (82). If we graft this adapted notion of the performative ends rather than essences of mixed race to passing, the pass is better understood as a political event rather than an identity experiment.[25]

In Philip Roth's *The Human Stain*, for instance, the main character's passing is not an ontological effect in which race is a precondition. Rather, race is a performative doing that requires recurrent enactments of "blackness" or "whiteness." Set in 1998, *The Human Stain* traces the rise and fall of Coleman Silk, a light-skinned African American who passes as a Jew, first in his youth as a competitive boxer and later as dean of a liberal arts college. He is dismissed from the school on charges of racism, and at age seventy-one, he begins an affair with a thirty-four-year-old illiterate janitoress, Fania, at the school—the occasion for more than one literary tribute to Viagra in the novel—and dies at the hand of her anti-Semitic ex-boyfriend.[26]

Passing in *The Human Stain* is often onstage—literally: the first time Silk performs a "pass," he is in a ring at a public boxing competition. At age sixteen, he deeply savors both the thrill of the secret ("The power and pleasure were to be found . . . in being counterconfessional in the same way you were a counterpuncher" [100]) and the thrill of flooring a West Point cadet, a representative of "the patriotic center, the arrow of his country's unbreakable spine" (101): "all he saw as this white guy was going down was someone he wanted to beat the living shit out of" (101–102). He is, ironically, no more black than when he passes for white here, for he recognizes that the "sweet flood of fury" (102) that drove him to victory derives from his sense that the match is racial payback for all the nationally sanctioned discrimination he and his family daily endure without redress.

But boxing while passing does not merely translate into some local form of black reparation. In Roth's novel, passing is always political multitasking. Silk's first fight against the white cadet is contrasted with his final fight, against a black competitor, Beau Jack. Silk beats him in under two minutes, much to the displeasure of Solly Tabak, the white promoter, who tells him to "'[f]eel the nigger out in the first round, see what he's got, Silky, and give the people their money's worth'" (116). Silently, Silk refuses: "I'm supposed to let the guy hit me in the head four, five, ten extra times in order to put on a show? Fuck the show" (117). But when Solly confronts him afterwards with, "You could have stopped the nigger in the fourth round instead of the first and gave the people their money's worth . . . Why's that, wise guy?" Silk tells Solly he knocked him out "[b]ecause I don't carry no nigger" (117). His betrayal of course is all the more poignant since he *is* the black man he's carrying. It is too simple, however, to identify this as merely a moment of racial self-hatred. For it is also an exemplary moment of racial performance, of what sociologist Amanda Lewis calls "everyday race-making," those frequent, interpersonal micro-exchanges that performatively renew and enact the sociological macro-categories of race.[27] To be precise, the scene makes clear that for Silk, whiteness requires more than just remaining racially undeclared. Although his manager advises him not to "bring [race] up. You're neither one thing or the other" [98], passing requires actively staging himself inside and outside the ring as unequivocally white in part by self-consciously rendering "impassable" the distance between Beau Jack and himself. Earlier in the narrative, Silk is called the same epithet and the "impact was devastating" (103); it is no accident, then, that the same expression from Silk's lips—as casually, cruelly rendered—becomes a speech act (re)creating the racial divide and securing his chosen side on it.

This kind of "doing" that Silk's passing requires is never a singular deed, as I suggested before; its significance emerges as one in a series of narrative acts. Here is another revelatory example: early in the novel, Silk's brother, Walt, tells him that if Silk is committed to a life of passing, he should never dare "show [his] lily-white face" (145) at home again.

Implying that Silk's choice of whiteness reflects a flowery cowardice that unmans him, Walt locates himself as unimpeachably black (and masculine) by contrast. Many years later, Silk uses the same expression to challenge his lawyer, Primus Nelson—who, significantly, has teased Silk about his use of Viagra to combat impotence—telling him that he never again wants "to see your smug lily-white face" (81). Silk's slur is lost on the lawyer, who is only confused by it. Nelson, unaware of Silk's and Walt's associations of whiteness with a feminized betrayal and weakness, asks himself, "why *white*?" (82). The slur cannot satisfy Silk's bid to reclaim male pride since, still passing as white, he cannot racially distinguish himself from Nelson and therefore cannot claim the same masculinizing blackness that his brother does when defining himself against Silk. The insult's many failures reveal how racial meanings are generated through situational performances of, and contingent narrative contexts for, race.

And the narrative stakes of this realization—or lack of it—are high, since in this case, when Silk names whiteness, he risks betraying his blackness. As John Fiske notes, whiteness is ex-nomic, characterized by its function as an unmarked—that is, unsaid—norm: to name whiteness, then, is to racialize it. But what these exchanges between Silk and his brother, and between Silk and Nelson, further suggest is that naming whiteness also tends to racialize reflexively those who name whiteness as being non-white themselves. That is, since white people rarely call each other white, Silk's calling out the whiteness in Nelson risks identifying him as black, something he recognizes himself when he notes that he made this insult to Nelson "strategically . . . yet not nearly so mindfully as he might have" (81). Part of Silk's passing requires his allegiance to the ex-nomic condition of whiteness; hence the lawyer's pause when Silk breaks the tacit contract of whiteness. In both cases, racial ascriptions are tendered in order to masculinize or to emasculate, and serve Roth's greater narrative end of establishing male potency in a world, the novel suggests, that conspires against it.

Scenes such as these suggest ways in which understanding race as performance springs the intellectual trap of race as mistake; they move us from arguing whether or not passing exists to examining, more usefully in my opinion, the multiple narrative and experiential ends that the practice of passing serves. One of the most troubling and poignant ends is suggested by Silk's final boxing match. The match is set in the late 1940s, and layered with explicit historical and literary references. These range from Jack Johnson's famed boxing matches against racist white competitors some thirty years earlier to the "Brown Bomber," Joe Louis, renowned as a national hero after avenging an earlier loss to Germany's Max Schmeling in 1938, and from the welterweight "Sugar" Ray Robinson, whose career spanned the forties through the mid-fifties and whose record Silk speculates he could surpass (99) to Ralph Ellison's excruciating "Battle Royale" scene in *Invisible Man* in which the young protagonist, a promising scholar like Silk, is forced to box blindfolded for white entertainment.[28]

The evocative weave and welter of all these associations create a host of unstable effects. On the one hand, we have the historical record: Jack Johnson defeated Canadian Tommy Burns on December 26, 1908, in the World Boxing Championship held in Sydney. Johnson's achievement prompted a white response: in 1910, the white fighter James Jeffries fought Johnson in a contest widely understood by all to be a battle of the races. Despite the race riots that followed in which whites incited violence against blacks, Johnson's win was a moment of immense pride for many African Americans. Years later, black poet William Waring Cuney captured the excitement in "My Lord, What a Morning":

O my Lord
What a morning,
O my Lord,
What a feeling,
When Jack Johnson
Turned Jim Jeffries'
Snow-white face
to the ceiling.

The poem echoes Silk's own satisfaction in flooring the white cadet the first time he passes, the fantasy of "snow white" now a feminized sign of a princess laid to rest, the pasty face turned skyward as though in Snow White's fabled coma. Another oft-noted fight that haunts Silk's fights is the second heavyweight title match between black champion Joe Louis and the white former champion Billy Conn. Historical accounts note Louis' victory by knocking out Conn in the eighth round. But the mere record of the victory does not capture the profound power that the cultural memory of the Brown Bomber, the son of an Alabama sharecropper, had within African American communities across the country who listened to the radio broadcast of the match. Louis' victories were experienced vicariously and collectively, becoming symbolic triumphs over oppression.[29]

But Silk's racial performance is only in part made potent by and through these historical referents because the referents themselves are constantly reinterpreted in the novel. Joe Louis, mentioned several times by Silk's father, is *not* figured for him as the national hero whose win against Schmeling was hailed by both whites and blacks as a strike against Hitler and Nazism, for instance, but is referred to as a vulnerable black man who in 1936 was "knocked out cold" (96) by Schmeling's overhand right punch. In the novel, Louis becomes representative of the fights that Silk had seen in the army "among [black] soldiers staged at night for the troops where fighters were not only knocked out like Joe Louis but so badly cut up nothing could be done to stop the bleeding" (97). When Silk begins boxing and when his father condemns it on these grounds, Louis had not yet made his comeback, but the father's image of black men as spectacle for whites nonetheless shadows Silk's final boxing match. Thus these referents are not simply imported into but evolve within the text. Silk also evokes but then refigures Louis. In this final match, Silk seems at first textually and racially aligned with Louis as a heroic black man doing the unthinkable: trouncing a white man before other white men. Further, Silk's "Fuck the show" (117) in response to Tabak's call to throw the match seems to signal Silk's racial pride. That is, his challenge to Tabak seems to stand as a recognition and refusal of the history of black boxing feeding white sadism, and also as a refusal to repeat the fate of Ellison's young and humiliated protagonist (and his father's perception of Louis' fate as well). But even if a (black) Silk stands up to (white) Tabak before the fight, he claims his win as a white man putting down, both verbally and physically, his black peer when he insults Beau Jack with "nigger" (117) after trouncing him.

In such moments inhere the contradictory politics of passing, the kind of miasmic effect that prompts Eve Sedgwick to conclude that performance itself is always just "kinda subversive, kinda hegemonic."[30] But as Amy Robinson insists, such conclusions become "self-indulgent" if they avoid the political imperative that the "relevance of the subject of passing" exists "precisely in its thoroughgoing complicity with those institutions that we daily negotiate in an ongoing attempt to imagine a political context in which structural change is not merely a fantasy relegated to the theatrical frame" (237). The question, then, is not simply whether to judge Silk's passing in this scene as a purely liberatory or a reactionary gesture, for as Robinson suggests, we must take for granted that it is both. However uncomfortable the implications, the proud iconoclasm of "Fuck the show" and the racial perfidy of "I don't carry no nigger" do not cancel each other out, nor can they be neatly quarantined from one another. Rather, Silk's iconoclasm, his autogenesis—the liberation he seeks as "one of the great *pioneers* of the I" (108)—occurs through, not despite, this participation in racism.[31]

This is not just the cost of individualism; in the novel, it is what makes individualism possible. Silk quite consciously decides he must metaphorically "murder" his mother "on behalf of his exhilarating notion of freedom!" (138), to "live his life on the scale he wants to live it" (136). Only by having the "bulwarks gone" (109) of family and of racial community can he be

free to be whatever he wants, free to pursue the hugest aim, the confidence right in his bones to be the particular I. Free on a scale unimaginable to his father. As free as his father had been unfree. Free now not only of his father but of all his father had ever had to endure. The impositions. The humiliations. The obstructions. The wound and pain and the posturing and the shame—all the inward agonies of failure and defeat. Free instead on the big stage. Free to go ahead and be stupendous. Free to enact the boundless, self-defining drama of the we, they, and I. (109)

Thus, only by passing does he imagine that he can be emancipated not only from white racism but also from racial collectivity, which he views as similarly oppressive: "Never for him the tyranny of the we that is dying to suck you in, the coercive, inclusive, historical, inescapable moral *we* with its insidious *E pluribus unum*. Neither the we of Woolworth's [civil rights protests] nor the we of Howard [University]" (108). Ironically, social justice movements and historically black colleges and universities—both of which sought to change the status quo—get conflated here *with* the status quo, with American mainstream moralism and dogmatism. For this reason, Silk wants to transcend race: "All he'd ever wanted, from earliest childhood on, was to be free: not black, not even white—just on his own and free" (120). "Free" here is clearly associated with American individualism, but his ode to personal "resolve" (121) dramatizes the contradiction of American freedom: it is represented as at once non-racial ("not black, not even white") and yet, since it apparently necessitates his passing, a freedom available to him only as white—or the next best thing to it.

V. RACIAL PASSING AND JEWISH CONVERSION

Passing as Jewish is both the transition to and the provisional destination of whiteness in Senna's and Roth's novels, a triangulated process that reminds us that the performative nature of passing often requires a convoluted negotiation of available and mediated images, tropes, stereotypes, perceptions, politics. As Michael Rogin documents in *Blackface, White Noise: Jewish Immigrants in the Hollywood Melting Pot*,[32] in the field of representation, blackness and Jewishness are joined at the hip: Jews, he argues, became white, and simultaneously American, through and against blackness, acquiring national credentials through their popular performances of minstrelsy. The "conversion of Jews [to Americans] by blackface" involves appropriating "an imaginary blackness to Americanize the immigrant son" (80). In effect, "Jewish movie blackface . . . engendered Crevecoeur's new man, the American" (70). As does *The Human Stain*, Senna's *Caucasia* also represents passing as a variation on a representatively American pastime: the finding and losing of oneself at will. I "disappeared into America," Birdie writes in the opening paragraph, "the easiest place to get lost" (1), a refrain echoed later in the text when she remembers her mother telling her that "America's a good place to get lost" (380). By passing as half-Jew, according to her WASP mother, they can lose themselves in possibility: as Birdie puts it, passing made "the world . . . our pearl" (131). If Jews are converted to "white" Americans through blackness, as

Rogin argues, then blacks perhaps can be converted to white by performing Jewishness—and through that whiteness, the logic suggests, also become enfranchised as part of the national polity. Rogin argues that such moves reinforce, by underscoring, racial hierarchies (34), since Jewish blackface only "loosens up white identities by taking over black ones" (34). So are black identities "loosened up" by taking over white Jewish identities? If so, at what expense to both blacks and Jews?[33]

In Roth's and Senna's novels, the effort at national enfranchisement through ethnic conversion yields asymmetrical results. On the one hand, Judaism represents a continuum of blood and faith that leads to an ontological confounding that passing can manipulate. Standing both physically and culturally left of center to white, Silk exploits the "off color" dimension to Jews. When the narrator, Nathan Zuckerman, first sees Silk, for instance, he reminds him of "one of those crimp-haired Jews of a light yellowish skin pigmentation who possess something of the ambiguous aura of the pale blacks who are sometimes taken for white" (16). Zuckerman's vision of Jews passing for black people passing for white, in contrast with Silk's efforts as a black man passing as Jewish passing as white, hints at precisely the productive instability and interchangeability among proximates that makes passing both viable and attractive for Silk. But more powerfully, both Birdie's mother and Silk are drawn to the Jewish persuasion because Jews are persuasively associated with certain American myths of self-invention in the novels, what Roth refers to as a "new being" (342) and what R. W. B. Lewis calls the "American Adam." The salient aspects of this archetypal American identity involve a self-creation that requires rejecting what Ralph Waldo Emerson in "Self-Reliance" (1841) termed the corpse of memory, leaving behind the past and, in the masculine tradition of narrative self-discovery, finding the fresh green breast of a frontier in which to realize fully one's unfettered potential. Immigrant success best captures this Adamic ideal in *The Human Stain*; Jews stand in closest relation to, and as a vehicle of, whiteness in part because they best represent, according to Silk, immigrant achievement and assimilation. As he characterizes Dr. Fensterman, Jews "were like Indian scouts, shrewd people showing the outsider the way in, showing the social possibility, showing an intelligent family how it might be done" (97).

This is not to say that the novel uncritically celebrates Jewish success. Even before Silk begins passing, he and Fensterman certainly represent dubious political partners: Fensterman, who has experienced discrimination as a Jew, nonetheless cynically proposes to give the Silks three thousand dollars if Silk, then still black and in high school, agrees to sacrifice his valedictorian status in favor of Fensterman's son (85). The unscrupulous boxing promoter, Tabak, similarly represents intra-ethnic exploitation. But Jews are nonetheless appealing to Silk because they embody the American spirit of self-invention. Silk's wife, Iris Gittelman, for instance, comes from a family who "claimed to be American, even called themselves Jews, these two uneducated immigrant atheists who spat on the ground when a rabbi walked by. But they called themselves what they called themselves freely, without asking permission or seeking approval" (127). Judaism is admired here as representing exemplary American independence: they are imagined as attractively secular, anarchist (the Gittelmans supported Sacco and Vanzetti, the narrator notes), and self-determining. And, of course, the ability to script one's own self is precisely what Silk aims to do through passing.

But passing as Jewish also gives Silk an even more particular thrill. Marrying Gittelman and passing himself off to his wife and the rest of the world as Jewish "raises everything to another pitch, gives him back his life on the scale he wants to live it" (136). His decision not to pursue a "Negro girl" (136) is revelatory here. Silk rejects her not because she is black but because she identifies rightly the hubris motivating his passing. Chiding him, she points out that his passing is nothing extraordinary, that Greenwich Village composes "the four freest square miles in America," and that there is someone passing "on every other block. You're so vain, you thought you'd dreamed it up yourself" (135).[34] Silk's addiction to the "elixir of the secret" (135) necessary to his flattering self-conception informs his passing. He tells himself that "even if there *are* a dozen more guys like [me] hanging around the Village," only *he* has "that gift . . . secretive in [a] grand and elaborate way" (135). The uniqueness afforded him by the secret of his *Jewish* passing, for Silk, is not so much an end run around American racism as it is an opportunity to become the incomparable native son.

In *Caucasia*, Birdie's mother, too, regards Judaism as a "cultural thing" (131), but appealing because it unites, not because it differentiates. Judaism, she reasons, is only one step removed from being African American: Jews and blacks share a "tragic history, kinky hair, good politics. . . . It's all there" (140). She resists the subsumption of Jewishness to whiteness, however, saying Birdie wasn't really passing, "because Jews weren't really white, more like an off-white." Even Birdie concedes that acting Jewish is "the closest I was going to get to be black and still stay white" (140). Her passing becomes a mode of staying black—in contrast to Silk's desire to slip into racelessness. At least for a little while, she half believes that her Jewish "act" in New Hampshire serves to confirm rather than surrogate her black identity: "Strange as it may sound, there was a safety in this pantomime. The less I behaved like myself, the more I could believe that this was still a game. That my real self—Birdie Lee—was safely hidden beneath my beige flesh, and when the right moment came, I would reveal her, preserved, frozen solid in the moment in which I had left her" (233).

Wearing a Dunbarian "mask"[35] as an attempt at racial retention, Birdie reinforces through her "pantomime" her racial identity to the very degree that her performance is at variance with it. Her pantomime is a defensive buffer between game and reality, but it only highlights the mutually constitutive nature of performance and reality. Acting white risks making her white, she begins to think, as her pantomime hyperbolically exaggerates a distinction that cannot hold. The behaviors that Birdie performs silently sanction her white friends' casual use of "nigga, spic, fuckin' darkie" (233), the backdrop and context for her "game." She hopes her passing will keep the black self paused in time and secreted within, a hibernation that will become the very basis through which her racial identity and family genealogy are not abandoned. But she realizes that in this instance, at least, performing whiteness will make her irresistibly complicit with white racism.

If Senna's characters are continually trying to locate themselves in society, to recover racial affiliation and kinship, Roth's novel, in contrast, celebrates the virtuosic realization of the self's expressivity as a *release* from society, family, race. *Caucasia*'s Birdie finds liberation *in* communities of racial affinity, whereas Silk in *The Human Stain* recognizes that his passing—this "act committed in 1953 by an audacious young man" (145)—means, as the saying goes, he has "'lost himself to all his people'" (144). But he dismisses this as mere nostalgia, the "imprisonment" of family history and "ancestor worship" (144). As suggested earlier, Silk's "pass" is also, in part, a reactionary response to black social activism, his attempted escape not just from white racism but from, the narrator tells us, hungry "propriety," the bigger evil "masquerading" as America's core values, "that dominatrix in a thousand guises, infiltrating . . . women's rights, black pride, ethnic allegiance" (153). Such tirades suggest why the repressiveness associated with society in this novel is only gratuitously associated with racism; it is racial and sexual political correctness that Silk sees as the hegemonic order to be resisted.[36]

For all Silk's talk about racial transcendence—wanting to be "not black, not even white" (120)—by novel's end, this "ex-colored man" is, I would argue, some proxy for an aging white man. Passing ends up being largely an occasion to explore white masculine social and physical impotency, and given the narrative space devoted to the castrating effects of both prostate cancer (36) and feminist scholars (273), the performance of race starts to look more like performance anxiety.[37] At times, then, the novel suggests that Silk thinks "identity politics" is his undoing, even though it is anti-Semitism that finally does him in. Left hanging are certain disturbing equivalencies in which anti-Semitism, feminism, and black activism are all cast as carnivorous ideologies making a bloody feast of individualism. In *The Human Stain*, the problem with passing is not so much that you will be found out, but rather that p.c. will find *you* out. Roth's novel moves us beyond the usual moral and epistemological pieties about fraudulence or authenticity in passing, and seems to offer a bid to move beyond "identity politics," as negatively represented in the text, as well.

Yet the identity that Silk tries to pass into, the one he thinks will free him of race, religion, and nation, is, I have suggested, white, Jewish, and specifically American. If anything, *The Human Stain* warns of the dangers and costs of pretending that identity is *not* salient, for it makes more difficult the analysis of why some identities are marked as racial, religious, or national and some are not, makes it more difficult to analyze the social circumstances in which some identities are cast as oppressive and some are seen as liberatory, makes it more difficult to notice why "identity politics" somehow always belong to someone else's identity and politics. As Linda Martín Alcoff argues, in her exhaustive critique of the recent wave of anti-identitarianism and those who would do away with racial identity in particular: "[R]acial eliminativists are generally concerned about group identity of any sort, which they see as scripts that compromise moral commitments and constrain individual choice. . . . [But] identities are not analogous to scripts that we are consigned to play out. Nor are we boxed in by them, constrained, restricted, or held captive."[38] As I hope my readings of these novels suggest, social change can occur not by jettisoning but by mobilizing identity, by examining how and when a passer's unique position affords insight into structures of injustice and inequity.

VI. PASSING INTO THE FUTURE OF *THE INTUITIONIST*

I end with Colson Whitehead's *The Intuitionist* because the futuristic possibilities of passing in this novel repudiate the idea either that passing forces one into existential limbo, a permanently liminal state betwixt and between racial categories, *or* that passing is a speedway out of the landscape of race altogether. *The Intuitionist* is not interested in passing as a vehicle to a post-race, post-identity world—in other words, its brave new world does not have at its center Silk's "new being" (*The Human Stain* 342), free of all social commitments and allegiances of identity—"women's rights, black pride, ethnic allegiance" (153). But neither does it concern a search for racial identity and communion, at least not in the way that such a quest structures *Caucasia*.

Rather, *The Intuitionist* offers an accord between *Caucasia*'s investment in race and identity and *The Human Stain*'s efforts to divest both; it does so through its insights into the very heart of passing's cultural power and utility, the fact that these identity questions are always tied to larger social and national dramas over cultural boundaries and borders. Passing is always linked to what Betsy Erkkila calls the "phobias and fantasies of blood mixture and contamination in the national imaginary [that] . . . account for the fact that despite the country's constitutional commitment to an ideology of justice, freedom and rights, the American republic continues as a house divided in which some are more equal, more human, and more entitled than others."[39] Those who can pass not only inherit the legacies of mixed race heritage; they put that heritage into practice in a way that marks the transgression of, and thus lays bare, the paradox of unequal entitlements in the land of equality. This is why passing creates such cultural anxiety and yet why, too, it holds so much progressive potential. *The Intuitionist* taps some of that potential by understanding the performance of passing as always politically implicated in the larger possibilities for social change.

Set in a vaguely post–civil rights era metropolis with distinctly pre–civil rights era racist sensibilities, *The Intuitionist* follows Lila Mae, the city's first black female elevator inspector. In the novel, elevators represent technological progress—the promise of upward mobility, racial uplift, religious ascent, faith in transcendent verticality—but also the profound failure of such teleological commitments to address social inequity. Lila Mae is a member of the Department of Elevator Inspectors, which is in the midst of a near-religious quarrel between two schools of thought and instruction about elevator and funicular theory: Empiricism and Intuitionism. Empiricists methodically inspect elevators through observation and data collection; Intuitionists rely on instinct and impression. Lila is a skilled Intuitionist, gifted with the near-metaphysical ability to divine any elevator's ailments. But an elevator—the "Fanny Briggs," Number Eleven—that she has recently inspected inexplicably collapses, and she finds herself used as a pawn in the Intuitionists' and Empiricists' struggle for political power. In her efforts to reestablish her always challenged professional reputation, Lila Mae discovers the "luminous truth" (230)—that Fulton, the visionary founder of Intuitionism, was "colored" and passing as white. She suspects that his foundational canon of texts, universally assigned in technical institutes and schools—"from the groundbreaking *Towards a System of Vertical Transport* to the more blasphemous parts of his oeuvre, *Theoretical Elevators* Volumes One and Two" (31)—contains coded racial commentary, and that Intuitionism itself is a wickedly clever send-up of a world that refused to recognize his abilities. Intuitionism, it turns out, has only been passing as inspired Truth; it is "all a big joke"

(32) perpetrated by Fulton. This is the kind of joke that slips the yoke, as Ellison put it, "motivated not so much by fear as by a profound rejection of the image created to usurp his identity. Sometimes it is for the sheer joy of the joke; sometimes to challenge those who presume, across the psychological distance created by race manners, to know his identity."[40]

The joke of his passing extends to both the content and the form of the novel. *The Intuitionist* passes as a dystopic naturalist novel, replete with grotesque one-dimensional characters who seem socially and genetically over-determined in an indifferent universe, only to transmogrify into a realist novel with characters of psychological depth, qualified agency, and unpredictable futures. It passes as detective fiction—opening with a catastrophic accident that we are initially led to believe is the result of worldly political intrigue and sabotage. In fact, we discover, the inexplicable fall of the Fanny Briggs is a sign of *the* Fall, a glimpse into a postlapsarian world in which the social and racial order will suddenly and utterly collapse. The detective novel's epistemological requirement—that the world can be known—dissolves into science fiction's conceit—that worlds can be imagined. Thus revelation and discovery of the "answer" that Fulton is passing, too, is not the climax but only a complication in *The Intuitionist*. Knowing that Fulton passed does not unify the narrative vision. Rather, it fragments at the end of the novel into Faulknerian first-person multiplicities, first Fulton's posthumous perspective, then Lila Mae's prophetic séance, rendered in a stew of semi-omniscience and stream of consciousness. The narrative slippage between genres enacts one of the challenges of passing that is thematized in the novel itself: the call to surrender generic expectations and commitments, to reconsider and remake acts of interpretation. The fated elevator is, after all, named after Fanny Briggs, famed as a slave who taught herself to read, just as Lila Mae must constantly acquire new cultural literacies (230).

VII: NEW WORLD CONVENTIONS

As I suggested at the outset, by violating standard protocols—aesthetic, social, racial—passing throws them into relief. But it need not necessarily reify them in the process; in *The Intuitionist*, passing can point the way to figuring subversive new norms. Passing requires an adjustment of perspective, a recognition that norms can be generated anew. The novel, in fact, teases with the suggestion that urban architecture can anticipate and enable fresh conventions, unexpected normative subjects—and, by implication, new societies organized with both at their center. As Fulton writes in his *Theoretical Elevators*:

Take capacity. The standard residential elevator is designed to accommodate 12 passengers, all of whom we assume to be of average weight and form. This is the Occupant's Fallacy. The number 12 does not consider the morbidly obese, or the thin man's convention and necessity of speedy conveyance at the thin man's convention. We conform to objects, we capitulate to them. We need to reverse this order. . . . Our elevators ought to be variable in size and height, retractable altogether, impervious to scratches, self-cleaning, possessing a mouth. The thin man's convention can happen at any time; indeed, they happen all the time. (38)

The "thin man's convention" reorients the marginal as the norm. It is a radical revolution upending the world by de-naturalizing norms that pose as self-evident and apolitical.[41] The tone in this and so much of the novel's description is deadpan, flat, naturalistic, and both its absurd form and its content enact the destabilizing of normative expectations that is so often the basis of black humor.[42] According to Fulton, the thin man's convention is spontaneous and independent of human machination; it need not wait for the gradualist engines of time and change. Like passing, the "thin man's convention" transforms the political epistemologies underwriting the status quo. Fulton can pass because whites cannot see past themselves as the norm, cannot imagine any others. They only perceive the "skin of things" (239), are "slaves to what they could see . . . built on what things appear to be" (239); thus they perceive neither his "negrescience" (151) nor the fact that Intuitionism is a "lie," a "world he invented to parody his enslavers" (241). He exploits black "invisibility" (148), in the Ellisonian sense of the word, and uses whites' blindness to "pierce" the Du Boisian "veil" (100) in order to perceive a "world beyond this one" (240). But even though the elevators he designs reflect the desire to ascend in a world that will not "let a colored man rise" (240), he remains suspicious of any "doctrine of transcendence" (240)—including racial transcendence.

For Fulton is not overcoming race; that is, he is not passing from what he "is" to what he "is not." Rather, he is passing into Du Bois' projected dream in "Of Our Spiritual Strivings" of "the worlds I longed for,"[43] passing from the present to an alternate future. Passing reflects Fulton's "keen longing for the next [world], its next rules" (232), a way of living in *"another world beyond this one"* (240). These are what Robin D. G. Kelley calls "freedom dreams."[44] Fulton, in fact, prophesizes a sort of Second Coming—what he calls the "second elevation" (198)—a racial reality never fully characterized except to the extent that it expressly celebrates neither black cultural nationalism *nor* rainbow integration. Fulton dies before he completes this written divination—or more accurately, his passing away is characterized as being "pulled into the future" (253). The secret "truth" of passing in this novel is not simply that one might be exposed posing as a person from another race but that one might reveal an altogether alternative universe:

[Lila Mae] thinks what passing for white does not account for: the person who knows your secret skin, the one you encounter at that unexpected moment on that quite ordinary street. What Intuitionism does not account for: the catastrophic accident the elevator encounters at that unexpected moment on that quite ordinary street, the one who will reveal the device for what it truly is. The colored man passing for white and the innocent elevator must rely on luck, the convenience of empty streets and strangers who know nothing, dread the chance encounter with the one who knows who they are. (231)

What the elevator "truly is," Lila Mae realizes, is something that has "reached out to her and told her she was of its world" (255), revealed to her a vision of both cataclysm and rebirth. The unexplained fall of the elevator represents the dissolution of all ontological and epistemological frameworks, cues her "that the frail devices she had devoted her life to were weak and would all fall one day like Number Eleven. All of them, plummeting down the shafts like beautiful dead stars" (255). With this revelation, Lila Mae understands that she, like Fulton, is no longer someone working peripherally "in the margin" (252) but rather "a citizen of the city to come one day" (255). Fulton argues that the "thin man's convention" can "happen at any time" (38) and, in fact, her new centrality is the realization of that principle. She is the chosen one, called to be the architect of an enlightened elevator, of new technologies that will serve as the "ferry across Earth to Heaven" (98), will move not vertically but laterally, will move sideways not upwards.[45] If Lila Mae, like Fulton, is a black person passed over by the world, by novel's end she orchestrates the passing of one world to another.

This sense of passing as "passing over," as a kind of death, or at least a stepping into the unknown, is reinforced by Fulton's absence from the text. On the one hand, Fulton is central to the novel's world: his unknown biography is the occasion for all manner of speculation and intrigue, and his theories define and dominate the academic debates. But he is dead and gone by the time Lila Mae begins her investigation of him; readers are offered very little of his background and even less of his physical appearance. Instead, he appears synaptically through bits of his writing, partial representations that themselves are meta-commentaries on the possibilities and limitations of racial legibility. His absent presence is a clever refusal of the visual obsession with the mixed race body, a performance of mixed race that never requires Fulton's appearance yet works Oz-like behind the curtain. This refusal of the visual performance of race is a central concern of Chapter Five.

Working within a genre that was thought long dead, *Caucasia*, *The Human Stain*, and *The Intuitionist* make relevant a literary form assumed unfit for racial new millennialism; they find in passing a particularly timely medium to explore the ongoing relevance of race amid the recent rise in anti-identitarianism and post-racialism. And as passing makes its transition into the twenty-first century, the conventions of both genre and politics are transformed. Certainly, unlike the protagonist of James Weldon Johnson's *Autobiography of an Ex-Colored Man*, none of the protagonists in these new passing novels feel that they have sold their "birthright for a mess of pottage."[46] Gone is the biblical moral of Esau and in its place we find Roth's searing critique of moralism itself. Gone, too, is monoracial complacency, replaced by Senna's ironic "mestizo imperative."[47] And also gone are civil rights–era politics, replaced by Whitehead's radical racial jeremiad.

With so much gone, so much overturned, what then is left? What makes these passing novels like or unlike earlier twentieth-century passing novels? On the one hand, they very much share in the literary and cultural work of earlier passing novels. William Wells Brown, Charles Chesnutt, Frank Webb, Sutton Griggs, Frances E. W. Harper, Edward Johnson, and James Weldon Johnson revised available narrative modes—from sentimental romance to sensationalistic realism—to initiate what William Andrews calls the "novelization" of slave narratives.[48] James Weldon Johnson actually parodies the passing form itself in order to suggest that passing is the consequence, not the cause, of cultural alienation. Like the earlier works, these passing novels mix generic conventions, experimenting with passing as both a thematic and a structural concern, in order to expand the traditional boundaries and received definitions of black letters. This holds most true for *Caucausia* and *The Intuitionist*, particularly in the case of Fulton and Birdie, who are interested in creating new worlds that are re-raced not "e-raced" (in contrast with *The Human Stain*'s Silk, who tries to escape race in this world).

How do these new millennial passing novels fit into the new canon of mixed race literature? In a sense, they fit mixed race literature back *into* an African American literary canon. The revival of the passing novel form makes visible the literary-historical continuities with these much earlier works, in which contemporary debates about mixed race emerge as thematic extensions of earlier questions about the limits of blackness. The novels' experiments with passing as a device disrupting traditional novelistic representations of blackness similarly yoke the books to the ongoing development of African American literary forms inaugurated in the late nineteenth century. That said, these novels also freshly reinvent passing as a literary intervention and cultural commentary precisely because of the way they engage new millennial discourses of mixed race as historically distinctive. If, as Fabi argues, earlier passing novels were pivotal in moving African American literature from the autobiographical to the fictional at the turn of the last century, then *Caucasia* and *The Intuitionist* similarly facilitate the move of literature frequently understood as dealing with the mixed race experience from personal memoir to fictional modalities. If the vast majority of writing on mixed race has been published—and as I argue in Chapter One, canonized—in the form of personal narrative, the work of Senna and Whitehead suggests how the passing novel form can tap the greater social and literary possibilities posed by the challenges of mixed race representation.

As I explore in the next chapter, one of these possibilities involves a move from representing mixed race as a personal issue, most often explored in the first-person memoir, to thinking of the self's development within a web of social relations and in the context of national aspiration, the domain of the bildungsroman. Traditionally, the bildungsroman represents the progress of the individual as the incorporation into modern society. Chapter Four explores Emily Raboteau's *The Professor's Daughter* and Danzy Senna's *Symptomatic* as mixed race coming-of-age novels that take this premise of the bildungsroman and turn it on its head.

"People just like us"

EMILY RABOTEAU'S *THE PROFESSOR'S DAUGHTER*, DANZY SENNA'S *SYMPTOMATIC*, AND THE MIXED RACE ANTI-BILDUNGSROMAN

We were a breed of our own.

Emma in *The Professor's Daughter*[1]

I think we should start our own nation. . . . We could buy an island. . . . And we could fill it with people just like us.

Greta in *Symptomatic*[2]

I. MODERNITY AND THE MIXED RACE ANTI-BILDUNGSROMAN

As I suggested in Chapter Three, the narrative mode of the European bildungsroman focuses on the social incorporation of the individual, the integrative merging of self into society. Novels about a mixed race experience seem exemplary of the genre: the individual feels out of place in society, searches for his or her family (usually a father or his history) by which the protagonist can establish some sense of social location and reconciliation with society—a "breed of our own," "our own nation." Most importantly, this plot is associated with, as are most bildungsromans, national progress and modernity. Enrique Lima argues that this tethering of modernity and progress with the renunciation of the individual to society is disrupted in the ethnic bildungsroman. Those who were disenfranchised by what passed for European progress experienced not a cultural and literary march forward but rather an "uneven development," as he terms it. This unevenness—distinct from "backwardness"—must be understood in the context of the colonial violence, capitalist exploitation, and disenfranchisement of individuals marginalized in a society's racial order.[3] Thus genre and progress cannot, he suggests, be so neatly aligned: literary history is not simply the inexorable advance of both form and modernity, the "great genre of socialization."[4] The problematic situation of reconciling the desires of the individual with the imperatives of the social order is resolved in the European bildungsroman, which found a symbolic solution to this dilemma by making socialization the endpoint of individualism. Lima suggests that writers on the colonial periphery of capitalist modernity, those who would never be enfranchised within society, refunctionalized the bildungsroman to address their different historical realities and alternative modernities. These "peripheral" bildungsromans resignify the story of the relationship of the individual's freedom to society's mandates and the possibility of inclusion. They do so in ways that challenge many of the commonplaces about literary history and the novels as literary "progress," at least to the extent that the narrative form plots the self's ascent into socialization.

In the mixed race bildungsroman, the challenge to the implied indexical relation between the novel and modernity differs from either the traditional European or the ethnic bildungsroman as characterized by Lima. The protagonist is certainly peripheral, but not characterized as atavistic. In fact, correspondence between the novel and modernity is actually magnified: the mixed race protagonist is represented as modernity itself. Unlike the protagonist in either the European or the indigenous bildungsroman, the protagonist in the mixed race bildungsroman is often represented as not requiring social education—he or she is already modern. In fact, the idea that the racially mixed individual is a modernizing agent of a new multicultural world order is often an explicit theme in these works. But like the native bildungsroman to which Lima refers, the biracial characters in the texts that this chapter examines, Emily Raboteau's *The Professor's Daughter* and Danzy Senna's *Symptomatic*, do not feel incorporated into the society or the social progress that they are supposed to represent. The mixed race protagonists, in particular, challenge this popular image of the "modern minority." They not only fail to lead society in its development; ironically, given the high media exposure of "Generation Ambiguous," they are most often represented in the novels as feeling invisible.

These anti-bildungsroman characters do not come of age by coming into society. Rather, their experiences critique the racial and economic basis by which individuals are incorporated, and both to some extent abandon the social contract altogether: Senna's character moves back to what she sees as the peripheral West—versus the East Coast "Source of power" (6)—living alone, unemployed, and emotionally off the grid. Raboteau's Emma moves outside the country altogether, becoming an expatriate in Brazil where "she was beginning to suspect that there wasn't anything wrong with her head, but rather something wrong with her country" (*The Professor's Daughter* 271). The two novels are less an example of what Ruth Colker calls "living the gap"[5] than of pointing out the gap at the center of modernity's myth of racial and literary progress. Senna's and Raboteau's mixed race protagonists often feel invisible, but these novels are not a cry for better legal representation or more refined racial categorization. Rather, they critique a social order that would "deploy the figure of the racial hybrid as an alibi for a nationalism that reinvents the racial logics it claims to have broken."[6]

II. "THE SAME PERSON IN DIFFERENT BODIES"

The Professor's Daughter focuses predominantly on Emma Boudreaux's search for herself by coming to terms with the divorce of her interracial parents, the sudden disability of her older brother, and her discovery of her paternal grandfather's lynching. The daughter of an illustrious black Princeton professor from very humble origins, she and her brother, Bernie, are extremely close, in part because both "didn't look black." The title of the book refers, of course to Emma, but it also references *The Professor's Daughter* (1997), a young adult graphic novel about Victorian lovers, one of whom is a mummified ancient Egyptian pharaoh, hinting at the near-incestuous love between Emma and her brother, whose tragic accident leaves him catatonic, also lives in the borderland between the living and the dead. It also evokes an even more interesting connection: *The Professor's Daughter* (1971) by the British novelist Piers Paul Reed, which was, Danzy Senna notes in her memoir, *Where Did You Sleep Last Night?*, a "literary thriller" based loosely on Senna's own parents' interracial relations.[7]

At first Emma appears to be the quintessential mixed race type. She, especially, remains what she calls a "a question mark":

When people ask me what I am, which is not an everyday question but one I get asked every day, I want to tell them about Bernie. I don't, of course. I just tell them what color my parents are, which is to say, my father is black and my mother is white.

People don't usually believe me. You look_____(fill in the blank) *Puerto Rican, Algerian, Israeli, Italian, Suntanned, or maybe Like you Got Some Indian Blood, but you don't look like you got any Black in you. No way! Your father must be real light-skinned.* (2)

Emma is subject to the signal "What are you?" question, and to precisely the indignities of disbelief that Adrian Piper interrogates in "Passing for White, Passing for Black."[8] Because she and her brother share her mother's straight hair—and it is hair, she posits, that "really makes you black in the eyes of others" (2)—her racial status is ever suspect. She is, to various degrees, rejected by extended family (her cousins call her a "stuck-up white prissy" [9]), her fellow peers (her "culture counselor," Karim, from the "Af-Am Center," refuses to speak to her [21–22]), and her boyfriends, who eventually leave her for women they think are more race-appropriate marriage partners. She loses her virginity to her college teaching assistant from "London by way of Bombay," because Poresh wooed her with a cheap line uniquely geared towards a mixed race naïf: "We are both stuck between two worlds. I belong to two cultures, while you are suspended between childhood and womanhood." She sees it as an auspicious omen that "[o]ur skin was the exact same color. I was sure this meant something" (230). But in fact, being culturally "between" or being the same color means nothing, as he has long ago agreed to an arranged marriage.

In contrast, she has a symbiotic relationship with her brother, Bernie, who tells her that she is an "extension of himself" (2). She believes that "I grew up in his skin" (20). It is community-making in miniature; siblinghood as the first occasion to form an interpersonal bond that is at once part blood kin and ethno-racial, protective and yet ultimately defensive in relation to other people, including their own mother. In Senna's *Caucasia*, similarly, the two sisters also feel as one, also develop a private language, Elemeno, and also seem to share a wholly private mutual understanding. But it is also an experiment in the limits of such bonding. In *Caucasia*, Birdie is kept away from her sister for years by their parents' marital separation; in *The Professor's Daughter*, Bernie has become a paralyzed, insensible "vegetable" (3), a "raceless, faceless thing" (27) because of a freak accident that electrocuted him. In both novels, family is the place that seems, at first, to hold the best promise of racial and spiritual symmetry: "we were the same person in two different bodies" (2).

The pre-vegetative Bernie is seen as a prophet, "The *New* New Negro" who inspires academic lectures by his father's colleague Professor Lester, about the "liminal space between black and white America," in which there "can be no life on the hyphen" (22). Lester, who tries to give Bernie an education in being a black man by bringing him to the Million Man March (against his father's wishes), sees race as already and always socially determined as separated. For him, Bernie's biracialism represents Du Boisian double consciousness and speaks to the condition not of mixed race identity but of Black America, with its "warring selves" (22)—directly quoting from Du Bois' definition of the psychic tension inhering within all African Americans. He argues that the "'mulatto' cannot be both black and white just as he cannot be neither black nor white. These terms are mutually exclusive and mutually imperative" (22). But, in fact, Du Bois argues in "Of Our Spiritual Strivings" (1903) that white (which for Du Bois does nominal double duty as "American") and black cannot and should not be separated:

The history of the Negro is the history of this strife,—this longing to attain self-conscious manhood, to merge his double self into a better and truer self. In this merging he wishes neither of his older selves to be lost. He would not Africanize America, for America has too much to teach the world and Africa. He would not bleach his Negro soul in a flood of white Americanism, for he knows that Negro blood has a message for the world.[9]

Du Bois' concept of blackness differs both from Lester's adaptation of double consciousness as Manichean divide and from mixed race advocates' concept of biracialism as resolution of that divide. As that famous quote suggests, Du Bois understands double consciousness as a function of the structural and social tensions of being black in white America: moving from the biological determinism of the nineteenth century, he argues that race is not a genetic condition but a cultural process and psychological orientation. This important shift in race discourse implies, then, that race as a cultural process makes social change possible, and, furthermore, that black people have a psychic depth and emotional interiority that, as Du Bois theorizes in "Of Our Spiritual Strivings," "Criteria of Negro Art" (1926), and elsewhere, not only rivals but exceeds whites' lauded ability to appreciate beauty, tragedy, theater, art, and nature. Racial hierarchies are fictions maintained by social and political institutions, Du Bois insists; and, contrary to popular opinion, black people are not brutes but, rather, the bearers of the most refined and exquisite sensibilities. They do not have to play cultural catch-up; once the legal and social obstacles that disadvantage black people are removed, Du Bois maintains, black people can bring their considerable cultural gifts to the global table and acquire parity as "co-workers in the kingdom of culture." Du Bois' original notion of double consciousness, then, was never simply reduced to a question of biracial identity or loyalty (am I black or white?) but was always an occasion to set in motion questions about social justice and enfranchisement (How can one be black in America? How can one be a citizen in a country that does not recognize one's humanity?). That is, the excruciating experience of "twoness," as he describes it, is produced not by black pathology but by a national sickness that perversely weakens the nation itself through exclusion of some of its best citizenry. Du Boisian double consciousness calls for social change and institutional reform, not individual therapy or identity stances. He hopes that change can be accomplished through a multilateral and mutually beneficial integration—versus either assimilation or separatism. The twoness represented by Emma and Bernie is the direct result of and response to this history. Bernard Boudreaux, Jr., Emma's father, offers his own experiment with integration, revealing that he *married a white woman so my children wouldn't inherit our misery*" (220, italics in original). Emma's and Bernie's biraciality is the result of his effort to interrupt the generational momentum of racism, an experiment he eventually realizes is totally unsuccessful. Marriage as a form of integration, miscegenation as a form of political intervention, and biraciality as an identity unshackled from the past prove a profound failure in the novel. The children are not an escape from history; they are birthed from it.

Du Bois makes a point of distinguishing miscegenation from integration, since whites often interpreted black desire for political power as an excuse to make legal their putative desire for white mates. Du Bois is never interested in arguing for conjugal integration, and in fact often dismisses it as a red herring meant to distract from the more important political arguments. But later in his career, he becomes more cynical about the possibilities for even political and cultural integration; by 1935, he argues passionately in "Does the Negro Need Separate Schools?," "A Nation Within a Nation," and elsewhere for separate schools in the belief that equal education opportunities are simply unavailable in the traditional school system, and pleads, as well, for self-sufficient economic institutions that would free black people from whites' constant hampering of their professional development and financial security. But at the turn of the nineteenth century, Du Bois still believes that mining the critical possibilities of double consciousness—with its gift of "second sight" into a racist social order—could bring clearer critical vision to the nation as a whole. Although Emma and Bernie never exercise this second sight, they seem poised to access such critical vision, not because they are transcendent of race and history but precisely because they are the most intimately connected to it, as Bernard Boudreaux, Jr.'s story suggests.[10]

At the outset of the novel, Bernie and Emma represent themselves as one, but racial similitude is recurrently exposed as an unreliable model for community-making—not only because families are infamous for producing children that look nothing like each other or their parents, but also because one's sibling may leave physically or mentally. Any kinship based on symmetry is always revealed as imaginary, fraught, a child's dream. In *The Professor's Daughter*, this sibling unity is, finally, represented not as something desirable to return to or to re-create, but rather as a conjoining that distorts. Emily feels that she "has been in her brother's skin" (20) and at first believes Bernie's claim that she is his female half—"I'm the he of you and you're the she of me" (26)—and thus feels like the "ghost limb of an amputee" (21) when he is absent. If his presence completes her, without him she feels she is "unfinished," "halfway something and halfway something else, without definition" (261)—rather like what the Japanese call "mizuko," a "baby that doesn't get born." Loosely translated, it means "water child". . . . [Like] a glass only partially filled with liquid—its body is unfulfilled but not without form. Mizukos have presence, and agency. They are capable of haunting; they are capable of being born into another body" (261). The condition of being mixed race has left her feeling only partially realized, formed but unborn, as though miscarried or aborted like the mizukos. She understands this partial birth as a fulfillment of another's coming into being, agreeing with Bernie that she is his female half, "an extension of himself" (2): "*I wasn't finished yet when I came. I came too fast and left part of me behind. That was you. You came to finish me up*" (2, italics in original).

"Finishing up" someone else is a problematic mission in life to embrace; nonetheless, part of what enables a sense of continuity between the siblings carries with it a patronymic legacy that Bernie feels he has inherited and must enact, though he is unclear how. The legacy brings with it the unspoken, unspeakable rumor that his paternal grandfather died a violent and unjust death, and it bequeaths to him, and ostensibly Emma, an inarticulate rage from the grave. His grandfather, a gifted athlete, is lynched for his sports prowess, for being "too good at baseball" (26); his father, an acclaimed academic, is accused of losing touch with his black heritage because "it ain't all in the books" (18). And so Bernie, named after both his father and his grandfather, believes that he and Emma are "put here to finish something. They got Bernard Number One before he could do it. Bernard Number Two has failed in every respect to get it 'cause he's blind. I'm Number Three. Number One came back in me. In us. . . . You think it's a coincidence we chose to descend through the same womb into the world?" (26).

This compact seems to have been of Bernie's own half-dreamed design, however, a psycho-spirituo-historical-racial bargain that Emma buys into but that slowly evaporates once Bernie becomes vegetative. But before his catastrophic injury, "Bernie was my we" (18), and Emma shared in the racial fury and unrest that define both brother's and grandfather's experiences.

III. OF RASHES AND RACIAL MADNESS

Emma's own inheritance of double consciousness, as both blessing and curse, is manifested physically through chronic rashes, eczema, dermatitis, and other skin disturbances that range from "red pinpoint spots" on her face to raised bumps that look like "spider bites" (102). Described variously as "inflamed eruptions" and "stigmata" (107), they are often "violently itchy, like something live crawling under her skin" that she would attempt "to dig out," once by raking two forks across her skin till it bled (107). Throughout her adolescence, Emma's parents take her to dermatologists, herbalists, and other skin specialists, but nothing yields the slightest improvement. In fact, it turns out that Emma can bring on the rash at will (105), and that her symptoms are signs of what Harry Elam, drawing on the Martinican psychiatrist and philosopher Frantz Fanon, terms "racial madness." Fanon, Elam explains, "believed that the madness, the mental disorder and the melancholia of the colonial subject, was a direct product of the social and political circumstances of colonialism" and, furthermore, that "the symptoms of madness" were linked to "the cause of freedom . . . to the abuses of racism and oppression as well as to the struggles of liberation."[11]

Her brother asks if she can transfer her rashes to him, her own contagion, her own kind of legacy, to pass on. She cannot, but the rashes become associated for both of them with the expression of a racialized anger similar to Bernie's angry saxophone playing. They claim they are "mad," and make a point of distinguishing their madness from their mother's (she says she too is "mad," mad at them for playing loud music). Their mother, they say, would not understand their kind of mad because she would have "to look like us" (107), making this the requisite for entrance into an exclusive "club" (107). But if looking similar creates the kinds of racialized experiences that bond Emma and Bernie, it also makes her "invisible," as Emma says. Her biracial appearance obscures her from the vision of others in Ellisonian fashion because others see what they imagine, project upon her.

Yet, despite the deforming and uncomfortable effects of her rashes, they are actually what draws attention in a way that she appreciates because it renders her crisis visible:

In spite of all the name-calling, I didn't really mind. As a matter of fact, I grew to enjoy the attention the rash attracted. There was something magic in it. I normally felt invisible, but the rash made people stare. It lured my mother's attention away from Bernie, who outshone me at everything except for school. It won sympathy from my teachers. It dominated my biracial features, which my classmates found perplexing. Most important, when it was bad enough, the rash demanded my father's compassion. (102)

The rashes are, in part, an adolescent bid for attention. But the "magic" of the rashes is not simply their ability to garner sympathy and compassion for Emma. It is their ability to make people stare, to look, to notice. To her peers, her mixed race body does not communicate, does not register; it only perplexes. As Rosemarie Garland-Thomson argues in her brilliant *Staring: How We Look*, "We stare when ordinary seeing fails, when we want to know more. So staring is an interrogative gesture that asks what's going on and demands a story. The eyes hang on, wanting to recognize what seems illegible, order what seems unruly, know what seems strange."[12]

Emma's body seems to demand a story, and part of her burden is that she feels the walking requirement to tell one, even as she realizes that no narrative can satisfy the interrogatives. As I suggest in the Introduction, staring, in its violation of all polite protocols, can nonetheless be an occasion for productive engagement that can prompt a perceptual refocusing:

Triggered by the sight of someone who seems unlike us, staring can begin an explanatory expedition into ourselves and outward into new worlds. . . . Because we come to expect one another to have certain kinds of bodies and behaviors, stares flare up when we glimpse people who look or act in ways that contradict expectation. Seeing startlingly stareable people challenges our assumption by interrupting complacent visual business as usual. Staring offers an occasion to rethink the status quo. Who we are can shift into focus by staring at who we think we are not. (6)

Emma contradicts expectations, but it turns out that being blotchy, not biracial, is what makes her usefully "stareable," in Garland-Thomson's sense. As she tells it, her rash trumps her "biracial features"; the lesions interrupt seeing as usual, cause readerly reflection on the status quo. The problem is not that her racial mix fails to register her identity; it is that her biracial features do not chronicle the real story, the racial injustices that lurk beneath her skin and beneath the surface of official history. In and of itself, her biracial appearance does not challenge interpretation. *But the undiagnosed rashes do.* They signify on top of her illegible skin, one sign on top of another—both equally livid, equally indecipherable— yet the layering of their intelligibility creates a double negative "magic" that wins for her "sympathy" and "compassion."

More significantly, the skin eruptions on top of her already unsettling skin create a palimpsest of symptoms that signify beyond the self—they are the "red traveling welts" (105) of historical unease. In *The Professor's Daughter,* in fact, the rashes are explicitly linked to the restless ghost of her grandfather. When half of Emma's face grotesquely swells as the result of having touched "graveyard dust" (125), or what her father calls "goofer dust" (124), he tells her: "That's the punishment when you mess with a bigger power than yourself" (125). He had experienced the same bifurcated swelling when he touched his father's ashes. When he admits that he had actually eaten his grandfather's goofer dust, we come to understand just how profound are the consequences. If Emma's rash makes her a "two-faced shape shifter" (123), then her father's monstrous ingestion leads her to wonder if he is not "schizophrenic" even as she is "relieved . . . just to know the rash was larger than I was" (126). It leads her later to speculate on the true "nature of depression":

As far as she could see, it wasn't just anger turned inward, or grief, or something generic she'd gotten from Bernard's side, or a chemical imbalance in need of correction by a head doctor and pharmaceuticals. Though it might have been all those things, more important, it was a thing you could escape. (270)

Emma's rashes are like the odd, roving, ever-changing symptoms of something that *Symptomatic*'s protagonist constantly experiences throughout the novel, and that exists as a constant but unnamed irritant. They always occur after racialized exchanges—when she is about to break up with a white boyfriend, for example: "At night, I lay awake for hours listening to my body speak to me: the grumbles and aches and pricks and itches— evidence, I suspected, of a problem growing larger inside me" (21).

She also feels curiously, persistently ill in an apartment she sublets that houses the racial history of others:

My body continued to send me signals that I was coming down with something, a full-fledged winter flu. Achy bones. A mildly sore throat. Vague symptoms of a problem, but not enough to see a doctor. . . . When I was there, I felt ill. My symptoms were mild and vague. They roamed my body, like tinkers searched for new temporary homes where they could not be caught. Nausea one day, a dull ache behind my eyes the next. A rash on my neck like something crawling just beneath my skin. (81–82)

The tinkers, the nausea, the ache, the rashes in both *The Professor's House* and *Symptomatic* illustrate what Paul Gilroy terms "postcolonial melancholia," a new millennial world in which the race and racism in all their complex possibilities and perversities not only go unnamed but have been characterized as outdated. Race is only obliquely mentioned, rarely addressed, and barely glimpsed. Gilroy notes that in the postcolonial order, even the "desire for redress" becomes unimaginable because the hurt itself is represented as so attenuated, diffused, and broadly distributed. This is precisely the world of both these novels, in which racism is also as hard to pinpoint and diagnose as the rashes and aches that both protagonists have—they are *symptomatic*, as Senna's novel suggests, but of what? They register symptoms because the causes are so hard to name. This difficulty results in part because when there are bids for recognition or recompense, Gilroy argues, they are described as merely the "politics of blackmail."[13]

In seeking an explanation for the widespread reluctance to engage racism analytically, historically, or governmentally, we may observe charitably that questions about "race," identity, and differentialization have a very distant, mid-twentieth-century ring to them. They sometimes feel anachronistic because they try to return contemporary discussions to a moral ground that we feel we should have left behind long ago. Gilroy suggests that many people are inclined to be impatient about being asked to revisit aspects of the political and moral debates over race, yet "[t]hat return is necessary because consideration of these questions has only a minimal presence in today's incomplete genealogies of the global movement for human rights, which are inclined to imagine that conflict between 'race' and more inclusive models of humanity was concluded long ago" (14).

Neither novel directly engages with politics, economics, capitalism, or racism. The protagonists indifferently hold jobs but not careers; they aspire to nothing or no one in particular; they do not explore political options and organizations. Racism is only obliquely thematized in the novels. In that, these novels are unlike the bildungsromans of Ralph Ellison or Richard Wright; the protagonists' growth, if there is any, seems completely uncoupled from social movements. From that perspective, we cannot call these novels radical projects in decolonization. But it is precisely the dramatization of this absence of a political life, the foregrounding of the dissolution of political will in the twenty-first century fin de siècle that marks the decolonizing impulse of the mixed race anti-bildungsroman. The fictional world of these novels re-creates the post–civil rights *Geist*, and in doing so prompts the kind of critical social reflection in readers that the characters themselves cannot quite achieve. The willed absence and invisibility of ways of talking about race and racism, of Emma's grandfather, of the legacy of the "peculiar institution," are representative of postcolonial melancholia: the vague, shrouded ennui that both of the protagonists experience. The random, distracting, mobile skin eruptions bear highly visible, if silent, witness to the cultural malaise, to the lack of social progress.

There is a suggestion of a way out of the malaise in *The Professor's Daughter*, for Bernie's disability indirectly begets Emma's healing. When he drops out of her life, he also drops out of racial categorization and thus out of the family's racial history altogether: "My father is black and my mother is white and my brother is a vegetable" (3). His skin has become de-racialized—like "leather" (23)—and his accident the catalyst that has broken the racial logic that had fixed them as the third point on the diamond, the triangulated link between the grandfather, their father, and Bernie. The implication is, too, that Emma breaks what has amounted to a particularly masculinist legacy. She and her brother assume that together they were meant to right their grandfather's death through some vague but powerful act, but by novel's end, there is the sense that her racial education is no longer triangulated through men, family, or even nation as either they leave her or she leaves them behind.

IV. "THE THING ABOUT MULES . . . IS THEY CAN GO EITHER WAY"

Symptomatic is similarly obsessed with the socially progressive potential for affiliated networks and with the less savory assumptions often tacitly informing who gets in or is left out of such networks: the racial gatekeeping, the class biases, the gender protocols, and the visual ascriptions governing entrance into a society of peers. From the beginning of the novel, the biracial protagonist—unnamed, in the tradition of Ralph Ellison's *Invisible Man* and James Weldon Johnson's *Autobiography of an Ex-Coloured Man*—longs for connection, but she also prefers being "out of context" (9). Biracial—or "'*nusu-nusu*,' Swahili for girls like me. Literal translation: *partly-partly*" (48)—the light-skinned, straight-haired protagonist intentionally disidentifies[14] with any particular crowd, "avoids being locatable" (135), and does not mind that her boyfriend can never quite place her (14). In part she cultivates this epistemological haze in order to resist the inevitable racial cataloging and its predictable reduction of her to a heuristic: "You know how it goes. The disclosure, followed by the edifying speech. My body, the lesson" (35).

But it also reflects anxiety about the social requirements that always seem to come with belonging, even in—or perhaps especially in—intimate relations. The friends of her white boyfriend, Andrew, for instance, bond through racist humor: one friend performs a grotesque blackface charade, complete with stage dialect, of a cleaning woman they had all known in college, then they make fun of black names ("are those names supposed to be creative, or is it all just an epic spelling mistake? Like dyslexia on a mass scale?" [13]), and sum up with a story about a black couple on *The Newlywed Game* who, when asked where was the strangest place she and her husband had ever "made whoopee" says, "Uh, I'ze gon halfta say in da butt" (14). The jokes leave Andrew "flushed with affectionate pleasure" (14) for his classmate chums, but drive her to the questionable sanctuary of a bathroom. As her father tells her, "[H]umor, above all else, was what bound each of us and separated each of us from one another. Humor was the great moment of truth. What we thought was funny was how we defined ourselves, whether we knew it or not" (42). Andrew's friends are the "closest thing he has to family" (5), united through "in-jokes." It is a moment for the protagonist that exposes the suspect processes of exclusivity that bind and renew even seemingly innocent friendships, and it is the catalyst for her breakup with him.

Interracial intimacy has often been posed as the answer to racism by claiming to be above or beyond its historical cycles.[15] However, all the protagonist's relations with men—black and white—function as crucibles for racism (inter- and intra-) rather than buffers from it. One of her boyfriends, Claude, a black Stanford graduate student, for instance, rejects her because he cannot "see himself in her" (105), cannot handle what he calls the "dissonance" between her racial identity and her appearance. The narcissistic terms by which she can be embraced—his words suggest she must mirror him back to himself—reflect his own racial insecurities (he, too, we are told, is very light-skinned). As Claude puts it, "mules" like her can

go either way. They either get the best of both worlds—the strength of the donkey and the showmanship of the thoroughbred horse—or the worst of their lineage—the braying stubbornness of a donkey and the genetic weakness, rubbery limps and low I.Q. of an overbred horse. . . . In other words, chicks like this? They either end up genius messiahs, or craven hybrid monstrosities. But they'll never be ordinary. (201–202)[16]

Ivers Greene similarly offends: "Are you a quadroon?" he abruptly asks, to which she responds, "No. . . . That's not the word I'd use to describe myself . . . I'm half. And anyway, that word seems pretty archaic." He just laughs at her: "Oh. You don't like that kind of language. It's impolite. You must be one of those 'new people' I keep reading about in the papers" (103). Greene ends up dismissing her tentative "I guess so" by also cracking crude jokes about whether, as "someone who could go either way," she says "motherfucker" or "muthafucka" (105). The lurking hostility informing *both* lovers' identical concerns about whether the protagonist can go "either way" suggests straight male anxiety about the mulatta's sexual and racial loyalties.

But if her heterosexual relations merely repeat historical canards about the mulatta, sororial community does not release her from history's claims either. The protagonist's experimental immersion in a same-sex community—an old-fashioned 1930s women's boardinghouse (3)—proves disappointing. The organization's logo is an image of an older woman joylessly giving a piggyback ride to a younger woman, and the organization's motto—"she ain't heavy, she's my sister"—speaks to even more uneasy models for sisterhood. Neither the image of elder-mentor as beast of burden nor the male-bonding 1970s classic "He Ain't Heavy, He's My Brother," which literalizes the logo to comic effect, represents the kind of relationship she is seeking. The appealing symmetry of their sororial unity hides, it seems, this asymmetrical bondage—one generation's duty to another. She does not want the differential relations (the older, the younger, the wise, the ingénue), especially to the extent that such a relationship plots all their relationships: younger women are apprenticed to older, wiser women, women who then become responsible for lifting up the next generation. It is a pattern and a prescription that the protagonist does not want to inherit: "Everything is designed to make you feel part of a community but . . . I felt a loneliness so complete it makes my teeth hurt" (3).

The protagonist eventually finds her doppelgänger in a biracial woman twice her age, Vera (aka Greta Hicks), who also is passing—passing four times over: as white, as Greta, as a journalist at the magazine where the protagonist works, and as her mulatta comrade-in-arms. There seems an instant bond—"these quirks of DNA . . . were not supposed to change anything. But they did. As soon as Greta had told me [that she was biracial], I'd felt an invisible wall fall away between us" (49). As people from "Nowhere, Everywhere" (48), they share a potential kinship. The protagonist recognizes that their "natural" bond is constructed, motivated by their shared desire for similarity. The protagonist notices, for instance, "[t]he slight resemblance to each other. Nothing obvious, but we could have been related . . . the same straight brown hair and olive skin, and the same vague look about our features" (48) only *after* Greta tells her that she is the daughter of a German woman and a black GI. She retroactively creates racial identification out of a desire for communion.

For the protagonist, Greta's corporeal blur is not cause for an existential crisis about the "gulf between visibility and knowability, the irrecuperable chasm between representation and identity,"[17] but an occasion for wishful self-recognition, a way of turning their "same vague look" into the basis for connection.

Their creation of an "imagined community"[18] climaxes in Greta's fantasy about the two of them starting a mixed race nation, a world where they would no longer be exoticized, aesthetized, or fetishized, a world unto themselves. "I think we should start our own nation," Greta tells her. "We could buy an island. . . . And we could fill it with people just like us" (50). The expression "people like us" not accidentally evokes the title of Lawrence Otis Graham's controversial guide to the light-skinned elite, *Our Kind of People: Inside America's Black Upper Class*,[19] with its history of the infamous "paper-bag tests" deciding who was light enough to be let into social events. In a scene that I will discuss later, the same expression is also used by the protagonist's white colleague, who, believing that the protagonist is white, rants about affirmative action stealing his professional opportunities to advance (83). So "people like us" in the novel signals the risks of in-group racial cohesion. Indeed, Greta's vision is an imperialist dream and capitalist privilege: she wants to "buy an island—one of those Tahitian joints that Marlon Brando got himself" and then, assuming there is no indigenous population with sovereignty rights, she would simply import "people like us." Oblivious to such implications, Greta suggests she would be the "minister of defense" of, apparently, a national army conscripted to protect the mixed race nation. The protagonist, interestingly enough, imagines this new nation very differently, as not a military but a spiritual model along the lines of the Nation of Islam, with herself more harmlessly holding the position of "minister of information" and selling "bean pies to passing sailors" (50). Greta is more ambitious, even claiming for them their own "mixed race" poetic manifesto, complete with the promise of occult pleasure domes for the adventurer: she recites Samuel Taylor Coleridge's "Kubla Khan," sure that the "mixed race" nation will be like Xanadu (50). They even have a theme song—a misinterpretation of Mick Jagger's "Wild Horses": Greta sings the line *"Raceless lady, you know who I am"* over and over again, saying it is "our song, girl," despite the protagonist's insistence that the word is "graceless" not "raceless" (72).[20]

The mixed race Xanadu is more than colonialist ideal; it is also a commercial enterprise. In a spoof on the appetite for skin and hair products marketed for the mixed race consumer, *Symptomatic* features Greta taking the protagonist to a "color diagnostician," who gives her some "swatches" that she is ordered to carry in her wallet as she learns how to clothe herself in the right shades to match her unique skin tone as a mixed race person (66). The protagonist swoons before the appeal at first, seduced by the prospect of being at the very center of a new world: "And now you'll see," Greta tells her. "The world is made up of people wearing the wrong colors. Except you and me, of course" (67). Through such scenes, *Symptomatic* parodies the community-building efforts of mixed race organizations across the country that refer subscribers to websites marketing products specifically designed for them. Since the two women are united not only by their experience as "optical illusions" (84, 115) but also by consumer placement, the protagonist finds perfect fellowship in Greta:

She was always available to me when I wanted to tie one on, and she was always sympathetic, no, empathetic—to my every grumble and complaint. She agreed with everything I said, and we spent many hours comparing our experiences of being "optical illusions," as she called us. . . . Sometimes I felt as if we'd known each other a lot longer than we had—as if she had always been there in my life, hovering beside me, a dotty spinster aunt. . . . she was always there for me, steady and comforting . . . she would call before bed to make sure I'd gotten home okay. And if she didn't, I would call her, just to speak to somebody. And she was always there to pick up on the first ring. (84–85)

Greta appears to her as doting aunt, solicitous mother, selfless confidante, "hovering" fairy godmother, the projected answer to her need.

But by novel's end, hovering comradeship proves but one step from the slippery slope of obsessive stalking, and Xanadu is exposed as a claustrophobic den of obscenity and insanity, as in a rage Greta destroys the protagonist's apartment, writes on the wall in giant Magic Marker letters "XANADU" (194), and then ties her up. This transformation between the two is a meditation on community writ large, the tensions inherent in competing interests and self-investments in the other. For if the protagonist enjoys being the center of attention here, by the novel's end she is reduced to the gagged plaything of Greta, silent, without agency, an unwilling audience to her self-pitying self-aggrandizements (205). Early on in their relationship, the protagonist is reminded of the "odd" (84) intimacy of coworkers, of intense friendships united only by circumstance, opportunity, and the curious, fleeting alliance of needs that make them "slightly unreal, without consequence, and therefore peaceful" (85). The protagonist realizes that she and Greta are "strangers after all" at the very moment that they also "toast to sisterhood" (73).

V. HOMEOPATHY AND HOMOEROTICISM

In *Symptomatic*, the problem with mixed race bonding is not that its intimacies are similarly provisional but that they can foster a deceptive species of exclusionism, become color-struck in their own way. The protagonist finally rejects it altogether as too self-referential. Her crazy twin gives her *too* much of the mulatto-love she has been craving, her mimicry becomes mockery as Greta starts to parrot everything the protagonist says (128, 137). In fact she starts to imagine others are also mimicking her (109), as if Greta has apprenticed others to copy her. Theirs becomes a community that does not look outward but only inward, as they mirror each other's obsessions: it is true that Greta stalks her (120), but the protagonist also stalks Greta at one point (171), dissolving their distinctions. Mirroring Greene's view that his erstwhile girlfriend, against whom he had to have a restraining order, at least made him feel that he was "never alone" (160), the protagonist admits the mutually constituted attraction between her and Greta in which their positions as desired/desiree, pursued/sought are constantly being inverted. After all, when Greta reclaims her apartment and her space, the protagonist by then has become the interloper, the one who has borrowed clothes without asking, who has overstepped the boundaries. Greta has mixed up all their clothing, translated borrowing into ownership (195), but so has the protagonist, wearing Greta's winter coat, using her bath products and toiletries. As they grow closer, Greta/Vera capitalizes on and exploits the protagonist's problems with her boyfriends—Andrew, Claude, and Ivers—by ranting about how black men want her as white, white men want her as black (151), and says even dating other mixed men would be simply redundant (115), a doubling rather than a resolution of being "nusu-nusu."

This Möbius strip of duplication and inversion, the community that collapses difference in the name of it, is the very thing that finally cures her of her "symptoms," the vague racial malaise that plagues her throughout the novel. Curing "like with like," as her mother puts it, is the homeopathic answer to everything: "You have to give the body small doses of the problem . . . to remind it what it's fighting against, and to trigger it into action" (140–141). As I suggested earlier, throughout the novel the protagonist manifests symptoms not unlike Emma's in *The Professor's Daughter* ("grumbles and aches and pricks and itches—evidence, I suspected, of a problem growing larger inside me" [21]). These symptoms of social ills, pricks of the social conscience, are rousing reminders of the need for defensive "action" (141). As a character suggests in Senna's first novel, *Caucasia*, "the mulatto in America functions as a canary in a coal mine," the "gauge of how poisonous American race relations were."[21] Her symptoms are warning chirps from the canary, I would suggest, that the climate in the coal shaft is getting dangerous. They are aimed, among other things, at pulling the protagonist from her sanguine belief that she can do progressive work deep within the bowels of a company that produces superficial commercial media. Awarded a prestigious fellowship to work there, the protagonist nonetheless is challenged by her father for accepting the post; he finds the commercial magazine "problematic." She argues that "that only proves that they need more people like me on the inside. People who can identify a problem, name it, fix it. (He smiled and shook his head and started unloading groceries.) But it seeps inside, baby doll, he said. It seeps inside" (16). Although she agrees with her father's critique of the magazine she will work for, it is only at the novel's end that she realizes that change cannot occur from within corporate America, which itself is never named, never fully drawn in the text. Its power is diffuse, only obliquely glimpsed. Her father's comment that the magazine is "problematic" is the harshest critique we hear; it is not a challenge to change but only an expression of mild concern. For the magazine's power poses as benign, even benevolent, as senior people in the organization take her to dinner, celebrate her fellowship, appear to mentor her. The magazine's ability to shape reality is only hinted at when, for instance, her editors coax her away from writing a slightly alternative story, or away from representing underrepresented voices in her journalism. Only when she leaves her job and New York does she break out of the complacency and passivity that come down like a miasma over her and that characterize this peculiar form of postcolonial melancholia.

The homeopathic "cure" involves being galvanized in action, "seeing 'race' as moral as well as political and analyzing it as part of a cosmopolitan understanding of the damage that racisms are still doing to democracy"[22] (Gilroy 33). But the protagonist in *Symptomatic* seems always just on the eve of action. She is, in one way, very much like Ellison's invisible man—"in a state of hibernation," subversively lying in wait for the right time to emerge,[23] a racial specter unseen by those around her. Her interest "of disappearing into someone else's story. Of watching and not being seen" (6) becomes a tension between a removed critic of, and being complicit with, the "status quo" (6); her cure is meant to move her from political passivity to activism. Her passivity is part of the post–civil rights era depression that is the narrative climate for the mixed race anti-bildungsroman. Horrified by her boyfriends' racism, for instance, she does not speak out and up, she does not launch into righteous indignation and protest, she does not turn the dinner party into a teachable moment. We get the sense, instead, of political exhaustion and impotence: "I thought of things I could do or say—things I'd already done and said. But I was all of a sudden so sleepy. I yawned, barely able to move from my seat by the window" (15).

At first, it appears the cure is realized through homoerotic bonding in *Symptomatic*, as the desire to create a community of racial look-alikes translates into same-sex longing. On the one hand, Greta defensively insists that her attraction to the protagonist is not erotic—she's "not into women," and her interest in the protagonist is not a "dyke come-on," she says; she wants her merely to be a partner in "building a new reality" because "we're a new race, a new people" (155). Greta tells the protagonist that she has always wanted a "girl like her," so she would no longer feel like a "half-caste misfit" that "everybody wanted but no one loves" (203).

Greta's affection, however, often comes after insulting the one she loves. Her call for another foot soldier to serve the new nation is a possessive recruitment, more suggestive of a lover's compact in the Garden of Eden. Jealous of what she assumes is the protagonist's interest in Ivers Greene (124), she launches into an attack, like Greene's, anxious about her racial proclivities, the fear that she can go either way:

Well he might not be your boyfriend now, but he will be. . . . If it's not him, it'll be someone else. Not a white boy. You're done with that. It'll be some coon with a hankering for high-yella ass. You'll fall head over heels and next thing I know you'll be doing the jitterbug up in Harlem with Mr. Milky Way, discovering your black heritage astride his dick. And I'll just be some sandpile you used to play in. . . . It's two-faced bitches like you that give us a bad name. (124)

Both the straight and the queer loves' attraction towards the protagonist is animated by fantasies that the biracial person will sexually betray herself and others across racial lines. But it also fuels her lovers' revulsion, for in the next moment, Greta embraces her in a gesture both tender and aggressive—as the protagonist explains,

her hair tickling my cheek, and the softness of her bosom pressed against my chest. I heard her whispering in my ear, "You're not alone. I'm here. I'm here now." I could smell the cocoa butter on her skin. I felt her hands massaging the back of my skull, its cranial hardness. (125)

The protagonist sees herself in the mirror—and notices Greta also looking at herself in the mirror (127)—creating the "strange sensation of being surrounded by her—one version in front of me and the other behind" (126). It is an erotic suffocation. In fact, Greta/Vera's presence subtly inflects and infects all her relations: even when the protagonist has sex with Ivers, she is distracted by Greta/Vera's vulgar nighttime callers (179), internalizing the callers' messages that she is a white bitch in need of a black stud. And their dream of Xanadu, by then, seems less like a Tahitian vacation than a suicide pact, as Greta promises her that she will take her "so far away where no one will ever find us. It'll be beautiful, I promise. And we'll be together" (104).

Greta is Vera's own masturbatory invention, after all, a woman sketched by her imagination, a fiction for her own manipulations. This tendency toward invention is evident from the outset, for Greta actually conceives of the protagonist as a friend months before they get to know each other. She finds out that Greta has been telling a colleague, Dorothea, that she can't wait to introduce her to this "friend of mine" who is "just like me" (66), even though, as the protagonist notes later, "we barely knew each other" (67). Thus the curious vacillation between erotic possibility and clinical mundanity, between seduction and daily self-maintenance, in the scene when Greta begins to wax her legs before the protagonist (148–150), pulling down her pants and then later exposing legs gleaming with oil. It is as if Greta can no longer distinguish her desire from the protagonist's. In fact, since for Greta the protagonist is only a projection of herself at this point, the waxing is about self-arousal, an onanistic display, as if the protagonist were Greta watching herself. The protagonist's desires are different only in degree, not kind. She too seeks a merging, sleeping in her sheets that "smell like someone else's skin" (111) and seeing her own body as twinned, with breasts that look like they belong to "two different women" (44). Greta needs the protagonist as a mirror in order to give Greta back to herself: "[Y]ou forget who you really are. The original you? That's what I forgot. Until I met you" (203).

VI. "LIKE SOMEWHERE ELSE I'D LIKE TO BE"

Jonathan Dollimore explores how so-called "deviant desire brings with it a different kind of political knowledge, and hence inflects both desire and politics differently,"[24] but worries that the "celebration of the exotic cultural/racial other is merely the counterpart of the racist's demonizing of the other" (22). If cross-sex, same-race reproduction structures hegemonic relations, as he suggests, then what social structure is generated by same-sex, mixed race desire? Miscegenation is, at least in part, as Eva Saks argues, about the way representations of sex secure norms of identity (national and/or racial) and lines of property; miscegenation—the "taboo of too different"—is, she maintains, historically and legally associated with incest and sodomy—"taboo of too similar," since these "crimes" rely on "a pair of bodies which are mutually constitutive of each other's deviance. . . . [Thus] neither body can represent the norm, because each is figured as deviance from the other." According to this reasoning, same-sex or intra-familial relations fall beyond the pale because the "pair of bodies . . . upon conjunction . . . are too similar to each other and too different from the 'norm.'"[25] In that sense, homoeroticism shares with miscegenation the threat to lines of blood and property because they upset patronymic influence, disrupting "blood" reproduction and inheritance, the dispersal of property along those bloodlines. Similarly, Phillip Brian Harper argues that anti-miscegenation sentiment and homophobia "derive their impetus largely from a common organizing principle: the sanctity of the private realm by which to control the flow of economic capital."[26] Under these terms, Greta and the protagonist are potentially transgressive because they are too similar (shared gender) and too different (offspring of crossed races)—they are doubly taboo. Their union is threatening in part because it is supposedly doubly sterile: it not only removes the woman from male sexual circulation (and thus potential progeny), but it also brings together two "mules," already associated with infertility. Actually they are triply taboo, and potentially the most radical, because their mixed race couple-dom turns the racial too-different into a shared same: Greta is all about making their two too-similar bodies a norm, to make the deviant normative, to place them at the center rather than on the periphery of the world.

But their sameness multiplied is not necessarily progressive, since same-sex coupling can also prove fundamental to the *maintenance* of class, sex, and especially racial norms, suggesting how, in Judith Butler's terms, "homosexuality [or any same-sex coupling] and miscegenation . . . converge at and as the constitutive outside of a normative heterosexuality that is at once the regulation of a racially pure reproduction."[27] How does that work in *Symptomatic*? On the one hand, Greta turns the protagonist away from heterosexual companions (Andrew, Greene) and defines their relation beyond that pale. But Greta also identifies *with* the men, suggesting that the protagonist will dump her like she putatively did them (124). Greta evokes precisely the old myth of a mulatta's sexual unreliability (the idea that she can go "either way") that Ivers and Claude did, only this time in the service of regulating a homoerotic and miscegenated—not heterosexual, "racially pure"—norm. Separating the protagonist from her lovers, coworkers, and family, Greta sees them all as threatening competitors for the protagonist's affection and attention, but also as competition for her own position as surrogate for all of them:

I'm the best fucking friend you'll ever have, and when all your boys, white, black, Puerto Rican, have come and gone—and mark my words, they will disappear—and Lola has sold you down the river, which she will, mark my words, when all them motherfuckers have left you high and dry, I'll be here beside you. (153)

Greta imagines that she—as the protagonist's double and racial proxy—will be the only one standing. Joseph Roach argues that all performance is surrogation, a standing in of one thing for another.[28] But what is Greta "standing in for" when she imaginatively orchestrates everyone's absence? She is, on the one hand, surrogating all others with herself, but only in order to also create a surrogate *of* herself. When Greta dresses the protagonist in a matching silver dress and then turns her into a doll (205), she is the caricatured projection of herself, a proxy by which she, ironically, knows herself, feels herself affirmed. Hers is a desire for the other which *is* the self, an incestuous yearning and cannibalistic competition, as we see in the climax when Greta tries to slash her abdomen: "The inside. The mystery space. What my mother calls the 'invisible world'" (208). They are joined at the uterus, the place where life begins; it is as if Greta sought a transfusion—"My blood seeping out into the space between us"—that would umbilically join them as blood kin. This ultimate joining, violent as it is, is also deeply appealing, and not only for Greta. The protagonist also is overcome with a "warm, a perfumey heat that engulfed me. . . . The blood felt warm, like somewhere I'd like to be" and they dance a "crazy dance" (208).

VII. HALF-LIT COMMUNITIES

I always found half-lights more blinding than utter darkness,
and my eyes didn't know which way to adjust.
The protagonist in *Symptomatic*[29]

The warning against the lure of narcissism stands as a challenge to mixed-race nationalism. But *Symptomatic* also offers the suggestion of an alternative politics for a protagonist seeking to lay claim to the unique perspectives of a *"partly-partly"* (48) while still resisting the mulatto mystique and all the politically suspect perks of this new "Talented Tenth."[30] In both of Senna's novels discussed here, the characters always limn mixed race identity with attention to its relation to community, and always with a delicate sense of how the individual is racially situated in social and historical matrices.[31]

The "half-lights" of pre-dawn or dusk that the protagonist early on finds blinding nonetheless encourage her to adjust her vision so that she glimpses the cleaning woman who looks like her grandmother (20), the disappointed downtrodden (20), the pregnant drug addict (44), the boy begging for change and the nannies of color (61), the colorless, genderless homeless person (63–64), and those whom she sees as slightly "deformed" (53) in some way, like herself. They become visible in the dim light, suggesting a community of affiliation and connection that is not tied by family or skin color, color swatches, shared humor, or even a political agenda. They are connected by a sense of mutual recognition. These insights are always subtly linked to issues of social equity and justice in the novel. Just as for Birdie in Senna's *Caucasia*, not knowing exactly who or what one is— that is, not having personally settled the question about what being "half" (*Symptomatic* 103) means—does not prevent feeling empathy for folks in the margins, for people who are often just as blurry around the edges. In *Symptomatic*, for instance, one of the many odd, recurrent figures that flit in and out of the narrative is a beggar in a wheelchair. The protagonist cannot figure out his or her race, gender, or age: "I stared hard into its face, trying to decide once and for all. Boy, girl, old man, or old woman. No clue. Even the voice was unclear" (62). Greta, who has been pestering her to put out some fifty dollars for a color analysis, merely frowns at the beggar, but the protagonist "tossed some silver" (63) to him or her. The protagonist's hard staring here is different from her visual self-regard in the mirrors, different from her journalist's watchfulness, different from Greta's dismissive glance. Nor is it an act of aggression. Her staring at "it" performs the necessary ethical work of recognition. As Garland-Thomson explains:

If staring has done its work, the next time people see such bodies, they will be familiar, if only vaguely. . . . Recognition . . . is essential not simply for individual self-realization but, more important, as the cornerstone of an ethical political society. . . . Recognition, then, relies on a combination of identification and differentiation. The trajectory of recognition is this: I recognize you by seeing your similarity and your difference to me, and then I make your strangeness familiar. In other words, I see you as you are. (158)

The protagonist stares in an effort at empathetic recognition, a way to make familiar the strangeness of "it," one of the most "potentially mutually revivifying aspect of staring encounters" (158).

One of the most striking moments in the novel then involves this small, glancing moment of recognition, and occurs also when, after her boyfriend's chums sicken her with their livid racist jokes about their dorm's black washerwoman, the protagonist bumps into an actual cleaning lady working before dawn in her office building and the pairing of these moments moves from the spectacle of a generalized "it" to the specificity of an individual. Unlike the ignorant mammy figure described earlier, this woman is "old enough to be my grandmother," "tiny," with netted hair, "skin the color of molasses" (21)—a "real life" version of a woman made so light of pages earlier. The protagonist's heartfelt "I'm sorry," and the woman's familiar "Don't be, baby. Don't be," make clear that they both understand she is apologizing not only for accidentally running into her; she is also ashamed that such an elderly woman should have to perform onerous menial and physical labor, ashamed because she recognizes her as "family" in the most catholic sense of the word, ashamed because she recognizes her responsibility to her and, by implication, to the many other invisible laborers working before and after hours in their shared environment.[32] The juxtaposition of scenes highlights the political implications and real-life costs of her boyfriend's pals just having a "good time." It also offers a quiet moment of mutual connection of kinship, unromanticized, across socioeconomic lines, that clearly calls for self-reflection even if no action is taken.

The protagonist's "community," if we can call it that, is prompted by occasional contact but not necessarily organized movement, is interpersonal but not necessarily scaled up into community mobilization, and it implies membership among the other liminal figures in the novel, most of whom never meet. These moments are marked by the protagonist's keen appreciation of the race/gender/class inequities at play. In that sense, it remains unclear how these looks translate into a politics, or become anything more than a fleeting sense of anxiety that never galvanizes the character into action. But they do throw her inaction into relief and make her paralysis itself the crisis and the focus. If there is one way in which the novel suggests that these moments can lead to social change, it is through her internship work. One of her assignments, for instance, is to interview mothers about "new high-tech playground designs," but in all Central Park she can find no mothers to interview, for "[a]ll the women were brown, and the children were white, and none of them were related." She interviews the women of color caring for their white charges, but her editor is uninterested in quoting "nannies" (61). The protagonist's wry description bespeaks her acute awareness of all of it: the privileged absence of white motherhood, the censoring of the "brown" underclass, the editorial monitoring of what stories "work" (61) or not, which voices are fit to be heard. Ultimately, however, she is not allowed to publish her observations, and the commercial media are represented as a vehicle that eclipses rather than exposes social commentary.

Nonetheless, she bears witness to these inequities because of her ability to move up and down the class ladder, in and out of her white boyfriend's expensive Village apartment, the prestigious offices downtown, and finally Greta/Vera's sublet in what she calls a "transitional" (38) Brooklyn neighborhood. The protagonist registers every shift in advantage and opportunity. (She recognizes this ability to move as itself a middle-class luxury, for though her internship pays little, it is a prestigious fellowship from a prestigious school that most likely promises her a secure living.) But she is always pulled from her comforts and from the risk of narcissism. In the midst of her self-ruminations always crowd a host of other people in greater need; a flaneur of sorts in the early mornings, she strolls and watches women on/of the street: "stared at the women I saw. . . . I saw disappointment in the deep lines etched around a mouth. Rage in the cracks between the eyebrows. Wide eyes signified a bewildered hurt. A jaw jutting forward spoke of unfulfilled desire" (19–20). If she cannot read herself—perhaps exactly because she makes herself a study—she is open to reading, unsentimentally but sympathetically, the faces of those from whom others turn away. She notes the hypocrisy of her "Old Money" boyfriend, who prefers (at a distance) the "working class [which] he found romantic" to the middle class with their supposed "bourgeois pretensions" (69). He prefers playing down and out by taking Greyhound buses rather than Amtrak trains, but she likes the latter precisely because you "saw poor people riding side by side with rich flying-phobics. And everything in the middle. And it seemed on those journeys that the lines broke down. There was camaraderie among the riders, as if for those hours on the train, they were one" (70). That ideal middling space of heterogeneity is the America that the protagonist loves (in opposition to her boyfriend, who sees it as the "bane of America" [70]). This "womb" (70) of the Amtrak cabin, as she calls it, is a space literally on the fly, in transit and transitive, a generative oasis, perpetually suspended even as it moves through time and space.

VIII. DOUBLED CONSCIOUSNESS

As suggested in the Introduction, all sorts of meditations on sight and insight dominate Senna's novels. *Caucasia*'s Birdie is constantly peering as through a glass darkly in search of herself—any and all reflective surfaces seem to do: mirrors, teapots, still water, the sheen of photographs, faces reflected and half glimpsed through car and bus windows (121, 180, 230, 249, 263, 293, 297, 336, 361, 380). *Symptomatic*'s protagonist is similarly obsessed, compulsively drawing a face with her finger on the fog of bathrooms and windowpanes (74):

I drew the outline of a face in the fog. I had been doodling this same face since I was a little girl, on napkins and glass, an anxious tic I resorted to whenever I felt out of place. It was a crude sketch of a woman. She had big eyes with long lashes, a long nose, full bow lips, and wavy lines around her face to signify hair. Ambiguous. Guarded. There was a certain refracted quality to the features that made her hard to place. I don't know who she was supposed to be—only that her face calmed me, like an old friend who shows up at just the right moment. Now I watched the fingerprints that were her fade into the mirror. (15)

The self-comforting image is of the protagonist (ambiguous, guarded) but also an always evaporating projection of what she wishes to be. Her gazing upon her image replicates the distanced, almost professional, watching that she herself does of others as much as of herself. As Garland-Thomson puts it, "We stare to know, and often we stare to know ourselves. Being caught off-guard by a surprising version of ourselves in some reflective surface is one of the primal scenes of staring. . . . Encountering ourselves face-to-face before the mirror, we become both subject and object of our stares. The work of self-scrutiny can be affirming or alienating, but always absorbing" (51–52). The protagonist's finger-drawing on the mirror is not mere self-absorption or obsession with how others see her, but an effort at self-creation through the mediation of the mirror, which itself, as Garland-Thomson notes, represents how we think others see us.

Less an example of the Lacanian mirror stage of identity formation than a bending of Du Boisian double consciousness, the protagonist looks at an image of herself looking back in an effort to pinpoint the vectors of identity. Du Bois suggests that double consciousness means "always looking at oneself through the eyes of others," a process yielding "no true self-consciousness, but only lets him see himself through the revelation of the other world";[33] *Symptomatic*'s young woman, too, finds no self-knowledge through others' perception of her—even when, unlike in Du Bois' account, they perceive her not as black but as white. At a bar with a Southern colleague on a "rant" about how if he had been born black, affirmative action would have catapulted him to "editor of the magazine by now," and how the 1950s was "the golden age for people like us" (83)—"us" meaning white people—the protagonist, who does not reveal her heritage to him, "stared at my own face in the mirror" and thought *"This is what they see when they look at you,"* a "sallow face" with "slightly stricken" eyes (83). All she sees in such moments is their perception of her, painful because just as white preconceptions of black people led to "measuring one's soul by the tape of a world that looks on in amused contempt and pity" (Du Bois 615), *Symptomatic*'s protagonist, suffering from white preconceptions of *white* people, bears witness to even more explicit racism. Her colleague's confession of hostility and jealousy is in some ways an experience especially peculiar to a girl like her, who passes by default—whose body will be read according to limited white perceptions of who "looks black" if she does not explicitly realign them—and brings with it its own ethical challenges.[34]

Since the protagonist cannot control the gaze of others, she seeks to control her own by creating what bell hooks calls "the oppositional gaze" of females of color who would be spectators instead of spectacle.[35] Her doodling of herself is one such example, in which she is both seer and seen, an activity duplicated in a "doodle" (94) by Ivers Greene, whose doodle is Menchu, an ambiguous "poodle-monkey" (102) that he often draws into his photographs. He describes it as a watcher half in and half out of his pictures, as someone that "doesn't like labels" (102). The protagonist tries to bypass the other's gaze, to become the seer, to watch herself—even to the point of constructing her *own* doubles upon which to gaze in search of "true self-consciousness." The novel is crowded by "ambiguous" strangers who resemble and watch her, as well by Greta, who, too, seems in part conjured into existence by the protagonist.[36] Rather than yield self-consciousness, however, it leads to a political cul-de-sac.

Perhaps the vision of this double double consciousness—doubled consciousness—is best graphically rendered in the novel's pagination: it is a reverse mirroring: a signifying on doubling that leads to a vertiginous double vision that in turn can lead to a politically insightful double consciousness. This metacritical gesture is no easy feat, and the vertiginous process of trying to "see" race is enacted for readers in the book's sly reverse double pagination at the top of each page—one number printed backward on the page as if one were looking at it in a mirror, and then laid right next to it, on the same page, is the following number, which refers to the page opposite, left blank. The first impression is that it is a typing error; the second, equally mistaken, is that since they are laid side by side, one number is the mirror opposite of the next, but in fact it is not. Rather, each follows the other in standard sequence—although always one faces backward—yet even by the end of the book, one never gets over the subtle dizziness and hallucinatory effect of the layout, the feeling, as the protagonist puts it on that same page, that one is "dreaming." Naomi Baron invokes the canary metaphor that Senna also uses in *Caucasia* to describe the cultural function of mixed race:

How do you recognize a phenomenon that gives no visible trace? Miners working deep under the earth have long been aware that lethal gases they can neither see nor smell might spell sudden death. Their solution? The hapless canary. For if the caged bird they brought along into the mine succumbed to the silent killer, the miners knew to evacuate immediately. Only by the aftermath—the canary's demise—was the presence of danger established. Like gases in mines, changes in language are often difficult to document. . . . Punctuation is the canary.[37]

↛ | 5

my belongings into my Samsonite suitcase, stuffed my bed-
ding into a garbage bag, and wrote the housemistress a note.
I flew down the hall past bewildered housemates, shouting
good-bye over my shoulder, then disappeared into the mild
autumn air in a shining yellow cab.

The décor of his place was collegiate, preppy, hard angles
and minimal furniture and stacks of books like leaning tow-
ers in every corner. A framed portrait of President Lincoln,
something he'd picked up at a flea market, hung over his bed.
On his bookshelf was a stack of vinyl records—Miles Davis
stared down pensively, a witness to our coupling.

"Am I dreaming?" he asked. "I need to know."

"You're not dreaming. I'm really here."

"Prove it," he whispered.

FIGURE 4.1. Text capture to show pagination device in Danzy Senna, *Symptomatic: A Novel* (New York: Riverhead Books, 2004). From *Symptomatic* by
Danzy Senna, copyright © 2004 by Danzy Senna. Used by permission of Riverhead Books, an imprint of Penguin Group (USA) Inc. Reprinted by permission of
International Creative Management, Inc.

As in the novel, trying to divine racial affiliation by even the most studi-
ous *looking* also turns out to be just a tease. The text's play on punctuation in the page numbering is a warning, pointing not to the challenge of
divining race but to the invisible threat of a suffocating political malaise.
In Senna's *Caucasia*, the mixed race person is herself "the canary in the
coalmine . . . the gauge of how poisonous American race relations were"
(393). The "mulatto," like *Symptomatic*'s punctuation, is a political hi-
eroglyphic requiring a different kind of interpretive reading.

And this, finally, is one of the less visible calls to arms in *Symptomatic*: the need to move from watching (which leads only to crossed eyes)

to action, from spectatorship to participation, from staring to social recognition, especially if it enables the staree to look back. This is perhaps one of the richest opportunities for a progressive politics of mixed race, for it not only refigures one of the most common conditions of mixed race—being stared at—but it also remakes the common tendency to try to make race intelligible into an occasion to make race into an intelligence about oneself and an other. This involves a willingness to allow one to look back, and it is not an easy process for the protagonist, who has used journalistic detachment as a defense against always being the subject of the stare. She at first uses this explanation with her mother, saying that her profession as a journalist justifies her watching: "The sense I got of disappearing into other people's stories. Of watching and not being seen. Then and only then do the secrets reveal themselves to you" (6).

Her mother thinks her daughter's idea that disinterested observation can somehow lead to revelation is just "silly," and finds journalism, like all nonfiction, disingenuous because "there is no such thing as no agenda." She insists that even the magazine employing her daughter is suspicious because magazines "sustain the status quo in subtle, invidious ways. They keep us separated from each other, all the while homogenizing us into oblivion" (6). Her mother's critiques, uttered as she performs yoga asanas, are associated with a West Coast liberalism that at first seems tame in comparison to the vibrant East Coast, the "center of power," as she describes it. But in the end, the novel, in fact, does suggest that watching is a luxury, and a deceptive one at that, since people of mixed race are already politically implicated, as the protagonist discovers. Watching is a defensive response, in part, to the fact that, like many mixed race people, the protagonist is always stared at. The possibility for community and social change occurs only when *Symptomatic*'s protagonist gives up the indulgence of just looking, and with that, gives up what in the end amounts to political disengagement, of "disappearing—the delicious sense of my body fading into thin air and only my eyes remaining, two brown laser points observing somebody else's story but never being a part of it" (139). This could as easily be a description of the novel's readers as they might imagine themselves—cocooned, disembodied, reading another's story with putatively no need to become a part of it. *Symptomatic*, then, is also a critique of a readerly model that encourages or allows readers to remain at bay even if it does not outline the terms of engagement.

Looking, as a potent means for ethical interpersonal connection, exists *in potentia* in both *The Professor's Daughter* and *Symptomatic*. The glance, the look, the hope that one will, in fact, be seen and understood, is what prompts both protagonists to consider how others are seen and understood, to think beyond themselves—whether it is Emily's recognition that her rash tells history beyond herself, or whether it is the protagonist's recognition of the nannies, the cleaning women, the disabled. The affirmative gaze that these characters seek, and occasionally grant, also momentarily takes them out of a stupor that in both their cases seems at once existential and political, a condition of their being "paused" somehow in the world. Both novels suggest ways in which looking at mixed race bodies need not merely involve the more frequent hostile diagnosis or disbelief.

But neither are these anti-bildungsromans calls for great visibility and political recognition in the ways we have come to expect from civil rights groups. In fact, the brief moments of empathetic looking in the novels, charged as they are with possibility, represent an alternative to what Kobena Mercer calls the constant "problem of the visual" in which the modernist equation of "visibility and empowerment"—so important in the early to mid-twentieth century for ethnic minorities—has been turned on its head. As Mercer reminds us, drawing on Herman Gray's work on race in the media, a simple move from invisibility to hypervisibility does not necessarily work as a political aesthetic strategy in the postcolonial and post–civil rights era, for "even though media images of blackness are more visible than ever before, we witness the deepening of racial inequalities in U.S. politics as evidence of the structural decoupling of culture and politics" (158).[38] The global corporatization and commercialization of blackness have produced a "heightened visibility [which] appears to merely mask a growing sense of disenfranchisement and disillusionment with politics per se" (158). In contrast, *Symptomatic* and *The Professor's Daughter* explore the possibilities of a mediated sight—the readjusted view of "half-lit" communities—that emphasizes the processes of mutual recognition rather than (or as a precondition for) the politics of representation. The form and plot of these mixed race anti-bildungsromans, then, offer a refreshing counter to the premises of modernity inhering in European bildungsromans that do not imagine people of color as agents of progress. They represent a type of ethnic literature that does not explicitly dramatize protest, but *not* because, like early-twentieth-century writers, they are torn between the competing tensions between art for art's sake and art as politics. Rather, *Symptomatic* and *The Professor's Daughter* aesthetically enact the cultural suppression of civil rights issues; the absence in the text registers the absence of a political language or mandate at the turn of the new century.

Chapter Five explores the ways in which mutual recognition is both enriched and complicated by the fact that others' looking is always interested, that racial gazing is always deeply informed by investments in particular national narratives of history and memory. As Dave Chappelle's "The Racial Draft" and Carl Hancock Rux's *Talk* suggest, these narratives are often publicly staged, traded, and negotiated in a collaboration that is committed a priori to certain images and ideas about mixed race. The social theatricality of race—the tacit recognition of an always present audience in racial formation, and of the collaborative construction of racial identity—becomes the meta-content of the television show and dramatic play that I explore in this next chapter. If Raboteau's and Senna's works suggest that the productive stare at the mixed race person is sometimes an occasion for new understandings, Chappelle's and Rux's works make clear that such connections are never innocent: they are always motivated and shaped by the needs for certain kinds of stories that tropes of mixed race enable. These are powerful, historically reiterated stories that the nation tells about itself. That is not to say that these memorialized narratives over-determine the possibility for meaningful interpersonal connection and social change. The passing novel and the anti-bildungsroman take us beyond the photographic norming of the anthology and the individualism of the memoir; Chappelle and Rux show us how the collective negotiations over the meaning of mixed race, as fraught as they are by various investments, can lead to aesthetic experiments in racial representation that are both socially conscious and distinctively counter-visual.

CHAPTER FIVE

"They's mo' to bein' black than meets the eye!"

PERFORMING MIXED RACE IN
DAVE CHAPPELLE'S "THE RACIAL DRAFT"
AND CARL HANCOCK RUX'S *TALK*

IN 1970, Charles Edward Gordone's play *No Place to Be Somebody: A Black-Black Comedy in Three Acts* won the Pulitzer Prize for Drama, the first ever given to an African American and the first given to an off-Broadway play. *No Place to Be Somebody* is about a black bartender challenging a white mob syndicate, but it is also, more broadly, a meditation on what it means to be black. In a long spoken-word monologue, one of the central characters, Gabe, explains:

> They's mo' to bein' black than meets the
> eye!
> Bein' black, is like the way ya walk an'
> Talk!
> It's a way'a lookin' at life! . . .
> They's mo to bein' black than meets the
> eye![1]

Gabe is an actor too light-skinned to be cast as black and too black to be cast as white (often assumed to be a representative of Gordone himself, who faced similar challenges), so his injunction for a more-than-meets-the-eye blackness is also a test of racial casting. Being black, he intimates, requires its performance—it is enacted through ways of walking, ways of talking, ways of looking—that recognize preexisting racial codes and expectations for behavior but do not necessarily require their re-inscription. Certainly Gabe's comment reflects an understanding that blackness is something that is on display as well as something that can *dis*-play with a viewing audience expecting race to be presented in full view before their discerning eye and for their entertainment. "They's mo' to bein' black than meets the eye" suggests that appearance is insufficient to determine blackness, that the "mo'" of being black is actually backstage. Not out of sight necessarily, but not in the usual line of vision: as the Reverend in the Prologue to Ralph Ellison's *Invisible Man* famously puts it, "Now black is . . . an' black ain't."[2] In that same spirit, *No Place to Be Somebody* is a challenge to both the performer of and the audience for blackness, an effort to reorient sight so that determining race is not so much a matter of appearance but one of apprehension, not of visibility but of vision. As John Berger argues, "The way we see things is affected by what we know or what we believe."[3] In the play, the knowing that affects the seeing is constantly changing, and so Gabe's image of blackness evolves with it. Just as important, that seeing, as Berger suggests, is always relational: "We never look at just one thing; we are always looking at the relation between things and ourselves" (9). Mixed race prompts us to consider that race, too, is an image that is never perceived as "one thing" or the possession of just one person. Rather, mixed race functions as a relation among things and people.

In the previous chapter I explore alternatives to the usual emplotments of identity development and social engagement in the mixed race anti-bildungsroman; in this chapter, I consider two dramatic stagings of mixed race in which these debates about identity as relational and social refigure some of the most cherished public rituals of national memory. Focusing on one of the most popular television episodes, "The Racial Draft" (2004),[4] from *The Dave Chappelle Show* by the renowned comedian/producer Dave Chappelle, and the Obie-award-winning play *Talk* (2002), by celebrated poet/playwright/novelist/essayist Carl Hancock Rux, I examine how both productions enact debates about mixed race that occasion a re-visioning and a re-membering of the national order. Both productions turn the eye to the way race both indexes and establishes relations of all sorts—personal, social, professional, economic, political—and to how mixed race is a negotiation among many differently invested and differently empowered parties. In both cases, the critiques about the global commercialization and academic professionalization of mixed race are not the end but the beginning of Chappelle's and Rux's efforts to clear ground in order to go beyond the narrow protocols of "black representational space,"[5] so often confined by expectations of people of all colors who are invested in historically specific notions of racial art.

"The Racial Draft" and *Talk* are most keenly alert to how these relations are arbitrated by self-appointed experts whose business it is to parse racial value, to deliberate placement, and whose own professional status depends on the exercise of this judgment. At the center of both format and plot in Chappelle's and Rux's productions are panels of judges gathered to assess the meaning of race and identity prompted by the interpretive dilemma posed by persons of mixed race (See Fig C.4). This crisis of determining race, Chappelle and Rux suggest, is in many ways a red herring marshaled for entertainment—institutionalized and professionalized as a blood sport in both athletics and academe. The business and pleasure of settling who's who racially involves attributing value and wielding arbitrary power. Most importantly, both Rux and Chappelle make clear that the rules of the game encourage turning a blind eye to historical injustices or exploitation because the respective evaluators, invested in deliberating merit and ranking involved in "settling the question" of race, are never neutral arbitrators. These "deciders" often have their own reputations to uphold and so are less than disinterested in certain racial outcomes, their assessments motivated by a plethora of personal and institutional concerns.[6] And despite their pontificating and deliberating, the question of racial ambiguity is never resolved. Its resolution, in fact, is beside the point, as both *Talk* and "The Racial Draft" critique the way race has become a commercial enterprise in which hand-wringing about racial choice and categorization tends to distract from questions of equity and aesthetic expression.

Significantly, as I will explore in this chapter, although mixed race is the explicit occasion for and central source of anxiety in both productions, "The Racial Draft" and *Talk* choose generally *not* to represent mixed race onstage as part of their cultural re-visioning. This blacking out of mixed race, I explain, paradoxically opens up an important conceptual space that foregrounds, as Darby English puts it in *How to See a Work of Art in Total Darkness*, "racial blackness's ultimately discursive character . . . blackness as it is relationally defined and erratically constituted."[7] Like the art installations that English examines, race in "The Racial Draft" and *Talk*—untethered to any freestanding, straitjacketing notion of "black culture"—is understood as "public, participatory, and thereby perpetually innovated" (3). In "The Racial Draft" and *Talk*, real-life figures Mariah Carey, Halle Berry, and Lenny Kravitz, as well as the fictional character Aymes, are referenced but never seen. (Notably, Tiger Woods, played by Chappelle, does appear in "The Racial Draft," but his depiction relies more on iconic attire associated with golf prowess—Nike hat, golf shirt, golf glove, golf club—to signify Woods than any effort to represent mixedness. As I explore later in the chapter, this kind of racial marking makes clear that the physical body of the mixed race person is not the site of racial intelligibility. By largely opting out of the racial eye-balling of the mixed race body, Rux's and Chappelle's works represent an artistic response very different from nineteenth- and twentieth-century figurations of the mixed figure in literature, film, and drama. These earlier media tend to dwell long on the body, hair, face, and sound of the mixed race person. By absenting the mixed race body altogether from the scene, Rux and Chappelle deny the eye's demand that it parse the mixed race body and redirect the gaze from skin, color, and physiognomy to the social, historical, and artistic questions that both raise.

I. PLAYBOOKS AND PLAYSCRIPTS OF RACE IN "THE RACIAL DRAFT"

Born after the civil rights era and critical of many of its pieties and legacies, Chappelle gained popularity among the under-35 crowd. *The Dave Chappelle Show* on Comedy Central's cable channel was the network's top-watched show in 2004; the DVD of the show's first season was the top-grossing DVD of any television series to date. Held up as an icon of what Nelson George calls the "post-soul" epoch,[8] Chappelle is allied with the unofficial site for post-soul, Okayplayer (okayplayer.com), the cutting-edge online community of neo-soul musicians, artists, MC's, and DJ's known for their experimentations with black cultural expression and pop-cultural critique.[9] One particular episode of *The Dave Chappelle Show*, "The Racial Draft," offers a sly send-up of the racial tug-of-war over mixed race celebrity-hood. What we need, Chappelle claims—after explaining that he and his Filipina wife argue over whether "Cablinasian" Tiger Woods' athletic gifts come from his black or Asian side—is a procedure, a "draft," that identifies those of multiple racial heritage "once and for all." Set up in the genre of a sports show newscast, a panel of suited "experts" provides commentary in "real

FIGURE 5.1. "The Racial Draft," Dave Chappelle and Neal Brennan, writers/ producers. Originally aired on Comedy Central network, October 2004.

time" on the Racial Draft, which is modeled on the hype and suspense of the televised drafts for the National Football League—we hear the rousing NFL theme song in the background—and the National Basketball Association. With Chappelle performing the roles of "draft prospect" Tiger Woods, a white draft representative, and himself as a sports commentator, participants are happily traded from one monoracial group to another: Tiger Woods is claimed as "100% Black"; "the Jews" get Lenny Kravitz; "the Asian" delegation drafts the black hip-hop group Wu-Tang Clan; Condoleezza Rice is eagerly traded to the whites as part of the Colin Powell deal; the white group gets to keep white rapper Eminem by returning O. J. Simpson to the blacks. Significantly, no one kind of mix is culturally weighted or guarantees a draft selection outcome—thus no relevance is given to the fact that the Asian-Black Woods goes black while the Jewish-Black Kravitz goes Jewish, foregrounding the sense that in subsequent rounds the draft of both could go another way.

"The Racial Draft" exploits commercial culture by signifying on the medium itself: Chappelle's show is on the show of race. And by self-consciously foregrounding the spectacular nature of race itself, he invites us to question the spectacle. In particular, the performances of racial identity make visible the production of blackness as it emerges from the debates about mixedness and as it informs national rituals of identity. The episode is not just making light of race by making sport of it; rather, it uses the metaphor of sports to speak to the way race *is*, in fact, very much a national game, pastime, hobby, and public spectacle reenacted annually. "The Racial Draft" recognizes race as prime-time entertainment even as the real-life drama of race, as many have noted, is avidly watched in the news (O. J.), in courtrooms (Clarence Thomas/Anita Hill), and in the streets (1992 L.A. riots).[10] Many scholars have noted the ends to which the media spectacle of race has been put; Chappelle's "Racial Draft" is a metacritical comment on the cultural processes of specularization itself. The *Show* uses the metaphor, ironically, to foreground these literal realities; and in that sense, the literary conceit indexes actual social practices, calls the "plays" on the field, arguably better than any non-metaphorical accounting could.

"The Racial Draft" stands in for real life to the extent that its format graphically replicates the way we are all implicated in the game, for it situates everyone as racialized subjects both in the show *and* outside of it. It does this in several ways. First is the complex, nested format of this particular episode—*The Dave Chappelle Show* works within the draft ESPN-style "show," and within that, the action onstage as candidates are drafted, all of which operate as a visual extension of the sports metaphor and as meta-commentary on the racial scene. So, for instance, the panel of experts (two whites and Chappelle as requisite token) reflects the disproportionate number of white surveyors of the racial action "downstairs" onstage or on the playing field. The panel suggests that for the most part whites are the experts, blacks and people of color the object of their expertise. People of color play the game, but white people putatively understand it: they are the connoisseurs, the evaluators, the arbiters of race. The white panelists bring us "color," which in sports broadcasting euphemistically refers to the biographical tidbits, the detailed interpretation of just completed action on the playing surface, or the revelation of the players' off-field activities, but which in "The Racial Draft" refers literally to *people* of color. "We" are cast as both the fictional audience in the skit *and* the audience watching *The Dave Chappelle Show* on television—watching and enjoying at once both scenes, replicating our double position as voyeur and participant as we observe but also identify with both the *Show* and the show-within-the-show, identifying variously and unevenly perhaps with the panelists, the delegations, and the draftees. As in the "real" NFL draft, the expert panel must wait with the audience to hear the draft picks; they are our proxy at such moments. Like the implied and actual audiences, they offer their guesses and are often proved wrong. Their roles are carefully scripted to appear, paradoxically, improvised.

Ironically, though, the actual cast at times *did* improvise and go off script during the live taping of the show. We find this out from the audio commentary that accompanies the Season 2 DVD, in which Chappelle and the other writer/producer of the *Show*, Neal Brennan, discuss this and other episodes. This spontaneous improvisation not only frets the distinction between "live" and rehearsed time, embedding the audience in the action; it also upends what might be called "hierarchies of knowing." These hierarchies are associated with concentric time frames: the sense that Chappelle and his *Show* are in the "now" and "in the know," and that he and it frame the boundaries of the "The Racial Draft" such that the episode operates within a subordinate, if parallel, space and time of the imagination. "We" are supposedly situated in Chappelle's more knowing "now," at a comfortable remove from and putatively entertained by those seemingly less knowledgeable (at least of the presence of an "us" observing them). But the improvisation breaks down that comfortable hierarchy, for it reveals that even those supposedly most "in the know" (such as the show's producers) are at times ignorant—Brennan at one point in the audio commentary twice confesses to Chappelle that he does not understand a couple of the racial jokes, even casually wonders if one of the quips is "racist." Such commentary between Chappelle and Brennan unwittingly reproduces the racial drama they are watching—perhaps even some of the tension that led to Chappelle's frustration with the *Show*, since many of the racial in-jokes Brennan does not "get," but still admits to laughing at, are precisely those that might enlighten a white audience.

II. THE SPACE-TIME OF RACE

As I suggest above, time itself is not just telescoped; it is collapsed, as the show-within-the-*Show* gives us simultaneous putatively live broadcasts—the staged live of the draft merges with the semi-scripted live of the panel, which in turn merges with the living viewing audience shown supposedly in real time on the *Show*—not to mention the audience watching Chappelle on television or on video at any given time. The audience (both in and outside the show) are also *fans* and as in the real racial draft, this fan-audience also lives and dies for their team, feels as though their fate is linked with the outcomes. These distinctions between the two audiences within and the one implied without, between the panel and the "live" draft and between Chappelle as show host–qua sports expert–qua everyday black man, quickly slip and merge in the simultaneous present of the theater. As S. E. Wilmer argues, this is characteristic of "stage space," which is always "simultaneously historical, contemporary, and imaginary such that mythical and stereotypical figures can co-occupy it and engage with more realistic figures, both living and dead."[11] The apparatuses of the show work against passive spectatorship, for the palimpsest of time-spaces and characters implicates everyone, including Chappelle. Chappelle is not so much playing different characters at different times as he is inhabiting at once the multiple and always racialized subject positions that he always must: he may be the privileged insider—either as head of his own show or as a panel "expert"—but he is also, as I will discuss, the black butt of the white commentators' racial digs more than once. Building on Joseph Roach's theory of surrogation, the *Show* stands in for real life.[12] But one has to ask who is surrogating for whom in "The Racial Draft," for its transparent paralleling of audiences, of time frames, and of racial scenes does not so much substitute representation for real life as it uses representation to sharpen focus on the real-life politics of race.

III. RACE TO THE NTH DEGREE

Chappelle gives us the opportunity to re-see race, in part, by rendering it hyberbolically visible. The exaggerated typecasting of socially iconic representatives (Puerto Ricans for Latinos; Chinese for Asians; Hassidim for Jews; 1970s Blaxploitation/Funk for Blacks—amusingly played by rapper Mos Def) who purportedly speak for the entire "race" all too obviously mark each group. To play the "Jew," an actor dresses as a conservative Hassidic, with side curls and yarmulke. Chappelle himself plays the white representative: in chalky whiteface, a cheap six-dollar wig, a stilted, flat affect—he makes no attempt at verisimilitude. His whiteface is quite self-consciously not about resemblance at all; it's about *dis*semblance, an explicit caricature, a drawing of attention to the representation rather than the real. The performative dimension of race in the draft is one of the most self-reflexive elements in the show, a comment on the artifices of race. As Harry Elam, Jr., argues, "The inherent 'constructedness' of performance and the malleability of the devices of the theater serve to reinforce the theory that blackness, specifically, and race, in general, are hybrid, fluid concepts whose meanings depend upon the social, cultural and historical conditions of their use."[13] The fluid and historically specific artifices of race have everything to do with the real lived experience of race, not least because they inform how we experience, and even perceive, race. Even the recognition of color as a significant distinction requires certain visual competencies and social contexts to register, an idea suggested by the Chappelle-qua-commentator's comment about Woods "looking blacker already" as soon as he is drafted as Black. Racial identity in "The Racial Draft" is distinguished not so much by self-evident bodily marks as by sartorial shorthand, social positioning, linguistic codes, and economic consequence. And all of these in the episode denaturalize the way that, as Linda Alcoff puts it, "social systems of exclusion and discrimination operate" through "visible identities, naturalized as marked on the body without mediation" (165).[14] Instead what is made visible in this episode is those racialized systems of exclusion and discrimination, the ways the playing field of race is rendered uneven and unequal.

IV. FREE AGENTS AND OPEN AUCTIONS

One of the most important ways the episode makes these things visible is by using the metaphor of an NFL draft as a kind of corrective lens for those who would myopically see mixed race as a choice, a personal exercise of free will that is free of those systems. The episode treats as naïve romance the idea that race is, or even should be, merely about self-selection. Sacking the near-sacred myth of identity as a wholly private affair, "The Racial Draft" does not for a moment indulge the idea that being "mixed race" or any race is, was, or even should be, solely about individual self-definition. It certainly lays waste to founding documents of the mixed race movement that assert individuals' absolute autonomy over their racial identification.[15] After all, a draft takes as a given that your identity and status are the pick of authorized others. As in the NBA or NFL, being drafted means someone else owns the rights to you. Indeed, the episode suggests that racial identity is a public commodity with a value decided according to certain protocols—according to the "rules of the game," as it were. Furthermore, drafts (be they sport-wise or even military) are formal agreements that bring with them mutual responsibilities, duties to fulfill in addition to rewards to receive. This all makes the concept of racial belonging in the skit a double entendre, since belonging in "The Racial Draft" is both an affective and a contractual relation, not entirely unlike the quasi-legal sense of responsibilities that people of color often feel in relation to their community.[16] "The Racial Draft," therefore, does not so much collapse the twin discourses of kinship and race as it exploits the fact that they are already yoked. That Chappelle's interracial marriage is the occasion for this episode is especially significant, since the stakes for him are at once familial and political: Chappelle's own biracial children are, by implication, the ones being drafted.

But the staging of the "draft" also uncomfortably evokes an uglier cousin the slave auction, with its similar traffic in the sale of bodies. It is, after all, primarily the draftees' flesh that excites financial interest. They are reduced to the sum of their parts—legs, arms, muscles, and sinew all evaluated and savored for their potential to perform—and to the calculation of their statistical profile. In football, for instance, weight, girth, how many repetitions of 225 pounds one can lift, how fast one can run the forty-yard dash, how high the vertical leap, all represent the individual's "goods." Even the Wonderlic Test, administered to draftees to test their ability to understand plays, measures only a narrow skill set and, furthermore, tends to racialize "instinct" (read: black) from "intellect" (read: white).[17] This traffic is not only commercial but also prurient in nature, those sold offering the purchasers both erotic and economic potential: as one of the white commentators (Robert Petkoff) notes in response to a suggestion that Oprah Winfrey be claimed by the whites (a high proportion of her viewing audience is white women), that she has "thick thighs" and "no felonies" and, therefore, would be a "great pick-up." The sports patois, "pick-up," refers simply to who is picked in the draft, but it also suggest that Oprah is available as a sexual score, and by implication that all the other players—male and female—are as well. The "pickup" is a nod to the hetero- and homoerotics on the playing field *and* in draft team headquarters where the deal-making takes place. The draftees are offered up for bidding as objects of desire whose own desirous interests matter very little in the draft.

So what of those who wish to resist society's and one's parents' racial desires and ascriptions? Is race entirely over-determined by others? Among the most hostile and sustained criticisms of the episode were those of mixed race bloggers and online forums, who felt that Chappelle, like Aaron McGruder, was taking away their racial rights, that the draft celebrates compulsory racial conscription.[18] It appears to offer a confirmation of all the fears and resentments of those who cry oppression by society's monoracialist bias.[19] And, in fact, in "The Racial Draft," a separate mixed race identity is not on the table, as it were; there is no distinct delegation of mixed race advocates bidding for the players. Draftees have no choice in their selection; nor are they portrayed as even wanting one. "The Racial Draft" does not give the slightest nod to any of what Alcoff calls the "three possible ways to name and characterize mixed race identity: 1) as a generic "mixed" identity; 2) as a mixed identity of a specific type, such as mestizo; 3) as a combinatory identity straddling two or more identities" (282). In fact, the entire question, so often raised by mixed race advocacy groups, about the need for racial self-determination is given no airtime in the show. One wonders why this omission, why even the possibility of a distinct mixed race identity and delegation is eclipsed, especially after the addition in the 2000 Census of the "mark one or more" category and all the political chatter about it (something Chappelle and his writers could hardly have missed). But "The Racial Draft" is not simply mimetic; it is diagnostic: there is no space devoted to a hybrid constituency because in the show's logic no one can really opt out of the racial rules altogether. Race is not a solo performance or a rebel act of free will, "The Racial Draft" implies; everyone is already implicated (including Chappelle himself), and thus race cannot simply be transcended, certainly not by personal fiat. Furthermore, even if there were a separate voting contingent of mixed race people, there is no reason to think it would change any of the game rules; it might merely add an additional lobby without changing any of the terms by which race is bargained.

This idea that one cannot opt out of the draft is highlighted by the career of mixed race actor Vin Diesel, conspicuously not mentioned in "The Racial Draft." Vin Diesel declares himself a free agent in his film short, *Multi-Facial*, suggesting that he is outside all this racial rigmarole by marketing himself as capable of performing any and all races. In 1994, the struggling actor self-produced the quasi documentary, later accepted for the 1995 Cannes Film Festival. The film is both guileless enactment and self-conscious commentary of the commercial dilemmas for actors who do not fit the racial stereotypical roles allotted by Hollywood casting agencies. It shows Diesel fruitlessly going from actor's call to actor's call, trying unsuccessfully to enact the racial stereotypes requested by the writers and producers: a black street thug, a Latino wife-beater, and so on, a dilemma historically shared by many light-skinned actors, including, as I mentioned, Gabe in *No Place to Be Somebody*. At first Vin Diesel appears merely to be merging the script of the tragic mulatto ("woe is me; I fit in nowhere") with a social critique of Hollywood racial typecasting. With his producing partner, George Zakk, he runs One Race Productions, whose very name suggests that race distinctions should matter little. But arguably *Multi-Facial* merely markets mulattohood in the service of typecasting, capitalizing on therapeutic discourses of self-help to make a shameless commercial appeal: "hire me and I can be any race you want me to be." In fact, since the film, he has openly touted a racially ambiguous identity, refusing in the press to declare his race, although his official website reveals him as "biracial"—African American/Italian American.

This bid to financially benefit from the versatility of mixed race is part of a larger trend, appearing in some of the articles in the Seattle-based national magazine *Mavin: The Intelligent Magazine of the Mixed*

Race Experience, for example, which speculate on the market value of your "exotic" image in the media—the spring 2000 issue of *Mavin* offers headline articles, "Cashing In on That Mixed-Race Look" and "Exotica Erotica: The Multiracial Woman," which acknowledges the long history of exoticizing women of mixed descent only to conclude that we must not be "arrogant" because indeed, mixed race women are "beautiful, different, mysterious" (37). In the barely tongue-in-cheek "Mulattos for Dummies" in the Spring 1999 edition of *Mavin*, James Kerrin says, "It's high time that we mixed folks stop trying to be 'righteously race-less' for a moment and capitalize on what has become a national obsession. (I am still kicking myself that I didn't push the 'Cablinasian Ken Doll' idea to Mattel immediately after the Masters.) The combination of self-help and mulatto mystique is certain to make one of us rich. Now who's gonna step up to the plate and exploit ourselves?" (13). In this sense, commercialism has dovetailed with the often crusading dimension to many of these contemporary multiethnic publications as the voice of a "new age." Indeed, Vin Diesel refers to himself as just such a success story: reportedly, *Multi-Facial* caught Steven Spielberg's attention and landed the actor a role in *Saving Private Ryan* as an Italian soldier.

But here, too, though Vin Diesel's "mixed race identity" may be lucrative, it is no end run around the game of race. Quite the contrary: "free agency" is perfectly accommodated by "The Racial Draft," just as being a free agent in the NFL draft is one of many positions within the system rather than any counter to it. Free agency is understood to be provisional and circumstantial, both on the turf and in the field of late-night television. In fact, in the NFL, those who opt to be a free agent ironically tend to have fewer, not more, options than those who do not.

Yet, as a companion to this indictment of race as individual choice or self-invention—of those who imagine that they, unlike everyone else, have an opt-out clause in the racial and social ordering of the world—"The Racial Draft" also renders a scathing indictment of the mercurial investments of monoracial groups. Their bickering and bartering is largely represented as silly partisanship: each group only trying to lay claim to the fame or prestige of anyone they can associate with. It seems a vulgar battle in which each group is self-interested, complete with its own cheering section and "nationalist" banners and 1970s-era rhetoric. They seem antithetical to Neal's "post soul babies" representing that generation of people who have no "nostalgic allegiance to the past (back in the days of Harlem, or the thirteenth-century motherland, for that matter) but are firmly in the grasp of the existential corners of this brave new world."[20]

But "The Racial Draft" does not, finally, represent race as a relic of the "old world" with outdated imperatives. It makes an important distinction between race as a mere marketplace commodity animated by coarse speculation and the acknowledgment that race is a social negotiation informed by legitimate need. That is, Chappelle certainly does critique the mercantile element to ethnic and racial groups' lobbying, yet he also simultaneously validates many of the groups' monoracialist reasons *for* lobbying. Chappelle's satire of how race is marketed, commercialized, and sold gets at the structural and institutional bases for racial inequity in ways that calls for "right to choose" with regard to one's race do not begin to address. The episode's critical insight into the economics of race is the very heart of the show's humor and social analysis, for the recognition in "The Racial Draft" that race involves more than personal choice is not so much to concede the system of racial attribution that is in place as it is to enable an indictment of the valuations underwriting it. For instance, we hear from the black commentator (Chappelle)—who catches the news flash through his earpiece—that Tiger Woods immediately loses all his national sponsors once he is drafted as unequivocally black.[21] No one on the panel is surprised. The loss of sponsorship, an American audience well knows, is the potential flip side to Woods' commercial success. The loss of sponsorship as a racial (versus athletic) issue was always present in the marketing of Woods. We see it, for instance, in the American Express ads that have featured Woods embracing his Asian mother on the golf course, foregrounding the credit card mogul's putatively pan-racial embrace of its clients. Ironically there is an earlier, complementary ad showing Woods embracing his black father. That son-and-father hug seems to hail black nationalism, the triumph of black people in the historically racist world of golf, but also risks appearing narrowly political when positioned against the later ad with the mother-son Thai-black kiss.

In another example, the Latino constituency preemptively tries to claim Elián Gonzales as one of their own. A white moderator says he is confused, saying the boy is "already" Latino, but the spokesperson for the group insists they want to draft him before the whites try to, a defensive move recognizing that particularly sympathetic and telegenic children will be assimilated as white, that some people of color are more desirable than others (at least at certain times and places)—referencing the privileged status of the Cuban refugee population who emigrated to the United States during the Cold War—and that whites might raid another race for certain politically useful members.[22] Significantly, the Latinos in "The Racial Draft" are represented as an "ethnorace," to use Goldberg's term, because, as Alcoff argues, there is, finally, little metaphysical or political point in distinguishing between race and ethnicity (229, 240); race in this context is better understood as indexing shifting collaborations in the context of racialization than as explaining internal cultural and regional diversity (241). The Latino constituency, after all, votes as a united block without in any way minimizing their internal hybridity: their representative sports not only a bright shawl and an "attitude," but also the Puerto Rican national flower (the Flor de Maga) *and* a necklace with a Cuban flag pendant. The Latinos perceive whites' taking Elián to their bosom as a hostile act, an empty gesture of largesse that is discontinuous with the wider interests of some in the Latino community (adopting a motherless child from Cuba does not automatically translate into greater cross-cultural understanding or political support for programs like bilingual education in schools, and so on).

Thus what may at first seem like the fixed, self-evident nature of the groups, manifested by the flattened, two-dimensional, stereotypical "look" of each, is undermined by each group's compositional volatility and shifting collaborations. In short, Chappelle is not simply challenging the viability of mixed race identification by recalling outdated civil rights–era racial profiles. For this same reason, it is important to note that despite the typing and the clear race-based alliances in the groups participating in the draft, no simple notion of race or of racial fealty is advanced. The Wu-Tang Clan members—who named their group after the 1981 Hong Kong martial art film, *Saho Lin and Wu Tang*—appear simply thrilled to "become" Asian, for instance, when selected. The show assumes from the outset that the race debate is not about metaphysics or biology but about competing interests and associations.

This movement across and within racial-ethnic lines also generates anxiety, however, for racial crossovers are often informed by and yet willfully blind to the economic and political costs. It is no accident that the black people drafted into some other ethnic or racial group trouble the limits of blackness: the Wu-Tang Clan[23] reflects the commercial crossover of hip-hop music; the Hassidim have been a flashpoint for Black-Jewish tensions since the Crown Heights incident in Brooklyn (memorialized by Anna Deavere Smith's *Fires in the Mirror* [1992]); Elián Gonzales has come to be a flashpoint for the ongoing political fallout between black "natives" versus immigrants. The episode, I argue, does not demonize racial lobbies and their recruitment of members, because it recognizes that race is already so often about entertainment, about commerce, about the economic values associated with, and differentials between, races. Thus racial identity, complex and shifting as it may be, is not simply waved aside as unimportant; nor is racial experience, however it may vary, merely dismissed as irrelevant to understanding how society works. "The Racial Draft" offers in the same moment both a critique of *and* a competing, cogent justification for why people have been, and continue to be, committed to race for both pragmatic and intellectual reasons.

Part of the basis for this justification comes from the episode's implication that monoracially identified groups are not simply 1970s throwbacks, blindly committed to the one-drop rule. Race in "The Racial Draft" is a "doing," not a done deed, not some given characteristic or blood inheritance. It must be *performed*, must be enacted and continuously renewed, reaffirmed, reasserted; its boundaries are historically elastic and adaptable to needs or interests. And sometimes these boundaries are up for challenge by other interested parties: as in the case of the Gonzales draft, race must be reaffirmed preemptively lest it be stolen, appropriated, or, as in the case of Colin Powell, come "under review," or as in the trade of O. J. Simpson, deemed "white" then "black again" when traded back to the blacks so the whites can keep Eminem. Simpson and Powell are of interest to whites because they represent what Herman Gray calls "exceptional blackness," blackness understood to be in the service of whiteness. To say that race is performative, therefore, does mean that any person of color can be white or vice versa, that somehow racial identity, untethered by biology, is interchangeable, a free-market item to be traded arbitrarily. Rather, the saliency of race emerges within the context of bargaining, negotiation, and cultural expectation that makes sense of and gives importance to racialized performances.[24]

V. MAKING WHITE

In fact, "The Racial Draft" makes clear that whites, too, act as a collective, interested group. This refusal to leave whiteness unmarked or to let whites be a neutral observer in the draft is made even more explicit by the way the panel's comments reflect the individual's peculiar racial orientation. This orientation is established from the outset when one of the white commentators responds to Chappelle's opening comment ("Wow,

FIGURE 5.2. "The Racial Draft," Dave Chappelle and Neal Brennan, writers/ producers. Originally aired on Comedy Central network, October 2004.

FIGURE 5.3. "The Racial Draft," Dave Chappelle and Neal Brennan, writers/ producers. Originally aired on Comedy Central network, October 2004.

that's the first lottery a black person's won in a long time, Billy") by say- ing "Yes, and they will probably still complain." Then later when O. J. is traded back to the blacks, the white panelists do a private "dap dap" hand gesture of pleasure in white solidarity. Their handshake operates as an iron sign of the cultural appropriation of black cool at the same time it hints at a collective white mentality that is cynical about ever satisfying black complaints about inequities; the second evokes a white identity relieved to be rid of not only a black man whose accused crime is the murder of a white woman but also the very fact of his marriage to her. Giving O. J. back to the blacks seems the climax of the effort to visually "blacken" him on the *Newsweek* cover.[25] It racializes both of the white commentators and further distinguishes them from the black commentator (Chappelle), who glimpses the "dap dap" in his peripheral vision and merely shakes his head as if to acknowledge it's the "same ol', same ol'," suggesting his own cynicism about ever reforming white perspectives.

This attention to white racial performances emerges as a central feature of the episode. But, as Alcoff speculates, given whites' heightened access to visibility and the power it wields, whiteness should be made even *more* visible (205). Would visibility work towards encouraging a progressive white identity, she wonders? Might whites cultivate what she calls a *white* "double consciousness"? (223). In her argument, this double consciousness is not entirely symmetrical with the Du Boisian definition but her equation is appealing, especially if we adapt an often overlooked aspect of Du Bois' version, the idea that even if double consciousness interrupts self-knowledge, it also brings with it the "gift of second sight," uniquely privileged insight into others' perceptual apparatuses, which are then codified into social institutions. This means double consciousness is not merely private angst over what others think of oneself but, more profoundly, an enlightened, if sobering, recognition of one's social and institutional positioning, which is perhaps necessary, if not sufficient, for the beginning of personal self-reflection and social change.

I would suggest that this "second sight" is dramatized for whites in "The Racial Draft": they are given a rare opportunity to see themselves as others see them, and that can be the beginning of an "acknowledgement of the historical legacy of white identity constructions in the persistent structures of inequality and exploitation" (223). White people in "The Racial Draft," for instance, are not just made visible to others; they are potentially made visible to themselves, albeit at a distance. The very fact that the white people in the show *exaggerate* certain white attitudes may enable a kind of attenuated identification (white people may sense a resemblance to their own positions but not identify to the extent that they cannot still distance themselves as the subject of the joke) that skirts defensiveness while still implicating them. White people, furthermore, are not just always made visible as the all-powerful default: if the white sports commentators seem to be unimpeached in their sense of superiority when the white representative appears onstage to claim his draft, white authority *is* made absurd. The white spokesperson is booed by the audience as he steps forward, is frustrated because no one will listen to him since he takes for granted that white privilege demands deference ("Hey, a white man is speaking!" he blusters), is portrayed as blindly incompetent because he cannot speak the language of the "natives" ("Ungawa!" he cries to the jeering crowd of constituencies of color, mimicking Tarzan's mumbo-lingo when he tried to speak "African"), and is seen as pathetically self-deceived when he chides as "childish" the black representative for trying to trip him onstage, then boasting like a juvenile and without irony that he himself cannot be tricked because *he* is the "biggest hustler."[26]

In that sense, *The Dave Chappelle Show* makes race visible in a way that does *not* simply, as he says, "decide once and for all" racial identification (though he claims it will at the show's outset), but rather makes it an invitation to ongoing interpretation, a potential social heuristic. Although I am cautious about the transformative potential of commercial television and popular culture as a site for social change, I do think that "The Racial Draft" brings to light and to the screen the idea that race is not simply an imposition to shed or a legal fiction to dismiss; instead, people of color are bonded not only by social oppression but also by the opportunity for social insight.

VI. SLIPPING THE YOKE:
HUMOR AND SOCIAL CHANGE

America is a land of masking jokers. We wear the mask for purposes of aggression as well
as for defense; when we are projecting the future and preserving the past. In short, the
motives hidden behind the mask are as numerous as the ambiguities the mask conceals.

Ralph Ellison, "Change the Joke and Slip the Yoke"[27]

But just what are the transformative potentials and political possibilities for comedy television shows like Chappelle's to, as Ellison put it, "change the joke and slip the yoke"? There are, on the one hand, so many limitations to the genre and the technological form of television that many have seen it as politically bankrupt despite its power. Chappelle's breakdown after his second season—in which he reportedly walked away from a $52 million contract and disappeared to South Africa without telling anyone (including his wife) in 2005—is a case in point. Chappelle has explained his sudden exit as a response to his fear that his jokes are inadvertently reinforcing racist dogma rather than advancing social commentary. In an interview with Chappelle, *Time* reporter Christopher John Farley characterizes his rationale for his flight to Durban as what he describes as a "spiritual retreat": white people "started laughing at the wrong jokes for the wrong reasons at the wrong times."[28] He has specifically referred to a November 2004 taping of a sketch about magic pixies that embody stereotypes about the races:

The black pixie—played by Chappelle—wears blackface and tries to convince blacks to act in stereotypical ways. Chappelle thought the sketch was funny, the kind of thing his friends would laugh at. But at the taping, one spectator, a white man, laughed particularly loud and long. His laughter struck Chappelle as wrong, and he wondered if the new season of his show had gone from sending up stereotypes to merely reinforcing them. "When he laughed, it made me uncomfortable," says Chappelle. "As a matter of fact, that was the last thing I shot before I told myself I gotta take f_____ time out after this. Because my head almost exploded."

This anxiety about the line between racial send-up and racist reinforcement was dismissed by his cowriter, Brennan, who claims "indecisiveness" was Chappelle's only problem:

Dave would change his sketches so much, and it just got to the point that the show never would have aired if he had his way. . . . He would come with an idea, or I would come with an idea, pitch it to him, and he'd say that's funny. And from there we'd write it. He'd love it, say, "I can't wait to do it." We'd shoot it, and then at some point he'd start saying, "This sketch is racist, and I don't want this on the air." And I was like, "You like this sketch. What do you mean?" There was this confusing contradictory thing: he was calling his own writing racist.[29]

Clearly, Chappelle was not allowed to question controversial material once under way, and Brennan turns that against him, suggesting it is Chappelle's own writing that is racist, even as he makes clear that the pitch is frequently Brennan's. Thus despite the fact that Chappelle is purportedly in control of the content of his program, he cannot fully control its collaborative development (in fact Brennan implies that Chappelle should *not* have "his own way") or its political reception.

The case of the short-lived *The Richard Pryor Show* is an eerily simi-lar precedent for some of the difficulties of commercial artistic venues for social critique and influence, because even though the performer had titular claim to it, *The Richard Pryor Show* (1977) turned out not to be his show at all. Pryor, after leaving a successful gig on *The Ed Sullivan Show* doing what he called "white bread humor," eventually landed a lucrative NBC contract for *The Richard Pryor Show*. But, slotted during a designated "Family Hour," opposite *Happy Days* and *Laverne and Shirley*, and highly censored, the show received miserable ratings and he completed only four of the ten contracted episodes. Extremely frustrated and reportedly in tears over his lack of control over the time slot and the program's content, the comedian told his new staff, "I don't *want* to be on TV. I'm in a trap. I can't do this." As Billy Ingram reports it, the show's writers "tried to convince him that he could do something special on television, and labored for days trying to convince the comedian to change his mind and go forward with the show."[30] The contrast between the great hope that the public reach of television offers, as recommended by the writers—the idea that one can do something "special" in that medium—and the impotence experienced by Pryor, the feeling that he could do nothing at all against the media industry and its bureaucratic machinery, is representative of many critical discussions about television's potential (or lack of it) for social critique and transformation.

More generally, those binaries between idealized optimism and dis-missive cynicism inform debates about the role of popular art and cul-ture as sites for social change. On the one hand, there was the belief that network television's historic move to give a show to a black man suggested an unprecedented level of black artistic and financial control. It hinted at political shifts in the country's racial attitudes. Like any black performer following the steps of Bert Williams, Dick Gregory, and other commercially successful and socially insightful performers of color, Pryor was certainly not naïve about the constraints and compro-mises involved with working in the entertainment industry, but here it seemed that the show could be a unique personal vehicle through which he could both advance his own career and operate more freely as social critic—ostensibly the best of both worlds in which he could merge self-

and community interests. Yet, for both Pryor and Chappelle, working under what at least appeared to be the best possible circumstances, the shows' political effects and outcomes were uneven, hard to measure, and even harder to orchestrate. As Herman Gray notes, television shows that represent race, despite powerful institutional and commercial imperatives to reinforce the racial status quo, *can* have progressive dimensions to them, even if the shows that do manage to explode racial hierarchies are often sporadic in their challenges:

The reigning wisdom in critical television studies of race is still that television representations of blackness work largely to legitimate and secure the terms of the dominant cultural and social order by circulating within and remaining structured by them. . . . Just as often, however, there are alternative (and occasionally oppositional) moments in American commercial television representations of race, especially in its fragmented and contradictory character. In some cases, television representations of blackness explode and reveal the deeply rooted terms of this hierarchy.[31]

Chappelle's "The Racial Draft" offers a provocative pop-cultural engagement with mixed race that is precisely such a site, a performance that is both artistically inventive and politically astute. Clearly, Chappelle is not simply aligning himself with those who think it is high time we stopped taking race so seriously and just go "post-ethnic."[32] He is very alert to the way racial "hybridities are always in the process of, on the one hand, being appropriated and commodified by commercial culture and, on the other, of being rearticulated for the creation of oppositional 'resistance cultures.'"[33] The humor in *The Dave Chappelle Show*—like that in Spike Lee's movie *Bamboozled,* Jon Stewart's *The Daily Show* episode on mixed race, "The Afrospanicindioasianization of America" (April 6, 2006),[34] or the *Da Ali G Show*, starring British comedian Sacha Baron Cohen as the character Ali G—is controversial. But controversial humor in and of itself does not necessarily provoke political inquiry and insight. The Freudian model of comedy, after all, exposes the obscene and repressed in order to control and circumscribe the taboo, while Chappelle's comedy seems less a containment than an unleashing.[35] Luigi Pirandello argued that "the contrapuntal art of comedy is directed at playing off life's incongruities"—the tension between aspiration and limitation, between idealism and expedient materialism, truth and delusion—such that humor "evokes and attracts contrary" impulses, and "these naturally divide the spirit," so that laughter is "troubled and obstructed by something that stems from the representation itself."[36] And the laughter in "The Racial Draft" is very often uneasy, troubled; in fact the "obstruction" is sometimes perceived as Chappelle himself, not the social injustices he exposes. But as Glenda Carpio discusses in her wonderful analysis of Chappelle's work in *Laughing Fit to Kill*, Chappelle is balancing "paradoxes . . . the need to redress a breach that cannot be redressed and the need to create community even while evoking a divisive past and an equally, if different, divisive present" (116). "The Racial Draft" is not a prescription for but a reminder of those paradoxes of past and present.

VII. UPSTAGING RACE IN *TALK*

True learning has to involve unlearning—we all to have to "forget what we think we know" in order to arrive at the next relevant idea. And this is extremely dangerous, because knowledge means death.

Carl Hancock Rux[37]

Social memory is always reciprocally linked to social forgetting; every act of recall entails an act of oblivion.

Jonathan V. Crewe, "Recalling Adamastor"[38]

Carl Hancock Rux's *Talk* dramatizes not the sports scene but the academic mis-en-scène of mixed race, and takes up precisely the challenge posed by Chappelle's "The Racial Draft": how to unsettle past commitments to certain notions of race that so intricately and ritualistically inform people's present pleasures, their professions, their national histories? What kinds of acts of remembering and forgetting are necessary to maintain these commitments, and how can we move beyond these Pavlovian racial responses in order, as Rux suggests above, to "arrive at the next relevant idea"? As I explore in this chapter, humor as a device for social revelation (Chappelle's aim) is retrieved through memory in *Talk*, although it is the recall of its failure to amuse that most creatively instructs and entertains.

Early on in the play, a Moderator assures the other characters onstage and the audience that he welcomes "all of you . . . into this curious room of forgetting what had been remembered" (17).[39] This welcome to participate is both a complaint about forgetfulness—since the play centers on remembering a forgotten artist—and a call to action that requires "social forgetting," the letting go of moribund or memorialized truths in the service of social change. The predicament of memory in *Talk* has to do with the ethical challenges in deciding when to recall, what to forget, and why it all matters so much. It is also, not incidentally, a play about race. The play focuses on the anxious bickering, scandalous gossip, invented rumors—in short, talk—about whether the main character, a writer named Archer Aymes, is black, mulatto, a black man passing for white, a white man passing for black, or a con man playing "some game of race representation" (104). At times the issue of race in the play is characterized as moot, relegated to a footnote to Aymes' larger aesthetic project, dismissed as an abstract epistemological query—i.e., how can we ever know what "race" is anyway?—or miniaturized into an aside about one man's solipsistic angst. But as Jonathan Crewe reminds us, individual memory and identity are always socially mediated and of social consequence (25), and the mixed race figure, in particular, functions as what Pierre Nora calls les *lieux de mémoire*, "products of the interaction between history and memory, the interplay between the personal and collective."[40] In fact, Aymes' ambiguous racial status generates a furor in the play not just over his artistic legacy but over historical accounts of the turbulent and socially transformative 1960s and 1970s in the United States. I argue that the play represents no mere academic squabble: the political stakes of cultural memory are high, as Aymes becomes a palimpsest of different scholars' and activists' competing recollections of, and investment in, certain narratives of U.S. racial history and politics. In particular, Aymes' miscegenated self, which haunts as both corporeal specter and historical spectacle in *Talk*, works on- and offstage not just to unsettle taxonomies of race; the anxiety over his mixed race identity points to a larger racial crisis at the very center of cultural memory itself.[41]

Commissioned by the Foundry Theatre in New York, developed at the Sundance Theatre Laboratory in 2001, *Talk* was first produced by the Foundry Theatre at the Joseph Papp Public Theater in March 2002 and directed by Marion McClinton (who has also directed several of August Wilson's plays). The play is staged as an academic conference qua commemorative tribute to the biracial author and activist Archer Aymes—the supposed offspring of the white Sir Norman Victor and "a Negro concubine"—who died mysteriously after breaking into and destroying a museum as part of a civil rights protest. The Moderator, a young black professor, has discovered a manuscript of Aymes' forgotten novel, and he invites putative experts on Aymes to participate in a conference, modeled on Plato's *Symposium*, at the New York Museum of Antiquities, what one character calls the "House of Memory" (85). Named after characters in the *Symposium*'s dialogues, the panelists include Ion, a pretentious white academic who holds forth on what he sees as Aymes' disingenuous performance of blackness; Phaedo, Aymes' maudlin white lover and the leading actress in his only film; Meno, a retired TV talk show host and self-promoting buffoon; Crito, a black jazz musician, Vietnam vet, and Aymes' musical collaborator; and Apollodoros,

FIGURE 5.4. Scene from *Talk* by Carl Hancock Rux in a production by Foundry Theatre at the Joseph Papp Public Theater in March 2002. © 2002 The Foundry Theatre.

part Greek chorus member and part self-described "performance artist
. . . Barfly. Bitch" (17). In their role as experts, they resemble the sports
commentator panel in "The Racial Draft."

Yet once gathered, none of the participants can quite remember
Aymes' age or his appearance, no one can agree on his political commitments, his aesthetic motivations, where he published—the *New Yorker*?
the *New York Post*? the *New Age*? *Esquire*? (36–37), or his place in
literary history, variously arguing that he is a Beat poet, a modernist,
a postmodernist, an avant-gardist, a surrealist, a proto-hip-hop artist,
or one in a line of misunderstood black artists, from the gay Harlem
Renaissance writer Richard Bruce Nugent to *New Yorker* journalist
Anatole Broyard, who passed for white (48).[42] No one can even confirm
that Aymes' one literary monograph (around which the conference is
centered), titled *Mother and Son*, was really written by him, or whether the film and jazz music famously associated with the book was the
result of true artistic collaborations or cynical postmortem appropriations by others eager to associate their name with his. No one, finally,
can agree on what he lived or died for—whether he took his own life
or was killed in prison by the police who arrested him for his desecra-
tion of the museum, how exactly the museum protest was linked to his
civil rights agitation, or what happened to the corpse, which has gone,
inexplicably, missing—which leads to much discussion about the need
to find or re-member his physical body as well as consideration of the
corpus of his work. In this sense *Talk* is meta-commentary on the theoretical and experiential limits of cultural memory: Rux states that "[t]
he only way for [the Moderator] to know the answer to his questions
is to be led by the panelists into a *milieu de mémoire*—an environment
of memory."[43] The putative goal of the conference, to honor Aymes'
memory, is disrupted by the problem of memory itself. Since all of the
panelists remember him differently, the Moderator's naïve hope of recovery through consensus is lost. By the play's end, any challenge to
the idealization of memory as mimetic re-creation of the past, any nostalgic longing and competition for the "true" Aymes, is replaced by an
anxious but more critically self-reflective understanding of the shifting,
provisional, and vertiginous sense of the man, his race, and history it-

self. Furthermore, this understanding that objectivity is impossible, not even necessarily desirable, is represented as a precursor to social change, not as an obstacle to it.

VIII. HISTORY AS ENDNOTE

The reluctance to give up the search for Aymes onstage is whetted by the playscript's hundreds of rich and sometimes obscure cultural and literary references, which function like detective novel clues but which are burlesqued in magnificently elaborate but fictitious endnotes (141–158)—seventeen single-spaced pages!—and in a ten-page General Index of historical names and facts (159–169), both of which extend the parody and generate a compelling read quite distinct from, maybe even in competition with, the playscript proper. Far more than stage directions or dramaturgical guide, the endnotes and index mimic and mock genres of truth, if you will; they offer extensive and impressively erudite research about theater, literary history, cultural history that we recognize as true in every detail except in their references to Aymes, and so they seduce—coerce, really—directors, actors, anyone who reads the playscript into thinking that Aymes just might be continuous with history—that readers and viewers can locate him among the historical details, scholarly essays, society gossip, and stray errata. The play's text and notes are filled with references to and background on everyone from Canada Lee to André Breton, Jean Genet to Allen Ginsberg, Adrienne Kennedy to Jack Kerouac, Truman Capote to Norman Mailer, Fannie Hurst to Nat Hentoff to James Renwick, Jr. Like Toni Morrison's novel *Paradise*, *Talk* also teases with genealogies and maps and historical references, high and low, as if such facts could ever stand as self-explanatory, let alone offer therapeutic curatives to the problem of race, of identity, of history.[44] I include a representative endnote here (rather than endnote the endnote) because this textual material is as central to the play's interpretation as that which is performed onstage:

lvii. Several films made since Aymes' *Mother and Son* was released in 1968, have (arguably) been inspired by the author's film and/or novel, most notably Alexander Sokurov's *Mother and Son* (1999). Russian filmmaker Sokurov offers an agonizingly slow and beautiful story of a son's final day with his mother as a metaphor for the death of Russia. Though Sokurov has denied Archer Aymes as the inspiration for his film, critics say otherwise. Rudolf E. Kuenzli, Director of the International Dada Archive and professor of Comparative Literature at the University of Iowa wrote: "as a filmmaker [Sokurov is] is a disciple of imperiled futurism and maternal longing, a prodigal but faithful son of Stan Brackhage and André Tarkovsky . . . but Sokorov's [sic] film fails in comparison with its predecessor. Sokurov insists that his film remains faithful to its primary influence—German Romanticism—suggesting that Archer Aymes' *Mother and Son* is a hallucinatory parable, structured, ironically enough, after the Russian literary tradition of fictional autobiography and elegy. . . . I argue a filmmaker's influences are irrelevant. What matters most, when you're eating popcorn in the dark, are the results: Alexander Sokurov made memorable cinematography, Archer Aymes made memoristic art. (153)

This endnote, mimicking and mocking every academic convention— from the dutiful but snotty "[sic]" pointing out a misspelling, and the faithful accounting of critical debate, to the requisite supporting quote that somehow obscures as much as illuminates—is a send-up of professional history-making, and ultimately of the desire to find Aymes amid the facts and affiliations. As Antonio Gramsci describes it, history is an "infinity of traces without . . . an inventory."[45] So in lieu of an inventory, the characters rely on associations: "Associations are very important!" Meno declares at one point. "Everyone's interested in associations. Very interested! I'm always interested in a man's associations—how else do you know a person or judge his character?" (33). It is to reduce History to gossip and reputation (47), or, further, to expose History's teleology as arbitrary, associative, influenced by power, by relations, by who says what about whom or who sees who with whom.

The desire to believe in the truths of History is not only the characters' but, Rux implies, also the readers' (since only readers of the playscript would see these endnotes). His play challenges the unspoken and tenacious hope that if we just knew enough history, knew whom someone met and when, then we might place him or her in right relation to both aesthetic and civil rights histories. Because Sukorov and Kuenzli are, in fact, real people whose biographies are more or less represented faithfully in the endnotes, the play—by this association with and accumulation of "true" facts—suggests that Aymes too might be real. This and *Talk*'s other endnotes poke fun at the project of endnoting as fastidious sleuthing and graduate-school truth-telling. By implication, it punctures the very possibility that we might thus secure the definitive basis by which to determine "correct" history, to judge "good" art, and to understand ourselves in relation to both. Mixed race is a trope for both the importance and the impossibility of this kind of historical desire. The play recognizes its symbolic potential; in fact it functions entirely as a symbol in which the "real" body of the person of mixed race heritage is only incidental—just as it is in "The Racial Draft."

Thus it is no accident that Aymes is an absent figure. He is all the more pervasive because of it, for his body's significance lies not in its bone and blood but in the narrative discourses making him so readily interpretable and so culturally available on so many levels. One way that Aymes is made present is through the panelists' putatively respectful resurrection of him: "This is the body of a man we are handling. Please, let none of us mishandle him" (91). They conjure him, certainly, through citation—he emerges through a short quote here or there read by a panelist, or a clip from the film he supposedly made projected onto a background screen in the Foundry Theatre production. But Aymes gains salience not merely through the references to his own words or from images that generate facsimiles of him, for these recollections and fragmented, self-interested memories only produce the person remembering. That is, Aymes secures the most substantive narrative presence in the play to the degree that he brings into relief other characters' projections of themselves. Called up in the endless service of the panelists' own authoritative versions of Aymes, each panelist mediates his or her own identity through his or her account offered of Aymes, garnering academic or artistic importance from relation to and through him. Importantly, his mixed race status—the ways in which his ambiguity opens up interpretative possibility—makes him an endlessly usable figure in others' self-figurations.

IX. MIXED-UP LIVES

This is not a play about discovery of Aymes as an other, therefore, but about the discovery of Self through an Other. For example, Phaedo's claims that she was fundamental to Aymes' inspiration for his one film smack of self-involvement:

PHAEDO: He said I was his muse. I became agitated, told him I did not want to be that—would not be like one of the tragic beauties fueling the genius of god-like men. He never brought it up again . . . and then . . . well I found my way into it.

ION: Found your way into it?

PHAEDO: I knew the pulse of it—how the role should be performed.

ION: But before the film was completed, Archer [Aymes] abandoned the project, didn't he?

PHAEDO: No! He did not abandon it!

THE MODERATOR: But he didn't complete it either—did he? . . . Phaedo, if it was really his film . . . why did he leave . . . in the middle of production?

PHAEDO: I don't know.

THE MODERATOR: (Accusatory) You don't know what? Did the man have anything to do with the film at all? . . . She made a movie, signed his name to it—used him—just like Meno did! . . . It's no wonder the man—. (83)

Aymes apparently disappears after this, and the Moderator makes it clear that he blames Phaedo, in part, for taking over Aymes' film project. It is apparent from her own statements that she overrode his decisions ("We . . . were having one of many disagreements about how a scene should be shot . . . but his was no different from any other argument . . . the crew agreed with me . . . they usually did and that incensed Archer" [84]). Nevertheless, she ironically claims that she understands his true artistic intent better than anyone gathered—"the evidence of what he intended is in his films" (107). That is, her intent is reflected in his films, if we take her at her word. Importantly, she insists that his/her intent had nothing to do with race: he wanted a "multicultural cast—both black and white with no true focus on ethnicity. That he was black or biracial is of no consequence. This conference is about his work—race was not the point of his work" (107), something vigorously contested by Ion, who insists that Aymes was looking for "some artistic act of political activism" (78). Ion argues that not only was Phaedo's vision completely opposed to that of Aymes but she actually altered the film and then entered it into a festival in his name. When the film won an award, Aymes did not recognize it as his own (79). Ion's scathing indictment of Phaedo challenges Phaedo's implication that their interracial affair—a black man with a white woman—somehow took them beyond race, that it typified a kind of artistic race transcendence. As Phaedo puts it: "We were no different, Archer and I. His black male body. My white female body—it was the same body." To which Meno says incredulously, "Huh?" (75). The audience is coaxed by Meno's and Ion's reactions to suspect that Phaedo's aesthetics are a self-serving convenience and in direct contradiction to Aymes' apparent interest in the political exigencies and artistic contingencies of race and gender. Her high modernist art-for-art's-sake position requires the erasure of race because her position validates her involvement as pivotal rather than parasitic.

Crito, albeit in very different ways, also makes Aymes a crucible for his own identity: in his case, as a civil rights activist. If Phaedo argued for an art without politics, Crito fights for art as politics. A struggling jazz musician, Crito has made a living off an album he said was based on a jailhouse meeting with Aymes when they were incarcerated after civil rights "Mule Train" march protests. But soon the Moderator begins to realize that Crito's elaborate lore about the co-creation with Aymes of a song that made Crito's career "was a lie too" (118):

THE MODERATOR: [You] said you were in a jail cell with him for three weeks, said he refused to talk . . . so he hummed . . . communicated to you by hummin' or some shit . . . and you went to Vietnam and you remembered his hummin' . . . and when you got home, you recorded his hummin' into a hand-held tape recorder and then made a chart of the music, and spent years composing it . . . until you made your first album, Mother and Son, Volume I: Track I: "The Sound of Archer Aymes." (118)

It turns out, however, that Ion has done some careful investigation proving that Crito has lied about when and where he met Aymes (he may have spent one night in jail with him at best), and it becomes clear that, in fact, Crito is not channeling Aymes' music at all: he has not gained insight through proximity, is not the guardian of his prophetic humming. This revelation is devastating to the Moderator, who "listened to that song . . . over and over . . . I listened to that song" (122) only to have Crito admit that "Truth is . . . MOTHER AND SON, VOLUME I . . . truth is, VOLUME I didn't have a goddamned thing to do with nothin' Archer said in his jail cell. . . . Not a GODDAMNED thing!" He promises that the next album, VOLUME II—soon as he can "get me a record label"—will actually "tell the shit!" but by now the Moderator realizes the score: "So you were using Aymes, too?" (122). Ion suggests a probable narrative for the relationship between Aymes and Crito, implying that exploitation cannot fully account for the intra-racial dynamics at play: they borrowed each other's lives, he insists, out of mutual self-interest:

ION: What agreement was made between the two of you? What conversation transpired? Why did he assume your life? Why did he live in your house in Marks—like Valéry, hiding out from the world, taking time to understand what the next step would be—Plato's cave. You meet Aymes, who turns his performance over to you . . . lives in your house on a plantation—an authentic Negro experience—giving you passageway to come to New York: an exchange. Multiple selves. Each life observing the other. (123)

Ion concludes by saying that Crito and Aymes were "exchanging lives" (124), and argues, in fact, that Aymes' putative suicide might have been a murder, that Crito sought to keep the life he had borrowed. The Moderator mourns, "The music, a lie. The movie, a lie. The book, a lie" (121), but in fact Ion avers something more complex: that Aymes, perhaps ambivalent about the relation of race to his art—suggested by everyone at the conference—was at least at one point a willing participant in the mirage, and allowed himself to be cannibalized by others' interests. As Ion explains, "Aymes was replicating and sampling, borrowing and reproducing—and being sampled and reproduced by Phaedo" (78).

This sampling itself is earlier offered as Aymes' own "hiphop" aesthetic, characterized as duplicitous innovation. As Ion describes it,

Aymes was recontextualizing . . . not unlike today's hiphop. . . . Its popularity is reliant upon the act of sampling, and by taking these instrumental lines out of context and setting them in another context—taking what was old and putting it in something new—we are tricked into believing that what we are listening to is new, is different, but it's not. That's what Aymes' book did—recontextualized—tricked people, like today's Jay-Z. (41)

But if we tweak Ion's insight to suggest that sampling is not necessarily derivative or deceptive but a creative act of transformative borrowing, then Ion's example of rapper Jay-Z's sampling a line from the song "Hard Knock Life" in the Broadway musical *Annie*, in order to make it speak to "gangsta life and gangsta ambitions" (42) seems brilliant adaptation rather than black trickery. Furthermore, to the extent that sampling values hybridity, fusion, amalgamation, and cross-pollination of traditions, its miscegenating processes seem perfect analogs to Aymes' own mixedness, for he too is a mélange of his parents' different racial as well as social stations, and his work a brew of high and low cultural forms, and of historically black and white artistic impulses. Sampling unsettles all the categories it draws on (once we know that Jay-Z drew on *Annie*, we listen to both the Broadway song and Jay-Z's songs differently) and resists its own reification: it is a looping process rather than one type of music. The problem with sampling and being sampled in Aymes' case is not that it renders his work misleading (as Ion suggests) but that it walks a fine line between ethical collaboration and opportunistic appropriation, especially given the racial politics of sampling. Haunting *Talk* are the many examples of and debates about white appropriation of black expressive forms (blues, jazz, swing, now hip-hop, from George Gershwin to Elvis Presley to Eminem) in which whites capitalize on black music and art but fail to recognize the cultural debt or share the economic wealth (just as the economic power of whites remains in place in "The Racial Draft" even as bodies of color are traded and accrue value). Aymes may have participated in this sampling aesthetic, but the problem is that the others consumed him entirely—hence the repetition throughout the play that there is "no body" left (124–125). When does borrowing become stealing? When does collaboration become co-optation?

It is essential to note that Aymes' ambiguous racial status most felicitously enables the other characters' narcissistic accounts of their self-importance. That is, precisely because his ambiguity is the site of much anxiety, it also offers immense possibility, and is recruited to make Aymes proxy and party to a host of neuroses, fantasies, and projections. As Ralph Ellison put it, "[T]he whole of American life [is] a drama acted out on the body of a Negro giant, who, lying trussed up like Gulliver, forms the stage and scene upon which and within which the action unfolds" (85).[46] Rux extends this critique of the utility of blackness in order to examine the peculiar expediencies of mixedness. All the panelists in the symposium, black and white, realize themselves through his enabling hybridity: "Aymes is everybody on that panel," Rux suggests in an interview.[47] "Aymes is not someone outside of ourselves; he is us. He is black, he is white, he takes on the quality of all of the other characters' desires for him and for themselves. Which is why they're ripping that body up, why they're claiming him as their own." Even the Moderator, at the play's end and as indicated by the director's notes, assumes Aymes as his own persona (137), narrating Aymes' thoughts as his own.

However, this is not just a play about the reduction of race to cynical self-interested or casual speculation by a few individuals. In *Talk*, as in "The Racial Draft," the mulatto makes evident the way personal acts are both structured by and mediate material effects and social conditions. As I note in the Introduction, Eva Saks has cogently argued that U.S. national anxiety about miscegenation is less about taboo sexual relations and more specifically about establishing patriarchal lines of property, about the transmission of material goods within the white community, and the corresponding disinheritance of the black mother and any children born of an interracial union.[48] In Aymes' case, this disinheritance is not just economic but artistic. His inheritance is complicated because the (white) father's legacy is supposedly not his to claim.[49] That is, Aymes could not lay claim to the white Beat sensibility—they could "say and do what they wanted to" (53). He felt he could not "legitimately" imagine himself their artistic heir because, the Moderator notes, "the forefathers were their fathers—NOT HIS! . . . And their controversies would only fuel their celebrity—prolong it—while Aymes would always be just another colored entertainer, tap-dancing in the wings!" (53). Well into the late twentieth century, de jure and then de facto laws required that children follow the so-called "condition of the mother." The play extends this concept to suggest that Aymes' white paternal legacy grants him not only no civic or political enfranchisement but also a fraught birthright to black expressive cultural traditions.

X. BODIES OFFSTAGE

Yet rather than bemoan the absence of the mixed race body from the stage, the play seems to beg the question, Do we need a new politics of representation that is, as Herman Gray argues, released from a language of visibility/invisibility equating political representation only with being heard and seen?[50] After all, Ayme's absence the stage, his offstage presence, disrupts the tendency to fetishize the racial body as spectacle. How does one stage mixed race without enjoining all the conventions of and expectations for racial representation, without triggering the visual obsession with seeing race writ on the body in predictable ways? Karen Shimakawa and others have examined strategies of subverting the over-determining performance of the racial type, and Rux's absenting of Aymes altogether can be considered within this context.[51] Furthermore, the play neatly dramatizes how truly incidental the presence of the "real" Aymes would be anyway. After all, there seems little point in recovering Aymes' mixed race self; he is already completely imbricated throughout and central to all the characters' narratives.[52]

Ironically, Ion accuses Aymes of another kind of disappearing act, saying his racial identity as mixed is fraudulent, that he is merely some kind of white-black man trying to borrow the "cultural dowry,"[53] to use Norman Mailer's choice expression, of black people in order to legitimate himself—a desperate effort to borrow blackness, like a white person, to make himself into a "real" black person. Aymes' posturing was a convoluted response to Western representations of African and African Americans, Ion argues, from Picasso to Baudelaire (104–105), who represented "Negroes" as "some romantic . . . some exotic . . . dangerous other—the outcasts" (106). Aymes, Ion concludes, bested white appropriations of blackness: "So the Negro kept for survival the art of the primitive . . . but the hipster, Mailer said, absorbed the existentialist synopsis of the Negro . . . The hipster could be considered . . . a WHITE NEGRO . . . as was—ARCHER AYMES!" (106).

Or if not, mimicking white theft of black cool, Ion speculated, Aymes might have been attempting to become and to create blackness. He wanted, Ion thought, to

fulfill the character of the Negro and he wanted to suffer as a Negro—an authentically black avant-garde postmodernist. Tried to pull himself away from white associations . . . and became a Negro integrationist. But he couldn't assimilate as easily as he would have liked to. . . . He didn't have a black soul, had failed to purchase one with his art, that is. (109)

But this and trite white debates by other characters about whether Aymes stopped writing because of Du Boisian double consciousness or whether he had tried to create a "postmodern Negro identity" (102–103) for which there were "no models" yet in African American arts and letters (35)—all portray him as either a victim trapped in a racial past or a prophet before his time. His brief career and disappearance seem a victimless crime; or at least the responsibility for his failure seems circumscribed by what is characterized as the politics of black identity and art. Aymes' death is condescendingly represented as a shame, but the panelists at first do not recognize their own complicity or historical accountability because their recall involves a simultaneous and selective ignorance, what Mieke Bal terms "the communal fictionalizing, idealizing, monumentalizing impulse," which thrives in a conflicted culture: "Because memory is made up of socially constituted forms, narratives, and relations, but also amenable to individual acts of intervention in it, memory is always open to social revision and manipulation."[54]

Bal's suggestion that cultural memories can work towards a reactionary forgetting of conflict is important, since Crito and the Moderator are constantly trying to remind the panelists and the audience about the importance of the civil rights crises, trying to link the Mule Train civil rights protests in the South with Aymes' museum protest in the North—both challenges to the status quo that none of the others want to hear (112). In that sense, the play invokes the mulatto as a vehicle for political revolution (as did Langston Hughes in his play *Mulatto* and Lorraine Hansberry in her *Les Blancs*, discussed in my Introduction) when Aymes smashes the Museum of Antiquities, full of Greek urns and busts, littered with what stage directions describe as "the characteristic objects of an older period in a world long past" (9). The museum is, not accidentally, "the institutional setting in which the history of art can be accessed and pressured to mean what the authorities who manage culture for us want it to mean."[55] Spurred on by a will to remember—by a conscious effort to limit forgetfulness—*lieux de mémoire* seek "to post the problem of the embodiment of memory in certain sites where a sense of historical continuity persists."[56] The urns have to go, *Talk* maintains, not just to destroy memory's embodiment of historical continuity in order to challenge paradigmatic models of understanding human relations, especially the iconic mother-son dynamic, evoked by the title of Aymes' work.[57] These paradigms, which claim universality, are challenged through racial particularity to suggest that these are not transhistorical halls of "great" thinkers, history, types, iconic models, rehearsed familial dramas.

XI. MEMORY AS REALITY CHECK

The racial challenge to this communal idealizing comes from the percolating of counter-memories within the scene of memory itself. These are what Crito calls "ruptures" (43) of memory by memory—he terms this process "addictive subversive memory" (110). Specifically, studded throughout the play we find these moments, bracketed in the script by icons (Ω Ω) that signify, according to the play's Key, "a heightened or subtle change of reality distinguishable in the gradual distortion of environment and behavior." The most revelatory is Meno's participation in an excruciating moment of racial mockery. It is the moment when we find Meno suddenly remembering a memory within a memory, memory as present experience—"I just remembered" (90), he says—recalling the time he hosted Aymes' first and only television appearance. While Aymes is in the Green Room preparing for the show, Meno comes out in grotesque blackface before the unknowing Aymes appears and reads the opening lines from Aymes' *Mother and Son* to the audience: "His mother saw that his hair was black. All of it. He had all of his hair and all of it—black" (12):

—So I come out in this . . . these dark sunglasses, and this little wig, you know, little tight black curly wig, and cork, and I was—cork all over my . . . like from the death trail—and I was reading, reading from his book out loud with . . .

using . . . you know, black slang, you know, like Kerouac would do, black slang, like the old . . . the old days. . . . Café Society!—his hair, I say his hair was buh-LAAK. . . . "Dadio," I say, "I say his mu-tha . . . his mu-tha saw, she saw dat his hair was buk-LAAK. Buh-lakuh dan buh-LAAK! Buh-Lakk, buh-LAAK!" Oh it was sooo funny! You shoulda seen the audience, everybody was laughing, with the little wig and sunglasses. . . . Well, then I introduce Aymes. And Aymes comes out—he didn't see the skit because he was in the green room—and so he comes out, he starts reading "His hair was black, blacker than black. . . ." The audience . . . everybody—oh God!—soooo funny. . . . Right away, everybody's on the floor—oh how they laughed—it was sooo funny. You should've seen his face. Everybody was laughing, the audience loved it. Oh God, they ate it up! (90–91)

The blackface performance replicates the a priori over-determination of any black artist, the minstrel scene that precedes and overwrites anything the artist might say, any art the black artist might tender before a white audience. But the re-creation leads to reflection. The stage directions read, "Meno returns to his seat. His hands are shaking. He pops a pill" (91). This subversive memory emerges as an inside joke that turns inside out, for Meno first tells the story as one of self-congratulation, is busy in the act of telling a tale to be remembered, adding to the lore about Aymes, and then suddenly the scenario of memory-making jogs him into self-reflection, a reenactment leading to retrospection, in which he realizes that his self-aggrandizing appears grotesque. In this way, remembering Aymes means Meno remembering his own complicity with the writer's artistic erasure. And then this rogue memory—a subversion of the original—becomes part of the public record. What raises this private epiphany to the possibility of social critique is the contemporary audience's witness to and implied contract with this revised public account of Aymes. The audience is reminded through the canned laughter in the scene that they sit where another audience sat also before Meno, laughing when they are not, and it enables a critical distance paralleling Meno's, a defamiliarization that potentially leads them, too, to "a reality check." A "reality check," according to Harry J. Elam, Jr., is a moment that

traumatically ruptures the balance between the real and the representational. It is a moment that, in the dissonance, generates demands that the relationship between the real and representation be renegotiated. Reality checks brusquely rub the real up against the representational in ways that disrupt the spectators and produce new meanings.[58]

In fact, the audience realizes that it was after this that Aymes stopped writing, that it was not personal neurosis or racial gatekeeping but the violence of minstrelsy, the harm of misrepresentation, that silenced his creativity. Significantly, the play opens with the Moderator quietly, respectfully, reading these same lines from *Mother and Son*, a postmortem righting of Meno's act. When it erupts, addictive subversive memory in *Talk* involves not the recovery of prelapsarian coherence—what Meno sees as the original variety show "good time," his recounting of the "good ole days." Rather, it foregrounds the compulsive, unstable fracture lines within the practice of memory.

Implied in the play is the hope that this very unpredictability and fracturing—what Brent Hayes Edwards calls racial *décalage*—can occasionally productively arbitrate between memories that offer competing representations of reality. These revisionist memories work not so much because they naïvely collapse differences in time and across space and homogenize a simplistic racial identity but because they potentially function, as *décalage*, as "a time-lag, a gap or interval of time and space which articulates a difference across time and perspective, but which also allows for movement just as a joint articulates and allows for the movement of limbs."[59] Edwards is drawing on Stuart Hall's foundational "Race, Articulation, and Societies Structured in Dominance," which invites an understanding of identity as imbricated in a complex structure through which we can see, as Edwards puts it, "difference within unity" (11). Black identity does not require mimetic identification, as Hall puts it,

where one structure perfectly recapitulates or reproduces or even "expresses" another; or where each is reducible to the other. . . . The unity formed by this articulation is necessarily a "complex structure," a structure in which things are related, as much through their differences as through their similarities . . . [and] there will be structured relations between its parts, i.e. relations of dominance and subordination.[60]

Reviews of the play seem to miss completely this possibility. Michael Feingold's review of the Joseph Papp performance of *Talk* in April 2007 is representative of this mistake:

Because his digressions are so much more to the point than the mythic paradigm he is trying to construct, Hancock Rux has not really solved his play. Archer Aymes is too transparently a pretext for everything else, and the Moderator's obsession with him too impertinent an interference with the fact-finding mission that ought to be at the drama's core. Nor are these the only problems with the script's elaborately fractured context, which is echoed—often gorgeously, but too often excessively—in the glittering, shadow-shifting ornateness with which Marion McClinton has staged the Foundry Theatre's production.[61]

This idea that play is a project to solve, that it "ought to be" a "fact-finding mission," as Feingold puts it, is to reduce art to instrumentalism and in many ways to enact the critical practices that the play critiques. It also, more seriously, fails to see the larger social and aesthetic critique which is at the "drama's core." Theater itself provides the conditions for this subversive memory, encouraging us to move from talk to action, or rather to seeing talk as a form of action. *Talk*, in this sense, is crucial to the production of cultural memory, which is, to cite Diana Taylor's familiar definition, as "a practice, an act of imagination and interconnection."[62]

What that history actually is and should be has been a political, cultural, and aesthetic project since the nineteenth century—as Arthur Schomburg put it in 1925, "The American Negro must remake his past in order to make his future."[63] If history is collective memory, then much of African American literature and drama has been about challenging normative, officially sanctioned memory, from the NAACP's boycott of *The Birth of a Nation*—which rewrote Reconstruction as a triumph of the KKK and which President Woodrow Wilson praised as "history writ with lightning" in the movie's opening frames—to W. E. B. Du Bois' Pageant plays, which grant African Americans a grand pre-slavery history; and from August Wilson's refiguration of Hayden White's master narratives with his play cycle to Kara Walker's black paper silhouettes that expose slavery's unspokens. And I would include Rux's *Talk*, with its smashing of the "Museum of Antiquities" and what his character Apollodoros calls the sacred "house of memory" (85). Chappelle's "The Racial Draft" similarly bends the sacred rituals and hallowed icons of sports culture and history—disturbing the annual ceremony of the NFL draft so sanctified in American culture. Raboteau's *The Professor's Daughter* insists on exhuming the cemetery dust of the past. McGruder's comic strip, too, conjures history to reclaim it in public discourse about mixed race, referencing everyone from Angela Davis to Margaret Mitchell in Huey's re-education of Jazmine.

I WOULD LIKE TO CONCLUDE by returning to the line in Gordone's play that names this chapter—"They's mo' to bein' black than meets the eye!"—in order to note the particular kind of political aesthetics emerging from "The Racial Draft" and *Talk*, as well as from the earlier works I discuss throughout. Filmmaker Isaac Julien argues that "blackness as a sign is never enough. What does that black subject do, how does it act, how does it think politically . . . being black isn't really good enough for me: I want to know what your cultural politics are."[64]

We can connect this insight to the concerns of mixed race, not as a challenge to prove one's cultural politics, as Hall implies, but as a reminder that mixed race as a sign is also not "good enough." However well-meaning, many of the most common signatures of mixed race—checking census boxes, installing mixed race people on television, film, fiction, and stage, requiring mixed race–sensitive school curricula—are signs that do not necessarily fulfill the greater promises of mixed race doing, acting, thinking. To repeat the question I raise in my Introduction, is it not what or who these mulattoesque writers and artists are but what they do and where they can take us?

Like all the creative works I have examined, "The Racial Draft" and *Talk* offer incisive, creative meta-commentaries on the personal and popular investments in mixed race that are embedded in everyday cultural practices. These works resist uplifting bromides, prescriptive blueprints, coffee-table photo albums, political manifestos, instruction manuals, or special healthcare products. They do not model a harmonious way or a right way. But they do "finger the jagged grain,"[65] inviting provocative forms of aesthetic reflection and creation out of daily injury. They do not anesthetize political restlessness by creating art for art's sake; rather, they galvanize by registering a need for more responsive modes of artistic and political engagement. Their aesthetic modes are not reduced to mere instrumentalist vehicles for social change; none call for a congressional lobby or census reform, and intentionally none of these post–civil rights novels, installations, drama, comics, skits bear the pamphleteer's gloss or script specific forms of action or community building. Here, art *is* the political change, not the ornamental gloss to it.

What perhaps makes this political aesthetics most distinctive is its embrace, even exaltation, of the mutual, processual nature of race and its imbrication in a web of social relations. Importantly, this recognition that racial identity is not of one's own making does not lead these artists to concede the "What are you?" interaction as the only or the representative example of the participatory creation of mixed race's meaning. That query has come to signal how others' anxieties about perceived racial ambiguity tend to hijack all discussions. Instead, these works explicitly address and move beyond the constantly repeated fear of many mixed race advocacy groups that recognizing that one's identity as not solely an individual or family affair automatically grants others the power to determine one's identity ("others" often characterized as bullying monoracial organizations or the ham-fisted Big Government). In Chappelle's and Rux's theatrical productions we see the play or skit as an alternate metaphor and model for others' involvement in the production of racial identity—not as an intrusion but as a necessary given, for the performances are realized only through a community joined in the co-creation of the meaning of mixed race in processes that do expect or require either like-mindedness. Their stages offer both the opportunity for and mediations on forms of social belonging that fully recognize, actively negotiate, and—most importantly—turn into creative grist all the given power hierarchies, social locations, and complicated investments that individuals bring to the collective performance.

These artists extend a principle that I also see in the earlier work of the twentieth-century "poet laureate of the race," Langston Hughes, who wrote and directed theater and musical productions, for "[t]heater enabled Hughes to conjoin the social imperatives of his art with a collaborative practice; in fact, the artistic collaborative was both a means to and an end of his political objectives."[66] Most of the works I explore in this book similarly consider the ethical-artistic imperative, very often through formal aesthetic structures and strategies that explore the creative consequences of identity as public collaboration: *The Boondocks'* and *Maintaining*'s graphic re-imagining and re-imagings of the mixed race body toy with the visual prescriptives and social contexts that bring mixed race identities into view and give them meaning in time and on the page; *Caucasia*'s, *The Human Stain*'s, and *The Intuitionist*'s reinvention of the passing novel point not to individual quests for self-knowledge but to the twenty-first-century performances of identity as social experience and of social consequence; *Symptomatic* and *The Professor's Daughter* re-situate the mixed self in relation to so-called post–civil rights society through their narrative refiguration of the bildungsroman plot; Chappelle's and Rux's theatricalization of the cultural and communal playscripts of mixed race stage modes of memory callback and reality check.

Notes

1. Ruth La Ferla, "Generation E.A.: Ethnically Ambiguous," *New York Times*, December 28, 2003. The theme appears frequently in the popular press and in the many books that flood the marketplace on this subject: Alon Ziv's *Breeding Between the Lines: Why Interracial People Are Healthier and More Attractive* (2006) is representative. See also "Mixed Race, Pretty Face?" *Psychology Today*, http://www.psychologytoday.com/articles/200512/mixed-race-pretty-face. For consistency's sake, since there exists no popular or critical consensus, I use "mixed race" throughout as both an adjective (without hyphens) and a noun (without capitalization), and as more or less synonymous with other common terms applied to and invoked by those interested in this phenomenon, which include "multiracial," "biracial," "interracial," and so on. From here onward I generally remove quotes from "mixed race" as a concession to this increasingly general usage, although my aim is to question precisely the normative assumptions associated with the expression itself, so the quotation marks are always implied. Some use the expression in reference to parentage, immediate or distant, of different races, but I discuss the post-1990s usage of mixed race at further length in the Introduction as a term that has become associated with distinctly new millennial identities, experiences, and movements.

2. See Jeffrey Santa Ana, "Feeling Ancestral: The Emotions of Mixed Race and Memory in Asian American Cultural Productions," *positions: east asia cultures critique* 16, no. 2 (Fall 2008): 457–482.

3. "Post soul" is Mark Anthony Neal's expression in *Soul Babies: Black Popular Culture and the Post-Soul Aesthetic* (New York: Routledge, 2002). "Post soul babies" represent that generation of people who have no "nostalgic allegiance to the past (back in the days of Harlem, or the thirteenth-century motherland, for that matter) but firmly in the grasp of the existential corners of this brave new world" (5). Neal's definition of "post-soul aesthetic" is associated with the "soul babies," born between the March on Washington in 1963 and the *Regents of California v. Bakke* case on affirmative action in 1978. See Todd Boyd, *The New H.N.I.C.: The Death of Civil Rights and the Reign of Hip Hop* (New York: New York University Press, 2002), who argues that "the post-soul generation exists somewhere between the poles of both the race man and the nigga, between the true civil rights generation and between the hip hop generation" (6).

4. Maria P. P. Root, *The Multiracial Experience: Racial Borders as the New Frontier* (Thousand Oaks, CA: Sage, 1995).

5. Stanley Crouch, "Race Is Over," *New York Times*, September 26, 1996.

6. See Holland Cotter, "Beyond Multiculturalism, Freedom?" *New York Times*, Arts and Leisure, July 13, 2001, and Cotter's review of "black and post-black art" exhibitions from New York to Baltimore, "'Black' Comes in Many Shadings," *New York Times*, Arts and Leisure, August 13, 2004. In this 2004 piece, Cotter suggests a new twist on the controversy over the term "post-black" that emerged when the curator, Thelma Golden,

introduced a group of young African American artists, "Freestyle," at the Studio Museum in Harlem as "post-black artists . . . who didn't feel obliged to refer to ethnicity or racial history in their work." Importantly, Cotter concludes that the post-black is not necessarily "new": the exhibition, which included work by African Americans from the nineteenth century, "provides solid proof that post-black art has been part of the American picture for almost a century, and probably longer."

7. Debra J. Dickerson, *The End of Blackness: Returning the Souls of Black Folk to Their Rightful Owners* (New York: Pantheon Books, 2004). Dickerson joins black conservatives John McWhorter and Shelby Steele in their critiques of the black middle class in particular.

8. Anthony Appiah, "Towards a New Cosmopolitanism," *New York Times Magazine*, January 1, 2006, 30–37.

9. Naomi Zack, *Race and Mixed Race* (Philadelphia: Temple University Press, 1993): "An American who identifies herself as mixed black and white race is a new person racially, because old racial categories do not allow her the option of identifying this way. It is such a person's very newness racially that gives her the option of racelessness. To be raceless in contemporary racial and racist society is, in effect, to be *anti-race*" (164).

10. Ellis Cose, in *Color-Blind: Seeing Beyond Race in a Race-Obsessed World* (New York: HarperCollins, 1998), advocates a "race-neutral" world.

11. See Dinesh D'Souza, *The End of Racism: Principles for a Multiracial Society* (New York: Free Press, 1995). D'Souza argues that racism is no longer an important factor in American life, even suggesting a repeal of the Civil Rights Act of 1964.

12. Paul Gilroy, *Against Race: Imagining Political Culture Beyond the Color Line* (Cambridge, MA: Belknap Press of Harvard University Press, 2000).

13. G. Reginald Daniel, *More Than Black? Multiracial Identity and the New Racial Order* (Philadelphia: Temple University Press, 2001).

14. See Walter Benn Michaels, "Autobiography of an Ex-White Man: Why Race Is Not a Social Construction," *Transition* 73 (1998): 122–143.

15. Robin Wilson's *Chronicle of Higher Education* article, reviewing thirty-five years of black studies departments, is titled "Past Their Prime?" and cites Shelby Steele, opining that "universities never had a legitimate reason for establishing black-studies programs . . . these programs are dying of their own inertia." Wilson's article as a whole questions the raison d'être of black studies altogether, suggesting it is an antiquated relic of the civil rights era. *Chronicle of Higher Education* 51, no. 33 (April 22, 2005): A9.

16. As Morrison puts it in "Unspeakable Things Unspoken: The Afro-American Presence in American Literature":

> For three hundred years black Americans insisted that "race" was no usefully distinguishing factor in human relationships. During those same three centuries every academic discipline . . . insisted "race" was *the* determining factor in human development. When blacks discovered they had shaped or become a culturally formed race, and that it had specific and revered difference, suddenly they were told there is no such thing as "race," biological or cultural, that matters and that genuinely intellectual exchange cannot accommodate it. . . . It always seemed to me that the people who invented the hierarchy of "race" when it was convenient for them ought not to be the ones to explain it away, now that it does not suit their purposes for it to exist.

> *The Norton Anthology of African American Literature*, ed. Henry Louis Gates, Jr., and Nellie Y. McKay, 2nd ed. (New York: W. W. Norton, 2004), 2300–2301. Originally published in *Michigan Quarterly Review* 18 (Winter 1989): 1–34.

17. Susan Koshy, "Why the Humanities Matter for Race Studies Today," Special Topic: Comparative Racializations, *PMLA* 125, no. 5 (October 2008): 1542–1549. Koshy provides an excellent analysis of the need for the humanities in analyzing contemporary racial formations. I take only slight issue with what I see as an unnecessary privileging of comparative racial studies over and against civil–rights era race studies (1548). Treating comparative studies as the "next wave" risks eclipsing what looking at black and white can still yield *along with* multiple racial inter-articulations, and risks also suggesting an ever-upward progress in critical thinking that might too confidently assume the complete exhaustion of all previous paradigms.

18. Jon Michael Spencer, *The New Colored People: The Mixed-Race Movement in America* (New York: New York University Press, 1997).

19. The first essay in Du Bois' *The Souls of Black Folk* is "The Spiritual Strivings of Black Folk," in which he offers his definition of "double consciousness." "Of Our Spiritual Strivings." *The Souls of Black Folk*. (1903) in *The Norton Anthology of African American Literature*, ed. Henry Louis Gates, Jr. and Nellie Y. McKay, 693–699, 2nd ed. (New York: W. W. Norton, 2004).

20. See Peter Weiss, *Aesthetics of Resistance*, Vol. 1, *A Novel* (Durham, NC: Duke University Press, 2005).

21. W. E. B. Du Bois, "Criteria of Negro Art" (1926), in *W. E. B. Du Bois: Writings*, ed. Nathan Irvin Huggins, 995 (New York: Library of America, Viking, 1986). This simple formulation is, of course, much more complex: in distinguishing Walter Pater's modernist ideal of "art for art's sake" from his own claim of art as propaganda, Du Bois suggests that the claim that art is apolitical masks politics. All art, Du Bois argues, subtly and irresistibly advances a kind of racial interestedness, what Harold Cruse would later call "cultural particularism."

22. From the Registration call for Pride's Fusion 2009 Summer Program for Mixed Heritage and Transracially Adopted Youth, http://www.fusionprogram.org/ (accessed April 7, 2010).

23. See Justin Grant, "Who Needs the NAACP?" September 2, 2008, http://abcnews .go.com/US/story?id=5649192&page=1 (accessed April 8, 2010).

24. Paul Gilroy, Introduction to *Postcolonial Melancholia* (New York: Columbia University Press, 2005), 14.

25. Koshy, "Why the Humanities Matter for Race Studies Today," 1548.

26. George Lipsitz, *The Possessive Investment in Whiteness: How White People Profit from Identity Politics* (Philadelphia: Temple University Press, 1998), 26. On the relation between mixed race identification, presumptive whiteness, and the "end of race," see also David Roediger's excellent *Colored White: Transcending the Racial Past*, American Crossroads, vol. 10 (Berkeley: University of California Press, 2002).

27. Danzy Senna, "Passing and the Problematic of Multiracial Pride (or, Why One Mixed Girl Still Answers to Black," in *Black Cultural Traffic: Crossroads in Global Performance and Popular Culture*, ed. Harry Justin Elam, Jr., and Kennell A. Jackson, 85 (Ann Arbor: University of Michigan Press, 2005).

28. Susan Eckert, "The Birth of the Multiracial American" (December 5, 2007), http://racism.suite101.com/article.cfm/birth_of_the_multiracial_american (accessed April 7, 2010).

29. Danzy Senna, "The Mulatto Millennium," in *Half and Half: Writers on Growing Up Biracial and Bicultural*, ed. Claudine Chiawei O'Hearn, 12–27 (New York: Pantheon, 1998).

INTRODUCTION

1. Lezley Saar's delightful *Mulatto Nation* installation lives on in cyberspace. Start at http://www.mulattonation.com/ (accessed March 28, 2010). *Mulatto Nation* offers sections devoted to Birth of a Nation, Founding Mothers and Fathers, Mulattoville Athenaeum, Alienation, and Materialism and the Mulatto (including the Souvenir Gift Shop, which features "Baby Halfie Brown Head").

2. The "reborn" baby movement involves creating newborn dolls so highly lifelike that their owners often treat them like real babies. Some claim they are mistaken for real if the owner appears with them in public. http://www.reborn-baby.com/ (accessed April 5, 2010). Baby Halfie is perhaps more akin to the very popular Japanese make-your-own destructible dolls available on www.kidrobot.com or www.myplasticheart.com. See Ellen Tani on the tension between play and violence in doll sculpture and culture in her exhibition notes to "Kid Mutiny," June 13–July 13, 2008, District of Columbia Arts Center, curated by Ellen Tani, curatorial project mentor J. W. Mahoney. See press release at http://artdc.org/forum/index.php?topic=9393.0 (accessed March 28, 2010). For an important reading also of the cultural unease expressed by dolldom and the complex aesthetics of "cuteness," see Sianne Ngai, "The Cuteness of the Avant-Garde," *Critical Inquiry* 31 (Summer 2005): 811–847. Unlike Barbie, Baby Halfie's erased genitalia do not represent, as Ann DuCille puts it, "a seemingly innocent space for the displacement of adult ambivalence about sexuality . . . the unclean thoughts of grown-ups into the immaculate conceptions of children." *Skin Trade* (Cambridge, MA: Harvard University Press), 1996), 19. It offers not so much the fetish work of Barbie's "Victoria Secret . . . presexual space" but the resistance to sex as a simple gender marker just as it resists color as a simple race marker.

3. This is the motto for the store Dolls Like Me, Inc., which provides dolls of "every hue" because "despite our desire to develop strong, healthy, sensitive and aware children, there is still a painfully meager sampling of toys that resemble America's growing population of multicultural children." I do not want to dismiss this admirable desire to counter the historical power of white dolls' ruling aesthetic or parents' interest in supporting a child's self-esteem, but rather to call attention to the way that these and other dolls marketed as multiracial often tend to reproduce standardized and standardizing markers of race, gender, and class that then become automatically identified with mixed race. http://www.dollslikeme.com/store/pg/6-About-Us.html (accessed November 8, 2009).

4. DuCille, *Skin Trade*, 16, 37.

5. Patricia J. Williams, *Seeing a Color-Blind Future: The Paradox of Race* (New York: Farrar, Straus, and Giroux, 1997), 4.

6. I discuss the Topsy-Turvy doll also in relation to "Presenting Negro Scenes Drawn Upon My Passage Through the South and Reconfigured for the Benefit of Enlightened Audiences Wherever Such May Be Found, By Myself, Missus K.E.B. Walker, Colored," by artist Kara Walker, in "Introduction: Working Relations and Racial Desire" in my *Race, Work, and Desire in American Literature, 1860–1930* (Cambridge: Cambridge University Press, 2003), 5. The Walker image, of a black woman carrying the head of a white woman, similarly evokes the violence of replaceable heads.

7. See James Gaines, "From the Managing Editor," *Time*, special issue on "The New Face of America: How Immigrants Are Shaping the World's First Multicultural Society," 2. Many scholars have tendered excellent readings of this *Time* issue, including Donna Haraway, Lauren Berlant, Joane Nagel, and Michael Rogin. See especially Evelynn M. Hammonds' excellent discussion of this image in "New Technologies of Race" in

Processed Lives: Gender and Technology in Everyday Life, ed. Jennifer Terry and Melodie Calvert, 107–122 (New York: Routledge, 1997). I briefly offer a different context for and interpretation of the cultural work of this image in Chapter One.

8. Danzy Senna, "The Mulatto Millennium," in *Half and Half: Writers on Growing Up Biracial and Bicultural*, ed. Claudine Chiawei O'Hearn, 12 (New York: Pantheon, 1998).

9. An example of the kind of call to somewhat self-aggrandizing action is represented by an October 14, 2005, press release by the mixed race organization MAVIN, announcing its bus drive across the country—called the Generation MIX National Awareness Tour—by "mixed race young people" to "raise awareness" about "multiracial youth," encouraging them to be "race ambassadors to provide insight into how to create a cohesive, multicultural America in the 21st century." http://www.mavinfoundation.org/news/media.html (accessed July 2007).

10. See Ariela J. Gross, *What Blood Won't Tell: A History of Race on Trial in America* (Cambridge, MA: Harvard University Press, 2008). Black Seminoles, also known as estelusti, were the result of "political, social and sexual mingling" of Native Americans and escaped slaves in colonial Florida in the late seventeenth century (141–142). Although some later reclassified themselves as white on the census, Melungeons were counted as "free people of color," and were most likely "'tri-racial' amalgamations of Africans, Portuguese (including Portuguese-African), Indian, English, and others who came into the hill country of the Carolinas and Tennessee in the eighteenth century" (64).

11. See Kimberly McClain DaCosta, *Making Multiracials: State, Family, and Market in the Redrawing of the Color Line* (Stanford: Stanford University Press, 2007), especially "The Making of a Category" (21–46), and Kim M. Williams, *Mark One or More: Civil Rights in Multiracial America* (Ann Arbor: University of Michigan Press, 2006). Both are among the most trenchant critiques of the political implications of mixed race identification.

12. Cited on the first page of the Population Estimates Program sponsored by the U.S. Census Bureau at http://factfinder.census.gov/home/en/official_estimates_2008.html (accessed October 3, 2009).

13. In a response to a reporter asking President-elect Obama at his first news conference, on November 7, 2008, what kind of dog the First Family would get, Obama says they could get a dog from the pound that would be a "mutt" like himself. See also "Obama Checks Simply African American," Blackpolitics.com (April 2, 2010), http://blackpoliticsontheweb .com/2010/04/02/obamas-census-choice-simply-african-american/ (accessed April 5, 2010).

14. Drawn from Michele Elam, "Why Obama Is Black Again," Thinking Twice column, *Stanford Report* (January 29, 2009), http://humanexperience.stanford.edu/race-elam.

15. Shirlee Taylor Haizlip, *The Sweeter the Juice: A Family Memoir in Black and White* (New York: Free Press, 1995), excerpted from a meditation of hers that appears in the front matter.

16. See George M. Fredrickson, *White Supremacy: A Comparative Study in American and South African History* (New York: Oxford University Press, 1982), especially chapter 3, "Race Mixture and the Color Line," 94–135.

17. Jon Michael Spencer, *The New Colored People: The Mixed-Race Movement in America* (New York: New York University Press, 1997), 26, 35.

18. Sharron Hall, "It's Time for Foundation," in *Mixed Heritage: Identity, Policy, and Practice*, ed. Jessica Mai Sims, 24–26 (London: Runnymede Press, 2007). Hall's article is part of a special issue of Runnymede Perspectives devoted to "Mixed Heritage" in the UK.

19. See Lisa Nakamura, "Mixedfolks.com: 'Ethnic Ambiguity,' Celebrity Outing,

and the Internet," in *Mixed Race Hollywood*, ed. Mary Beltran and Camilla Fojas, 64–83 (New York: New York University Press, 2008). The complete name of the mixedfolks.com website is "MixedFolks.com Representing People" and has links to "Our People" and the "MF Community." For the ways in which visual technologies generate racial identities, see also Susan Courtney's excellent *Hollywood Fantasies of Miscegenation: Spectacular Narratives of Gender and Race, 1903–1967* (Princeton, NJ: Princeton University Press, 2005).

20. Ronald Sundstrom, "Being and Being Mixed Race," *Social Theory and Practice* 27, no. 2 (April 2001): 295.

21. The idea that race mixing will enact social change is certainly not a new perspective: the child of the conservative black Harlem Renaissance writer and critic George Schuyler and a white woman, Josephine Cogdell, Philippa Duke Schuyler was raised by her parents as an example to the world of the brilliant transcendence of race. Unfortunately, Philippa came to deny her racial background, passing variously as white, Malaysian, and Spanish and seeking a late-term abortion in Mexico because the father was black. See Kathryn Talalay's biography, *Composition in Black and White: The Life of Philippa Schuyler: The Tragic Saga of Harlem's Biracial Prodigy* (New York: Oxford University Press, 1995).

22. Tony Kushner, *Angels in America: A Gay Fantasia on National Themes*, Part II, *Perestroika* (New York: Theatre Communications Group, 1994), 77–78.

23. Maria P. P. Root, *The Multiracial Experience: Racial Borders as the New Frontier* (Thousand Oaks, CA: Sage, 1995).

24. As Tavia Nyong'o argues, "Does miscegenation in fact corrode white supremacy? Or does the conjugal union of the races work as a depoliticizing catchall, preempting a more critical engagement with the traumas of the American past?" *The Amalgamation Waltz: Race, Performance, and the Ruses of Memory* (Minneapolis: University of Minnesota Press, 2009), 5.

25. Roland G. Fryer, Lisa B. Kahn, Steven D. Levitt, and Jörg L. Spenkuch, "The Plight of Mixed Race Adolescents," National Bureau of Economic Research Working Paper Series, vol. w14192, http://ssrn.com /abstract=1179862 (accessed July 2008); and Kevin R. Binning, Miguel M. Unzueta, Yuen J. Huo, and Ludwin E. Molina, "The Interpretation of Multiracial Status and Its Relation to Social Engagement and Psychological Well-Being," *Journal of Social Issues* 65, no. 1 (2009): 35–49. See also the Stanford Business School article on this research, http://www.gsb.stanford.edu/news/research/binning_multirace.html.

26. Cited in Maria P. P. Root and Matt Kelley, eds., *Multiracial Child Resource Book: Living Complex Identities* (Seattle: MAVIN Foundation, 2003): Matt Kelley and Maria P. P. Root, "Introduction," xiv–xvi; Ramona E. Douglass, "The Evolution of the Multiracial Movement," 12–17; Velina Hasu Houston, "Multirace and the Future," 223–228; Nicholas A. Jones and Amy Symens Smith, "A Statistical Portrait of Two or More Races in Census 2000," 3–10.

27. Paul Spickard, "The Subject Is Mixed Race: The Boom in Biracial Biography," in *Rethinking "Mixed Race*," ed. David Parker and Miri Song, 76–98 (Sterling, VA: Pluto Press, 2001).

28. Some popular children's books include Marguerite W. Davol, *Black, White, Just Right!*, illustrations by Irene Trivas (Morton Grove, IL: Albert Whitman and Company, 1993); Kim Wayans and Kevin Knotts, *Amy Hodgepodge: All Mixed Up!* (New York: Grosset and Dunlap; Penguin, 2008); Donna Jackson Nakazawa, *Does Anybody Else Look Like Me?: A Parent's Guide to Raising Multiracial Children* (Cambridge, MA: Perseus Publishing, 2003). An oft-cited parent guide is Marguerite A. Wright, *I'm Chocolate,*

You're Vanilla: Raising Healthy Black and Biracial Children in a Race-Conscious World (San Francisco: Jossey-Bass, 1998).

29. Mixed-Race People History Month is novelist Heidi Durrow's designation; she features mixed race people's accomplishments on her blog, Mixedchicks.com. Her celebration on the blog of playwright August Wilson as mixed even though he vigorously self-identified as black throughout his life and passionately advocated for more black directors and black theater, represents some of the controversial challenges of creating a mixed history month that Durrow herself acknowledges. http://lightskinnededgirl.typepad .com/my_weblog/2007/05/may_is_mixed_ra.html (accessed October 4, 2009).

30. I use the term from R. W. B. Lewis' foundational *The American Adam: Innocence, Tragedy, and Tradition in the Nineteenth Century* (Chicago: University of Chicago Press, 1955), which explores John Hector St. John de Crèvecoeur's idea of the American as a self-styled "new man," an innocent Adam in a new country that could release him from his historic past. Lewis argues that this Adamic image informed and continues to inform all major models of what it means to be American.

31. Heather Dalmage, "Patrolling Racial Borders: Discrimination Against Mixed Race People," in *Multiracial Child Resource Book: Living Complex Identities*, ed. Maria P. P. Root and Matt Kelley, 19 (Seattle: MAVIN Foundation, 2003).

32. Maria P. P. Root, "A Bill of Rights for Racially Mixed People," in *Racially Mixed People in America* (Thousand Oaks, CA: Sage, 1992). Reprinted in *Multiracial Child Resource Book: Living Complex Identities*, 32. Root's "Bill of Rights" has been adopted as the motto for the Web organization Intermix and remains an unofficial charter for many mixed race advocacy groups. The literature of mixed race educational advocacy is not unlike the performative assertions in Black Arts poetics, in which the emphatic creation of a declarative "I" and a "we" against a "you" betrays an anxiety that there is no sufficiently collective "we" from which to distinguish "you." See Philip Brian Harper, "Nationalism and Social Division in Black Arts Poetry of the 1960s," in *African American Literary Theory: A Reader*, ed. Winston Napier, 460–474 (New York: New York University Press, 2000).

33. Paul R. Spickard and Rowena Fong, "Pacific Islander Americans and Multiethnicity: A Vision of America's Future?" Abstract. *Social Forces* 73 (1995): 1365. See also Paul R. Spickard, *Mixed Blood: Intermarriage and Ethnic Identity in Twentieth-Century America* (Madison: University of Wisconsin Press, 1991).

34. As Kiyomi Burchill documents in "Beyond the Box: The Post-Census Politics of the Multiracial Movement," Stanford University undergraduate honors thesis (May 19, 2006), the "Republican Speaker of the House of Representatives Newt Gingrich, whose constituent Susan Graham was the co-founder of Project RACE, lent his support for Rep. Petri's bill, H.R. 830 in the 105th Congress (which he named the 'Tiger Woods Bill') that would require the census to include a multiracial category, arguing before a house committee that he wished for the day there would be only one box for 'American.' The bill was defeated. UC Regents decision was in 2004 and the proposal, put forward by Ward Connerly, was defeated 12–1." Connerly has made clear his desire to do away with both affirmative action programs and, indeed, racial categorization itself in *Creating Equal: My Fight Against Racial Preferences* (New York: Encounter Books, 2000). Most recently, the "Racial Privacy Initiative," known also as "Proposition 54: Classification by Race, Ethnicity, Color, or National Origin," was placed on the October 7, 2003, California state election ballot as an initiative constitutional amendment and actively enlisted the support of multiracial organizations. Both Gingrich and Connerly have publicly aligned themselves

with many of the mixed race advocates' stated goals, especially those that might disable race-based policies in the name of libertarian "privacy rights." For a comprehensive description of the conservative movement's interest in mixed race, see Williams, *Mark One or More.*

35. Elissa Gootman, "Proposal Adds Options for Students to Specify Race," *New York Times*, August 9, 2006, http://www.nytimes.com/2006/08/09/education/09ethnic .html?ex=1155787200&en=8d33409d61a82656&ei=5070&emc=eta1. Gootman's article cites Gary Orfield, director of the Civil Rights Project then at Harvard, as critical of the Education Department's push to include multiracial self-identification options on school enrollment because it would "harm the ability of researchers and civil rights groups to track race on campus."

36. Maria P. P. Root, "50 Experiences of Mixed Race People: Racial Experiences Questionnaire" (1996). See http://www.drmariaroot.com/doc/50Experiences.pdf (accessed October 1, 2009). By naming what she sees as the normative challenges of being mixed, Root also scripts a normative experience through documents like "50 Experiences of Racially Mixed People" with a questionnaire format that invites readers to situate themselves within the boundaries of the mixed race communal experience outlined for them. See also "Mix It Up!" *O: The Oprah Magazine*, April 2006, 270–279. Many mainstream journals, including Oprah's O, similarly generate and norm the appearance of the broad constituency. One article, "Mix It Up!" for instance, includes a photo-collage documenting interracial families whose offspring represent "beauty without borders" (270). In that same section, Lise Funderburg suggests that her multiracial town of Mt. Airy in Philadelphia represents a kind of ideal Mr. Rogers' America—specifically citing Walt Whitman's "I contain multitudes." She concludes, "It is always a beautiful day in my neighborhood" (279).

37. To their credit, both Root and Kelley argue that a multiracial identity should "advocate for progressive racial and social justice across all lines" (Introduction to *Multiracial Child Resource Book*, xvi), but the only activism they discuss is focused on revising the census for multiracial identification.

38. Many of my points here are drawn from my editorial "2010 Census: Think Twice, Check Once," *Huffington Post*, March 8, 2010, http://www.huffingtonpost.com/michele -elam/2010-census-think-twice-c_b_490164.html (accessed April 7, 2010). On related issues of classification, see David Theo Goldberg, "Made in the U.S.A.," in *American Mixed Race: The Culture of Microdiversity*, ed. Naomi Zack, 237–256 (Lanham, MD: Rowman and Littlefield, 1995); Michael Omi, "Racial Identity and the State: The Dilemmas of Classification," *Law and Inequality: A Journal of Theory and Practice* 7 (1997): 7–23; John Powell, "The Colorblind Multiracial Dilemma: Racial Categories Reconsidered," *University of San Francisco Law Review* 31 (1997): 789–806. Deborah Ramirez offers perhaps the most exhaustive critique of the political costs for these bids for multiracial identifications at the level of the "box" in "Multicultural Empowerment: It's Not Just Black and White Anymore," *Stanford Law Review* 47, no. 5 (May 1995): 957, 968.

39. March 22, 2010, e-mail to author from the Association of Multiethnic Americans (AMEA), amea2010census@gmail.com, Subject line "URGENT: Census 2010 Info Packet for Multiracial Individuals and Families." Citations from this press release and "Most Commonly Asked Questions and Answers" quoted from attachments to this e-mail. Although it offers a disclaimer that "[t]he information contained herein . . . does not necessarily reflect the views of the U.S. Census Bureau," the press release does claim AMEA's official association as one of the U.S. Census National Partners (one of dozens

of interest and community groups that advocate for constituencies to the bureau and, more controversially, claim to speak as the voice for multiracial interests). Their "Most Commonly Asked Questions and Answers" erases debates about the organization's right to be the official national representative of "Multiracial Individuals and Families" and erases as well any controversy over how to complete the census. Two of the more controversial instructions are presented merely as fact: the document warns constituents that "You have been misinformed if you are told that if you choose one or more races on the 2010 Census that this takes away from any single-race population numbers. In fact, multiracial identified people are counted among each of the single-race categories they select, which *adds to*, NOT *takes away from*, other populations. It therefore benefits all communities" (italics and capitalization in original). A surprisingly direct response to the many arguments the group has had and continues to have with the NAACP and other traditional civil rights organizations about this subject, the claim of mutual benefit remains hotly contested, and for good reason since the government must still disaggregate racial statistics and at times counts those who check both "black" and "white" as "black" for Voting Rights Act purposes. The same document also advises against checking the "Some Other Race" option or writing in "unique, community-based terms such as 'Hapa,' 'Multiracial/ethnic,' 'Biracial,'" etc.—options also equally available and legitimate on the census—since, the AMEA states, they will not be "considered a multiracial identity" and will not, therefore, "be counted in the overall multiracial population." People are free to identify as they wish, the document concedes, but the implication is very clear: the AMEA is the authoritative body dispensing authoritative directives: if you want to belong, if you want to be counted among us, you have to do it in this format and with our language.

40. According to a James Irvine Foundation 2005 research brief, "'Unknown Students' on College Campuses," in their occasional refusal to check any box on, for example, college admissions forms, people who identify as mixed race often join with white students who fall into the "race/ethnicity unknown" category: "Our findings suggest that overall, a sizeable portion of students in the unknown category are white, in addition to multiracial students who may have selected white as one of their categories." http://www.irvine.org/assets/pdf/pubs/education/UnknownStudentsCDI.pdf.

41. David Horowitz's dismissive opinion in "American Apartheid" in Salon.com, http://www.salon.com/july97/columnists/horowitz2970718.html/index.html.

42. Michael Omi and Howard Winant, *Racial Formation in the United States: From the 1960s to the 1990s*, 2nd ed. (New York: Routledge, 1994), 3. See also C. Matthew Snipp, "Racial Measurement in the American Census: Past Practices and Implications for the Future," *Annual Review of Sociology* 29 (2003): 563–588, on the census as a "racial cosmology . . . affecting public perceptions about the racial hierarchy of American society" (563). For a history of census designations of people of mixed descent, see Ann Morning, "New Faces, Old Faces: Counting the Multiracial Population Past and Present," in *New Faces in a Changing America: Multiracial Identity in the 21st Century*, ed. Loretta I. Winters and Herman L. DeBose, 41–67 (Thousand Oaks, CA: Sage, 2003). Also see Joel Perlmann, "Reflecting the Changing Face of America: Multiracials, Racial Classifications, and American Intermarriage," in *Interracialism: Black-White Intermarriage in American History, Literature, and Law*, ed. Werner Sollors, 506–534 (New York: Oxford University Press, 2000).

43. See Francis Winddance Twine, *Racism in a Racial Democracy: The Maintenance of White Supremacy in Brazil* (New Brunswick, NJ: Rutgers University Press, 1997);

Suzanne Bost, *Mulattas and Mestizas: Representing Mixed Identities in the Americas, 1850–2000* (Athens: University of Georgia Press, 2003); and Charles V. Hamilton et al., eds., *Beyond Racism: Race and Inequality in Brazil, South Africa, and the United States* (Boulder, CO: Lynne Rienner Publishers, 2001).

44. Halle Berry and her mother, who live near each other in Los Angeles, are close by all accounts, and her mother's choice to identify her as black has never been associated with personal rejection. See http://en.wikipedia.org/wiki/Halle_Berry (accessed October 4, 2009). Dozens of mixed race blogs, however, registered fury that Berry identified as black, which they saw as "dissing" her mother.

45. As I suggest in "Obama's Mixology," whatever others' debates over Obama's blackness, he consistently represents biracialism in the context of broader civil rights both to the public and to multiracial advocates in particular. See The Root.com (*Washington Post*), October 30, 2008, http://www.theroot.com/views/obamas-mixology (accessed April 5, 2010). His refusal of post-racialism was evident at least as early as 2005. When the MAVIN Foundation, which identifies itself as "the nation's largest mixed race advocacy organization," sent five people in their twenties to travel the country raising awareness "of America's mixed race baby boom" on a bus tour called Generation MIX, they met with Obama in Washington, DC, at his offices (April 25, 2005). It "was really exciting because he's mixed race," one of the participants noted in the foundation's film documentary of the tour, *Chasing Daybreak*. One gets the clear sense from the documentary that Generation MIX hoped to find in Obama a representative who could serve as a legislative whip for mixed race identity and concerns in the Senate. But in his meeting with the Generation MIX group, Obama soberly tells them:

> Well you know, I don't think that you can consider the issue of mixed race outside of the issue of race. And I do think that racial relations have improved somewhat, and I think to the extent that people of mixed race can be part of those larger movements and those larger concerns then I think that they serve as a useful bridge between cultures. But, you know, what I am always cautious about is persons of mixed race focusing so narrowly on their own unique experiences that they are detached from larger struggles, and I think it's important to try to avoid that sense of exclusivity, and feeling that you're special in some way. I think you are maybe unique in your experiences and [that] may allow you to reach out to more people, but ultimately the same challenges that all of you face are the same challenges that a lot of young people face, which is how you can make an impact on the world that is positive.

The message hit home: in particular, one participant, Geetha Lakshminarayanan, took to heart his message that they need to "be careful not to separate ourselves," and to understand the mixed race movement in the context of the civil rights agenda more broadly. Quotes from *Chasing Daybreak: A Film about Mixed Race in America*, directed and edited by Justin Leroy, produced by Matt Kelley (MAVIN Foundation, 2006). More on the documentary can be found at www.chasingdaybreak.com.

46. Race mixing is "de way," Cora says, a normative practice only the more potent because unspeakable. See Langston Hughes, *Mulatto*, in *Five Plays by Langston Hughes*, ed. Webster Smalley, 30–31 (Bloomington: Indiana University Press, 1963). For a deeper analysis of the play, see Michele Elam and Harry Elam, "Blood Debt: Reparations in Langston Hughes' *Mulatto*," *Theatre Journal* 61, no. 1 (March 2009): 85–103.

47. W. E. B. Du Bois, "The Concept of Race," *Dusk of Dawn* (1940), in *W. E. B. Du Bois: Writings*, ed. Nathan Irvin Huggins, 630 (New York: Library of America, Viking, 1986).

48. In the apocalyptic vision of "The Comet," only the threat of complete human extinction warrants cross-racial desire, as if only the end of the world could witness an end to racial antipathy. W. E. B. Du Bois, "The Comet," *Darkwater* (1920), in *The Oxford W. E. B. Du Bois Reader*, ed. Eric J. Sundquist, 619 (New York: Oxford University Press, 1996).

49. From W. E. B. Du Bois, *Dark Princess: A Romance* (1928), introduction by Claudia Tate, 311 (Jackson: University of Mississippi Press, 1995).

50. From Langston Hughes' famous poem "Harlem" (1951): "What happens to a dream deferred?/Does it dry up like a raisin in the sun . . . ?" In *The Norton Anthology of African American Literature*, ed. Henry Louis Gates, Jr., and Nellie Y. McKay, 2nd ed. (New York: W. W. Norton, 2004), 1308–1309.

51. For an extended analysis of this scene, see Michele Elam and Paul C. Taylor, "Du Bois' Erotics," in *Next to the Color Line: Gender, Sexuality, and W. E. B. Du Bois*, ed. Susan Gillman and Alyce Weinbaum, 209–233 (Minneapolis: University of Minnesota Press, 2007).

52. W. E. B. Du Bois, "The White World," *Dusk of Dawn* (1940), in *W. E. B. Du Bois: Writings*, ed. Nathan Huggins, 652–680 (New York: Library of America, Viking, 1986).

53. See Adrian Piper, "Passing for White, Passing for Black," *Transition* 58 (1992):4–32.

54. Du Bois' and Hughes' recognition that race is an expedient contrivance is developed further in Lorraine Hansberry's play *Les Blancs* (1969) through the mixed race character, Tshembe. Lorraine Hansberry, *Les Blancs: The Collected Last Plays*, ed. Robert Nemiroff, introduction by Margaret B. Wilkerson (New York: Vintage Books, 1994).

55. Betsy Erkkila, in *Mixed Bloods and Other Crosses: Rethinking American Literature from the Revolution to the Culture Wars* (Philadelphia: University of Pennsylvania Press, 2005), similarly argues that "mixed-blood," better than terms like "hybridity," speaks to the "dialectics of blood and boundaries, mixture and crossing . . . that signify the anxieties about class mixture, black and female sexuality, sexual inversion, same-sex merging, and . . . capitalist exploitation that were expressed through the metaphorics of blood in the Americas" (x). See also Elise Virginia Lemire's excellent "Epilogue: 'Miscegenation' Today" in *"Miscegenation": Making Race in America* (Philadelphia: University of Pennsylvania Press, 2002), 145–147. In a similar vein, Suzanne Bost, in *Mulattas and Mestizas*, warns about celebrating these new "millennial mixtures" for many of the same reasons as I do, and also warns against the domestication of the potentially radical fluidity of racial intelligibility. Erkkila, Lemire, and Bost all offer much-needed historical analyses of earlier representations of mixed race that bear directly on contemporary discussions.

56. Saks, "Representing Miscegenation Law," 53–54.

57. A 2007 *Journal of Blacks in Higher Education* article reported research that proved that Ivy League race-sensitive admissions programs were primarily helping black students who were foreign-born or from upper-middle-class African American families. Henry Louis Gates, Jr., is quoted as saying that more than two-thirds of Harvard's black students are of "African or Caribbean descent or of mixed race." http://www.jbhe.com/news_views/56_race_sensitive_not_helping.html.

58. See Harryette Mullen's excellent foreword to *Oreo* (Boston: Northeastern University Press, 2000), xi–xxviii.

59. Anthony Appiah, "Towards a New Cosmopolitanism," in the *New York Times Magazine*, January 1, 2006, 30–37.

60. Mark Anthony Neal, *Soul Babies: Black Popular Culture and the Post-Soul Aesthetic* (New York: Routledge, 2002), 2–3. See also Trey Ellis, "Obama: Cultural Mulatto,"

Huffington Post (February 19, 2007), http://www.salon.com/ent/feature/2009/05/07/obama_spock/index.html (accessed November 7, 2009).

61. Bertram D. Ashe, "Theorizing the Post-Soul Aesthetic: An Introduction," *African American Review* 41, no. 4 (Winter 2007): 614.

62. This concept of blackness goes by many variants and names: Studio Museum of Harlem curator Thelma Golden calls it "post-black"; Hamza Walker calls it "renigged." Thelma Golden's "Post . . ." and Hamza Walker's "Renigged" essays both in the exhibition catalog (New York: Open Library) for "Freestyle," April 28–June 24, 2001, Studio Museum of Harlem.

63. Ashe, "Theorizing the Post-Soul Aesthetic," 615. Ashe is quoting from Senna's *Caucasia* (New York: Riverhead, 1998), 413.

64. Ellis, "Obama: Cultural Mulatto."

65. Cornel West, "The New Cultural Politics of Difference," in *The Cultural Studies Reader*, ed. Simon During, 203–204 (New York: Routledge, 1993). In that sense, blaxploration could be considered part of the new profile for "Black cultural workers" (212), as West defines them.

66. Jared Sexton, *Amalgamation Schemes: Antiblackness and the Critique of Multiracialism* (Minneapolis: University of Minnesota Press, 2008).

67. Samira Kawash, *Dislocating the Color Line: Identity, Hybridity, and Singularity in African-American Narrative* (Stanford: Stanford University Press, 1997); Eduardo Bonilla-Silva, *Racism Without Racists: Color-Blind Racism and the Persistence of Racial Inequality in the United States* (New York: Rowman and Littlefield, 2003); Lawrence D. Bobo and Victor Thompson, "Unfair by Design: The War on Drugs, Race, and the Legitimacy of the Criminal Justice System," *Social Research* 73, no. 2 (2006): 445–472; Lawrence D. Bobo, "Inequalities that Endure? Racial Ideology, American Politics, and the Peculiar Role of Social Science," in *The Changing Terrain of Race and Ethnicity*, ed. M. Krysan and A. Lewis, 13–42 (New York: Russell Sage Foundation, 2004); Lawrence D. Bobo and Devon Johnson, "A Taste for Punishment: Black and White Americans' Views on the Death Penalty and the War on Drugs," *Du Bois Review* 1 (2004): 151–180.

68. Orlando Patterson, "Race and Diversity in the Age of Obama," *New York Times Book Review*, August 16, 2009, 23. For the way racial formation underwrites American national identity, especially the way blackness continues to be constructed as the lowest social rung against which other races are ranked and defined, see Omi and Winant, *Racial Formation in the United States*.

For an account of how this divide shows no sign of changing with the times, see Barbara Ehrenreich and Dedrick Muhammad, "The Recession's Racial Divide," *New York Times*, September 12, 2009, http://www.nytimes.com/2009/09/13/opinion/13ehrenreich.html?_r=1 (accessed September 13, 2009).

69. Tommie Shelby, Introduction to *We Who Are Dark: The Philosophical Foundations of Black Solidarity* (Cambridge, MA: Belknap Press of Harvard University Press, 2005), 4.

70. Williams, *Seeing a Color-Blind Future*, 63–64.

71. John Berger, *Ways of Seeing* (New York: Penguin, 1991).

72. In the 1993 "The New Face of America" *Time* magazine article that I mentioned here, the "new" documentation is an attempt to in a sense re-register the nation's citizenry, a way of controlling racial difference and competing social realities through representation, not unlike the late-nineteenth-century realist literary gestures analyzed by both Amy Kaplan in *The Social Construction of American Realism* (Chicago: University of Chicago Press,

1988; rpt. 1992) and Kenneth Warren in *Black and White Strangers: Race and American Literary Realism* (Chicago: University of Chicago Press, 1995). As L. S. Kim and Gilberto Moíses Blasini argue, with the "shifts in [racial] identification come transformations in the nation's image of itself." L. S. Kim and Gilberto Moíses Blasini, "The Performance of Multicultural Identity in U.S. Network Television: Shiny, Happy Popstars (Holding Hands)," *Emergences: Journal for the Study of Media and Composite Cultures* 11 (Fall 2001): 287–307. Kip Fulbeck's *Part Asian, 100% Hapa* (San Francisco: Chronicle Books, 2006), which features headshots of multiracial individuals with "official" typed genealogies under which appear an individual's handwritten self-description, similarly makes the visual study of faces an index of mixed race intelligibility.

73. This argument, suggested by Peggy Phelan and others, maintains that "visibility is a trap . . . it summons surveillance and the law; it provokes voyeurism, fetishism, the colonial/imperial appetite for possession. . . . Visibility politics are addictive rather than transformational (to say nothing of revolutionary)." Peggy Phelan, *Unmarked: The Politics of Performance* (New York: Routledge, 1993), 10–11.

74. Jen Chau, founder of Swirl, Inc., a mixed race advocacy organization, and codirector of New Demographic, a diversity consulting firm in New York City, for instance, offers services to corporations that are interested in minority representation.

75. Linda Martín Alcoff, *Visible Identities: Race, Gender, and the Self* (New York: Oxford University Press, 2006).

76. Ralph Ellison, "Prologue," *Invisible Man*, 2nd Vintage International ed. (New York: Vintage International, 1995), 3.

77. Heather Dalmage argues that in racial border patrolling by the "race police," they "claim that race is a simple concept, demand that others comply, and make their presence felt through various actions. The most common action, by far, is the stare" (21). See her "Patrolling Racial Borders: Discrimination Against Mixed Race People," in *Multiracial Child Resource Book: Living Complex Identities*, ed. Maria P. P. Root and Matt Kelley, 19–25 (Seattle: MAVIN Foundation, 2003).

78. Rosemarie Garland-Thomson, *Staring: How We Look* (New York: Oxford University Press, 2009), 3, 6.

CHAPTER ONE

1. Teresa Kay Williams, Cynthia L. Nakashima, George Kitahara Kich, and G. Reginald Daniel, "Being Different Together in the University Classroom: Multiracial Identity as Transgressive Education," in *The Multiracial Experience: Racial Borders as the New Frontier*, ed. Maria P. P. Root, 359–337 (Thousand Oaks, CA: Sage, 1995).

2. A group sponsored by MAVIN, the mixed race advocacy organization, met with Senator Barack Obama in Washington, D.C., at his offices (April 25, 2005). The interview is included in the documentary *Chasing Daybreak: A Film About Mixed Race in America*, directed by Justin Leroy, produced by Matt Kelley (MAVIN Foundation, 2006). More on the documentary can be found at www.chasingdaybreak.com.

3. All collected in Root, *The Multiracial Experience*, 341–394.

4. Alejandra Lopez, in "The Population of Two or More Races in California," *Race and Ethnicity in California*, Demographics Report Series, no. 4 (Stanford University Research Institute of the Center for Comparative Studies in Race and Ethnicity, November 2001), notes that the percentage of people identifying as mixed-race or marking multiple racial designations is much higher for those under 18. It is no accident that the movement

is most popular among the young. Most mixed race organizations are a mixture of people 25 or younger, interracial couples with young children, and parents involved in interracial adoptions. Part of my argument is that the particular notion of mixed race circulated now is a distinctly post–civil rights era phenomenon that was coded quite differently before the 1950s.

5. For one of the many lists of mixed race courses, see http://www.eurasiannation .com/articlespol2003-04mixedstudies.htm (accessed March 10, 2004). The article "The Explosion in Mixed Race Studies," by Erica Schlaikjer, interestingly enough, had a banner picture of me as a supposedly representative mixed race faculty member teaching a course on the subject, although the picture was actually taken several years earlier for an unrelated promotional campaign for the University of Puget Sound and then sold to an advertising agency, gettyimages.com. Since 2006, I have taught many courses on mixed race politics and representation, though I had not in 2004 when the image was taken. Images from this photo shoot have since appeared also in a *Harper's Magazine* ad selling stock and bonds, the Hispanic Congressional website (where I am presumably Latina), the *Boston Globe* (representing an older-than-average non–English speaker returning to school), and elsewhere across the country. In many cases, the image is darkened, lightened, or placed in context among other images to represent a light-skinned woman of color.

6. These include the Association of MultiEthnic Americans (www.ameasite.org), Famlee (www.scc.swarthmore.edu/-thompson/famlee/home.html), Hapa Issues Forum (www.hapaissuesforum.org), My Shoes (myshoes.com), Interracial Individuals Discussion List (www.geocities.com/Wellesley/6426/ii.html), Project RACE (Reclassify All Children Equally), Inc. (projectrace.home.mindspring.com), www.eurasiannation.com, www .swirllinc.org, www.anomalythefilm.com, *Interracial Voice* (www.webcom.com/-intvoice), *MAVIN: The Articulate Journal of the Mixed-Race Experience* (www.mavin.net), and *Metisse Magazine* (www.metisse.com), among many others.

Many of the educational reforms just before and after the 2000 Census were advanced by white parents of grade-school children, minors whose identity is claimed on their behalf by their parents as bi- or multiracial; hence the focus on early childhood education.

7. I elaborate this argument in "Towards Desegregating Syllabuses: Teaching American Literary Realism and Racial Uplift Fiction," in *Teaching Literature: A Companion*, ed. Tanya Agathocleous and Ann C. Dean, 59 (New York: Palgrave Macmillan, 2003).

8. Chandra Talpade Mohanty, "On Race and Voice: Challenges for Liberal Education in the 1990s," *Cultural Critique* 14 (Winter 1989–1990): 186.

9. Kenji Yoshino, *Covering: The Hidden Assault on Our Civil Rights* (New York: Random House, 2007).

10. Teresa Williams-León and Cynthia L. Nakashimi, eds., *The Sum of Our Parts: Mixed Heritage Asian Americans* (Philadelphia: Temple University Press, 2001); Jonathan Brennan, ed., *Mixed Race Literature* (Stanford: Stanford University Press, 2002); Chandra Prasad, ed., *Mixed: An Anthology of Short Fiction on the Multiracial Experience* (New York: W. W. Norton, 2006).

11. Maria P. P. Root and Matt Kelley, eds., *Multiracial Child Resource Book: Living Complex Identities* (Seattle: MAVIN Foundation, 2003); Pearl Fuyo Gaskins, ed., *What Are You? Voices of Mixed-Race Young People* (New York: Henry Holt, 1997); Maria P. P. Root, ed., *Racially Mixed People* (Thousand Oaks, CA: Sage, 1992); Maria P. P. Root, ed., *The Multiracial Experience: Racial Borders as the New Frontier* (Thousand Oaks, CA: Sage, 1995); Loretta I. Winters and Herman L. DeBose, eds., *New Faces in a*

Changing America: Multiracial Identity in the 21st Century (Thousand Oaks, CA: Sage, 2002); *Of Many Colors: Portraits of Multiracial Families,* Photographs by Gigi Kaeser, Interviews by Peggy Gillespie, Introduction by Glenda Valentine (Amherst: University of Massachusetts Press, 1997) (selected as a Best Book for Teenagers by the New York Public Library); and Paul R. Spickard, *Mixed Blood: Intermarriage and Ethnic Identity in Twentieth-Century America* (Madison: University of Wisconsin Press, 1991). See also Mike Tauber and Pamela Singh, photographers, with an introduction by Rebecca Walker, *Blended Nation: Portraits and Interviews of Mixed-Race America* (New York: Channel Photographics, 2009).

12. The mission statements for most of the larger mixed race organizations and watch groups—MAVIN, AMEA (including New Demographics and Mixed Race Media Watch, etc.)—subscribe to this assumption that being seen is, to some extent, a political end in itself. For a fuller discussion of how mixed race organizations understand their relationships to civil rights, see Kevin R. Johnson, ed., *Mixed Race America and the Law* (New York: New York University Press, 2003).

13. Toni Morrison, "Unspeakable Things Unspoken: The Afro-American Presence in American Literature," in *The Norton Anthology of African American Literature,* ed. Henry Louis Gates, Jr., and Nellie Y. McKay, 2nd ed. (New York: W. W. Norton, 2004), 2306.

14. See Roderick Ferguson, *Aberrations in Black: Toward a Queer of Color Critique* (Minneapolis: University of Minnesota Press, 2003). Quote from "Editorial Review," http://www.amazon.com/Aberrations-Black-Critique-Critical-American/dp/0816641293/ ref=pd_sim_b_3/104-3761771-0121516?ie=UTF8 (accessed June 2, 2006).

15. William Byrd, *Histories of the Dividing Line Betwixt Virginia and North Carolina* (New York: Dover, 1967), 4.

16. The classroom is a social microcosm, as Andrea Lunsford, Paulo Freire, bell hooks, and others have argued; and in many ways it never was a room in an insular "ivory tower" but, rather, already existed and exists as an active site for social engagement. See Andrea Lunsford and John Ruszkiewicz, *The Presence of Others: Voices and Images That Call for Response* (New York: Bedford/St. Martin's Press, 2008); Paulo Freire, *Education for Critical Consciousness* (New York: Crossroad Publishing Company, 1974); bell hooks, *Teaching to Transgress: Education as the Practice of Freedom* (New Jersey: Routledge, 1994).

17. Kobena Mercer, "Welcome to the Jungle: Identity and Diversity in Postmodern Politics," in *Identity, Community, Culture, Difference,* ed. Jonathan Rutherford, 68 (London: Lawrence and Wishart, 1990).

18. Barbara Christian, "A Rough Terrain: The Case of Shaping an Anthology of Caribbean Women Writers," in *The Ethnic Canon: Histories, Institutions, and Interventions,* ed. David Palumbo-Liu, 256 (Minneapolis: University of Minnesota Press, 1995).

19. Kimberly McClain DaCosta, *Making Multiracials: State, Family, and Market in the Redrawing of the Color Line* (Stanford: Stanford University Press, 2007), 156.

20. Ibid., 172.

21. Sundee Frazier, *Check All That Apply: Finding Wholeness as a Multiracial Person* (New York: InterVarsity Press, 2002).

22. See Marguerite W. Davol, *Black, White, Just Right!* Illustrations by Irene Trivas (Park Ridge, IL: Albert Whitman and Company, 1993); Donna Jackson Nakazawa, *Does Anybody Else Look Like Me? A Parent's Guide to Raising Multiracial Children* (Cambridge, MA: Perseus Publishing, 2003); and Francis Wardle, *Tomorrow's Children: Meeting the Needs of Multiracial and Multiethnic Children at Home, in Early Childhood Programs,*

and at School (Denver: Center for the Study of Biracial Children, 1999).

23. Almost every mixed race advocacy organization has a website with resources of this nature and links to products and bibliographies. See, for example, http://www.mixedchicks.net/curlyhairproducts.html, http://real-kidz.com/, http://www.mixedstudentresources.com/?page_id=36, and http://www.ameasite.org/biblio.asp. These offer books for K–12 grouped according to "School Age" and "Teens," etc.

24. DaCosta, *Making Multiracials*, 169.

25. Quoted in Samira Kawash, who similarly argues that "hybridity is a challenge, not only to the question of human 'being,' but to the status of knowledge itself, the question of how and if we can *know* identity or hybridity. To rest with the conclusion that identity is really always hybridity deflects the real challenge of hybridity itself, a challenge posed to the very conditions of modern epistemology and subjectivity" (*Dislocating the Color Line: Identity, Hybridity, and Singularity in African-American Narrative* [Stanford University Press, 1997]). On hybridity, see also Robert C. Young, *Colonial Desire: Hybridity in Theory, Culture, and Race* (New York: Routledge, 1995).

26. See discussion of the racial politics of genre in Howell's patronage of Dunbar in chapter 2 of my *Race, Work, and Desire in American Literature, 1860–1930* (Cambridge: Cambridge University Press, 2003), 58–60.

27. Teresa Williams-León and Cynthia L. Nakashimi, eds., *The Sum of Our Parts: Mixed Heritage Asian Americans* (Philadelphia: Temple University Press, 2001).

28. For instance, see Geneviève Fabre and Michel Feith, eds., *Jean Toomer and the Harlem Renaissance* (Piscataway, NJ: Rutgers University Press, 2001). Their introduction, "Tight-lipped 'Oracle'," to Jean Toomer's *Cane*, is representative of the refiguration of Toomer as not simply complex but heroic—indeed, forward-thinking in a way, they imply, that his backward contemporaries simply could not understand:

> Toomer's definition of his identity—as of mixed ancestry, blue blood, and as American— at a time when the term mulatto had disappeared from Census forms and when curiosity for, or loathing of anything Negro was intense, was somehow disconcerting. Yet his declarations were more properly affirmations than denials and forced attention on the composite ethnic makeup of most Americans as well as on the arbitrariness of boundaries and categories of individuals as either/or. He experienced at his own expense the difficulties of proclaiming oneself neither white nor black; this is most evident in his dealings with editors and the publishing world. The pressure to be "tagged" . . . never deterred him from his conviction that his approach and treatment must be first and foremost artistic. (4)

The implication is that today's modern-thinking readers and publishers now agree that monoracialism is as negative a force as racist segregation and equally represses the free exercise of both identity and art.

29. Brennan, *Mixed Race Literature*, 3–4.

30. George Hutchinson, *In Search of Nella Larsen: A Biography of the Color Line* (Cambridge, MA: Harvard University Press, 2006). See also Gene Andrew Jarrett, *African American Literature Beyond Race: An Alternative Reader* (New York: New York University Press, 2006), who argues that black nationalist literary histories that privilege a certain kind of protest literature have ignored or devalued the "raceless" and "anomalous," as he calls it, fiction by writers like Frank Webb and Frank Yerby, among others.

31. Hutchinson, *In Search of Nella Larsen*, 1.

32. David Palumbo-Liu, ed., *The Ethnic Canon: Histories, Institutions, and Interventions* (Minneapolis: University of Minneapolis Press, 1995), 19.

33. Werner Sollors, *Neither Black nor White yet Both: Thematic Explorations of Interracial Literature* (New York: Oxford University Press, 1997), 10. See also his *Ethnic Modernism* (Cambridge, MA: Harvard University Press, 2008).

34. Sollors, *Neither Black nor White yet Both*, 13.

35. Ibid., 12.

36. Henry B. Wonham, ed., *Criticism on the Color Line: Desegregating American Literary Studies* (Piscataway, NJ: Rutgers University Press, 1996), 17.

37. Chandra Prashad, ed., *Mixed: An Anthology of Short Fiction on the Multiracial Experience* (New York: W. W. Norton, 2006). We could include also the beautifully written but very much in this same genre Richard Powers', *The Time of Our Singing* (New York: Farrar, Straus, and Giroux, 2003), which, though hailed by the *Christian Science Monitor*— "the best black novel to appear in America since *Beloved* has just been written by a white man"—nonetheless focuses in much the same way and with similar meditations as other texts of this kind on the "neither fish nor fowl" lives of two mixed race brothers. I would not include Natasha Trethewey's collection of poetry, often dealing with miscegenation, *Native Guard* (New York: Houghton Mifflin, 2006), in part because she situates her exploration so firmly within African American and American politics and traditions. I would distinguish, also, Edward Ball's very powerful *Slaves in the Family* (1999) and *The Sweet Hell Within: A Family History* (2001) because, although they explore race mixing, Ball places his family history and kinship in the context of historical responsibility, familial reparations, and black achievement, unlike many other memoirs of family race mixing. In fact, even as I signal the way all these texts have been marketed as part of a mixed race genre, it is not my aim to conflate them here by assembling them on the page together and, in doing so, to replicate the kind of packaging with which I take issue.

38. Brennan, *Mixed Race Literature*, 17.

39. Susan Graham was one of the earliest advocates of the multiracial census category, testifying with her child before the Office of Management and Budget. For a scathing criticism of her involvement, see Jon Michael Spencer, *The New Colored People: The Mixed-Race Movement in America* (New York: New York University Press, 1997).

40. Paul R. Spickard, *Mixed Blood: Intermarriage and Ethnic Identity in Twentieth-Century America* (Madison: University of Wisconsin Press, 1991), 92. As tempting as it is to include Cuban writers like Nicolás Guillén, Aimé Césaire, Eduoard Glissant, and many others who write about mestizaje, it is beyond the scope of what I can discuss here.

41. Ibid., 93.

42. Noel Ignatiev and John Garvey, *Race Traitor* (New York: Routledge, 1998).

43. See Harry Justin Elam, Jr., "Change Clothes and Go: A Post-Script to Post-Blackness," in *Black Cultural Traffic: Crossroads in Global Performance and Black Popular Culture*, ed. Harry J. Elam, Jr., and Kennell A. Jackson, 379–388 (Ann Arbor: University of Michigan Press, 2005).

44. Elizabeth McHenry, *Forgotten Readers: Recovering the Lost History of African American Literary Salons* (Durham, NC: Duke University Press, 2002), 261.

45. Ibid.

46. Harold Cruse, "The Integrationist Ethic as a Basis for Scholarly Endeavors," in *The Essential Harold Cruse: A Reader*, ed. William Jelani Cobb, 117–124 (New York: Palgrave Macmillan, 2002).

47. See Paula M. L. Moya ("Introduction: Reclaiming Identity") and Linda Martín Alcoff ("Who's Afraid of Identity Politics"), in *Reclaiming Identity: Realist Theory and the Predicament of Postmodernism*, ed. Paula M. L. Moya and Michael R. Hames-García (Berkeley: University of California Press, 2000).

48. Francis Wardle, "Academics Are Enemies of the Multiracial Movement," CSBCHome .org Blog Archive for the Center for the Study of Biracial Children, April 2, 2009, http:// csbchome.org/?p=24 (accessed June 30, 2009).

49. Michael R. Hames-García, "Which America Is Ours? Martí's 'Truth' and the Foundations of 'American Literature,'" *Modern Fiction Studies* 49, no. 1 (Spring 2003): 19–53. Special Issue, "Fictions of the Trans-American Imaginary," ed. Paula M. L. Moya and Ramón Saldívar.

50. Ibid., 30.

51. Ibid.

52. Paula M. L. Moya, *Learning from Experience: Minority Identities, Multicultural Struggles* (Berkeley: University of California Press, 2002), 156–158. Quoted in Hames-García, "Which America Is Ours?" 30.

53. Related to this notion of classroom conflict is the role of educators and the need for them to be self-critical as well. By this I am not suggesting the self-flagellating gestures that some white educators and critics in the early 1990s seemed compelled to make in prefaces to their articles or in opening their lectures with apologia (for being white). These have the inadvertent effect of waiving critical engagement with their own race with the justification that they do not share the same experience as minority students. But this does not advance analysis of experience; it quarantines it and the teacher, who has in effect, removed him- or herself from applying the critical discussion of racial experience except when it applies to "others."

54. Kimberlé Crenshaw, "Mapping the Margins: Intersectionality, Identity Politics, and Violence Against Women of Color," *Stanford Law Review* 43 (July 1991): 1241–1265.

55. Hortense J. Spillers, "The 'Tragic Mulatta': Neither/Nor—Toward an Alternative Model," in *The Difference Within: Feminism and Critical Theory*, ed. Elizabeth Meese and Alice Parker, 168 (Philadelphia: J. Benjamins, 1989).

56. See Calvin Hernton's early work on interracial love, first published in the mid-1960s, *Sex and Racism in America* (New York: Anchor Books, 1992), one of the earliest studies of the way racial stereotyping and race/power dynamics inform intimate interpersonal relations even if the couple sees themselves as a sanctuary from the world of race politics.

57. This is an argument commonly addressed in debates about reparations—see, for instance, Stephen Best and Saidiya Hartman, "Fugitive Justice," *Representations* 92 (Fall 2005): 1–16. Best and Hartman edited this special issue of the journal devoted to the questions of reparations and argued for a reconceptualization of redress discourses. The essays were drawn from the work of the Redress Project, begun at the University of California at Berkeley. See also DeWayne Wickham, "Today's Blacks Too Distant from Slavery? Think Again," *USA Today*, February 13, 2001, available at http://www.usatoday .com/news/opinion/columnists/wickham/2001-02-13-wickham.htm. Wickham argues that it is cynical and specious to suggest that those of mixed race do not deserve reparations because of some "diluted" heritage; in his view, "miscegenation was a spoil of slavery. White slave owners routinely had their way with slave women. The linear successors of these offspring are the most obvious proof of the cruelty inflicted upon slave families."

58. See Danzy Senna, "The Mulatto Millennium," in *Half and Half: Writers on Growing Up Biracial and Bicultural*, ed. Claudine Chiawei O'Hearn, 12–27 (New York: Pantheon, 1998).

59. Moya, *Learning from Experience*, 132.

60. This hardly needs elaboration, but for a reminder one need go no further than the tragic case of Philippa Schuyler. See Kathryn Talalay's excellent biography of the "mixed-race" genius who ended up repudiating any association with blackness: *Composition in Black and White: The Life of Philippa Schuyler: The Tragic Saga of Harlem's Biracial Prodigy* (New York: Oxford University Press, 1995).

61. An excellent and thoroughly documented glimpse into the complexity of two of these related histories, in the revolutionary period in the United States and during the same colonial period in South Africa, can be found in George Fredrickson, *White Supremacy: A Comparative Study in American and South African History* (New York: Oxford University Press, 1983), chapter 3.

CHAPTER TWO

1. M. M. Bakhtin, *Rabelais and His World*, trans. Hélène Iswolsky (Bloomington: Indiana University Press, 1984), 4. Quoted in Stephen Duncombe, ed., *Cultural Resistance Reader*, 83 (London: Verso, 2002).

2. Michael Moore, foreword to *A Right to Be Hostile: The Boondocks Treasury*, by Aaron McGruder (New York: Three Rivers Press, 2003).

3. McGruder's (with Reginald Hudlin and Kyle Baker) *Birth of a Nation: A Comic Novel* (New York: Crown Publishers, 2004), a hilarious twist on D. W. Griffith's racist film, *Birth of a Nation* (1915), features the secession of the city of East St. Louis, Missouri, and its creation as a new nation, Blackland, which has the faces of James Brown and Malcolm X on its money and celebrates as its national anthem the theme song from the 1970s sitcom *Good Times*. See also McGruder's *Public Enemy #2: An All-New Boondocks Collection* (New York: Three Rivers Press, 2005).

4. As the blog notes, "[I]n the two years the *Times Union* has run *Maintaining*, some readers have called jokes poking fun at stereotypes reverse racism," wrote Tracy Ormsbee. "Others praised the strip for being 'brave' and 'right on.' While with Universal Press, *Maintaining* ran in less than 20 newspapers—and had peaked at about 40, according to UPS' John Glynn, VP/rights and acquisitions." In explaining the conclusion of his contract, Creekmore states, "Unfortunately, *Maintaining* was never much of a financial success and recent market conditions have only exacerbated the situation. Universal Press Syndicate has chosen to opt out of its contract with my strip and I've decided to discontinue the production of the strip in order to concentrate on other projects." Quoted in http://gocomics.typepad .com/rcharvey/2009/08/index.html (accessed February 21, 2010).

5. Quoted in http://www.boondockstv.com/ (accessed July 8, 2009).

6. Quoted in http://www.creekification.com/maintaining.html (accessed July 8, 2009).

7. The article is listed on the TMA website as a Multiracial Media Advisory, June 17, 1999:

"The Multiracial Activist (TMA) Says 'Send the Racist Boondocks Comic Strip Back to the Boondocks,'" http://multiracial.com/site/content/category/1/53/2/ (accessed July 8, 2009). The journal also keeps a log of negative articles about mixed race in *The Boondocks* accessed through a link called "The Multiracial Activist: ISSUES - 'The Boondocks,'" http://multiracial.com/site/content/category/1/53/2/ (accessed July 8, 2009).

8. Project RACE also reprints with approval "The Multiracial Activist" article on McGruder, http://www.projectrace.com/hotnews/archive/hotnews-061899.php (accessed July 8, 2009). Creekmore, by contrast, has had favorable press even in the United Kingdom: see MaintainingMixed-Race NewsIntermix.org.uk.htm. See also his interview on "Mixed Chicks Chat," Episode 47 (April 23, 2008). Recording at http://www.talkshoe.com/talkshoe/web/talkCast.jsp?masterId=34257&pageNumber=4&pageSize=15 (accessed July 8, 2009).

9. Alan Gardner, "Review: *Maintaining* by Nate Creekmore," *Daily Cartoonist*, posted March 7, 2007, http://dailycartoonist.com/index.php/2007/03/07/review-maintaining-by-nate-creekmore/ (accessed July 9, 2009).

10. This reference is suggested also in the *New York Times* Television section article "The Comic-Strip Revolution Will Be Televised," by Lola Ogunnaike (October 30, 2005), 29, 39. Ogunnaike's article contemplates the repercussions of *The Boondocks'* debut on cable. The Cartoon Network pays Sony Pictures Television, producer of the series, an estimated license fee of $400,000 per episode, according to the article. The show premiered on November 6, 2005, in the late-night "Adult Swim" block. DVDs of Season 1 and Season 2 are now available, indicating that the series has been a success.

11. Quoted in Ben McGrath's profile of McGruder, "The Radical: Why Do Editors Keep Throwing 'The Boondocks' Off the Funnies Page?" *New Yorker*, April 19, 2004, 12. http://www.newyorker.com/archive/2004/04/19/040419fa_fact2 (accessed September 10, 2004).

12. Scott McCloud, *Reinventing Comics: How Imagination and Technology Are Revolutionizing an Art Form* (New York: HarperCollins, 2000), 10–11. That comics should be taken as literature and art are two of his six long-term goals for the art form and for the industry, goals that also include the idea that comics should include more gender balance and minority diversity.

13. McGrath, "The Radical." McGrath reviews the debacle at the *Nation*'s celebration at the Metropolitan Club on Fifth Avenue in New York in December 2003, at which McGruder was fêted but proceeded to insult most of those gathered.

14. Ibid., 17.

15. Philip Roth, *The Human Stain* (New York: Vintage International, 2001), 108.

16. Kimberly McClain DaCosta, "All in the Family: The Familial Roots of Racial Division," in *The Politics of Multiracialism: Challenging Racial Thinking*, ed. Heather Dalmage, 20 (Albany: State University of New York Press, 2004).

17. Susan Graham, cofounder of Project RACE (Reclassify All Children Equally), who urged adoption of a multiracial classification on forms requiring racial data, especially for children, was among the white mothers who successfully lobbied the Office of Management and Budget (OMB) in the late 1990s to change the 2000 Census category options. Jon Michael Spencer scathingly indicts Graham's crusade, not only because she trotted out her biracial child before the OMB in what he felt was an exploitative appeal to sentiment, but also because Graham insists that everyone from Halle Berry to Langston Hughes should (or in Hughes' case, she says, would have if he could have) identify as multiracial rather than black. The irony of mandating, in the name of free choice, that people of mixed race descent must identify as such is lost on Graham, as Spencer tells it. See Spencer, *The New Colored People: The Mixed-Race Movement in America* (New York: New York University Press, 1997), 59–61.

18. Erica Chito Childs, "MULTIRACE.COM: The Promise and Pitfalls of Multiracial

Cyberspace," in *The Politics of Multiracialism: Challenging Racial Thinking*, ed. Heather Dalmage, 143 (Albany: State University of New York Press, 2004).

19. See, for instance, the popular blog "The Multiracial Activist" (self-described as "a publication dedicated to the struggle for and preservation of civil rights"), an entry on Saturday, June 1999, 11:03:09-0500 from A. D. Powell, who claims that *The Boondocks* is a "new comic strip that attacks multiracial people and identity and fanatically supports the 'one drop' myth," and directs interested readers to http://www.uexpress.com/ups/comics/bo for a listing of *The Boondocks* episodes where he says that "the attacks on the biracial 'Jazmine' character and multiracial identity are these dates: April 28, April 29, May 5, 6, 8, 11, 12, 24, 26, 27, 28, 29." http://www.multiracial.com/readers/responses -boondocks.html (accessed September 19, 2005).

20. Jayne O. Ifekwunigwe, "Let Blackness and Whiteness Wash Through: Competing Discourses on Bi-racialization and the Compulsion of Genealogical Erasures," in *'Mixed Race' Studies: A Reader*, ed. Jayne O. Ifekwunigwe, 189 (New York: Routledge, 2004). Also Maria P. P. Root on black people: "People of color who have internalized the vehicle of oppression in turn apply rigid rules of belonging or establishing 'legitimate' membership" ("Within, Between, Beyond Race," in *'Mixed Race' Studies: A Reader*, ed. Jayne O. Ifekwunigwe, 144 [New York: Routledge, 2004]).

21. If McGruder's Huey assumes Jazmine is black, Spike Lee in *Bamboozled*, by contrast, makes clear in his portrayal of the character "1/32nd" (named so because it putatively reflects his ration of black blood) that racial inclusion is provisional. 1/32nd is upset because, since he looks white, he is not shot by the police like his brethren are; he is the only one of his gang, the Mau Maus, left alive and thus, in his mind, not martyred. The film makes quite clear its visual politics of race and affiliation: if you don't look black, you aren't. In both cases, 1/32nd's wailing and Jazmine's histrionic hand-wringing are rendered not merely self-indulgent but moot. Whether he or she "chooses" to be black is not a private decision but public attribution. And in the movie this attribution is based on split-second visual decisions—or as Malcolm Gladwell suggests, in a blink, whether that be Jazmine's frizzy "fro" or 1/32nd's white skin.

22. Judith Wilson, "One Way or Another: Black Feminist Visual Theory," in *The Feminism and Visual Culture Reader*, ed. Amelia Jones, 24 (New York: Routledge, 2003).

23. Daniel Witter, "Boondocks Creator Speaks on Finding a Voice," California State University, Sacramento *State Hornet*, October 13, 1999, http://www.csus.edu/hornet/archive/fall99/issue07/news12.html (accessed July 9, 2009).

24. In a statement protesting the claim in the *Palladium-Item* that President Barack Obama was not black because he was not a descendant of slaves (Debra Dickerson's argument), McGruder insists that the speech he made at Earlham College on Martin Luther King Day was "twisted around in a silly manner" by the press and "the claim that I asserted our new President was not Black is categorically false":

> I have seen an endless stream of Black pundits on TV pontificating about the significance of President Obama's election—many of them making reference to the 3/5th's clause in the constitution regarding slaves. The point I was making is that this is not an accurate comparison. Barack is the son of an immigrant, not the descendant of slaves. It's like comparing a half-Japanese man to the oppressed Chinese who built the American railroads. Yes, they are both Asian, but it is not an honest or accurate comparison. We all share the common experiences of being Black in America today—we do not all share a common history. A history that in part makes us who we are—and in some

cases (as with the psychological damage that still lingers from slavery) holds us back. These are not, I believe, insignificant distinctions.

Quoted in *Daily Cartoonist*. Posted January 21, 2009, http://dailycartoonist.com/index .php/2009/01/21/mcgruder-denies-report-regarding-obamas-race/ (accessed July 9, 2009). It is worth pointing out that he is trying to account for different historical experiences of black people in the Americas—and that those matter—without arguing that that requires a new racial categorization.

25. Margaret Mitchell, *Gone with the Wind* (1936) (New York: Warner Books, 1993), 5. An anonymous screenwriter ends the movie version with "There was a land of cavaliers and cotton fields called the 'Old South.' Here, in this pretty world, gallantry took its last bow. Here was the last ever to be seen of knights and their ladies fair, of master and slave. Look for it only in books, for it is no more than a dream remembered, a civilization gone with the wind."

26. Hortense J. Spillers, "Mama's Baby, Papa's Maybe: An American Grammar Book," *Diacritics* 17, no. 2 (Summer 1987): 67.

27. Will Eisner, *Comics and Sequential Art: Principles and Practices of the World's Most Popular Art Form* (Tamarac, FL: Poorhouse Press, 1985), 8. For excellent critical examinations of the relationship between comic art and politics, see also Andrea Lunsford with Adam Rosenblatt, "'Down a Road and Into an Awful Silence': Graphic Listening in Joe Sacco's Comics Journalism," in *Silence and Listening as Rhetorical Arts*, ed. Cheryl Glenn and Krista Ratcliff (Carbondale: Southern Illinois University Press, forthcoming, and Andrea Lunsford with Adam Rosenblatt, "Joe Sacco's Comics Journalism: Critique, Caricature, Compulsion," in *Contemporary American Comics: Creators and Their Contexts*, ed. Paul Williams and James Lyons (Jackson: University Press of Mississippi, forthcoming).

28. Henry B. Wonham, *Playing the Races: Ethnic Caricature and American Literary Realism* (New York: Oxford University Press, 2004), 4–5.

29. From McGruder's unpaginated introduction to *A Right to Be Hostile*.

30. Richard E. van der Ross, Foreword to Spencer, *The New Colored People*, x.

31. Even Riley, who most predictably rants, develops as a character, at least in the television version. In one episode, he begins by spray-painting a house, only to have the "white guy with an Afro" teach him about craft, about authorial humility, and ultimately, ironically, about the racial politics of art when Riley tries to claim credit for one piece of spray-paint art that he left anonymous and that is so good that no white person believes he is the artist.

32. Ronald Sundstrom, "Being and Being Mixed Race," *Social Theory and Practice* 27 (April 2001): 306–307.

33. Anthony Appiah, "Towards a New Cosmopolitanism," *New York Times Magazine*, January 1, 2006, 30–37,

34. http://www.intermix.org.uk/news/news_070607_01.asp (accessed July 11, 2009).

35. See Eval Amiran, "George Herriman's *Black Sentence: The Legibility of Race in Krazy Kat*," *Mosaic* 33, no. 3 (September 2000), and Jeet Heer's "A Cat-and-Mouse Game of Identity: George Herriman Played with Race in His Work and in His Real Life," *Toronto Star*, December 11, 2005. Herriman was a Creole African American born in Louisiana who passed as Greek, and as the product description for a 2004 DVD on Herriman, *George Herriman's Kinomatic Krazy Kat Kartoon Klassics*, directed by Ray Pointer, describes him, he is usually recognized as the first black comic strip artist:

KRAZY KAT was one of the great comic strips in history, and, was also one of the first comic strip characters to appear in an animated series starting in 1916. Krazy Kat appeared in four theatrical series over 24 years. But most of all, KRAZY KAT is important because its creator was a pioneer in a profession considered inaccessible for others of his kind because George Herriman was the first Black American cartoonist. http://www.amazon.com/George-Herrimans-KINOMATIC-KARTOON-KLASSICS/dp/B0006VMS5S (accessed July 11, 2009).

But the mixed-race blog discussion of Herriman's racial identity argues that he should be considered a "mixed race"—not a black—comic strip artist: http://dailycartoonist.com/index.php/2008/11/21/george-herrimans-mixed -race-and-its-influence-in-krazy -kat/ (accessed July 11, 2009).

36. Mixed Chicks Chat, Episode 47 (April 23, 2008), recording at http://www.talkshoe.com/talkshoe/web/talkCast.jsp?masterId=34257&pageNumber=4&pageSize=15 (accessed July 8, 2009). The episode is part of a series of weekly live podcasts by Heidi Durrow and Fanshen Cox. See http://www.mixedchickschat.com/.

37. All *Maintaining* comics published and accessed through gocomics.com. Dates for episodes correspond to their national publication through Universal Press Syndicate, which holds the copyright, and are archived on this site.

38. George Schuyler, "The Negro Art Hokum," in *The Norton Anthology of African American Literature*, ed. Henry Louis Gates, Jr., and Nellie Y. McKay, 2nd ed. (New York: W. W. Norton, 2004), 1171–1173. See also Langston Hughes' direct challenge to Schuyler (and to Countee Cullen) in his famous "The Negro Artist and the Racial Mountain" (1267–1271) and the biography of Philippa Schuyler and her own very troubled relation to racial identity. In *The Norton Anthology of African American Literature*, ed. Henry Louis Gates, Jr., and Nellie Y. McKay, 2nd ed. (New York: W. W. Norton, 2004).

39. Glenda Carpio, *Laughing Fit to Kill: Black Humor in the Fictions of Slavery* (New York: Oxford University Press, 2008), 4, 28.

40. See "Mixed Media Watch," for example: www.mixedmediawatch.com/.

41. Mixed Chicks Chat, Episode 47 (April 23, 2008).

42. Malcolm Gladwell, "Lost in the Middle," in *Half and Half: Writers on Growing Up Biracial and Bicultural*, ed. Claudine Chiawei O'Hearn, 112–124 (New York: Pantheon Books, 1998).

43. There are exceptions to the "we are so unique" thrust of many mixed-race advocacy organizations, one of which is Carmen Van Kerckhove's "Racialicious: The Intersection of Race and Pop Culture" website, http://www.racialicious.com/ workshops, and podcasts http://www.addictedtorace.com/, which regularly seek to expand articulation of mixed race experiences but maintain a consistent and sophisticated commitment to analyzing interracial politics, dynamics, privilege, and positionality in ways that encourage self-critiques of mixed race identity. Both also represent their anti-racist work as in concert and collaboration with (versus demonization of) the civil rights efforts of monoracially identified people and organizations. Kerckhove situates the "mixed race experience" within a larger attention to racialized experience—that is, her position is refreshingly not in the post-race camp, but rather on a continuum with other minority experiences.

44. Maria P. P. Root, *Love's Revolution: Interracial Marriage* (Philadelphia: Temple University Press, 2001).

45. See Calvin C. Hernton, *Sex and Racism in America* (1965) (New York: Anchor, 1992).

46. Stephen Henderson, quoted in Aldon Lynn Nielsen, *Black Chant: Languages of African-American Postmodernism* (Cambridge: Cambridge University Press, 1997), 5.

47. Mixed Chicks Chat, Episode 47 (April 23, 2008).

48. Tricia Rose, *Black Noise: Rap Music and Black Culture in Contemporary America* (Middletown, CT: Wesleyan University Press, 1994).

49. Sander L. Gilman, "Black Bodies, White Bodies: Toward an Iconography of Female Sexuality in Late Nineteenth-Century Art, Medicine, and Literature," in *The Feminism and Visual Culture Reader*, ed. Amelia Jones, 136–150 (New York: Routledge, 2002).

50. James Weldon Johnson, *The Autobiography of an Ex-Colored Man*, in *The Norton Anthology of African American Literature*, ed. Henry Louis Gates, Jr., and Nellie Y. McKay, 2nd ed. (New York: W. W. Norton, 2004), 883.

51. Cornel West, "The New Cultural Politics of Difference," in *The Cultural Studies Reader*, ed. Simon During, 217 (New York: Routledge, 1993).

CHAPTER THREE

1. I would distinguish the time-tethered orientation of some serial comics, especially those commenting on a particular political moment, from the ephemeral character of dramatic performances.

2. Senna's expression, coined in the title of her article "The Mulatto Millennium," in *Half and Half: Writers on Growing Up Biracial and Bicultural*, ed. Claudine Chiawei O'Hearn, 12 (New York: Pantheon, 1998).

3. From the front jacket to the reissue of *Flight* by Walter Francis White (Baton Rouge: Louisiana State University Press, 1998). For an excellent review of various types of historical literary passings, see Werner Sollors, *Neither Black nor White yet Both: Thematic Explorations of Interracial Literature* (New York: Oxford University Press, 1997), 246–284.

4. James Weldon Johnson, *The Autobiography of an Ex-Colored Man*, in *The Norton Anthology of African American Literature*, ed. Henry Louis Gates, Jr. and Nellie Y. McKay, 2nd ed. (New York: W. W. Norton, 2004), 803.

5. One of the finest, most nuanced discussions of these movies is Gayle Wald's *Crossing the Line: Racial Passing in Twentieth-Century U.S. Literature and Culture* (Durham, NC: Duke University Press, 2000).

6. M. Giulia Fabi, *Passing and the Rise of the African American Novel* (Urbana-Champagne: University of Illinois Press, 2001).

7. All citations drawn from these editions: Danzy Senna, *Caucasia* (New York: Riverhead Books, 1999); Danzy Senna, *Symptomatic* (New York: Riverhead Books, 2004); Philip Roth, *The Human Stain* (New York: Vintage International, 2001); Colson Whitehead, *The Intuitionist* (New York: Anchor Books, 2000).

8. Ellis Cose, *Color-Blind: Seeing Beyond Race in a Race-Obsessed World* (New York: HarperCollins, 1998.

9. John L. Jackson and Martha S. Jones, "Passed Performances: An Introduction," *Women and Performance: A Journal of Feminist Theory*, Special "Passing" Issue, ed. John L. Jackson and Martha S. Jones, 15, no. 1 (2005): 14. This volume usefully builds on earlier anthologies on passing, including Elaine Ginsberg's edited *Passing and the Fictions of Identity* (Durham, NC: Duke University Press, 1996) and María Carla Sánchez and Linda Schlossberg, eds., *Passing: Identity and Interpretation in Sexuality, Race, and*

Religion (New York: New York University Press, 2001).

10. From Maria P. P. Root, ed., *The Multiracial Experience: Racial Borders as the New Frontier* (Thousand Oaks, CA.: Sage, 1995).

11. Robyn Wiegman, *American Anatomies: Theorizing Race and Gender* (Durham, NC: Duke University Press, 1995), 22. See also two excellent examinations of race, sex, and the spectral in passing: Amy Robinson, "It Takes One to Know One: Passing and Communities of Common Interest," *Critical Inquiry* 20 (Summer 1994): 715–736, and Jennifer DeVere Brody, *Impossible Purities: Blackness, Femininity, and Victorian Culture* (Durham, NC: Duke University Press, 1998). Harryette Mullen offers an excellent discussion of the politics of racial optics in "Optic White: Blackness and the Production of Whiteness," *Diacritics* 24, nos. 2/3 (Summer 1994): 71–89.

12. Walter Benn Michaels, "Autobiography of an Ex-White Man: Why Race Is Not a Social Construction," *Transition* 73 (1998): 140.

13. See Ariela Gross on litigating whiteness, *Double Character: Slavery and Mastery in the Antebellum Southern Courtroom* (Princeton, NJ: Princeton University Press, 2000).

14. See Samira Kawash on the disconnect between social science studies of the actual practice of passing and the public fascination with the symbolic potency of the idea of passing in fiction (*Dislocating the Color Line: Identity, Hybridity, and Singularity in African-American Narrative* [Stanford: Stanford University Press, 1997], 126).

15. See Introduction for a discussion of Connerly and the discourse of rights in relation to mixed race politics.

16. See Walter Benn Michaels, "Race Into Culture: A Critical Genealogy of Cultural Identity," *Critical Inquiry* 18 (Summer 1992): 655–685, and "The No-Drop Rule," *Critical Inquiry* 20 (Summer 1994): 758–769.

17. Toni Morrison, preface to *Playing in the Dark: Whiteness and the Literary Imagination* (New York: Vintage Books, 1993), x.

18. Toni Morrison, "Unspeakable Things Unspoken: The Afro-American Presence in American Literature," in *The Norton Anthology of African American Literature*, ed. Henry Louis Gates, Jr., and Nellie Y. McKay, 2nd ed. (New York: W. W. Norton, 2004), 2300.

19. Paula Moya, "Postmodernism, 'Realism,' and the Politics of Identity: Cherríe Moraga and Chicana Feminism," in *Reclaiming Identity: Realist Theory and the Predicament of Postmodernism*, ed. Paula M. L. Moya and Michael R. Hames-García, 84 (Berkeley: University of California Press, 2000).

20. Lorraine Hansberry, *Les Blancs: The Collected Last Plays*, ed. Robert Nemiroff, introduction by Margaret B. Wilkerson (New York: Vintage Books, 1994), 92.

21. Paul C. Taylor, "Race, Rehabilitated," *Agora: Journal for Metafysisk Spekulasjon* 25, nos. 1–2 (2007): 314–331 (in translation from Norwegian). For another cogent critique of Michaels, see Michael Hames-García, "How Real Is Race?" in *Material Feminisms*, ed. Stacy Alaimo and Susan J. Hekman, 308–339 (Bloomington: Indiana University Press, 2008). For an excellent analysis of the ontology of race as applied to contemporary racial politics, see Ronald Sundstrom, "Being and Being Mixed Race," *Social Theory and Practice* 27, no. 2 (April 2001): 285–307.

22. Quoted in Lisa Lowe, *Immigrant Acts: On Asian American Cultural Politics* (Durham. NC: Duke University Press, 1996), 83.

23. Elin Diamond, Introduction to *Performance and Cultural Politics*, ed. Elin Diamond (New York: Routledge, 1996), 1–2.

24. Lowe, *Immigrant Acts*, 82.

25. For further discussions of performance in terms of this debate, see Diana Taylor, *The Archive and the Repertoire: Performing Cultural Memory in the Americas* (Durham, NC: Duke University Press, 2003), and Shannon Jackson's *Professing Performance: Theatre in the Academy from Philology to Performativity* (New York: Cambridge University Press, 2004). See, too, Philip Auslander, "Liveness: Performance and the Anxiety of Simulation," in *Performance and Cultural Politics*, ed. Elin Diamond, 198–218 (New York: Routledge, 1996).

26. In a fascinating case of so-called color-blind casting, in the 2003 movie made from the novel Coleman Silk is played by Anthony Hopkins and the cleaning woman is played by Nicole Kidman. Curiously enough, although in a *New York Times* Arts and Leisure spread a year before the release of the movie, there was no discussion, no recognition of controversy, over having a famous—and famously white—actor play the adult Silk (implying that if he looked white he might as well be white), the young man cast as the young Silk in the movie, then a Princeton student, Wentworth Miller, by contrast, was reportedly asked to bring pictures of his parents to the audition to prove he really was biracial—suggesting that in simultaneous operation for casting were two competing racial epistemologies. For an interesting review of the reviews of the film and the book in relation to expectations of "authenticity," see Rachel Gelder, "Passing and Failing: Reflections on the Limitations of Showing the Passer in *The Human Stain*," Special Issue, ed. John L. Jackson, Jr., and Martha S. Jones, *Women and Performance: A Journal of Feminist Theory* 15, no. 1 (2005): 293–312.

27. Amanda Lewis, "Everyday Race-Making," *American Behavioral Scientist* 47, no. 3 (November 203): 283–305. Lewis distinguishes between the "detailed macroprocesses of construction and formation" and "how those processes work themselves out in and on people's everyday lives. How is it that race is reproduced in day-to-day life? How do we become socialized into the racial schema, knowing what these categories mean for us and others?" (283).

28. See Ralph Ellison, *Invisible Man*, 2nd Vintage International ed. (New York: Vintage International, 1995), 21–26.

29. The power of Louis' win continues to appear in literature and drama—the broadcast of the fight, for instance, makes for a powerful scene in August Wilson's play *Seven Guitars* (1995), in which characters share the victory as they contemplate their own personal struggles against white hegemony.

30. Eve Sedgwick, "Queer Performativity: Henry James's *The Art of the Novel*," *GLQ: A Journal of Gay and Lesbian Studies* 1, no. 1 (1993): 1–16.

31. In my view this is one of the complications to Kathleen Pfeiffer's argument in *Race Passing and American Individualism* (Amherst: University of Massachusetts Press, 2003) that passing is best understood as just a legitimate realization of American self-initiative and self-invention. While I find her effort to move past seeing passing as merely self-hatred important and useful, her claim that light-skinned blacks who pass for white are no different from those Americans who create themselves in terms of class or religion certainly mirrors Silk's justification, but I hope my reading of this scene in *The Human Stain* makes clear that such bids for individualism do not, as Pfeiffer suggests, necessarily subvert the ideology of racial essentialism.

32. See Michael Paul Rogin, *Blackface, White Noise: Jewish Immigrants in the Hollywood Melting Pot* (Berkeley: University of California Press, 1996). For another

reading of the historical interrelations between black and white in representation, see Sander L. Gilman's marvelous "Black Bodies, White Bodies: Toward an Iconography of Female Sexuality in Late Nineteenth-Century Art, Medicine, and Literature," in *The Feminism and Visual Culture Reader*, ed. Amelia Jones, 136–150 (New York: Routledge, 2002). The issues of Gentile/Jewish passing as linked to similar issues of social justice are explored in films like *Gentleman's Agreement* (1948), directed by Elia Kazan, who also directed many of the "race passing" films of the period. See Gayle Wald, *Crossing the Line*, for excellent analyses of these films.

33. Such questions consider the larger implications as well of cases of "transraciality," to employ Michael Awkward's useful term in *Negotiating Difference: Race, Gender, and the Politics of Positionality* (Chicago: University of Chicago Press, 1995): "The adoption of physical traits of difference for the purpose of impersonating a racial other" (9)—as in the case of Michael Jackson—where "notions of essence and social practice are contiguous and intersecting" (192).

See also Daniel Itzkovitz, "Passing Like Me: Jewish Chameleonism and the Politics of Race," in *Passing: Identity and Interpretation in Sexuality, Race, and Religion*, ed. María Carla Sánchez and Linda Schlossberg, 38–63 (New York: New York University Press, 2001), who argue that "the 'natural place' of the Jew is in passing" (45). Also, on Jews as a "third race," see Philip Brian Harper, "Passing for What? Racial Masquerade and the Demands of Upward Mobility," *Callaloo* 21 (1998): 381–397.

34. Her comment hints at one possible inspiration for Roth's novel, the passing of New York reporter and essayist Anatole Broyard. See Henry Louis Gates, Jr., "White Like Me" (*New Yorker*, June 17, 1996, 66–81), although in an interview with Charles Taylor, Roth insists that he had begun the novel well before reading Gates' article and *The Human Stain* was not influenced by it.

35. I refer to Paul Laurence Dunbar's notion of racial masking in "We Wear the Mask" (1895). The first stanza seems particularly poignant in regard to Birdie's experience:

> We wear the mask that grins and lies
> It hides our cheeks and shades our eyes,—
> This debt we pay to human guile;
> With torn and bleeding hearts we smile,
> And mouth with myriad subtleties.

36. At times *The Human Stain* does play with racial stereotypes by representing Jews as gifted athletes and blacks as classically educated. See Ross Posnock, "Purity and Danger: On Philip Roth," *Raritan* 21, no. 2 (Fall 2001): 96. Posnock offers an excellent reading of the "epistemological moral" to *The Human Stain*, suggesting that the "ruthlessness of Coleman's self-making and the novel's high body count are reminiscent of the escalating carnage in the *Iliad*, Coleman's favorite book" and of the high tragic punishment that awaits the "American isolato" (98). Posnock astutely notes that Roth's more recent fiction goes beyond the white escapism of the "nasty primitivism" in Norman Mailer's "The White Negro" (1957), which "traffics in racial slumming grounded in white male privilege" ("Letting Go," *Raritan* 23, no. 4 [Spring 2004]: 10).

37. I am not conflating the author with the protagonist, but many critics have aligned them, suggesting that Silk's tirades against political correctness—associated with feminism, with race allegiances—echo Roth's. As Mark Krupnik puts it, "[R]eviews haven't paid sufficient tribute to Roth's rhetorical power in giving vent to his savage indignation toward the people who are always ready, in his view, to crush anyone who seems not to have hewed

to the current party line" (*Christian Century*, September 13, 2000, http://findarticles
.com/p/articles/mi_m1058/is_25_117/ai_65702752/). My point is simply that the ex-colored
man's concerns, as represented in the novel, are more resonant with those more commonly
associated with white men of a certain age in the United States.

38. Linda Martín Alcoff, *Visible Identities: Race, Gender, and the Self* (New York:
Oxford University Press, 2006), 286–287. As she notes in "Part One: Identities Real and
Imagined," the recent anti-identitarianism comes from "many oddly aligned fronts—
academic postmodernists, political liberals and leftists, conservative politicians, and
others—in academe as well as in the mainstream media" (5).

39. Betsy Erkkila, *Mixed Bloods and Other Crosses: Rethinking American Literature
from the Revolution to the Culture Wars* (Philadelphia: University of Pennsylvania Press,
2005), xi.

40. Ralph Ellison, "Change the Joke and Slip the Yoke," in *The Norton Anthology
of African American Literature*, ed. Henry Louis Gates, Jr., and Nellie Y. McKay (New
York: W. W. Norton, 2004), 1576.

41. The "thin man's convention" is tied to recent moves in disability studies to reshape
discourses of corporeal norms and spaces designed to reinforce them. See Tobin Siebers,
"Disability in Theory: From Social Constructionism to the New Realism of the Body,"
in *The Disability Studies Reader*, ed. Lennard J. Davis, 2nd ed. (New York: Routledge,
2006), 173–184.

42. See Glenda R. Carpio, *Laughing Fit to Kill: Black Humor in the Fictions of
Slavery* (New York: Oxford University Press, 2008). Carpio identifies this as the "humor of
incongruity [which] allows us to appreciate the fact that . . . African American humor has
been and continues to be both a bountiful source of creativity and pleasure and an energetic
mode of social and political critique" (6–7).

43. W. E. B. Du Bois, "Of Our Spiritual Strivings," *The Souls of Black Folk*, in
The Norton Anthology of African American Literature, ed. Henry Louis Gates, Jr., and
Nellie Y. McKay, 694 (New York: W. W. Norton, 2004).

44. Robin D. G. Kelley, *Freedom Dreams: The Black Radical Imagination* (Boston:
Beacon Press, 2002).

45. In this I differ somewhat from Madhu Dubey's discussion of Whitehead's novel in
Signs and Cities: Black Literary Postmodernism (Chicago: University of Chicago Press,
2003). She argues that "the imagery of uplift, verticality, and transcendence that surrounds
the black box [the secret to Fulton's new elevators] testifies to its modern lineage." But
the many articles of faith in verticality and transcendence are also searingly critiqued
throughout the novel. I agree with her claim that *The Intuitionist* offers "a way of doing
modernity differently, of getting it right the next time" (240), but I argue it is a modernity
that passes rather than rises.

46. The last line of Johnson's *Autobiography of an Ex-Colored Man*, in *The Norton
Anthology of African American Literature*, ed. Henry Louis Gates, Jr., and Nellie Y.
McKay, 2nd ed. (New York: W. W. Norton, 2004), 861.

47. Senna's expression, used in the acknowledgments to *Caucasia*, in which she thanks
Omar Wascow, "minister of information for the Mulatto Nation," for showing her the
"mestizo imperative." The expression is borrowed from Gloria Anzaldúa's *Borderlands–
La Frontera* theory of "the new mestiza." See Gloria Anzaldúa, *Borderlands: The New
Mestiza/La Frontera*, 3rd ed. (San Francisco: Aunt Lute Books, 2007). This theory lays
out a blueprint for racial equality that recognizes the interdependencies of discrimination.

"It is imperative that Mestizas support each other. . . . [As] long as Woman [man] is put down, the Indian and the Black in us all is put down" (106). According to Anzaldúa, "The future will belong to the mestiza. Because the future depends on the breaking down of paradigms, it depends on the straddling of two or more cultures" (102).

48. Fabi, *Passing and the Rise of the African American Novel*, 9. I explore, in particular, Frances E. W. Harper's approach to passing as an embrace of black culture and modernity in my *Race, Work, and Desire in American Literature, 1860–1930* (Cambridge: Cambridge University Press, 2003), 58–75.

CHAPTER FOUR

1. Emily Raboteau, *The Professor's Daughter: A Novel* (New York: Henry Holt, 2005), 20. All further citations are from this edition. To date, almost no scholarship exists on this novel, nor discussion of it within the mixed race community, suggesting it falls outside most generic expectations for the "mixed race novel."

2. Danzy Senna, *Symptomatic: A Novel* (New York: Riverhead Books, 2004), 51. All further citations are from this edition.

3. Enrique Lima, p. 2 from draft of chapter 3, "The Indian *Bildungsroman*: D'Arcy McNickle and Indian Assimilation. The Uneven Development of the Novel: The Theory of the Novel and the Indigenous Periphery of Capitalist Modernity" (*Comparative Literature*, forthcoming). Quoted with permission.

4. Cited in Lima. Sources include Jerome Hamilton Buckley, *Season of Youth: The Bildungsroman from Dickens to Golding* (Cambridge, MA: Harvard University Press, 1974); Todd Curtis Kontje, *The German Bildungsroman: History of a National Genre* (Columbia, SC: Camden House, 1993); Michael Minden, *The German Bildungsroman: Incest and Inheritance* (New York: Cambridge University Press, 1997); Franco Moretti, *The Way of the World: The Bildungsroman in European Culture*, 2nd ed. (London: Verso, 2000); Marc Redfield, *Phantom Formations: Aesthetic Ideology and the Bildungsroman* (Ithaca, NY: Cornell University Press, 1996).

5. Ruth Colker, *Hybrid: Bisexuals, Multiracials, and Other Misfits Under American Law* (New York: New York University Press, 1996), xii.

6. Tavia Nyong'o, *The Amalgamation Waltz: Race, Performance, and the Ruses of Memory* (Minneapolis: University of Minnesota Press, 2009), 4. Publisher's back jacket description.

7. Danzy Senna, *Where Did You Sleep Last Night? A Personal History* (New York: Farrar, Straus and Giroux, 2009), 132.

8. Adrian Piper, "Passing for White, Passing for Black," *Transition* 58 (1992), 4–32.

9. W. E. B. Du Bois, "Of Our Spiritual Strivings," *The Souls of Black Folk*, in *The Norton Anthology of African American Literature*, ed. Henry Louis Gates, Jr., and Nellie Y. McKay, 2nd ed. (New York: W. W. Norton, 2004), 695.

10. Interestingly, Raboteau says that "[t]o my mind, the book is not about race. It's about a family," but then cites a particularly racial genesis for the novel: "In particular, it's about the way an ugly moment in history (the lynching of the grandfather) affects the generations that follow." Quoted in Peter Biello, "Interview with Emily Raboteau," *Compulsive Reader*. December 20, 2005, Web audio, http://www.compulsivereader.com/ html/index.php?name=News&file=article&sid=11191 (accessed August 3, 2009). She goes on to explain her relation to the main character:

Emma is my mouthpiece in many ways. She looks like me, grew up in my hometown and went to the school I went to. She is invisible in the way I felt invisible before I wrote the book. I wrote it in an attempt to address a question I am asked routinely as a racially ambiguous person: "What are you?" That's not an easy question, though the answer people expect is a skin-deep one. (I have a black parent and a white parent.) I decided to answer this question in a more complex way, by writing a novel. It involves my history in both real and imagined ways.

11. Harry J. Elam, Jr., *The Past as Present in the Drama of August Wilson* (Ann Arbor: University of Michigan Press, 2004), 60.

12. Rosemarie Garland-Thomson, *Staring: How We Look* (New York: Oxford University Press, 2009), 3.

13. Paul Gilroy, *Postcolonial Melancholia* (New York: Columbia University Press, 2005), 14.

14. See José Esteban Muñoz, *Disidentifications: Queers of Color and the Performance of Politics*, vol. 2 (Minneapolis: University of Minnesota Press, 1999).

15. I offer an extended discussion of the politics of cross-racial friendship, and the idealization of interracial unions, the risks of miniaturizing and personalizing the complex dilemmas of race, in the introduction to my *Race, Work, and Desire in American Literature, 1860–1930* (Cambridge: Cambridge University Press, 2003), 12–15.

16. Greene's friend, Jarvis, argues by contrast that "mulattos these days are all ordinary and well-adjusted. Even a little boring. . . . Almost makes you miss the old head cases" (202). In either case, the mulatta is portrayed as either too monstrous or too banal to be of interest.

17. Samira Kawash, *Dislocating the Color Line: Identity, Hybridity, and Singularity in African-American Narrative* (Stanford: Stanford University Press, 1997), 132–133.

18. Benedict Anderson's expression. See *Imagined Communities: Reflections on the Origin and Spread of Nationalism* (London: Verso, 1991). As he explains, community is always "imagined because the members of even the smallest nation will never know most of their fellow-members." Moreover, "[i]t is imagined as a community, because, regardless of the actual inequality and exploitation that may prevail in each, the nation is always conceived as a deep, horizontal comradeship. Ultimately, it is this fraternity that makes it possible, over the past two centuries for so many millions of people, not so much to kill, as willingly to die for such limited imaginings."

19. Lawrence Otis Graham, *Our Kind of People: Inside America's Black Upper Class* (New York: HarperCollins, 2000).

20. Jennifer Beals' speech at the GLAAD Awards ceremony discusses the difficulties of growing up biracial, looking for songs about people "like me" when she was young and finding only Cher's hit "Half-Breed." http://www.youtube.com/watch?v=DRUFu_m_Nn4 (accessed August 30, 2006). Interestingly, in *Symptomatic*, during the infamous game of charades, one of Andrew's white friends plays Jennifer Beals, apparently unaware that she is not white.

21. Danzy Senna, *Caucasia* (New York: Riverhead Books, 1999), 393.

22. Gilroy, *Postcolonial Melancholia*, 33.

23. Ralph Ellison, *Invisible Man* (1952)(New York: Modern Library, 1994), 6.

24. Jonathan Dollimore, "Desire and Difference: Homosexuality, Race, Masculinity," in *Race and the Subject of Masculinities*, ed. Harry Stecopoulos and Michael Uebel, 22 (Durham, NC: Duke University Press, 1997).

25. Eva Saks, "Representing Miscegenation Law," *Raritan* 8 (1988): 53–54. On national/state investment in miscegenation and homosexuality regulation, see also Mark

Strasser, "Family Definitions and the Constitution: On the Antimiscegenation Analogy," *Suffolk University Law Review* 25 (Winter 1991): 981–1034.

26. Phillip Brian Harper, "Private Affairs: Race, Sex, Property, and Persons," *GLQ: A Journal of Gay and Lesbian Studies* 1, no. 2 (1994): 124.

27. Judith Butler, *Bodies That Matter: On the Discursive Limits of "Sex"* (New York: Routledge, 1993).

28. Joseph R. Roach, *Cities of the Dead: Circum-Atlantic Performance* (New York: Columbia University Press, 1996), 36.

29. Senna, *Symptomatic*, 19.

30. W. E. B. Du Bois' notion of black leadership in the first quarter of the century, in which a well-educated few guided the "masses." The "Talented Tenth," because they tended to be very light-skinned, were at times disparagingly referred to as the "mulatto elite," out of touch in terms of both class and color with those they claimed to represent.

31. See also George Lipsitz on the responsibility that cross-racial explorations should be carried out "with a self-conscious understanding of unequal power relations" in *Dangerous Crossroads: Popular Music, Postmodernism, and the Poetics of Place* (London and New York: Verso, 1994), 61.

32. Interestingly enough, *The Human Stain* also is drawn to the figure of the cleaning woman and also refuses the tendency toward condescending sentimentalism, Pygmalian improvement, hyperbolic minstrelsy. In Roth's vision, however, the custodial staff member is no grandmother but, rather, becomes Silk's "Voluptas" (*The Human Stain* 35), the goddess of satisfaction and delight.

33. Du Bois, "Of Our Spiritual Strivings," 615.

34. Adrian Piper in "Passing for White, Passing for Black," discusses precisely the curious burdens and responsibilities attendant upon such experiences, particularly when they occur in "polite society," when declaring one's racial affiliation might seem crass but not announcing it risks bringing upon oneself all sorts of accusations of fraudulence— or worse, snotty implications that one is not "really" black (*Passing and the Fictions of Identity*, ed. Elaine K. Ginsberg, 234–270 [Durham, NC: Duke University Press, 1996]). In her early performance interventions, Piper, a performance artist and philosopher, would hand out small formal cards at parties whenever someone made a racist comment in her presence printed with statements like "I am sure you did not know I was black when you made that racist comment."

See also Joseph R. Roach, "Kinship, Intelligence, and Memory as Improvisation: Culture and Performance in New Orleans," in *Performance and Cultural Politics*, ed. Elin Diamond, 219–238 (New York: Routledge, 1996): "[P]erformance is a particular class or subset of restored behavior in which one or more persons assume responsibility to an audience and to a tradition as they understand it" (219). This notion of performance is not the same as Judith Butler's concept of performance as discursive and derivative "citationality" (*Bodies That Matter*, 12–16).

35. See bell hooks, "The Oppositional Gaze: Black Female Spectators," in *The Feminism and Visual Culture Reader*, ed. Amelia Jones, 94–104 (New York: Routledge, 2003).

36. One such girl, for example, is "neither beautiful nor ugly . . . medium-length brown hair. . . . Fullish lips for a white girl. Brown eyes. . . . Staring at me and copying everything I did. When I blinked, she blinked. When I scratched my head, she scratched her head" (*Symptomatic* 109). Similarly, *Caucasia* ends with Birdie watching the receding face of a girl on a bus as it pulls away—"She was black like me, a mixed girl, and she was watching

me from behind the dirty glass. For a second I thought I was somewhere familiar and she was a girl I already knew. . . . Then the bus lurched forward, and the face was gone with it, just a blur of yellow and black in motion" (413). This search for someone "black like me" is a play on John Howard Griffin's 1961 classic, *Black Like Me*, about a white man who passed as black to interrogate racism.

This issue of discovering identity through racial transference occurs also in *Caucasia*. In that novel, Birdie also seeks herself in the face of another, especially her older sister, Cole; her descriptions echo those of Greta: "I scrutinized my sister's face for signs of my own. The resemblance was there, but it wasn't easy to explain. It was something in the expression. Or maybe I was just imagining it" (330). In fact, Birdie sees herself as continuous with her sister, a doubling without difference ("before I ever saw myself, I saw my sister. . . . That face was me and I was that face" [5]) until the darker-skinned Cole grows up and away to become the measure of Birdie's self-alienation (180), as does her near-but-not-close-enough resemblance to her girlfriend, Maria (70). The craving is really a form of narcissism, for Birdie does not want to merely be with Cole or Maria; she wants to be Cole, wants to be Maria. It is autoeroticism, not homoeroticism, that she is finally after.

37. Naomi S. Baron, *From Alphabet to Email: How Written English Evolved and Where It's Heading* (London: Routledge, 2000), 167. Quoted in Jennifer DeVere Brody, *Punctuation: Art, Politics, and Play* (Durham, NC: Duke University Press, 2008), 23.

38. Kobena Mercer, "Diaspora Aesthetics and Visual Culture," in *Black Cultural Traffic: Crossroads in Global Performance and Popular Culture*, ed. Harry J. Elam, Jr., and Kennell Jackson, 141–161 (Ann Arbor: University of Michigan Press, 2008). See also Herman S. Gray, *Watching Race: Television and the Struggle for Blackness* (Minneapolis: University of Minnesota Press, 1995), 230.

CHAPTER FIVE

1. Charles Gordone, *No Place to Be Somebody: A Black-Black Comedy in Three Acts*, introduction by Joseph Papp (New York: Bobbs-Merrill, 1969), 79. The play was first produced in 1967.

2. From the preacher's famous riff on blackness in Ralph Ellison, *Invisible Man* (New York: Modern Library, 1994; orig. 1952), 9. As Jennifer DeVere Brody argues in her completely fresh reading of this oft-cited moment in *Punctuation: Art, Politics, and Play* (Durham, NC: Duke University Press, 2008), the challenge of blackness is not simply that it is tied to the ocular expectation but that it is "simultaneously visceral and elusive, enveloping and intangible, material and conceptual" (63). She examines the use of typological composition, especially the ellipses in that and other passages, that work as analogs to the character of the Invisible Man, who is "ambivalent, singular but multiple, 'heard' but not seen, black but blank" (64).

3. John Berger, *Ways of Seeing* (New York: Penguin, 1977), 8.

4. "The Racial Draft" was first broadcast on the Comedy Central network in October 2004. The seven-and-a-half-minute skit appears in the first episode of the second season of *Chappelle's Show*. See Dave Chappelle and Neal Brennan, writers/producers, *Chappelle's Show*, Season 2 on DVD.

5. Darby English, *How to See a Work of Art in Total Darkness* (Cambridge, MA: MIT Press, 2007), 27.

6. These assessments also often trade on the ideology of merit and success that, as

Malcolm Gladwell argues, mistakenly relies on notions of individual talent and the "self-made man." Malcolm Gladwell, *Outliers: The Story of Success* (New York: Little, Brown, 2008), 18. Gladwell's critique of individual merit as the valorized result of "an individual person's choices or actions" (10) rather than the less recognized communal, cultural, and social structural systems in sports, health, education, and aviation safety has implications, as well, for racial "choice" and selection.

7. English, *How to See a Work of Art in Total Darkness*, 2. English is analyzing artist David Hammons' *Concerto in Black and Blue*, a 2002 installation that created an experience of "racially black darkness" that engaged the ways in which "black culture" is neither "primordial or preexistent," but instead given "social life in complex interactions, mediated by differently positioned subjects, languages, and forms" (3). Although I differ with English's critique of identitarian artistic gestures, his exploration of the performative dimension of race in the work of African American artists has its parallels in my approach to the literary and dramatic works I study here, especially to the extent that he finds in the art he examines "a remarkably capacious blackness" that is the "yield of a certain theatricalization" that resists easy categories such as "'the black artist' or 'the black experience'" (2).

8. Nelson George, *Post-Soul Nation: The Explosive, Contradictory, Triumphant, and Tragic 1980s as Experienced by African Americans (Previously Known as Blacks and Before That Negroes)* (New York: Viking, 2004).

9. As Danielle Heard describes the post-soul collaborative in her Ph.D. exam paper, "Black Comic/Black Critic: 'Reading' Culture and the Critical Pedagogy of the Post-Soul" (Cornell University, August 2006):

> Okayplayer was started by ?uestlove (Ahmir Thomson), drummer of The Roots, in the late 1980s as a musical collective, and it entered cyberspace in 1999. . . . Okayplayer is, in fact, more of a culture and worldview than a collective or a website, even as it revolves around underground and alternative black popular cultural figures. Dave Chappelle, while not formally affiliated with Okayplayer is nonetheless part of this community's fabric. Chappelle is close friends with ?uestlove and many of the artists on the label. . . . The "members" of the Okayplayer's "club," which one could extend to artists who are not necessarily on the label but who nonetheless interact in this circle, tend to constantly reference each other in their work. Dave Chappelle has featured all of the artists who performed on *Block Party* on his sketch comedy show.

10. Many of the essays in Toni Morrison's edited collection, *Birth of a Nation'hood: Gaze, Script, and Spectacle in the O. J. Simpson Case*, ed. Toni Morrison and Claudia Brodsky Lacour (New York: Pantheon, 1997)—especially Wahneema Lubiano, Kimberlé Crenshaw, and Claudia Brodsky Lacour, as well as Morrison herself—have explored the national ends to which the media spectacle of race is put.

11. S. E. Wilmer, "Restaging the Nation: The Work of Suzan-Lori Parks," *Modern Drama* 43, no. 3 (2000), 444.

12. Joseph Roach, *Cities of the Dead: Circum-Atlantic Performance* (New York: Columbia University Press, 1996), 36.

13. Harry Justin Elam, Jr., "The Device of Race: An Introduction," in *African American Performance and Theater History: A Critical Reader*, ed. Harry J. Elam, Jr., and David Krasner, 5 (New York: Oxford University Press, 2001).

14. They all take as a given that identity does not reside in visible features but emerges from shared, dominant interpretations of "visual markers on the body" (Linda Alcoff,

Visible Identities: Race, Gender, and the Self [New York: Oxford University Press, 2006], 6)—as in the case of Toi Derricotte, where race is reduced to "not skin tone" since that is a "continuously variable attribute" (204), and the fact that perception of identity is a "learned ability" which is context-dependent, complex, and fluid (187). On the history of whiteface, see Arthur Knight, *Disintegrating the Musical: Black Performance and American Musical Film* (Durham, NC: Duke University Press, 2002).

15. See my discussion of the primacy and unimpeachable privileges that Maria P. P. Root's "Bill of Rights for Mixed Race People" associates with the "I" in the Introduction. "Bill of Rights" is collected in *The Multiracial Experience: Racial Borders as the New Frontier*, ed. Maria P. P. Root, 7 (Thousand Oaks, CA: Sage, 1996).

16. Another example of what Kimberly McClain DaCosta calls the "'racialization of the family' (how racial premises came to be buried in our understanding of family, in which genetic/phenotypic sharing is coded to signify cultural sharing, intimacy, and caring) and the 'familization of race' (how it came to be that members of the same racial group feel a kin-like connection and how that familial understanding is used politically)." "All in the Family: The Familial Roots of Racial Division," in *The Politics of Multiracialism: Challenging Racial Thinking*, ed. Heather M. Dalmadge, 20 (New York: State University of New York Press, 2004).

17. The story of black quarterback Vince Young is an example of the racialization of the Wonderlic exam results. Drafted by the Tennessee Titans, Young had led the University of Texas to victory and a national championship in the Rose Bowl on January 1, 2006. The test is designed to score how well players can understand and implement plays (with the assumption that the quarterback is the "smartest" member of the team). Young—one of very few black quarterbacks in football—scored very low on his Wonderlic exam, although he excelled on the playing field. Rather than serving as a challenge to the legitimacy of a test that directs coaches to hire more whites than blacks, Vince Young's ability is often characterized as "instinctual," a bodily function rather than an intellectual attribute.

18. The comments posted on the Multiracial Activist website are especially hostile, arguing that Aaron McGruder promotes "hateful propaganda," that the NAACP and McGruder are the enemies of mixed race people, want only affirmative action "freebies" when the mixed race people, in contrast, only wish to be "counted accurately," and so on. For example, see multiracial.com/site/content/view/756/2 and www.projectrace.com/hotnews/archive/hotnews-061899.php - 16k – (accessed August 1, 2006).

19. Of the sort advanced by Ifekwunigwe and Root.

20. Mark Anthony Neal, *Soul Babies: Black Popular Culture and the Post-Soul Aesthetic* (New York: Routledge, 2002), 5.

21. It is worth noting how quickly Woods lost his endorsements when he became "black" in the media following revelation of his many extramarital affairs—his hyperlibidity was clearly associated not simply with moral turpitude but with historically "black" characteristics: sexual atavism and avariciousness.

22. For the debate about how Cubans moved from being perceived as a privileged class of "exiles" to just another immigrant group after the debates over the child's status, see PBS *Frontline*'s "Elián's Legacy," http://www.pbs.org/wgbh/pages/frontline/shows/elian/views/elianslegacy.html (accessed July 10, 2006).

Two interesting interviews with Dave Chappelle aired on NPR's *Fresh Air* in 2004: http://www.npr.org/templates/story/story.php?storyId=3886000 (accessed July 20, 2006) and http://www.npr.org/templates/story/story.php?storyId=4251776 (accessed July 20, 2006).

23. The Wu-Tang Clan also has one Jewish affiliate member named Remedy. His rap

song, "Never Again," details the horrors of the Holocaust.

24. Elin Diamond argues that "[e]very performance . . . embeds features of previous performances: gender conventions, racial histories, aesthetic traditions—political and cultural pressures that are consciously and unconsciously acknowledged" (introduction to *Performance and Cultural Politics*, ed. Elin Diamond, 1–2 [New York: Routledge, 1996]).

25. For a discussion of O.J.'s "blacking up," see "The Official Story: Dead Man Golfing," Toni Morrison's introduction to *Birth of a Nation'hood*, vii–xxviii.

26. It is true that the show does not illustrate the second part of white double consciousness, as Alcoff defines it: "a newly awakened memory of the many white traitors to white privilege who have struggled to contribute to the building of an inclusive human community" (223), but perhaps we could consider Chappelle's satire—including the performance of the white writer, Neal Brennan, and Petkoff, as self-conscious forms of race traitorism.

27. Ralph Ellison, "Change the Joke and Slip the Yoke," in *The Norton Anthology of African American Literature*, ed. Henry Louis Gates, Jr., and Nellie Y. McKay, 2nd ed. (New York: W. W. Norton, 2004), 1576.

28. "Dave Speaks," *Time* interview with Christopher John Farley, posted May 14, 2005. http://time-proxy.yaga.com/time/arts/article/0,8599,1061418-5,00.html, p. 5 of 7 (accessed June 23, 2006).

29. Ibid., p. 6 of 7.

30. Billy Ingram, "The Richard Pryor Show: September 13, 1977–October 20, 1977." http://www.tvclassics.com/pryor.htm (accessed July 16, 2006).

Given the textual exuberance and political intuition of *Oreo*, it should come as no surprise that three years after the publication of her novel, Ross accepted a position as a comedy writer for *The Richard Pryor Show*, convinced that Pryor could "make an impact as a socially-conscious black comedian." Harryette Mullen recounts Ross' struggle with Pryor to convince him to continue the show and the anomaly of her position as a black female comic writer (foreword to *Oreo*, xiv).

31. Herman Gray, *Watching Race: Television and the Struggle for Blackness* (Minneapolis: University of Minnesota Press, 1995), 10.

32. David A. Hollinger, *Postethnic America: Beyond Multiculturalism*, rev. ed. (New York: Basic Books, 2000). Hollinger calls the "postethnic perspective" a "cosmopolitan-inspired step beyond multiculturalism" (4) that he sees as too identity-focused and provincial.

33. Lisa Lowe, *Immigrant Acts: On Asian American Cultural Politics* (Durham, NC: Duke University Press, 1996), 82.

34. For a review of this episode of *The Daily Show* by Scott Butki, see http://blogcritics .org/archives/2006/04/06/202012.php (accessed August 29, 2006).

35. See Freud's *Jokes and Their Relation to the Unconscious* (1905). For an assessment of this theory of humor, see also Simon Critchley, *On Humour* (New York: Routledge, 2002), 2–3.

36. Pirandello, quoted in Glenda Carpio, "The 'Highest Joke': Laughter and Elegy in the Early Plays of Suzan-Lori Parks" (unpublished manuscript), 20. I am thankful to Glenda for many of these sources on humor. See also her *Laughing Fit to Kill: Black Humor in the Fictions of Slavery* (New York: Oxford University Press, 2008).

37. See interview between Carl Hancock Rux and Jocelyn Clarke (dramaturge) in "Season Preview Conversations," TCG Publications, http://www.tcg.org/publications/ at/2001/carl.cfm (accessed March 19, 2010).

38. Jonathan Crewe, "Recalling Adamastor: Literature as Cultural Memory in

'White' South Africa," in *Acts of Memory: Cultural Recall in the Present*, ed. Mieke Bal, Jonathan Crewe, and Leo Spitzer, 75 (Hanover, NH: Dartmouth College/University Press of New England, 1999).

39. *Talk* was commissioned by the Foundry Theatre in New York City and further developed at the Sundance Theatre Laboratory in 2001. It was first produced by the Foundry Theatre at the Joseph Papp Public Theater/New York Shakespeare Festival in March 2002, directed by Marion McClinton. It opened at Theater X (David Ravel, Producing Director) in Milwaukee, Wisconsin, in January 2003. The play itself is a generic hybrid, what Michael Eric Dyson calls "an intellectual tour de force," that mixes genres: "experimental theatre, Greek choruses, jazz-like rhetorical improvisation, post-structuralist theory, hip-hop and popular culture into a heady brew of critical reflection on Western intellectual life over the last seventy years" (back jacket of TCG edition). All quotations drawn from this edition: Carl Hancock Rux, *Talk* (New York: Theatre Communications Group, 2003).

40. Geneviève Fabre and Robert O'Meally, eds., Introduction to *History and Memory in African-American Culture*, 7 (New York: Oxford University Press, 1994).

41. On Pierre Nora's concept of the *lieu de mémoire*, see "Between History and Memory: *Les Lieux de Mémoire*," in *Acts of Memory: Cultural Recall in the Present*, ed. Mieke Bal, Jonathan Crewe, and Leo Spitzer, 284–300 (Hanover, NH: Dartmouth College/University Press of New England, 1999).

My bringing race into relief in *Talk* diverges from the general critical reception of the play. Interestingly, many reviewers make almost no mention of race in their reviews. See, for example, Michael Feingold's review in the *Village Voice* (April 2, 2002), http://www.villagevoice.com/theater/0216,feingold,33956,11.html (accessed March 19, 2010).

42. On the complexities of Anatole Broyard's passing, see Anatole's daughter Bliss Broyard, who published a biography of her father: *One Drop: My Father's Hidden Life—A Story of Race and Family Secrets* (New York: Little, Brown, 2007).

43. http://channel.creative-capital.org/project_52.html (accessed May 14, 2007). As I mentioned, the symposium degenerates into a Tower of Babel, and as people interrupt each other, the lines and memories begin to interpenetrate each other, creating no seamless and transparent picture or narrative of Aymes and the times, but rather a palimpsest that when performed is chaotic and unintelligible.

44. This intertextual layering is akin to that in "The Racial Draft," which evokes and exploits audience familiarity with sports history and which even offers the friction of endnote to text proper with the inclusion of the producer post-commentary in the CD that confuses more than illuminates the skit itself.

45. Antonio Gramsci, *Selections from the Prison Notebooks* (New York: International Publishers, 1971), 324.

46. Toni Morrison expands on the notion of the usefulness of blackness in her preface to *Playing in the Dark: Whiteness and the Literary Imagination* (New York: Vintage Books, 1993).

47. http://channel.creative-capital.org/project_52.html.

48. Eva Saks, "Representing Miscegenation Law," *Raritan* 8 (1988): 53–54.

49. Throughout the play, some characters suggest his father is black and his mother Greek, or some other combination. His ancestry becomes another part of the epistemological shell game central to the play, but I think both the director's notes and the racial logic of the play suggest that Aymes is the offspring of the master of the house and a "Negro girl."

50. See Herman S. Gray, *Cultural Moves: African Americans and the Politics of Representation* (Berkeley: University of California Press, 2005).

51. See Karen Shimakawa, *National Abjection: The Asian American Body Onstage* (Durham, NC: Duke University Press, 2002). If Shimakawa notes the "abjection" of Asian Americans onstage as an effort to disrupt the abjecting stereotype, Rux absents the mixed race figure as a way of pointing out and making a point of the complex ways in which he is absented—even as he is the putative focus of all the talk.

52. See also Alex Woloch's *The One vs. the Many: Minor Characters and the Space of the Protagonist in the Novel* (Princeton, NJ: Princeton University Press, 2003). He asks "what kind of narrative centrality is available for characters who are structurally subordinated within the social system" (Notes to Afterword, 372). Aymes, like Rufus in *Another Country*, as described by Woloch, is also the empty center around which the other characters revolve.

53. See Norman Mailer's "The White Negro: Superficial Reflections on the Hipster," *Dissent* 4, no. 3 (Fall 1957). Reprinted in *Advertisements for Myself* (Cambridge, MA: Harvard University Press, 2002; orig 1959), 369.

54. See Mieke Bal, introduction to *Acts of Memory: Cultural Recall in the Present*, ed. Mieke Bal, Jonathan Crewe, and Leo Spitzer (Hanover, NH: Dartmouth College/ University Press of New England, 1999), xiii.

55. Mieke Bal, "Memories in the Museum: Preposterous Histories for Today," 173, in Bal, Crewe, and Spitzer, *Acts of Memory*.

56. Pierre Nora, "Between Memory and History: *Les Lieux de Mémoire*," in *Acts of Memory: Cultural Recall in the Present*, ed. Mieke Bal, Jonathan Crewe, and Leo Spitzer, 282 (Hanover, NH: Dartmouth College/University Press of New England, 1999).

57. The mother-son in the title is variously implied to be Oedipal, but also an echo from a film (84) or some other cultural referent. It also evokes Langston Hughes' famous poem "Mother to Son." Like the endnotes, the mother-son paradigm, overwritten with associations, is deployed more as a tease than an answer to the play's interpretive options.

58. Harry Justin Elam, Jr., "Reality √," in *Critical Theory and Performance*, ed. Janelle Reinelt and Joseph Roach, 2nd ed. (Ann Arbor: University of Michigan Press, 2006), 173.

59. Brent Hayes Edwards, *The Practice of Diaspora: Literature, Translation, and the Rise of Black Internationalism* (Cambridge, MA: Harvard University Press, 2003), 12.

60. Quoted in ibid.

61. See http://www.villagevoice.com/theater/0216,feingold,33956,11.html (accessed September 13, 2009).

62. Diana Taylor, *The Archive and the Repertoire: Performing Cultural Memory in the Americas* (Durham, NC: Duke University Press, 2003), 82.

63. Arthur A. Schomburg, "The Negro Digs Up His Past," in *The Norton Anthology of African American Literature*, ed. Henry Louis Gates, Jr., and Nellie Y. McKay, 2nd ed. (New York: W. W. Norton, 2004), 963.

64. Stuart Hall, "What Is This 'Black' in Popular Culture (Rethinking Race)," *Social Justice* 20, nos. 1–2 (Spring–Summer 1993): 104–115.

65. Ralph Ellison, "Richard Wright's Blues" (1945), in *Shadow and Act* (New York: New American Library, 1964), 90.

66. Michele Birnbaum (Elam), *Race, Work, and Desire in American Literature, 1860–1930* (Cambridge: Cambridge University Press, 2003), 144.

Bibliography

Alaimo, Stacy, and Susan J. Hekman. *Material Feminisms*. Bloomington: Indiana University Press, 2008.

Alcoff, Linda. *Visible Identities: Race, Gender, and the Self*. New York: Oxford University Press, 2006.

———. "Who's Afraid of Identity Politics?" In *Reclaiming Identity: Realist Theory and the Predicament of Postmodernism*, ed. Paula M. L. Moya and Michael R. Hames-García, 312–344. Berkeley: University of California Press, 2000.

Alcoff, Linda Martín, Michael R. Hames-García, Satya P. Mohanty, and Paula M. L. Moya, eds. *Identity Politics Reconsidered*. New York: Palgrave Macmillan, 2006.

Amiran, Eval. "George Herriman's *Black Sentence: The Legibility of Race in Krazy Kat*." *Mosaic* 33, no. 3 (September 2000).

Anderson, Benedict R. O'G. *Imagined Communities: Reflections on the Origin and Spread of Nationalism*. Rev ed. London and New York: Verso, 2006; orig. 1991.

Anzaldúa, Gloria. *Borderlands: The New Mestiza/La Frontera*. 3rd ed. San Francisco: Aunt Lute Books, 2007.

Appiah, Anthony. "Towards a New Cosmopolitanism." *New York Times Magazine*, January 1, 2006, 30–37.

Ashe, Bertram D. "Theorizing the Post-Soul Aesthetic: An Introduction." *African American Review* 41, no. 4 (Winter 2007): 609–624.

Auslander, Philip. "Liveness: Performance and the Anxiety of Simulation." In *Performance and Cultural Politics*, ed. Elin Diamond, 198–218. New York: Routledge, 1996.

Awkward, Michael. *Negotiating Difference: Race, Gender, and the Politics of Positionality*. Chicago: University of Chicago Press, 1995.

Bakhtin, M. M. *Rabelais and His World*. Trans. Hélène Iswolsky. Bloomington: Indiana University Press, 1984.

Bal, Mieke. Introduction to *Acts of Memory: Cultural Recall in the Present*, ed. Mieke Bal, Jonathan V. Crewe, and Leo Spitzer, vii–2. Hanover, NH: Dartmouth College/University Press of New England, 1999.

———. "Memories in the Museum: Preposterous Histories for Today." In *Acts of Memory: Cultural Recall in the Present*, ed. Mieke Bal, Jonathan V. Crewe, and Leo Spitzer, 171–190. Hanover, NH: Dartmouth College/University Press of New England, 1999.

Ball, Edward. *Slaves in the Family*. New York: Ballantine, 1998.

———. *The Sweet Hell Within: The Rise of an Elite Black Family in the Segregated South*. New York: Harper Perennial, 2002.

Baron, Naomi S. *Alphabet to Email: How Written English Evolved and Where It's Heading*. London: Routledge, 2000.

Beals, Jennifer. "Jennifer Beals GLAAD Awards." November 28, 2005. Online video clip. http://www.youtube.com/watch?v=DRUFu_m_Nn4. Accessed August 30, 2006.

Beltran, Mary, and Camilla Fojas. *Mixed Race Hollywood*. New York: New York University Press, 2008.

Berger, John. *Ways of Seeing*. New York: Penguin, 1977.

Berry, Halle. Wikipedia entry. http://en.wikipedia.org/wiki/Halle_Berry. Accessed October 4, 2009.

Best, Stephen, and Saidiya Hartman. "Fugitive Justice." Special issue on "Redress." *Representations* 92, no. 1 (Fall 2005): 1–16.

Biello, Peter. "Interview with Emily Raboteau." *Compulsive Reader*. December 20, 2005. Web audio. http://www.compulsivereader.com/html/index.php?name=News&file=article&sid=11191. Accessed August 3, 2009.

Binning, Kevin R., Miguel M. Unzueta, Yuen J. Huo, and Ludwin E. Molina. "The Interpretation of Multiracial Status and Its Relation to Social Engagement and Psychological Well-Being." *Journal of Social Issues* 65, no. 1 (2009): 35–49.

Bobo, Lawrence D. "Inequalities that Endure? Racial Ideology, American Politics, and the Peculiar Role of Social Science." In *The Changing Terrain of Race and Ethnicity*, ed. M. Krysan and A. Lewis, 13–42. New York: Russell Sage Foundation, 2004.

Bobo, Lawrence D., and Devon Johnson. "A Taste for Punishment: Black and White Americans' Views on the Death Penalty and the War on Drugs." *Du Bois Review* 1 (2004): 151–180.

Bobo, Lawrence D., and Victor Thompson. "Unfair by Design: The War on Drugs, Race, and the Legitimacy of the Criminal Justice System." *Social Research* 73, no. 2 (2006): 445–472.

Bonilla-Silva, Eduardo. *Racism Without Racists: Color-Blind Racism and the Persistence of Racial Inequality in the United States*. New York: Rowman and Littlefield, 2003.

Bost, Suzanne. *Mulattas and Mestizas: Representing Mixed Identities in the Americas, 1850–2000*. Athens: University of Georgia Press, 2003.

Boyd, Todd. *The New H.N.I.C.: The Death of Civil Rights and the Reign of Hip Hop*. New York: New York University Press, 2002.

Brennan, Jonathan, ed. *Mixed Race Literature*. Stanford: Stanford University Press, 2002.

Brody, Jennifer DeVere. *Impossible Purities: Blackness, Femininity, and Victorian Culture*. Durham, NC: Duke University Press, 1998.

———. *Punctuation: Art, Politics, and Play*. Durham, NC: Duke Uuniversity Press, 2008.

Broyard, Bliss. *One Drop: My Father's Hidden Life—A Story of Race and Family Secrets*. New York: Little, Brown, 2007.

Buckley, Jerome Hamilton. *Season of Youth: The Bildungsroman from Dickens to Golding*. Cambridge, MA: Harvard University Press, 1974.

Burchill, Kiyomi. "Chapter 5: Rejecting a Multiracial Category: The Case of RE-52 and the University of California." In "Beyond the Box: The Post-Census Politics of the Multiracial Movement." Undergraduate honors thesis, Stanford University, May 19, 2006.

Butler, Judith. *Bodies That Matter: On the Discursive Limits of "Sex."* New York: Routledge, 1993.

Byrd, William. *Histories of the Dividing Line Betwixt Virginia and North Carolina*. New York: Dover, 1967; orig. 1929.

Camper, Carol, ed. *Miscegenation Blues: Voices of Mixed Race Women*. Toronto: Sister Vision Press, 1994.

Carpio, Glenda R. *Laughing Fit to Kill: Black Humor in the Fictions of Slavery*. New York: Oxford University Press, 2008.

Chappelle, Dave, and Neal Brennan, writers/producers. "The Racial Draft." *Chappelle's Show.* Season Two DVD. 2004. Originally aired on Comedy Central network, October 2004.

Chesnutt, Charles W. *Paul Marchand, F.M.C.* Jackson: University Press of Mississippi, 1998; orig. 1921.

Childs, Erica Chito. "MULTIRACE.COM: The Promise and Pitfalls of Multiracial Cyberspace." In *The Politics of Multiracialism: Challenging Racial Thinking,* ed. Heather Dalmage, 143–160. Albany: State University of New York Press, 2004.

Christian, Barbara. "A Rough Terrain: The Case of Shaping an Anthology of Caribbean Women Writers." In *The Ethnic Canon: Histories, Institutions, and Interventions,* ed. David Palumbo-Liu, 241–259. Minneapolis: University of Minnesota Press, 1995.

Colker, Ruth. *Hybrid: Bisexuals, Multiracials, and Other Misfits Under American Law.* New York: New York University Press, 1996.

Connerly, Ward. *Creating Equal: My Fight Against Race Preferences.* New York: Encounter Books, 2000.

Cose, Ellis. *Color-Blind: Seeing Beyond Race in a Race-Obsessed World.* New York: HarperCollins, 1998.

Cotter, Holland. "Beyond Multiculturalism, Freedom?" *New York Times,* Arts and Leisure, July 13, 2001.

———. "'Black' Comes in Many Shadings." *New York Times,* Arts and Leisure, August 13, 2004.

Courtney, Susan. *Hollywood Fantasies of Miscegenation: Spectacular Narratives of Gender and Race, 1903–1967.* Princeton, NJ: Princeton University Press, 2005.

Creekmore, Nate. Mixed Chicks Chat Interview. "Episode 47: Nate Creekmore: Creator/Illustrator of a Biracial Comic Strip." April 17, 2008. Web Audio. http://www.talkshoe.com/talkshoe/web/talkCast.jsp;jsessionid=34E5FAA18E1A45C69BA0F3B1816DBEF4.prod71_2?masterId=34257&pageNumber=5&pageSize=15. Accessed July 8, 2009.

Crenshaw, Kimberlé. "Mapping the Margins: Intersectionality, Identity Politics, and Violence Against Women of Color." *Stanford Law Review* 43 (July 1991): 1241–1265.

Crewe, Jonathan. "Recalling Adamastor: Literature as Cultural Memory in 'White' South Africa." In *Acts of Memory: Cultural Recall in the Present,* ed. Mieke Bal, Jonathan Crewe, and Leo Spitzer, 75–86. Hanover, NH: Dartmouth College/University Press of New England, 1999.

Critchley, Simon. *On Humour.* New York: Routledge, 2002.

Cross, June. *Secret Daughter: A Mixed-Race Daughter and the Mother Who Gave Her Away.* New York: Penguin, 2007.

Crouch, Stanley. "Race Is Over." *New York Times,* September 26, 1996.

Cruse, Harold. "The Integrationist Ethic as a Basis for Scholarly Endeavors." In *The Essential Harold Cruse: A Reader,* ed. William Jelani Cobb, 117–124. New York: Palgrave Macmillan, 2002.

DaCosta, Kimberly McClain. "All in the Family: The Familial Roots of Racial Division." In *The Politics of Multiracialism: Challenging Racial Thinking,* ed. Heather Dalmage, 19–42. New York: State University of New York Press, 2004.

———. *Making Multiracials: State, Family, and Market in the Redrawing of the Color Line.* Stanford: Stanford University Press, 2007.

Dalmage, Heather. "Patrolling Racial Borders: Discrimination Against Mixed Race People." In *Multiracial Child Resource Book: Living Complex Identities,* ed. Maria P. P. Root and Matt Kelley, 19–25. Seattle: MAVIN Foundation, 2003.

————, ed. *The Politics of Multiracialism: Challenging Racial Thinking*. Albany: State University of New York Press, 2004.

Daniel, G. Reginald. *More than Black? Multiracial Identity and the New Racial Order*. Philadelphia: Temple University Press, 2001.

Davis, Lennard J. *The Disability Studies Reader*. 2nd ed. New York: Routledge, 2006.

Davol, Marguerite W. *Black, White, Just Right!* Illustrations by Irene Trivas. Morton Grove, IL: Albert Whitman and Company, 1993.

Derricotte, Toi. *The Black Notebooks: An Interior Journey*. New York: W. W. Norton, 1999.

Diamond, Elin, ed. *Performance and Cultural Politics*. New York: Routledge, 1996.

Dickerson, Debra J. *The End of Blackness: Returning the Souls of Black Folk to Their Rightful Owners*. New York: Pantheon Books, 2004.

Dollimore, Jonathan. "Desire and Difference: Homosexuality, Race, Masculinity." In *Race and the Subject of Masculinities*, ed. Harry Stecopoulos and Michael Uebel, 17–44. Durham, NC: Duke University Press, 1997.

Douglass, Ramona E. "The Evolution of the Multiracial Movement." In *Multiracial Child Resource Book: Living Complex Identities*, ed. Maria P. P. Root and Matt Kelley, 12–17. Seattle: MAVIN Foundation, 2003.

D'Souza, Dinesh. *The End of Racism: Principles for a Multiracial Society*. New York: Free Press, 1995.

Dubey, Madhu. *Signs and Cities: Black Literary Postmodernism*. Chicago: University of Chicago Press, 2003.

Du Bois, W. E. B. "The Comet." In *The Oxford W. E. B. Du Bois Reader*, ed. Eric J. Sundquist, 611–622. New York: Oxford University Press, 1996.

————. "The Concept of Race." *Dusk of Dawn* (1940). In *W. E. B. Du Bois: Writings*, ed. Nathan Irvin Huggins, 625–651. New York: Library of America, Viking, 1986.

————. "Criteria of Negro Art" (1926). In *W. E. B. Du Bois: Writings*, ed. Nathan Irvin Huggins, 993–995. New York: Library of America, Viking, 1986.

————. *Dark Princess: A Romance*. Introduction by Claudia Tate. Jackson: University of Mississippi Press, 1995; orig. 1928.

————. "Of Our Spiritual Strivings." *The Souls of Black Folk*. In *The Norton Anthology of African American Literature*, ed. Henry Louis Gates, Jr., and Nellie Y. McKay, 693–699. 2nd ed. New York: W. W. Norton, 2004.

————. "The White World." *Dusk of Dawn* (1940). In *W. E. B. Du Bois: Writings*, ed. Nathan Huggins, 652–680. New York: Library of America, Viking, 1986.

DuCille, Ann. *Skin Trade*. Cambridge, MA: Harvard University Press, 1996.

Duncombe, Stephen. *Cultural Resistance Reader*. New York: Verso, 2002.

During, Simon, ed. *The Cultural Studies Reader*. New York: Routledge, 1993.

Durrow, Heidi. *The Girl Who Fell from the Sky*. Chapel Hill, NC: Algonguin Books, 2010.

————. "May Is Mixed-Race People History Month." *Light-skinned Girl: A mixed chick's mixed thoughts on a mixed-up world*. May 3, 2007. http://lightskinnededgirl.typepad.com/my_weblog/2007/05/may_is_mixed_ra.html. Accessed October 4, 2009.

Eckert, Susan. "The Birth of the Multiracial American." December 5, 2007. http://racism.suite101.com/article.cfm/birth_of_the_multiracial_american. Accessed April 7, 2010.

Edwards, Brent Hayes. *The Practice of Diaspora: Literature, Translation, and the Rise of Black Internationalism*. Cambridge, MA: Harvard University Press, 2003.

Ehrenreich, Barbara, and Dedrick Muhammad. "The Recession's Racial Divide." *New York*

Times, September 12, 2009. http://www.nytimes.com/2009/09/13/opinion/13ehrenreich
.html?_r=1. Accessed September 13, 2009.

Eisner, Will. *Comics and Sequential Art: Principles and Practices of the World's Most Popular Art Form*. Tamarac, FL: Poorhouse Press, 1985.

Elam, Harry Justin, Jr. "Change Clothes and Go: A Post-Script to Post-Blackness." In *Black Cultural Traffic: Crossroads in Global Performance and Black Popular Culture*, ed. Harry J. Elam, Jr., and Kennell A. Jackson, 379–388. Ann Arbor: University of Michigan Press, 2005.

———. "The Device of Race: An Introduction." In *African American Performance and Theater History: A Critical Reader*, ed. Harry J. Elam, Jr., and David Krasner, 3–16. New York: Oxford University Press, 2001.

———. *The Past as Present in the Drama of August Wilson*. Ann Arbor: University of Michigan Press, 2004.

———. "The Postmulticultural: A Tale of Mothers and Sons." In *Crucible of Cultures: Anglophone Drama at the Dawn of a New Millennium*, ed. Marc Maufort and Franca Bellarsi, 113–128. Brussels: Peter Lang, 2002.

———. "Reality √." In *Critical Theory and Performance*, ed. Janelle Reinelt and Joseph Roach. 2nd ed. 173–190. Ann Arbor: University of Michigan Press, 2006.

Elam, Harry Justin, Jr., and Kennell A. Jackson. *Black Cultural Traffic: Crossroads in Global Performance and Popular Culture*. Ann Arbor: University of Michigan Press, 2005.

Elam, Michele. "The 'Ethno-Ambiguo Hostility Syndrome': Mixed-Race, Identity, and Popular Culture." In *Doing Race: 21 Essays for the 21st Century*, ed. Hazel Rose Markus and Paula M. L. Moya, 528–544. New York: W. W. Norton, 2010.

———. "The Mis-Education of Mixed Race." In *Identities in Education*, ed. Amie MacDonald and Susan Sánchez-Casal, 131–150. New York: Palgrave-MacMillan, 2009.

———. "Mixed Race and Cultural Memory: Carl Hancock Rux's *Talk*." In *Signatures of the Past: Cultural Memory in Contemporary Anglophone North American Drama*, ed. Marc Maufort and Caroline De Wagter, 83–100. Brussels: Peter Lang, 2008.

———. "Obama's Mixology." The Root.com (*Washington Post*), October 30, 2008. http://www.theroot.com/views/obamas-mixology. Accessed April 5, 2010.

———. "Passing in the Post-Race Era: Danzy Senna, Philip Roth, and Colson Whitehead." Post-Soul Special Issue, *African American Review* 41, no. 4 (Winter 2007): 749–768.

———. *Race, Work, and Desire in American Literature, 1860–1930*. Cambridge: Cambridge University Press, 2003.

———. "Towards Desegregating Syllabuses: Teaching American Literary Realism and Racial Uplift Fiction." In *Teaching Literature: A Companion*, ed. Tanya Agathocleous and Ann C. Dean, 58–71. New York: Palgrave Macmillan, 2003.

———. "2010 Census: Think Twice, Check Once." *Huffington Post*, March 8, 2010. http://www.huffingtonpost.com/michele-elam/2010-census-think-twice-c_b_490164.html. Accessed April 7, 2010.

———. "Why Obama Is Black Again." Thinking Twice column, *Stanford Report*, January 29, 2009. http://humanexperience.stanford.edu/race-elam.

Elam, Michele, and Harry Elam. "Blood Debt: Reparations in Langston Hughes' *Mulatto*." *Theatre Journal* 61, no. 1 (March 2009): 85–103.

Elam, Michele, and Paul C. Taylor. "Du Bois' Erotics." In *Next to the Color Line: Gender, Sexuality, and W. E. B. Du Bois*, ed. Susan Gillman and Alyce Weinbaum, 209–233. Minneapolis: University of Minnesota Press, 2007.

Ellis, Trey. "The New Black Aesthetic." *Callaloo* 12 (Winter 1989): 233–243.
———. "Obama: Cultural Mulatto." *Huffington Post*, February 19, 2007. http://www.salon
.com/ent/feature/2009/05/07/obama_spock/index.html. Accessed November 7, 2009.
Ellison, Ralph. "Change the Joke and Slip the Yoke." In *The Norton Anthology of African
American Literature*, ed. Henry Louis Gates, Jr., and Nellie Y. McKay. 2nd ed., 1570–
1577. New York: W. W. Norton, 2004.
———. *Invisible Man* (1952). New York: Modern Library, 1994.
———. *Invisible Man* (1952). New York: Vintage International, 1995.
———. "Richard Wright's Blues" (1945). In *Shadow and Act*, 77–94. New York: New
American Library, 1964.
English, Darby. *How to See a Work of Art in Total Darkness.* Cambridge, MA: MIT
Press, 2007.
Erkkila, Betsy. *Mixed Bloods and Other Crosses: Rethinking American Literature from the
Revolution to the Culture Wars.* Philadelphia: University of Pennsylvania Press, 2005.
Fabi, M. Giulia. *Passing and the Rise of the African American Novel.* Urbana-Champagne:
University of Illinois Press, 2001.
Fabre, Geneviève, and Michel Feith, eds. *Jean Toomer and the Harlem Renaissance.*
Piscataway, NJ: Rutgers University Press, 2001.
Fabre, Geneviève, and Robert O'Meally, eds. Introduction to *History and Memory in
African-American Culture*, 3–17. New York: Oxford University Press, 1994.
Fanon, Frantz. *Black Skin, White Masks.* New York: Grove Press, 1967.
Favor, J. Martin. *Authentic Blackness: The Folk in the New Negro Renaissance.* Durham,
NC: Duke University Press, 1999.
Ferguson, Roderick. *Aberrations in Black: Toward a Queer of Color Critique.* Minneapolis:
University of Minnesota Press, 2003.
Frazier, Sundee. *Check All That Apply: Finding Wholeness as a Multiracial Person.* New
York: InterVarsity Press, 2002.
Fredrickson, George M. *Racism: A Short History.* Princeton, NJ: Princeton University
Press, 2002.
———. *White Supremacy: A Comparative Study in American and South African History.*
New York: Oxford University Press, 1982.
Freire, Paulo. *Education for Critical Consciousness.* New York: Crossroad Publishing, 1974.
Fryer, Roland G., Lisa B. Kahn, Steven D. Levitt, and Jörg L. Spenkuch. "The Plight of
Mixed Race Adolescents." National Bureau of Economic Research Working Paper
Series, vol. w14192. http://ssrn.com/abstract=1179862. Accessed July 2008.
Fulbeck, Kip. *Part Asian, 100% Hapa.* San Francisco: Chronicle Books, 2006.
Funderburg, Lise. *Pig Candy: Taking My Father South, Taking My Father Home: A
Memoir.* New York: Free Press, 2009.
———, ed. *Black, White, Other: Biracial Americans Talk About Race and Identity.* New
York: Harper Perennial, 1995.
Gaines, James. "From the Managing Editor." Special Issue. "The New Face of America:
How Immigrants Are Shaping the World's First Multicultural Society." *Time* (1993), 2.
Gardner, Alan. "McGruder Denies Report Regarding Obama's Race." *Daily Cartoonist*,
January 21, 2009. http://dailycartoonist.com/index.php/2009/01/21/mcgruder-denies
-report-regarding-obamas-race/. Accessed July 9, 2009.
———. "Review: *Maintaining* by Nate Creekmore." March 7, 2007. http://dailycartoonist

.com/index.php/2007/03/07/review-maintaining-by-nate-creekmore/. Accessed July 9, 2009.

Garland-Thomson, Rosemarie. *Staring: How We Look.* New York: Oxford University Press, 2009.

Gaskins, Pearl Fuyo, ed. *What Are You? Voices of Mixed-Race Young People.* New York: Henry Holt, 1999.

Gates, Henry Louis, Jr. "White Like Me." *New Yorker,* June 17, 1996, 66–81.

Gates, Henry Louis, Jr., and Nellie Y. McKay, eds. *The Norton Anthology of African American Literature.* 2nd ed. New York: W. W. Norton, 2004.

Gelder, Rachel. "Passing and Failing: Reflections on the Limitations of Showing the Passer in *The Human Stain.*" In special issue, ed. John L. Jackson, Jr., and Martha S. Jones. *Women and Performance: A Journal of Feminist Theory* 15, no. 1 (2005): 293–312.

George, Nelson. *Post-Soul Nation: The Explosive, Contradictory, Triumphant, and Tragic 1980s as Experienced by African Americans (Previously Known as Blacks and Before That Negroes).* New York: Viking, 2004.

Gilman, Sander L. "Black Bodies, White Bodies: Toward an Iconography of Female Sexuality in Late Nineteenth-Century Art, Medicine, and Literature." In *The Feminism and Visual Culture Reader,* ed. Amelia Jones, 136–150. New York: Routledge, 2002.

Gilroy, Paul. *Against Race: Imagining Political Culture Beyond the Color Line.* Cambridge, MA: Belknap Press of Harvard University Press, 2000.

———. *Postcolonial Melancholia.* New York: Columbia University Press, 2005.

Ginsberg, Elaine K., ed. *Passing and the Fictions of Identity.* Durham, NC: Duke University Press, 1996.

Gladwell, Malcolm. "Lost in the Middle." In *Half and Half: Writers on Growing Up Biracial and Bicultural,* ed. Claudine Chiawei O'Hearn, 112–124. New York: Pantheon Books, 1998.

———. *Outliers: The Story of Success.* New York: Little, Brown, 2008.

Goldberg, David Theo. "Made in the U.S.A." In *American Mixed Race: The Culture of Microdiversity,* ed. Naomi Zack, 237–256. Lanham, MD: Rowman and Littlefield, 1995.

Gootman, Elissa. "Proposal Adds Options for Students to Specify Race." *New York Times,* August 9, 2006. http://www.nytimes.com/2006/08/09/education/09ethnic.html?_r=1 &ex=1155787200&en=8d33409d61a82656&ei=5070&emc=eta1.

Gordone, Charles. *No Place to Be Somebody: A Black Black Comedy in Three Acts.* Introduction by Joseph Papp. New York: Bobbs-Merrill, 1969.

Graham, Lawrence. *Our Kind of People: Inside America's Black Upper Class.* New York: HarperCollins, 1999.

Gramsci, Antonio. *Selections from the Prison Notebooks.* New York: International Publishers, 1971.

Gray, Herman S. *Cultural Moves: African Americans and the Politics of Representation.* Berkeley: University of California Press, 2005.

———. *Watching Race: Television and the Struggle for Blackness.* Minneapolis: University of Minnesota Press, 1995.

Griffin, John Howard. *Black Like Me.* 35th Anniversary Edition. New York: Signet, 1996.

Gross, Ariela J. *Double Character: Slavery and Mastery in the Antebellum Southern Courtroom.* Princeton, NJ: Princeton University Press, 2000.

———. *What Blood Won't Tell: A History of Race on Trial in America.* Cambridge, MA: Harvard University Press, 2008.

———. "'Of Portuguese Origin': Litigating Identity and Citizenship Among the 'Little Races' in Nineteenth-Century America." *Law and History Review* 25, no. 3 (Fall 2007): 467–512.

———. *What Blood Won't Tell: A History of Race on Trial in America.* Cambridge, MA: Harvard University Press, 2008.

Haizlip, Shirlee Taylor. *The Sweeter the Juice: A Family Memoir in Black and White.* New York: Free Press, 1995.

Hall, Sharron. "It's Time for Foundation." In *Mixed Heritage: Identities, Policy, and Practice*, ed. Jessica Mai Sims, 24–26. London: Runnymede Press, 2007.

Hall, Stuart. "What Is This 'Black' in Popular Culture (Rethinking Race)." *Social Justice* 20, nos. 1–2 (Spring–Summer 1993): 104–115.

Hames-García, Michael R. "How Real Is Race?" In *Material Feminisms*, ed. Stacy Alaimo and Susan J. Hekman, 308–339. Bloomington: Indiana University Press, 2008.

———. "Which America Is Ours? Martí's 'Truth' and the Foundations of 'American Literature.'" *Modern Fiction Studies* 49, no. 1 (Spring 2003): 19–53, Special issue: "Fictions of the Trans-American Imaginary," ed. Paula M. L. Moya and Ramón Saldívar.

Hamilton, Charles V., Lynn Huntley, Neville Alexander, Antonio Ségrio, Alfredo Guimarães, and Wilmot James, eds. *Beyond Racism: Race and Inequality in Brazil, South Africa, and the United States.* Boulder, CO: Lynne Rienner Publishers, 2001.

Hammonds, Evelynn M. "New Technologies of Race." In *Processed Lives: Gender and Technology in Everyday Life*, ed. Jennifer Terry and Melodie Calvert, 107–122. New York: Routledge, 1997.

Hansberry, Lorraine. *Les Blancs: The Collected Last Plays.* Ed. Robert Nemiroff. Introduction by Margaret B. Wilkerson. New York: Vintage Books, 1994.

Harper, Phillip Brian. "Nationalism and Social Division in Black Arts Poetry of the 1960s." In *African American Literary Theory: A Reader*, ed. Winston Napier, 460–474. New York: New York University Press, 2000.

———. "Passing for What? Racial Masquerade and the Demands of Upward Mobility." *Callaloo* 21 (1998): 381–397.

———. "Private Affairs: Race, Sex, Property, and Persons." *GLQ: A Journal of Gay and Lesbian Studies* 1, no. 2 (1994): 111–133.

Hartfield, Ronne. *Another Way Home: The Tangled Roots of Race in One Chicago Family.* Chicago: University of Chicago Press, 2005.

Heard, Danielle. "Black Comic/Black Critic: 'Reading' Culture and the Critical Pedagogy of the Post-Soul." Ph.D. exam paper, Cornell University, August 2006.

Heer, Jeet. "A Cat-and-Mouse Game of Identity: George Herriman Played with Race in His Work and in His Real Life." *Toronto Star*, December 11, 2005.

Henry, Neil. *Pearl's Secret: A Black Man's Search for His White Family.* Berkeley: University of California Press, 2002.

Hernton, Calvin C. *Sex and Racism in America.* New York: Anchor Books, 1992; orig. 1965.

———. *Sex and Racism in America.* With a new introduction. 1st Evergreen ed. New York: Grove Press, 1988.

Hollinger, David A. *Postethnic America: Beyond Multiculturalism.* Rev. ed. New York: Basic Books, 2000.

hooks, bell. "The Oppositional Gaze: Black Female Spectators." In *The Feminism and Visual Culture Reader*, ed. Amelia Jones, 94–104. New York: Routledge, 2003.

———. *Teaching to Transgress: Education as the Practice of Freedom.* New York: Routledge, 1994.

Houston, Velina Hasu. "Multirace and the Future." In *Multiracial Child Resource Book: Living Complex Identities*, ed. Maria P. P. Root and Matt Kelley, 223–228. Seattle: MAVIN Foundation, 2003.

Hughes, Langston. *Five Plays by Langston Hughes.* Ed. Webster Smalley. Bloomington: Indiana University Press, 1963.

———. "Harlem" (1951). In *The Norton Anthology of African American Literature*, ed. Henry Louis Gates, Jr., and Nellie Y. McKay, 1308–1309. 2nd ed. New York: W. W. Norton, 2004.

———. "The Negro Artist and the Racial Mountain." In *The Norton Anthology of African American Literature*, ed. Henry Louis Gates, Jr., and Nellie Y. McKay, 1267–1271. 2nd ed. New York: W. W. Norton, 2004.

Hunt, Marsha. *Repossessing Ernestine: A Granddaughter Uncovers the Secret History of Her American Family.* New York: HarperCollins, 1996.

Hutchinson, George. *In Search of Nella Larsen: A Biography of the Color Line.* Cambridge, MA: Harvard University Press, 2006.

Ifekwunigwe, Jayne O. "Let Blackness and Whiteness Wash Through: Competing Discourses on Bi-racialization and the Compulsion of Genealogical Erasures." In *'Mixed Race' Studies: A Reader*, ed. Jayne O. Ifekwunigwe, 183–194. New York: Routledge, 2004.

———, ed. *"Mixed Race" Studies: A Reader.* New York: Routledge, 2004.

Ignatiev, Noel, and John Garvey. *Race Traitor.* New York: Routledge, 1998.

Intermix. "Nate Creekmore's *Maintaining*: Life Through the Eyes of a Mixed-Race Teen." http://www.intermix.org.uk/news/news_070607_01.asp. Accessed July 8, 2009.

Itzkovitz, Daniel. "Passing Like Me: Jewish Chameleonism and the Politics of Race." In *Passing: Identity and Interpretation in Sexuality, Race, and Religion*, ed. María Carla Sánchez and Linda Schlossberg, 38–63. New York: New York University Press, 2001.

Jackson, John L., and Martha S. Jones. "Passed Performances: An Introduction." *Women and Performance: A Journal of Feminist Theory.* Special "Passing" Issue, ed. John L. Jackson and Martha S. Jones. 15, no. 1 (2005): 9–16.

Jackson, Shannon. *Professing Performance: Theatre in the Academy from Philology to Performativity.* New York: Cambridge University Press, 2004.

Jarrett, Gene Andrew. *African American Literature Beyond Race: An Alternative Reader.* New York: New York University Press, 2006.

Johnson, E. Patrick. *Appropriating Blackness: Performance and the Politics of Authenticity.* Durham, NC: Duke University Press, 2003.

Johnson, James Weldon. *The Autobiography of an Ex-Colored Man.* In *The Norton Anthology of African American Literature*, ed. Henry Louis Gates, Jr., and Nellie Y. McKay, 803–883. 2nd ed. New York: W. W. Norton, 2004.

Johnson, Kevin R., ed. *Mixed Race America and the Law.* New York: New York University Press, 2003.

Jones, Amelia, ed. *The Feminism and Visual Culture Reader.* New York: Routledge, 2002.

Jones, Lisa. *Bulletproof Diva: Tales of Race, Sex, and Hair.* New York: Doubleday, 1994.

Jones, Nicholas A., and Amy Symens Smith. "A Statistical Portrait of Two or More Races in Census 2000." In *Multiracial Child Resource Book: Living Complex Identities*, ed. Maria P. P. Root and Matt Kelley, 3–10. Seattle, WA: MAVIN Foundation, 2003.

Kaeser, Gigi and Peggy Gillespie. *Of Many Colors: Portraits of Multiracial Families.* Introduction by Glenda Valentine. Amherst: University of Massachusetts Press, 1997.

Kaplan, Amy. *The Social Construction of American Realism.* Chicago: University of Chicago Press, 1988, rpt. 1992.

Kawash, Samira. *Dislocating the Color Line: Identity, Hybridity, and Singularity in African-American Narrative.* Stanford: Stanford University Press, 1997.

Kelley, Matt. *Chasing Daybreak: A Film About Mixed Race in America.* Directed by Justin Leroy. Seattle: MAVIN Foundation, 2006. www.chasingdaybreak.com.

Kelley, Robin D. G. *Freedom Dreams: The Black Radical Imagination.* Boston: Beacon Press, 2002.

Kim, L. S., and Gilberto Moisés Blasini. "The Performance of Multicultural Identity in U.S. Network Television: Shiny, Happy Popstars (Holding Hands)." *Emergences: Journal for the Study of Media and Composite Cultures* 11 (Fall 2001): 287–307.

Knight, Arthur. *Disintegrating the Musical: Black Performance and American Musical Film.* Durham, NC: Duke University Press, 2002.

Kontje, Todd Curtis. *The German Bildungsroman: History of a National Genre.* Columbia, SC: Camden House, 1993.

Koshy, Susan. "Why The Humanities Matter for Race Studies Today." Special Topic: Comparative Racializations. *PMLA* 125, no. 5 (October 2008): 1542–1549.

Krysan, M., and A. Lewis, eds. *The Changing Terrain of Race and Ethnicity.* New York: Russell Sage Foundation, 2004.

Kushner, Tony. *Angels in America: A Gay Fantasia on National Themes.* Part II. *Perestroika.* New York: Theatre Communications Group, 1994.

La Ferla, Ruth. "Generation E.A.: Ethnically Ambiguous." *New York Times,* December 28, 2003.

LaPlante, Alice. "Self-Identified Multiracial Individuals Realize Real Benefits." *Stanford Graduate School of Business News.* April 2009. http://www.gsb.stanford.edu/news/research/binning_multirace.html.

Lee, Spike. *Bamboozled.* New Line Cinema, 2000.

Lemire, Elise Virginia. *"Miscegenation": Making Race in America.* Philadelphia: University of Pennsylvania Press, 2002.

Lewis, Amanda. "Everyday Race-Making." *American Behavioral Scientist* 47, no. 3 (November 2003): 283–305.

Lewis, Elliott. *Fade: My Journeys in Multiracial America.* New York: Basic Books, 2006.

Lewis, R. W. B. *The American Adam: Innocence, Tragedy, and Tradition in the Nineteenth Century.* Chicago: University of Chicago Press, 1955.

Lewis, Sinclair. *Kingsblood Royal.* New York: Random House, 1947.

Lima, Enrique. "The Indian *Bildungsroman*: D'Arcy McNickle and Indian Assimilation. The Uneven Development of the Novel: The Theory of the Novel and the Indigenous Periphery of Capitalist Modernity." *Comparative Literature* (forthcoming).

Lipsitz, George. *Dangerous Crossroads: Popular Music, Postmodernism, and the Poetics of Place.* London and New York: Verso, 1994.

———. *The Possessive Investment in Whiteness: How White People Profit from Identity Politics.* Philadelphia: Temple University Press, 1998.

Lopez, Alejandra. "The Population of Two or More Races in California." *Race and Ethnicity in California.* Demographics Report Series, no. 4. Stanford University Center for Comparative Studies in Race and Ethnicity, November 2001.

Lowe, Lisa. *Immigrant Acts: On Asian American Cultural Politics.* Durham, NC: Duke University Press, 1996.

Lukács, György. *The Theory of the Novel: A Historico-Philosophical Essay on the Forms of Great Epic Literature.* London: Merlin Press, 1971.

Lunsford, Andrea, with Adam Rosenblatt. "'Down a Road and Into an Awful Silence': Graphic Listening in Joe Sacco's Comics Journalism." In *Silence and Listening as Rhetorical Arts,* ed. Cheryl Glenn and Krista Ratcliff. Carbondale: Southern Illinois University Press, forthcoming.

———. "Joe Sacco's Comics Journalism: Critique, Caricature, Compulsion." In *Contemporary American Comics: Creators and Their Contexts,* ed. Paul Williams and James Lyons. Jackson: University Press of Mississippi, forthcoming.

Lunsford, Andrea, and John Ruszkiewicz. *The Presence of Others: Voices and Images That Call for Response.* New York: Bedford/St. Martin's Press, 2008.

Macdonald, Amie A., and Susan Sánchez-Casal. "Introduction: Feminist Reflections on the Pedagogical Relevance of Identity." In *Twenty-First-Century Feminist Classrooms: Pedagogies of Identity and Difference,* ed. Amie A. Macdonald and Susan Sánchez-Casal, 1–30. New York: Palgrave Macmillan, 2002.

———, eds. *Twenty-First-Century Feminist Classrooms: Pedagogies of Identity and Difference.* New York: Palgrave Macmillan, 2002.

Mailer, Norman. "The White Negro: Superficial Reflections on the Hipster." *Dissent* 4, no. 3 (Fall 1957). Reprinted in *Advertisements for Myself,* 337–358. Cambridge, MA: Harvard University Press, 2002; orig. 1959.

Markus, Hazel Rose, and Paula M. L. Moya, eds. *Doing Race: 21 Essays for the 21st Century.* New York: W. W. Norton, 2010.

Matthews, David. *Ace of Spades: A Memoir.* New York: Henry Holt, 2007.

Maufort, Marc, ed. *Crucible of Culture: Anglophone Drama at the Dawn of a New Millennium.* Brussels: College of European Publ., 2002.

Maufort, Marc, and Caroline De Wagter. *Signatures of the Past: Cultural Memory in Contemporary Anglophone North American Drama.* Vol. 24. New York: P.I.E. Peter Lang, 2008.

MAVIN. Generation MIX National Awareness Tour. http://www.mavinfoundation.org/news/media.html. Accessed July 2007.

McBride, James. *The Color of Water: A Black Man's Tribute to His White Mother.* New Jersey: Riverhead Books, 1997.

McCloud, Scott. *Reinventing Comics: How Imagination and Technology Are Revolutionizing an Art Form.* New York: HarperCollins, 2000.

McGrath, Ben. "The Radical: Why Do Editors Keep Throwing 'The Boondocks' Off the Funnies Page?" *New Yorker,* April 19, 2004. http://www.newyorker.com/archive/2004/04/19/040419fa_fact2.Accessed September 10, 2004.

McGruder, Aaron. *The Boondocks: Because I Know You Don't Read the Newspapers.* Kansas City, MO: Andrews McMeel Publishing, 2000.

———. *Public Enemy #2: An All-New Boondocks Collection.* New York: Three Rivers Press, 2005.

———. *A Right to Be Hostile: The Boondocks Treasury.* New York: Three Rivers Press, 2003.

McGruder, Aaron, Reginald Hudlin, and Kyle Baker. *Birth of a Nation: A Comic Novel.* New York: Crown Publishers, 2004.

McHenry, Elizabeth. *Forgotten Readers: Recovering the Lost History of African American Literary Salons.* Durham, NC: Duke University Press, 2002.

Meese, Elizabeth A., and Alice Parker. *The Difference Within: Feminism and Critical Theory.* Vol. 8. Philadelphia: J. Benjamins Publishing, 1989.

Mercer, Kobena. "Diaspora Aesthetics and Visual Culture." In *Black Cultural Traffic: Crossroads in Global Performance and Popular Culture,* ed. Harry J. Elam, Jr., and Kennell Jackson, 141–161. Ann Arbor: University of Michigan Press, 2008.

———. "Welcome to the Jungle: Identity and Diversity in Postmodern Politics." In *Identity, Community, Culture, Difference,* ed. Jonathan Rutherford, 43–71. London: Lawrence and Wishart, 1990.

———. *Welcome to the Jungle: New Positions in Black Cultural Studies.* New York: Routledge, 1994.

Michaels, Walter Benn. "Autobiography of an Ex-White Man: Why Race Is Not a Social Construction." *Transition* 73 (1998): 122–143.

———. "The No-Drop Rule." *Critical Inquiry* 20 (Summer 1994): 758–769.

———. "Race Into Culture: A Critical Genealogy of Cultural Identity." *Critical Inquiry* 18 (Summer 1992): 655–685.

Minden, Michael. *The German Bildungsroman: Incest and Inheritance.* New York: Cambridge University Press, 1997.

Minerbrook, Scott. *Divided to the Vein: A Journey Into Race and Family.* New York: Houghton Mifflin Harcourt, 1996.

Mitchell, Margaret. *Gone with the Wind.* New York: Warner, 1993; orig. 1936.

"Mixed Media Watch." www.mixedmediawatch.com/.

"Mixed Race, Pretty Face?" *Psychology Today.* http://www.psychologytoday.com/articles/200512/mixed-race-pretty-face.

"Mix It Up!" *O: The Oprah Magazine,* April 2006, 270–279.

Mohanty, Chandra Talpade. "On Race and Voice: Challenges for Liberal Education in the 1990s." *Cultural Critique* 14 (Winter 1989–1990): 179–208.

Moore, Michael. Foreword to *A Right to Be Hostile: The Boondocks Treasury,* by Aaron McGruder. New York: Three Rivers Press, 2003.

Moretti, Franco. *The Way of the World: The Bildungsroman in European Culture.* 2nd ed. London: Verso, 2000.

Morning, Ann. "New Faces, Old Faces: Counting the Multiracial Population Past and Present." In *New Faces in a Changing America: Multiracial Identity in the 21st Century,* ed. Loretta I. Winters and Herman L. DeBose, 41–67. Thousand Oaks, CA: Sage, 2002.

Morrison, Toni. "The Official Story: Dead Man Golfing." In *Birth of a Nation'hood: Gaze, Script, and Spectacle in the O. J. Simpson Case,* ed. Toni Morrison and Claudia Brodsky Lacour, vii–xxviii. New York: Pantheon, 1997.

———. *Playing in the Dark: Whiteness and the Literary Imagination.* New York: Vintage Books, 1993.

———. "Unspeakable Things Unspoken: The Afro-American Presence in American Literature." In *The Norton Anthology of African American Literature,* ed. Henry Louis Gates, Jr., and Nellie Y. McKay, 2299–2322. 2nd ed. New York: W. W. Norton, 2004.

———. "Unspeakable Things Unspoken: The Afro-American Presence in American Literature." *Michigan Quarterly Review* 18 (Winter 1989): 1–34.

Moten, Fred. *In the Break: The Aesthetics of the Black Radical Tradition*. Minneapolis: University of Minnesota Press, 2003.

Moya, Paula M. L. "Introduction: Reclaiming Identity." In *Reclaiming Identity: Realist Theory and the Predicament of Postmodernism*, ed. Paula M. L. Moya and Michael R. Haines-García, 1–28. Berkeley: University of California Press, 2000.

———. *Learning from Experience: Minority Identities, Multicultural Struggles*. Berkeley: University of California Press, 2002.

———. "Learning How to Learn from Others: Realist Proposals for Multicultural Education." In *Learning from Experience: Minority Identities, Multicultural Struggles*, 136–174. Berkeley: University of California Press, 2002.

———. "Postmodernism, 'Realism,' and the Politics of Identity: Cherríe Moraga and Chicana Feminism." In *Reclaiming Identity: Realist Theory and the Predicament of Postmodernism*, ed. Paula M. L. Moya and Michael R. Hames-García, 67–101. Berkeley: University of California Press, 2000.

Moya, Paula M. L., and Michael R. Hames-García, eds.. *Reclaiming Identity: Realist Theory and the Predicament of Postmodernism*. Berkeley: University of California Press, 2000.

Moya, Paula M. L., and Ramón Saldívar, eds. "Fictions of the Trans-American Imaginary." Special issue of *Modern Fiction Studies* 49, no. 1 (Spring 2003): 1–18.

Mullen, Harryette. Foreword to *Oreo* by Fran Ross, xi–xxviii. Boston: Northeastern University Press, 2000.

———. "Optic White: Blackness and the Production of Whiteness." *Diacritics* 24, nos. 2/3 (Summer 1994): 71–89.

Multiracial Activist. "The Multiracial Activist (TMA) Says 'Send the Racist Boondocks Comic Strip Back to the Boondocks.'" June 17, 1999. http://multiracial.com/site/content/view/815/2/. Accessed July 8, 2009.

Muñoz, José Esteban. *Disidentifications: Queers of Color and the Performance of Politics*. Vol. 2. Minneapolis: University of Minnesota Press, 1999.

Nakamura, Lisa. "Mixedfolks.com: 'Ethnic Ambiguity,' Celebrity Outing, and the Internet." In *Mixed Race Hollywood*, ed. Mary Beltran and Camilla Fojas, 64–83. New York: New York University Press, 2008.

Nakazawa, Donna Jackson. *Does Anybody Else Look Like Me? A Parent's Guide to Raising Multiracial Children*. Cambridge, MA: Perseus Publishing, 2003.

Napier, Winston, ed. *African American Literary Theory: A Reader*. New York: New York University Press, 2000.

Neal, Mark Anthony. *New Black Man*. New York: Routledge, 2006.

———. *Soul Babies: Black Popular Culture and the Post-Soul Aesthetic*. New York: Routledge, 2002.

Ngai, Sianne. "The Cuteness of the Avant-Garde." *Critical Inquiry* 31 (Summer 2005): 811–847.

Nielsen, Aldon Lynn. *Black Chant: Languages of African-American Postmodernism*. New York: Cambridge University Press, 1997.

Nissel, Angela. *Mixed: My Life in Black and White*. New York: Villard, 2006.

Nora, Pierre. "Between Memory and History: *Les Lieux de Mémoire*." In *Acts of Memory: Cultural Recall in the Present*, ed. Mieke Bal, Jonathan Crewe, and Leo Spitzer, 284–300. Hanover, NH: Dartmouth College/University Press of New England, 1999.

Nyong'o, Tavia. *The Amalgamation Waltz: Race, Performance, and the Ruses of Memory.* Minneapolis: University of Minnesota Press, 2009.

Obama, Barack. *Dreams from My Father: A Story of Race and Inheritance.* New York: Three Rivers Press, Random House, 2004.

"Obama Checks Simply African American," Blackpolitics.com. April 2, 2010. http://blackpoliticsontheweb.com/2010/04/02/obamas-census-choice-simply-african-american/. Accessed April 5, 2010.

Ogunnaike, Lola. "The Comic-Strip Revolution Will Be Televised." *New York Times,* October 30, 2005, 29.

O'Hearn, Claudine Chiawei, ed. *Half and Half: Writers on Growing Up Biracial and Bicultural.* New York: Pantheon Books, 1998.

Omi, Michael. "Racial Identity and the State: The Dilemmas of Classification." *Law and Inequality: A Journal of Theory and Practice* 7 (1997): 7–23.

Omi, Michael, and Howard Winant. *Racial Formation in the United States: From the 1960s to the 1990s.* 2nd ed. New York: Routledge, 1994.

Palumbo-Liu, David, ed. *The Ethnic Canon: Histories, Institutions, and Interventions.* Minneapolis: University of Minnesota Press, 1995.

Parker, David, and Miri Song, eds. *Rethinking Mixed Race.* Sterling, VA: Pluto Press, 2001.

Patterson, Orlando. "Race and Diversity in the Age of Obama." *New York Times Book Review,* August 16, 2009, 23.

Perlmann, Joel. "Reflecting the Changing Face of America: Multiracials, Racial Classifications, and American Intermarriage." In *Interracialism: Black-White Intermarriage in American History, Literature, and Law,* ed. Werner Sollors, 506–534. New York: Oxford University Press, 2000.

Pfeiffer, Kathleen. *Race Passing and American Individualism.* Amherst: University of Massachusetts Press, 2003.

Phelan, Peggy. *Unmarked: The Politics of Performance.* New York: Routledge, 1993.

Piper, Adrian. "Passing for White, Passing for Black." *Transition* 58 (1992): 4–32.

Pointer, Ray, dir. *George Herriman's Kinomatic Krazy Kat Kartoon Klassics.* DVD. Inkwell Images, 2004.

Poovey, Mary. *Making a Social Body: British Cultural Formation, 1830–1864.* Chicago: University of Chicago Press, 1995.

Posnock, Ross. 'Letting Go." *Raritan* 23, no. 4 (Spring 2004): 1–19.

———. "Purity and Danger: On Philip Roth." *Raritan* 21, no. 2 (Fall 2001): 85–101.

Powell, A. D. "'The Boondocks' Comic Strip Promotes 'One Drop' Myth." Reader letters regarding "The Boondocks." June 6, 1999. http://www.multiracial.com/readers/responses-boondocks.html. Accessed September 19, 2005.

Powell, John. "The Colorblind Multiracial Dilemma: Racial Categories Reconsidered." *University of San Francisco Law Review* 31 (1997): 789–806.

Powers, Richard. *The Time of Our Singing.* New York: Farrar, Straus, and Giroux, 2003.

Prasad, Chandra, ed. *Mixed: An Anthology of Short Fiction on the Multiracial Experience.* Introduction by Rebecca Walker. New York: W. W. Norton, 2006.

Pratt, Mary Louise. *Imperial Eyes: Travel Writing and Transculturation.* New York: Routledge, 1992.

Project RACE. Reprint of "The Multiracial Activist (TMA) Says 'Send the Racist Boondocks Comic Strip Back to the Boondocks.'" June 17, 1999. http://www.projectrace.com/hotnews/archive/hotnews-061899.php. Accessed July 8, 2009.

Raboteau, Emily. *The Professor's Daughter: A Novel.* New York: Henry Holt, 2005.

Ragusa, Kym. *The Skin Between Us: A Memoir of Race, Beauty, and Belonging.* New York: W. W. Norton, 2006.

Ramirez, Deborah. "Multicultural Empowerment: It's Not Just Black and White Anymore." *Stanford Law Review* 47, no. 5 (May 1995): 957–992.

Redfield, Marc. *Phantom Formations: Aesthetic Ideology and the Bildungsroman.* Ithaca, NY: Cornell University Press, 1996.

Roach, Joseph R. *Cities of the Dead: Circum-Atlantic Performance.* New York: Columbia University Press, 1996.

———. "Kinship, Intelligence, and Memory as Improvisation: Culture and Performance in New Orleans." In *Performance and Cultural Politics,* ed. Elin Diamond, 219–238. New York: Routledge, 1996.

Robinson, Amy. "It Takes One to Know One: Passing and Communities of Common Interest." *Critical Inquiry* 20 (Summer 1994): 715–736.

Roediger, David R. *Colored White: Transcending the Racial Past.* American Crossroads, vol. 10. Berkeley: University of California Press, 2002.

Rogin, Michael Paul. *Blackface, White Noise: Jewish Immigrants in the Hollywood Melting Pot.* Berkeley: University of California Press, 1996.

Root, Maria P. P. "A Bill of Rights for Racially Mixed People." In *The Multiracial Experience: Racial Borders as the New Frontier,* ed. Maria P. P. Root, 3–14. Thousand Oaks, CA: Sage, 1995.

———. "50 Experiences of Mixed Race People: Racial Experiences Questionnaire." 1996. http://www.drmariaroot.com/doc/50Experiences.pdf (accessed October 1, 2009). Reprinted in the Yes! Magazine March 26, 2010, Education Connection Newsletter, "Curriculum & Resources: Understanding Multiracial America." http://www.yesmagazine.org/for-teachers/curriculum/curriculum-resources-understanding-multiracial-america. Accessed July 27, 2010.

———. *Love's Revolution: Interracial Marriage.* Philadelphia: Temple University Press, 2001.

———, ed. *The Multiracial Experience: Racial Borders as the New Frontier.* Thousand Oaks, CA: Sage, 1995.

———, ed. *Racially Mixed People in America.* Thousand Oaks, CA: Sage, 1992.

———. "Within, Between, Beyond Race." In *"Mixed Race" Studies: A Reader,* ed. Jayne O. Ifekwunigwe, 143–148. New York: Routledge, 2004.

Root, Maria P. P., and Matt Kelley, eds. *Multiracial Child Resource Book: Living Complex Identities.* Seattle, WA: MAVIN Foundation, 2003.

Rose, Tricia. *Black Noise: Rap Music and Black Culture in Contemporary America.* Middletown, CT: Wesleyan University Press, 1994.

Roth, Philip. *The Human Stain.* New York: Vintage International, 2001.

Rowe, John Carlos. *Post-Nationalist American Studies.* Berkeley: University of California Press, 2000.

Rowell, Victoria. *The Women Who Raised Me: A Memoir.* New York: William Morrow, 2007.

Rux, Carl Hancock. *Talk.* New York: Theatre Communications Group, 2003.

Saks, Eva. "Representing Miscegenation Law." *Raritan* 8 (1988): 39–69.

———. "Representing Miscegenation Law." In *Interracialism: Black-White Intermarriage in American History, Literature, and Law,* ed. Werner Sollors, 61–81. New York: Oxford University Press, 2000.

Sánchez, María Carla, and Linda Schlossberg, eds. *Passing: Identity and Interpretation in Sexuality, Race, and Religion*. New York: New York University Press, 2001.

Santa Ana, Jeffrey. "Feeling Ancestral: The Emotions of Mixed Race and Memory in Asian American Cultural Productions." *positions: east asia cultures critique* 16, no. 2 (Fall 2008): 457–482.

Scales-Trent, Judy. *Notes of a White Black Woman: Race, Color, Community*. University Park: Pennsylvania State University Press, 1995.

Schlaikjer, Erica. "The Explosion in Mixed Race Studies." *Eurasian Nation* (2003). http://www.eurasiannation.com/articlespol2003-04mixedstudies.htm. Accessed March 4, 2004.

Schomburg, Arthur A. "The Negro Digs Up His Past." In *The Norton Anthology of African American Literature*, ed. Henry Louis Gates, Jr., and Nellie Y. McKay, 963–967. 2nd ed. New York: W. W. Norton, 2004.

Schuyler, George. "The Negro Art Hokum." In *The Norton Anthology of African American Literature*, ed. Henry Louis Gates, Jr., and Nellie Y. McKay, 1171–1173. 2nd ed. New York: W. W. Norton, 2004.

Sedgwick, Eve. "Queer Performativity: Henry James's *The Art of the Novel*." *GLQ: A Journal of Gay and Lesbian Studies* 1, no. 1 (1993): 1–16.

Senna, Danzy. *Caucasia*. New York: Riverhead Books, 1999.

———. "The Mulatto Millennium." In *Half and Half: Writers on Growing Up Biracial and Bicultural*, ed. Claudine Chiawei O'Hearn, 12–27. New York: Pantheon, 1998.

———. "Passing and the Problematic of Multiracial Pride (or, Why One Mixed Girl Still Answers to Black)." In *Black Cultural Traffic: Crossroads in Global Performance and Popular Culture*, ed. Harry J. Elam, Jr., and Kennell A. Jackson, 83–87. Ann Arbor: University of Michigan Press, 2005.

———. *Symptomatic*. New York: Riverhead Books, 2004.

———. *Where Did You Sleep Last Night? A Personal History*. New York: Farrar, Straus, and Giroux, 2009.

Sexton, Jared. *Amalgamation Schemes: Antiblackness and the Critique of Multiracialism*. Minneapolis: University of Minnesota Press, 2008.

Shelby, Tommie. *We Who Are Dark: The Philosophical Foundations of Black Solidarity*. Cambridge, MA: Belknap Press of Harvard University Press, 2005.

Shimakawa, Karen. *National Abjection: The Asian American Body Onstage*. Durham, NC: Duke University Press, 2002.

Siebers, Tobin. "Disability in Theory: From Social Constructionism to the New Realism of the Body." In *The Disability Studies Reader*, ed. Lennard J. Davis, 173–184. 2nd ed. New York: Routledge, 2006.

Sims, Jessica Mai. *Mixed Heritage: Identities, Policy, and Practice*. London: Runnymede Press, 2007.

Singh, Amritjit, Joseph T. Skerrett, Jr., and Robert E. Hogan, eds. *Memory, Narrative, and Identity in Ethnic American Literature*. Boston: Northeastern University Press, 1996.

Snipp, C. Matthew. "Racial Measurement in the American Census: Past Practices and Implications for the Future." *Annual Review of Sociology* 29 (2003): 563–588.

Sollors, Werner. *Ethnic Modernism*. Cambridge, MA: Harvard University Press, 2008.

———. *Neither Black nor White Yet Both: Thematic Explorations of Interracial Literature*. New York: Oxford University Press, 1997.

———, ed. *Interracialism: Black-White Intermarriage in American History, Literature, and Law*. New York: Oxford University Press, 2000.

Spencer, Jon Michael. *The New Colored People: The Mixed-Race Movement in America.* New York: New York University Press, 1997.

Spickard, Paul R. *Mixed Blood: Intermarriage and Ethnic Identity in Twentieth-Century America.* Madison: University of Wisconsin Press, 1991.

———. "The Subject Is Mixed Race: The Boom in Biracial Biography." In *Rethinking Mixed Race,* ed. David Parker and Miri Song, 76–98. Sterling, VA: Pluto Press, 2001.

Spickard, Paul R., and Rowena Fong. "A Vision of America's Future?" Abstract. *Social Forces* 73 (1995): 1365.

Spiegelman, Art. *Maus I: My Father Bleeds History: A Survivor's Tale.* New York: Pantheon, 1986.

Spillers, Hortense J. "Mama's Baby, Papa's Maybe: An American Grammar Book." *Diacritics* 17, no. 2 (Summer 1987): 65–81.

———. "The 'Tragic Mulatta': Neither/Nor—Toward an Alternative Model." In *The Difference Within: Feminism and Critical Theory,* ed. Elizabeth Meese and Alice Parker, 165–188. Philadelphia: J. Benjamins, 1989.

Stecopoulos, Harry, and Michael Uebel, eds. *Race and the Subject of Masculinities.* Durham, NC: Duke University Press, 1997.

Stone, Judith. *When She Was White: The True Story of a Family Divided by Race.* Burbank, CA: Miramax, 2007.

Strasser, Mark. "Family Definitions and the Constitution: On the Antimiscegenation Analogy." *Suffolk University Law Review* 25 (Winter 1991): 981–1034.

Sundstrom, Ronald. "Being and Being Mixed Race." *Social Theory and Practice* 27, no. 2 (April 2001): 285–307.

Tademy, Lalita. *Cane River.* New York: Warner Books, 2001.

———. *Red River.* New York: Grand Central Publishing, 2007.

Talalay, Kathryn. *Composition in Black and White: The Life of Philippa Schuyler: The Tragic Saga of Harlem's Biracial Prodigy.* New York: Oxford University Press, 1995.

Tauber, Mike, and Pamela Singh, photographers. Introduction by Rebecca Walker. *Blended Nation: Portraits and Interviews of Mixed-Race America.* New York: Channel Photographics, 2009.

Taylor, Charles. *Modern Social Imaginaries.* Durham, NC: Duke University Press, 2004.

Taylor, Diana. *The Archive and the Repertoire: Performing Cultural Memory in the Americas.* Durham, NC: Duke University Press, 2003.

Taylor, Paul C. "Race, Rehabilitated." *Agora: Journal for Metafysisk Spekulasjon* 25, nos. 1–2 (2007): 314–331.

Trethewey, Natasha. *Native Guard.* New York: Houghton Mifflin, 2006.

Twain, Mark. *Pudd'nhead Wilson: And, Those Extraordinary Twins.* Edited and with an introduction by Malcolm Bradbury. New York: Penguin, 1986.

Twine, France Winddance. *Racism in a Racial Democracy: The Maintenance of White Supremacy in Brazil.* New Brunswick, NJ: Rutgers University Press, 1997.

van der Ross, Richard. Foreword to *The New Colored People: The Mixed Race Movement in America* by Jon Michael Spencer, ix–x. New York: New York University Press, 1997.

Van Kerckhove, Carmen. *Racialicious: The Intersection of Race and Pop Culture.* http:// www.racialicious.com/ workshops.

Wald, Gayle. *Crossing the Line: Racial Passing in Twentieth-Century U.S. Literature and Culture.* Durham, NC: Duke University Press, 2000.

Walker, Marianne. *Margaret Mitchell and John Marsh: The Love Story Behind "Gone with the Wind."* Atlanta: Peachtree, 1993.

Walker, Rebecca. *Black, White, and Jewish: Autobiography of a Shifting Self.* New York: Riverhead Books, 2002.

Wardle, Francis. "Academics Are Enemies of the Multiracial Movement." CSBCHome.org Blog Archive for the Center for the Study of Biracial Children. April 2, 2009. http://csbchome.org/?p=24. Accessed June 30, 2009.

———."Multicultural Education." In *The Multiracial Experience: Racial Borders as the New Frontier,* ed. Maria P. P. Root, 380–391. Thousand Oaks, CA: Sage, 1995.

———. *Tomorrow's Children: Meeting the Needs of Multiracial and Multiethnic Children at Home, in Early Childhood Programs, and at School.* Denver: Center for the Study of Biracial Children, 1999.

Warren, Kenneth W. *Black and White Strangers: Race and American Literary Realism.* Chicago: University of Chicago Press, 1995.

Washington-Williams, Essie Mae. *Dear Senator: A Memoir by the Daughter of Strom Thurmond.* New York: Harper, 2006.

Wayans, Kim, and Kevin Knotts. Illustrated by Soo Jeong. *Amy Hodgepodge: All Mixed Up!* New York: Grosset and Dunlap; Penguin, 2008.

Weiss, Peter. *Aesthetics of Resistance.* Vol. 1. *A Novel.* Durham, NC: Duke University Press, 2005.

West, Cornel. "The New Cultural Politics of Difference." In *The Cultural Studies Reader,* ed. Simon During, 203–220. New York: Routledge, 1993.

White, Walter Francis. *Flight.* Baton Rouge: Louisiana State University Press, 1998.

Whitehead, Colson. *The Intuitionist.* New York: Anchor Books, 2000.

Wickham, DeWayne. "Today's Blacks Too Distant from Slavery? Think Again." *USA Today.* February 13, 2001. http://www.usatoday.com/news/opinion/columnists/wickham/2001-02-13-wickham.htm. Accessed July 27, 2010.

Wiegman, Robyn. *American Anatomies: Theorizing Race and Gender.* Durham, NC: Duke University Press, 1995.

Williams, Gregory Howard. *Life on the Color Line: The True Story of a White Boy Who Discovered He Was Black.* New York: Plume, 1996.

Williams, Kim M. *Mark One or More: Civil Rights in Multiracial America.* Ann Arbor: University of Michigan Press, 2006.

Williams, Patricia J. *Seeing a Color-Blind Future: The Paradox of Race.* New York: Farrar, Straus, and Giroux, 1997.

Williams, Teresa Kay, Cynthia L. Nakashima, George Kitahara Kich, and G. Reginald Daniel. "Being Different Together in the University Classroom: Multiracial Identity as Transgressive Education." In *The Multiracial Experience: Racial Borders as the New Frontier,* ed. Maria P. P. Root, 359–379. Thousand Oaks, CA: Sage, 1995.

Williams-León, Teresa, and Cynthia L. Nakashimi, eds. *The Sum of Our Parts: Mixed Heritage Asian Americans.* Philadelphia: Temple University Press, 2001.

Wilmer, S. E. "Restaging the Nation: The Work of Suzan-Lori Parks." *Modern Drama* 43, no. 3 (2000): 442–452.

Wilson, Judith. "One Way or Another: Black Feminist Visual Theory." In *The Feminism and Visual Culture Reader,* ed. Amelia Jones, 22–33. New York: Routledge, 2002.

Wilson, Robin. "Past Their Prime?" *Chronicle of Higher Education* 51, no. 33 (April 22, 2005): A9.

Winters, Loretta I., and Herman L. DeBose, eds. *New Faces in a Changing America: Multiracial Identity in the 21st Century*. Thousand Oaks, CA: Sage, 2002.

Witter, Daniel. "*Boondocks* Creator Speaks on Finding a Voice." California State University, Sacramento *State Hornet*, October 13, 1999. http://www.csus.edu/hornet/archive/fall99/issue07/news12.html. Accessed July 9, 2009.

Woloch, Alex. *The One vs. the Many: Minor Characters and the Space of the Protagonist in the Novel*. Princeton, NJ: Princeton University Press, 2003.

Wonham, Henry B. *Playing the Races: Ethnic Caricature and American Literary Realism*. New York: Oxford University Press, 2004.

———, ed. *Criticism on the Color Line: Desegregating American Literary Studies*. Piscataway, NJ: Rutgers University Press, 1996.

Woodson, Carter G. *The Mis-Education of the Negro* (1933). Lawrenceville, NJ: Africa World Press, 2006.

Wright, Marguerite A. *I'm Chocolate, You're Vanilla: Raising Healthy Black and Biracial Children in a Race-Conscious World*. San Francisco: Jossey-Bass, 1998.

Yoshino, Kenji. *Covering: The Hidden Assault on Our Civil Rights*. New York: Random House, 2007.

Young, Robert C. *Colonial Desire: Hybridity in Theory, Culture, and Race*. New York: Routledge, 1995.

Zack, Naomi. *Race and Mixed Race*. Philadelphia: Temple University Press, 1993.

———, ed. *American Mixed Race: The Culture of Microdiversity*. Lanham, MD: Rowman and Littlefield, 1995.

Ziv, Alon. *Breeding Between the Lines: Why Interracial People Are Healthier and More Attractive*. Fort Lee, NJ: Barricade Books, 2006.

Index

Page numbers in *italics* indicate illustrative material.